Sefer Tagin Fragments from the Cairo *Genizah*

Études sur le Judaïsme Médiéval

TOME LXXXV

The titles published in this series are listed at *brill.com/ejm*

Cambridge Genizah Studies

Edited by

Ben Outhwaite
Geoffrey Khan
Michael Rand
Eve Krakowski

VOLUME 12

Sefer Tagin Fragments from the Cairo *Genizah*

A Critical Edition, Commentary and Reconstruction

By

Marc Michaels

BRILL

LEIDEN | BOSTON

The Library of Congress Cataloging-in-Publication Data is available online at http://catalog.loc.gov
LC record available at http://lccn.loc.gov/2020031604

Typeface for the Latin, Greek, and Cyrillic scripts: "Brill". See and download: brill.com/brill-typeface.

ISSN 0169-815X
ISBN 978-90-04-42635-1 (hardback)
ISBN 978-90-04-42636-8 (e-book)

This book is printed on acid-free paper and produced in a sustainable manner.

Dedicated to
Avielah Barclay-Michaels

אשת חיל **מצאתי** ורחק מפנינים מכרה
בטח בה לב בעלה ושלל לא יחסר

A woman of worth, *I have found*,
her price is far above rubies.
The heart of her husband safely trusts in her,
and he lacks no gain.

Proverbs 31:10–11 (almost)

Contents

Acknowledgements XIII
List of Assigned Sigla XVI
List of Figures, Tables and Reconstructions XVII
Note on Transliteration XIX

1 **Introduction** 1
- 1 The 'Strange Letters', Visual *Midrash* and *Sefer Tagin* 1
- 2 A Brief Introduction to *Tagin* 2
- 3 *Sefer Tagin*—A Manual for *Sofrim* (Scribes) 5
- 4 The Corpus of Textual Witnesses to *Sefer Tagin*—Core and Secondary Sources 9
- 5 Some Example Uses in *Sifrey Torah* 18
- 6 Adding to the Core Corpus, Oxford Bodleian MS. Heb. d. 33/3 (fol. 9), a Known Fragment from the Cairo *Genizah* 19

2 **A New (Partial) Witness** 21
- 1 T-S D1.42—Two New Pages from a Version of *Sefer Tagin* Identified from the Cairo *Genizah* 21
- 2 Dating and Locating T-S D1.42 24
- 3 Identifying Additional Joins, T-S AS 139.152, T-S NS 287.11 and T-S AS 139.144 26
- 4 An Additional Find, a Secondary Source T-S Misc. 24.182 from the Cairo *Genizah* 32
- 5 Dating T-S Misc. 24.182 33

3 **Transcription and Analysis** 39
- 1 Diacritical Conventions 39
- 2 Digital Composition and Font Construction 40

PART 1

4 **Critical Analysis of T-S D.142** 43
- 1 End of Listing of Instances for the First Special Letter *He* Form 43
- 2 Description and Example Forms of the First Special Letter *He* 55
- 3 Description and Example Forms of the Second Special Letter *He* 56
- 4 Listing of Instances for the Second Special Letter *He* 58

5 Description and Example Forms of the Special Letter *Vav* 62
6 Listing of Instances for the Special Letter *Vav* 65
7 Description and Example Forms of the First Special Letter *Zayin* 71
8 Listing of Instances for the First Special Letter *Zayin* 72
9 Description and Example Forms of the Second Special Letter *Zayin* 75
10 Listing of Instances for the Second Special Letter *Zayin* 77
11 Description and Example Forms of the First Special Letter *Ḥet* 78
12 Listing of Instances for the First Special Letter *Ḥet* 80
13 Description and Example Forms of the Second Special Letter *Ḥet* 83
14 Listing of Instances for the Second Special Letter *Ḥet* 86
15 Description and Example Forms of the Special Letter *Ṭet* 91
16 Listing of Instances for the Special Letter *Ṭet* 93
17 Summary—T-S D1.42 97

PART 2

5 Analysis and Reconstruction of Joined Fragments 101
1 Reconstruction of Additional Pages of Our New Core Source 101
2 Continuing the Listing for the Special Letter *Ṭet* 101
3 Description and Example Forms of the Special Letter *Yod* 111
4 Listing of Instances for the Special Letter *Yod* 113
5 Description and Example Forms of the Special Letter *Kaf* 131
6 Listing of Instances for the Special Letter *Kaf* 133
7 Description and Example Forms of the First Special Letter *Kaf Sofit* 145
8 Listing of Instances for the First Special Letter *Kaf Sofit* 146
9 Description and Example Forms of the Second Special Letter *Kaf Sofit* 159
10 Listing of Instances for the Second Special Letter *Kaf Sofit* 160
11 Description and Example Forms of the Special Letter *Lamed* 162
12 Listing of Instances for the Special Letter *Lamed* 164
13 Description and Example Forms of the Special Letter *Mem* 170
14 Listing of Instances for the Special Letter *Mem* 172
15 Description and Example Forms of the Special Letter *Mem Sofit* 179
16 Listing of Instances for the Special Letter *Mem Sofit* 181
17 Description and Example Forms of the Special Letter *Nun* 201
18 Listing of Instances for the Special Letter *Nun* 202
19 Description and Example Forms of the Special Letter *Tav* 207

20 Listing of Instances for the Special Letter *Tav* 209
21 Conclusion of *Sefer Tagin* 215
22 Summary—CG Joined Fragments 216

PART 3

6 Oxford Bodleian MS. Heb. 33/3 (fol. 9) 219
1 Critical Analysis of MS. Heb. d. 33/3 219
2 Continuing the Listing for the Special Letter *Nun* 219
3 Description and Example Forms of the Special Letter *Nun Sofit* 224
4 Listing of Instances for the Special Letter *Nun Sofit* 226
5 The 'Upside Down' *Nun Sofit* of *Ḥaran* 227
6 Continuing the Listing for the Special Letter *Nun Sofit* 231
7 Description and Example Forms of the Special Letter *Samekh* 233
8 Listing of Instances for the Special Letter *Samekh* 235
9 Description and Example Forms of the First Special Letter *'Ayin* 242
10 Listing of Instances for the First Special Letter *'Ayin* 244
11 Summary—Oxford Heb. 33/9 246

Appendix 1: Transcription and Annotation of T-S Misc. 24.182 247
Appendix 2: Enhanced Imagery of *Sefer Tagin* from Sassoon 82 (JUD. 022) 260
Bibliography 263

Acknowledgements

I wish to thank my PhD joint supervisor, Dr Ben Outhwaite, for his support and suggestions on the drafts of this monograph, for showing me the manuscript I had identified and for enabling permission to use imagery from CUL. Thanks are also due to Dr Kim Phillips for sharing his discovery of **T-S Misc. 24,182**, after early drafts of this monograph reminded him of the special letters forms he had seen on those fragments.

My thanks to Dr Ben Outhwaite (again) for his proof-reading skills and to my main PhD supervisor Professor Geoffrey Khan for his helpful suggestions, and to both for their general advice and specific transliteration guidance. My thanks also, to Nehemia Gordon, for reviewing this monograph and who, coming across Sassoon 82, took amazing photographs and alerted me to them. This assisted greatly with the decipherment of the damaged sections of that core text.

My gratitude to Mr. Jacqui E. Safra for his permission in reproducing imagery from Sassoon 82 (now JUD. 022), that resides in his private collection in Geneva. Also to Jolanda van Nijen (*Responsable administrative chez Collection d'art privée*) for her helpfulness in organising this. Additionally, to Dr. Justine Isserles who helped with manuscript dating and sent me images of MS Geunz 481. Also to Ephraim Caspi for early personal correspondence, sharing some articles with me and providing a couple of missing pages of Q651–652. Also for pointing me in the direction of Kreuzenstein, Sammlung Graf Wilczek, Inv.—**Nr.** 5667, HDSHDS.

A large thank you to the editors of the *Cambridge* Genizah *Studies* series and Brill for agreeing to publish this monograph and for their support in the publishing process. Particularly to Erika Mandarino, Assistant Editor, Ancient Near East and Jewish Studies for her guidance. Also to Cas Van den Hof of TAT Zetwerk for his guidance through the typesetting and proof-reading process.

Such a project would not have been possible without the opening up of the digital repositories in various academic institutions, notably the Cambridge University Library, the *Ktiv* digital repository though the National Library of Israel, the British Library, the Biblioteca Apostolia Vaticana, the Biblioteca Palatino, Parma, the Friedberg Jewish Manuscript Society *Genizah* project and the Books within Books project.

My thanks to Biblioteca Apostolia Vaticana for permission to use images of Vat. ebr. 1 and particularly to the British Library for their excellent open policy towards reproduction of their images. Also to the Alexander family for trusting me with the restoration of their precious family *Torah*, which provided some exquisite examples of letter forms from *Sefer Tagin*. Also to Ada Yardeni *z'l* for the inspiration to draw scripts that were not available for reproduction.

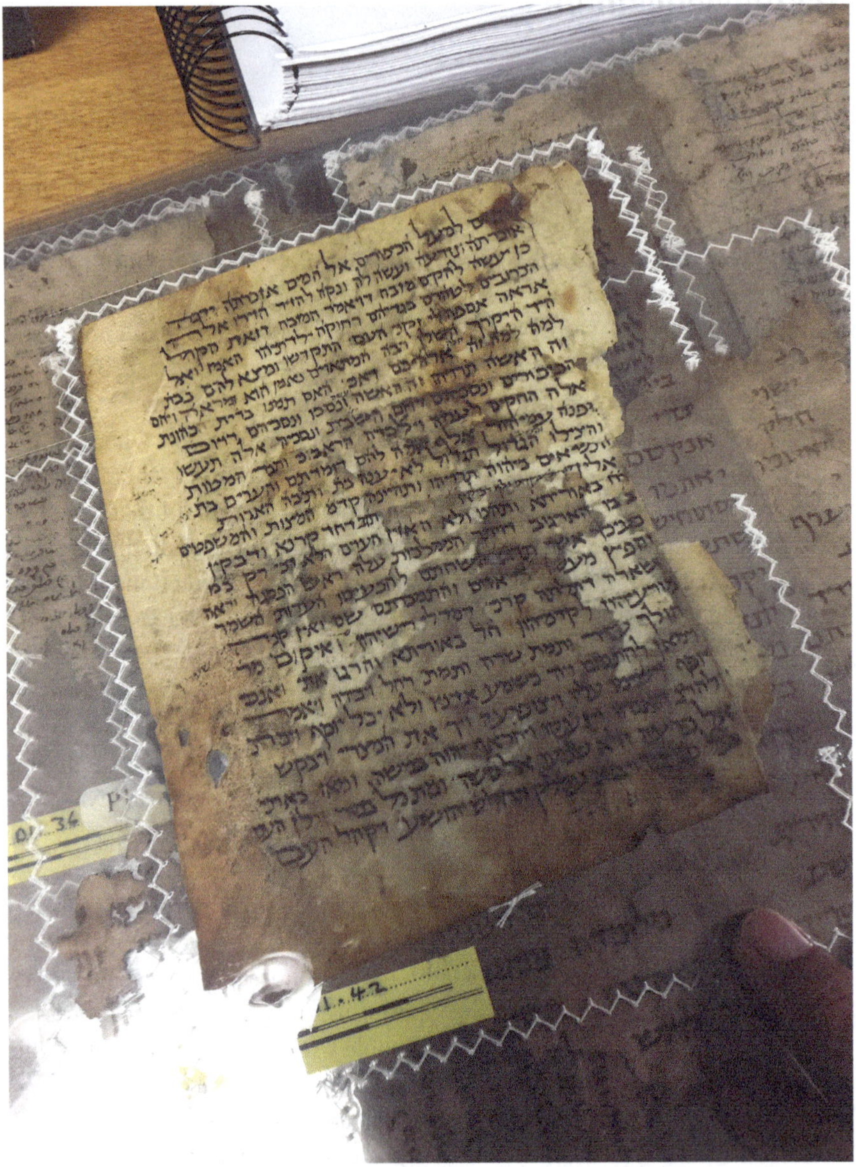

FIGURE 1 Examining T-S D1.42 in its protective pouch in Dr Outhwaite's office at CUL. Indeed, when first encountering the main fragment in reality as opposed to blown up on a computer screen, I was struck by how small the page was. This was no grand decorated manuscript—this was a small private note book for a learned scholar.

To my parents, Eileen and Rabbi Maurice Michaels for a loving upbringing that instilled in me a deep connection to Judaism and our heritage. To my son Aryeh, for listening to me talk about obscure texts, as well as discussing the latest superhero films and comics. However, my greatest thanks go to three scribes. My scribal teacher Vivian Solomon *z'l* who instilled within me his passion for the scribal arts and equipped me with the skills to be a *sofer STa"M*. To his teacher, Dr. Eric Ray *z'l*, whose fascination for the *ʾotiyot meshunot* rubbed of on his student's student. Finally to my wife, the first *soferet* of modern times, Avielah Barclay-Michaels for her love, patience and unstinting support, whilst I worked on this monograph.

Marc Michaels (Mordechai Pinḥas), M.A., *Sofer STa"M*
ʾAdar 5780/February 2020

List of Assigned Sigla

BH	*Badey ha-ʾAron uMigdal Ḥananʾel* in Recueil de commentaires cabalistiques—Hébreu 840, f103.
CG	Cambridge *Genizah Sefer Tagin*—collective term I have employed for CUL T-S D1.42 + CUL T-S AS 139.152 + CUL T-S AS 139.158 + CUL T-S AS 139.144 + top of T-S NS 287.11.
EPST	*Sepher Taghin* (ספר תגין), *Liber Coronularum*, (ed.) J.J.L. BARGES, Paris, 1866, pp. 1–28.
H	Ms Hébreu 837, ff. 148r–159r.
K	Kreuzenstein, Sammlung Graf Wilczek, Inv.—Nr. 5667, HDSHDS
P	MS Parma 2574 (DeRossi cat. no. 159), a manuscript of *Maḥzor Vitry le-Rabbeynu Simḥa*, ff. 240r–244v.
LMV	S. Hurwitz, *Maḥzor Vitry le-Rabbeynu Simḥa*, Nuremberg, 1923, pp. 674–683.
𝔐	Masoretic text of the *Torah*.
MV	Add. MS 27201, pp. 209r–215r.
MV2	Add. MS 27201, pp. 199v–209r.
OB	Oxford Bodleian MS Heb d.33/9.
ST	Sassoon 82 (JUD. 022), pp. 177–179.

List of Figures, Tables and Reconstructions

Figures

1 Examing T-S D1.42 in its protective pouch XIV
2 An example line from a *megillat 'Esther* that I wrote in 2018 2
3 A detail from *Tosafot* to *Menaḥot* 29b 3
4 An extract from *Shoneh Halakhot* explaining the secret of *She'atnez Gats* 4
5 Some very ornate *tagin* forms that have crossed my desk or I have seen in collections 5
6 Add. MS 27201, 209v 11
7 The forms of the letters from Sassoon 82 (JUD. 002) 11
8 CUL T-S D1.42 1V 22
9 CUL T-S D1.42 1r 23
10 CUL T-S AS 139.152-B 27
11 CUL T-S AS 139.152-F 28
12 CUL T-S AS 139.158-B 29
13 CUL T-S AS 139.158-F 30
14 CUL T-S AS 139.144-B 31
15 CUL T-S AS 139.144-F 31
16 Top of CUL T-S NS 287.11-F 31
17 CUL T-S Misc. 24.182 P1-B 34
18 CUL T-S Misc. 24.182 P1-F 35
19 CUL T-S Misc. 24.182 P2-B 36
20 CUL T-S Misc. 24.182 P2-F 37
21 My drawing of MS Heb. 33/9b 220
22 Sassoon 82 (JUD. 022) page 177 260
23 Sassoon 82 (JUD. 022) page 178 261
24 Sassoon 82 (JUD. 022) page 179 262

Tables

1 Sample scripts for comparison with our Cambridge *Genizah* fragments **CG.** 25
2 Forms for the first special letter *he* 57
3 Forms for the second special letter *he* 59
4 Forms for the special letter *vav* 64
5 Forms for the first special letter *zayin* 73
6 Forms for the second special letter *zayin* 76

7 Forms for the first special letter *ḥet* 79
8 Forms for the second special letter *ḥet* 85
9 Forms for the special letter *ṭet* 92
10 Forms for the special letter *yod* 113
11 Forms for the special letter *kaf* 133
12 Forms for the special letter *kaf sofit* 147
13 Forms for the second special letter *kaf sofit* 161
14 Forms for the special letter *lamed* 163
15 Forms for the special letter *mem* 171
16 Forms for the special letter *mem sofit* 180
17 Forms for the special letter *nun* 203
18 Forms for the special letter *tav* 210
19 Forms for the special letter *nun sofit* 225
20 A selection of the *nun sofit hafukha* from a number of *Sifrey Torah* 228
21 Forms for the special letter *samekh* 234
22 Forms for the first special letter *ʿayin* 243

Reconstructions

1 Folio showing 26 lines covering the conclusion of the listing for *ṭet*, that for *yod* and the start of *kaf* 136
2 Folio showing 23 lines listing part of letters *kaf* and *kaf sofit* 157
3 Folio showing 25 lines with the conclusion of the listing for the first form of *kaf sofit*, that for the second, for *lamed*, *mem* and the start of *mem sofit* 186
4 Folio showing 27 lines, showing the conclusion of the listing for the *mem sofit* and the start of *nun* 208

Note on Transliteration

There is no single accepted standard for transliteration and there are several systems in use. I have thus minimised the use of transliteration through this monograph, preferring to use the Hebrew characters. Use is therefore restricted largely to the names of the letters, the *parashiyyot* (weekly cycle of *Torah* readings) and some standard technical terms, e.g. *ḥaser* and *ma-le'*. Given that, and the hope that this work might be of interest to a wider public than academic scholars, rather than some regimes that are confusing to the lay-person, I have therefore selected and slightly adapted the more readily understandable transliteration conventions. The first is that employed in Berlin, Adele & Brettler, Marc Zvi, *The Jewish Study Bible* (TJSB), *2nd Edition*, Oxford University Press, 2014, shown on p. xx and the names of the *parashiyyot* given on pp. 2231–2232, with minor amends for consistency with the table below. Names of the letters are largely taken from *The Summary of the Phonetics and Phonology of the Consonants* table shown in Khan, Geoffrey, *The Tiberian Pronunciation Tradition of Biblical Hebrew, Volume 1*, Cambridge (FAMES), UK: Open Book Publishers, 2020, https://doi.org/10.11647/OBP.0163, pp. 608–610, though again slightly amended to maintain consistency with *The Jewish Study Bible* and the table below.

Character	Transliteration	Name	Character	Transliteration	Name
א	'	*'alef*	מ ם	m	*mem*
בּ ב	b, v	*bet*	נ ן	n	*nun*
ג	g	*gimel*	ס	s	*samekh*
ד	d	*dalet*	ע	ʿ	*ʿayin*
ה	h	*he*	פּ פ ף	p, f [ph]	*pe*
ו	v	*vav*	צ ץ	ts	*tsade*
ז	z	*zayin*	ק	q [k]	*qof*
ח	ḥ	*ḥet*	ר	r	*resh*
ט	ṭ	*ṭet*	שׁ	sh	*shin*
י	y	*yod*	שׂ	s	*sin*
כּ כ ך	k, kh	*kaf*	ת	t	*tav*
ל	l	*lamed*			

Quotes from other sources or quoted names of books or Jewish commentators may employ different transliteration conventions, dependent on their source, for example the addition of *he* at the end of a word will vary considerably between sources. Such as *Torah, Mishnah* and *Genizah* where the 'h' is more commonly present. Familiar words such as names of Biblical characters, Noah, Abraham, Sarah, Moses etc. are often, but not always, given in their Latin equivalent. I ask the reader to forgive any inconsistencies on my part and indeed any other errors you should find in this monograph.

CHAPTER 1

Introduction

1 The 'Strange Letters', Visual *Midrash* and *Sefer Tagin*

There are ancient traditions grouped together under the collective heading of אותיות משונות *'otiyot meshunot* (strange letters). They provide a visual *midrash* in that they tell a story, over and above the simple meaning of the text, merely through special adornment of the letters on the page. They include, bent, curled and spiral letters and those with many more decorative embellishments than would normally be the case.[1] There are a number of manuscripts and books that refer to these scribal idiosyncrasies and chief amongst these is ספר תגין ***Sefer Tagin*** (the book of 'serifs'/crowns) also known, perhaps more accurately, by its own description as ספר תאגי ***Sefer Tagey***.[2] This covers the forms of the letters that have different shapes or additional or specially shaped *tagin*.[3]

Being a practicing *Sofer STa"M* (scribe) means that I have checked and repaired many *Sifrey Torah* over the years. In so doing, I have had the privilege of seeing several which have been quite old and, as such, many contain examples of these special forms. Indeed, this is what initially piqued my interest in this subject and led me to this area of study.[4]

---

1 Rambam for example, amongst others exhorts scribes to: ויזהר באותיות הגדולות ובאותיות הקטנות ובאותיות הנקודות ואותיות המשנות כגון הפא"ן הלפופות והאותיות העקומות כמו שהעתיקו הסופרים איש מפי איש ויזהר בתגין ובמנינן יש אות שיש עליה תג אחד ויש אות שיש עליה שבעה וכל התגין כצורת זיני"ן הן דקין כחוט השערה (take care over the large letters and the small letters and the dotted letters, and the strange letters, such as the coiled letters *pe* and the crooked letters, such as the scribes have copied one from another—and take care over the *tagin* and the the number of them. For some letters have [only] one *tag* and some have seven on them. And all the *tagin* are in the shape of a [small] *zayin*—thin as a hair) from *Mishneh Torah, Hilkhot Sefer Torah* 7:8.

2 As per its own introduction, which begins הדין ספר תאגי (This is *Sefer Tagey* …). However, since it is more commonly known as *Sefer Tagin*, I have used that nomenclature throughout this monograph.

3 It also appears to cover the instructions ביה שמו—i.e. the six columns of the *Torah* that have to start with a particular letter. It can also be followed in manuscripts with discussions of the large, small and dotted letters. However, these are certainly not part of *Sefer Tagin*, and are derived from separate sources.

4 Indeed these are not as rare as one might think. Moshe Rosenwasser writes that 'it seems that the custom to write certain letters in the *Torah* in a strange form was very widespread, for I have found references to this custom in Spain, Germany, Italy, France, South Africa, and the Yemen. Similarly, I have found no early authority who declares this custom פסול *pasul*

 | DOI:10.1163/9789004426368_002

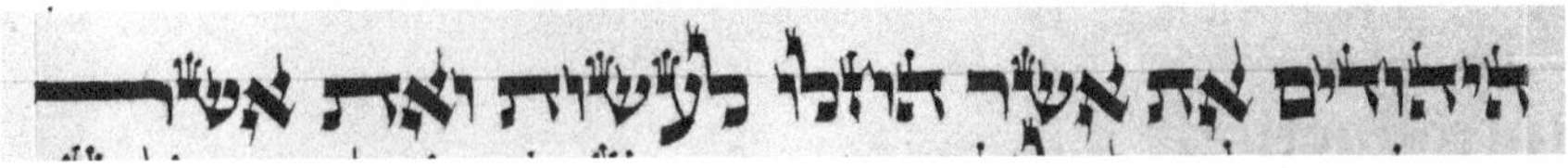

FIGURE 2 An example line from a *megillat 'Esther* that I wrote in 2018. It shows standard *tagin* as would be found in *Sifrey Torah, megillot 'Esther, tefillin* and *mezuzot*. Some letters have three, some just one and some none.

2 A Brief Introduction to *Tagin*

Tagin are the little decorative crownlets that make much of the difference between what is merely Hebrew block lettering and what one sees in the holy texts. Spelt תאגין or תגין (singular תגא (*taga*)) in Aramaic, in Hebrew they are often referred to as כתרים (crowns) as they crown the letter.[5] Because the most familiar *tag* arrangement is composed of three flourishes or strokes, each of which resembles a small letter *zayin*, they are often referred to as a זיון *ziyyun* (armour/dagger).[6]

Whilst there is no shortage of *midrashic* explanations and scholarly research (see bibliography), no-one quite knows what these embellishments really mean or their importance. Indeed, Rambam argues that their absence does not invalidate the writing as the core of the letter form is there.[7] However, the *halakha* dictates that certain letters should have these decorative flourishes, which the *sofer* creates by drawing ink upwards from the roof of the

(invalid) or cast doubt on it.' Rosenwasser, Moshe, האותיות המשונות שבתורה (*The Odd Letters that are in the* Torah), from המעין (The Spring), *Nisan* 5766. p. 24.

5 However, it should be noted that Yakir Paz argues that כתרים refer instead to marginal designs that resemble the Roman diadem or coronet, known as a κορωνίς *koronis*, marking a new *parasha* as a very elaborate *paragraphos* sign, bringing examples largely in Greek but also some Hebrew manuscripts (which are less convincing) of what he claims are vertical representations of the diadems worn by kings and emperors, with ties and tassels. See Paz, Yakir, קושר כתרים לאותיות: מנהג סופרי אלוהי בהקשרו ההיסטורי (*Binding Crowns to the Letters—A Divine Scribal Practice in Its Historical Context*) from רביץ—רבעון למדעי היהודית, שנה פו, חוברת ב— (תשע"ט) ג. 233–267. He also notes that despite the assertions in the *Talmud*, no *halakhot* do hang on these 'either from Akiva or any other sages' (op. cit., p. 234). Yaakov Elman notes similarly in *Jewish Interpretations of the Bible*, *TJSB*, op. cit. p. 1868.

6 I have translated this as a *zayin* type decoration throughout as, in modern Hebrew, this word has an unfortunate secondary meaning. This does not necessarily suggest that this was a *zayin* shape as we have seen it can be a line or a line with a ball on top. It is more a reflection of the weapon/dagger idea.

7 Rambam, *Mishneh Torah, Hilkhot Sefer Torah* 7:9. However, Rabbeynu 'Asher argues that a *Torah* lacking any *tagin* would be *pasul* (i.e. unfit, invalid). See *Shulḥan 'Arukh Harav* 36:5 and also the *Mishnah Berurah* 36:15 which requires that any *tagin* lacking should be added before the *Torah* is used in public reading.

FIGURE 3
A detail from *Tosafot* to *Menaḥot* 29b.

letter with the very thin tip of the quill (or down from little blobs towards the roof of the letter) held to be a mini *zayin* or are just straight lines, without the blob.[8]

The traditional halakhic source for the form of *tagin* is *Tosafot* to *Menaḥot* 29b as shown above from the standard Vilna edition.[9] The discussion centres around the form of the three *tagin* that adorn the letters שעטנזגצ, known by the mnemonic *She'atnez Gats*. Others only have one, בדק חיה[10] and some have none at all. *Tosafot* bring three opinions as to the form of this.

שעטנז גץ. יש מפרשים ג׳ זיונים השנים לצד שמאל אחד מלמעלה ואחד מלמטה והאחד לצד ימין כזה שעטנ״ז ג״ץ ובפי׳ שבת כתיבת יד רבי׳ ש״י צייר אחד מימין ואחד משמאל ואחד מלמעלה כזה עוד פי׳ שיש שעושין שלשתן למעלה כזה

8 *Pitḥey She'arim* gives a third option of a mini *vav* shaped *tag* where the blob faces the left of the line. Schechter, A. and Aurbach, U., פתחי שערים החדש—אוצר הלכות מזוזה, Jerusalem, 1990, p. 258.

9 The *tagin* themselves are said in *Menaḥot* 29b to originate directly from Sinai; as when Moses ascended the mountain he found God engaged in affixing crowns to the letters. When asked why, God replies that a man will arise—Rabbi 'Aqiva—who will derive from each *qots* (thorn) heaps and heaps of laws. Moses asks to see him and is transported to the future to 'Aqiva's classroom where he is unable to understand a thing and is somewhat disturbed to learn about 'Aqiva's painful end as a martyr.

10 The remaining letters that do not have a *tag* coincidentally spell out מלאכת סופר (work of a scribe).

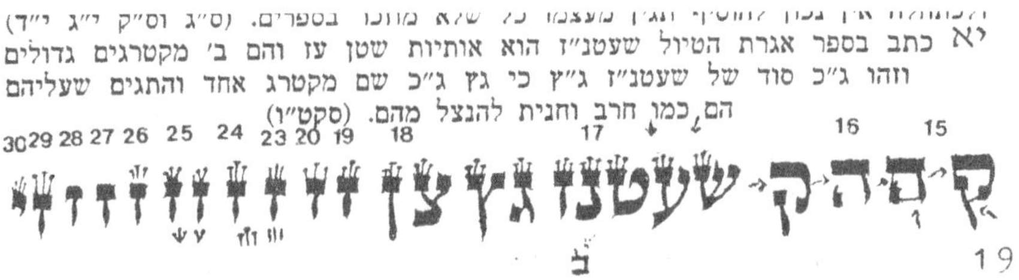

FIGURE 4 An extract from *Shoneh Halakhot* explaining the secret of *She'atnez Gats*—that they contain the names of three demons, Satan, 'Ez and Gats, and the *tagin* upon them are swords and daggers that protect us from them.

(*She'atnez Gats*—there are those that explain the three *zayin* type decorations as two on the left side, one above and one below and one on the right side as this [see image] ... and in the section *Shabbat* handwritten by R. S"Y draws with one on the right, one on the left and one above like this [see image] ... and further it is explained that there are those that make the three of them above like this [see image] ...).

This form as applied to the letters *She'atnez Gats* are also described by much later commentators as representing daggers.

Tagin thus became an indispensable part of how the letters on the parchment were to be displayed and retroactively given the status of having always been such and having been on the tablets God prepared for Moses, in the *Torah* that Moses wrote[11] and, on the stones Joshua erected in Gilgal.[12]

One other more modern development around *tagin* is that they perhaps represent the scribes' best chance of individual expression and show that despite the vast amount of rules and regulations the individualism of the scribe can still shine through. Considerable creative license can be seen with the splayed, fans, rainbows, fireworks, trees or dotted *tagin* that can be seen below, though some *sofrim* would frown on such a thing.

11 For example, Rambam in his responsa *Pe'er ha-Dor* (No. 68, p. 17b, ed. Amsterdam, 1765) explains that, 'the marking of the *tagin* in the *Sefer Torah* is not a later custom, for the *tagin* are mentioned by the Talmudists as the crowns on the letters ... the *Torah* that Moses wrote also contained *tagin*.'

12 Mentioned in the introduction to *Sefer Tagin*, הדין ספר תאגי דאסיק עלי הכהן מן שתים עשר אבנים שהקים יהושע בגלגל (This is the book of *Tagey* that 'Eli the priest, established from the twelve stones that Joshua erected in Gilgal).

FIGURE 5 Some very ornate *tagin* forms that have crossed my desk or I have seen in collections. Left to right, top row: a bridging rainbow effect. A fantastic splayed *lamed* on the word *hamelekh* (the king) from a *megillah* belonging to a synagogue in Edgware (more freedom is allowed when working on a *megillah* than with other works). A very ornate peacock tag in a *megillat ʾEsther* JER NLI 197/8=4 from the 19th Century and a tree *tag* from the same manuscript. F. Left to right, bottom row: Pomegranate *tagin* in a *megillat ʾEsther* from San Francisco (Photo by Avielah Barclay-Michaels, *Soferet*). Firework *tag* from an 18th century Polish *Torah*. Fan *tagin* in a row from a *Torah* that I repaired in 2006, from Stepney in London. However beautiful and decorative they may be, these are **not** part of the tradition represented by *Sefer Tagin*.
Note: JER NLI 197/8=4 available to view at: https://web.nli.org.il/sites/NLI/English/digitallibrary/pages/viewer.aspx?&presentorid=MANUSCRIPTS&docid=PNX_MANUSCRIPTS002590314-1#|FL44079935, reproduction permitted.

3 *Sefer Tagin*—A Manual for *Sofrim* (Scribes)

According to the Jewish Encyclopedia, 'the Aramaic language and the Masoretic style of *Sefer Tagin* would fix the time of its author as the Geonic period,[13] but the frequent references in the *Talmud* to the book suggest the probability of the existence of a different *Sefer Tagin* at a much earlier period.'[14] Yardeni notes that it is 'ascribed to Rabbi Naḥum the copyist, who lived at the end of the Second Temple period.'[15] and that 'there were evidently some early

13 Perani describes it specifically as 'Masorete's work composed in the eight century as cited by Saʿadyah [Gaon] between the ninth and tenth centuries', Perani, M., *Part 2: The Oldest Complete Extant Sefer Torah Rediscovered at the Bologna University Library: Codicological, Textual, and Paleographic Features of an Ancient Eastern Tradition* in *The Jews of Italy: Their Contribution to the Development and Diffusion of Jewish Heritage*, Academic Studies Press, Boston, 2019.

14 Crawford, H. and Eisenstein J., *Tagin* from *The Jewish Encyclopedia, Volume 11*. Funk & Wagnalls. New York, 1901–1906, p. 666.

15 Yardeni, Ada. *The Book of Hebrew Script: History, Palaeography, Script Styles, Calligraphy & Design*. Carta, Jerusalem, 2010, p. 269.

writings dealing with ornaments of the letters-signs and they were no doubt based on early scribal traditions'[16]

The book itself has an introduction which makes claims about its own authorship to lend itself authority. Various great historical personages are quoted as being part of the chain of tradition, to make it clear that these traditions have great validity by 'present[ing] their work as a legacy from the venerable past.

Antiquity implies authority.'[17] *Sefer Tagin* itself explains that these traditions are derived from the twelve stone pillars that Joshua set up[18] that contained the whole *Torah* and that these have been passed down איש מפי איש (from the mouth of one man to another). On these stones were inscribed the books of Moses, with the *tagin* in the required letters, according to Nachmanides on Deut. 27:8.

Sefer Tagin is also apparently mentioned in a *midrash* from *Shir ha-Shirim Rabba* though not in all extant versions. This *midrash* explains that, ר. לוי אמר ספר תגי הראה להם (R. Levi said *Sefer Tagi* appeared to them) and is the main subject of an important Hebrew article by R. Ephraim Caspi and R. Mordechai Weintroyb entitled על זמנו של ספר תגין (On the Time of *Sefer Tagin*).[19] They discuss the existence of this reference to *Sefer Tagin* as being in some of the early hand-written manuscripts of *Shir ha-Shirim Rabba* (3:4) but only in one of printed versions.[20] The importance of this statement is noted as if this is the case, then *Sefer Tagin* already existed in the time of R. Levi, who was amongst the first of the *ʾAmoraim*.

Sefer Tagin is, in effect, a manual for the *sofer* (scribe) that:

---

16 Ibid., p. 210.

17 Van der Toorn, Karel, *Scribal Culture and the Making of the Hebrew Bible*, Harvard University Press, Massachusetts, 2007, p. 34 As Van der Toorn further notes, 'texts were often attributed to great figures from the past as a way to impress their authority on the audience. The real author remained anonymous. These practices require that we first investigate ancient concepts of authorship. A review of the textual evidence, both biblical and cuneiform, leads me to conclude that anonymity was the rule in the literary production of the ancient Near East. This anonymity was not merely an omission of names [of the real author]; it is evidence of a particular notion of authorship.' Ibid., p. 28.

18 Described in Joshua 4:9.

19 Caspi, E. and Weintroyb, M., על זמנו של ספר תגין (On the Time of *Sefer Tagin*) from ירושתינו, Vol. 5, *Makhon Moreshet ʾAskenaz*, Bene Beraq, 5771.

20 They bring a table summary of those manuscripts and printed copies they have investigated and quote the text in each highlighting in parallel where the reference to *Sefer Tagin* appears and where it does not. Ibid., p. 310. It is possible, since this phrase is not in some versions, that is a later interpolation, but is just as likely an omission from some.

a) Gives a description of the form of a special letter that either has some oddity in its shape and/or is decorated with extra *tagin* over and above the norm. Most letters have only one special form, but some have two (e.g. *he, ḥet, zayin, kaf sofit, pe, pe sofit, tsade, qof*) or, in one case, three (*ʿayin*). *Meshunot* is thus a collective term that labels these special forms as different, which is not always just the shape. Conversely, whilst the book is called *Sefer Tagin*, the forms described do not always involve extra *tagin*.

b) Lists how many instances that there are in the *Torah* with this special form—there is not always universal agreement between the sources, as we will see.

c) Lists the words (sometimes within a short phrase) that identify where these instances occur in the biblical text. Often this is linked to a verse—e.g. the 'word' of [the verse beginning] 'word/phrase', such as the first example in *Sefer Tagin* in the very first sentence of the *Torah*, אלה̊ים דבראשית meaning [the *he*] of 'God' of [the verse beginning] 'in the beginning'. In some manuscript sources, these letters are also marked with a line or a circle or occasionally decorated fully in the prescribed form. Often there will be more than one letter decorated in a word or short phrase, in which case the text might add תרויהון (two of them) and sometimes even three תלתיהון (three of them).

The text will also refer to קדמאה (the first), which can either be the first occurrence of the word/short phrase in a certain section or the first letter in the word, if there are two of the same letters that could be decorated. Additionally, בתראה (the last) can also refer to the last time that word/short phrase occurs in a section or the last occurrence of that letter in the word/short phrase. Sometimes, it is not clear which is intended.

Usually each instance is separated by some kind of mark or dot, but occasionally this is forgotten or placed in error, which can lead to confusion over what is meant, or the conflation of two instances. We also see errors of metathesis,[21] dittography[22] or haplography,[23] in the sources, which add to the issues transmitted though subsequent copying.

The norm is for the כתיב *ketiv* (it is written) to be brought, but occasionally, the קרי *qeri* (it is read as) will be brought. It is also important to note

21 The inadvertent transposition of letters in a word.

22 The mistaken repetition of a letter, word, or phrase by a copyist.

23 When the scribe's eye inadvertently passes over from one word or phrase to another of similar nature, resulting in an omission. Or when repeated letters, words or phrases are omitted.

that despite these listings being words from the *Torah*, not one source, core or secondary, consistently follows the standard orthography seen in the Masoretic Text of the *Torah* (shown here as 𝔐). Thus words in the listing will be written *ḥaser* or *ma-le'* the *mater lectionis*, usually a *vav* or a *yod*, and so cannot be cannot be relied on as an accurate witness to the orthography in the *Torah*.

Finally, on rare occasions, no extant source brings what is likely to be the correct reading.

Razhabi[24] notes that the most well-known text of *Sefer Tagin* that we have, printed in Paris in 1866,[25] is both incomplete and contains errors. Though in part, he (incorrectly) holds this view because it does not refer to the other types of special letters (large, small etc.). Nonetheless, it is certainly the case that it has many errors when it is compared to extant manuscripts. Indeed, not one of the surviving manuscripts of *Sefer Tagin* is free from errors or corruptions (deliberate or otherwise). This has led Liss to comment that 'quite obviously, there existed a number of different traditions concerning tagin in the High Middle Ages'[26] and Isserles to note that 'the study of various medieval manuscripts and scrolls from Ashkenaz and Italy, as well as one early Sephardic scroll, reveals that there is hardly any copy which follows the rules precisely in the same way, attesting to a great diversity in the tagin tradition'.[27] In reality, this diversity is likely largely caused by uncertainty brought on by poor transmission of the original text over time and individual scribes adding or omitting instances when they were not sure and, to a certain extent, this has, in part, 'discredited' *Sefer Tagin*. This uncertainty, together with the nature of some of the more 'outlandish' forms of letters, which would be considered too far from the permitted form of the letter in stricter modern halakhic practice, means that some authorities do not encourage following this practice, over fears for the *kashrut* (validity) of the *Torah* for public use, and the doubts this brought.[28]

24 Kasher, M. and Razhabi Y., *Torah Shelemah Leviticus Vol. 29*. American Biblical Encyclopedia Society Inc. Jerusalem, 1978, p. 83, section 5, ספר התגין שלפנינו חסר הוא (The *Sefer Tagin* that is before us is defective).

25 Bargés, J. *Sepher Taghin: Liber coronularum*. Lutetiæ Parisiorum: Ex officina L. Guérin, Paris, 1866.

26 Liss, Hanna, *A Pentateuch to Read in: The Secrets of the Regensburg Pentateuch*, De Gruyter, 2017, p. 118.

27 Isserles, J. Oesch, J.M., and Hubmann, F.D., *The Torah Scroll Fragment from the Parochial Archives in Romont (Switzerland)* from *The Ancient Torah of Bologna: features and history*, Brill, Leiden, 2019, p. 214.

28 For example, the Ḥatam Sofer states that 'our scribes do not so any of this and this is

The sources for *Sefer Tagin* are indeed not consistent and do not agree with each other. My early researches suggested that more than 20% of the c. 1,914 instances that are required (by summing the numbers of instances given in the descriptions of letters) have some query or issue relating to them because of errors or disputes over which particular letter should be decorated. The closer examination of the texts, that has been a necessary part of this and wider work, suggest that this level of error is even higher.

Thus the discovery of additional fragments from manuscripts of *Sefer Tagin* in the Cairo *Genizah*, over and above the known corpus, is of enormous assistance in remedying some of these discrepancies and this will be treated in detail in parts 2–4.

4 The Corpus of Textual Witnesses to *Sefer Tagin*—Core and Secondary Sources

Before discussing those new finds, below is a list detailing the textual witnesses that specifically identify as **actual letter descriptions and listings from *Sefer Tagin*.** This constitutes a relatively small corpus.

The **core** sources include:

1. Biblioteca Palatina, **MS Parma 2574** (DeRossi cat. no. 159), a manuscript of *Maḥzor Vitry leRabbeynu Simḥa*,[29] from northern France. It is dated to end 12th–early 13th C. and, as such, is the oldest complete version extant.[30] The text of *Sefer Tagin* appears in ff. 240r–244v and follows the listing by letter order. Images of the forms of the letters are shown by each section and then summarised at the end—they do not always match. For the sake of brevity, I have assigned it the siglum **P**.

proper, for we do not really know how [to do] these things which were passed from man to man and are not in the *Mishnah*, they are confused in their explanation of the revelations and one should not rely upon them.' (Responsa *Yoreh De'ah* 275).

29 Simḥa ben Samuel of Vitry was a pupil of Rashi and a French Talmudist of the 11th and 12th centuries. Not all extant copies of this work contain the section on *Sefer Tagin*. Indeed, reportedly Jordan Penkover is of the opinion that *Sefer Tagin* is 'not part of the original *Maḥzor Vitri*, and was certainly not included by Simcha of Vitri' as noted in Perani, M., *Part 2: The Oldest Complete Extant Sefer Torah* ... op. cit. P is available to view at: https://web.nli.org.il/sites/NLI/English/digitallibrary/pages/viewer.aspx?&presentorid=MANUSCRIPTS&docid=PNX_MANUSCRIPTS000083855-1#|FL17263140 (first accessed 7/2/17).

30 Justine Isserles very kindly provided me information through email (dated 25/11/17) from her PhD thesis which explains that this manuscript is of North French origin, but with some relation to authorities in Provence. It has hard-point ruling and a pre-gothic book-hand script.

2. British Library, **Add. MS 27200—Add. MS 27201** (Margoliouth cat. n°605), northern France, c. 1242. See particularly Add. MS 27201 where *Sefer Tagin* begins after *Hilkhot Sefer Torah* ff. 209r–215r. It is written in Ashkenazi (French) square and semi-cursive script.[31] However, unlike the *Sefer Tagin* texts that show the order letter by letter, this shows the instances by *parasha* (*Torah* section). Similar to **P**, there is internal inconsistency in the forms presented of each letter form, with several variants presented in the manuscript. All images from this source are freely available to reproduce and © The British Library Board. It is given below as **MV**.
It is this London manuscript that was used in the printed edition by Hurwitz, S., *Maḥzor Vitry leRabbeynu Simḥa*, Nuremberg, 1923, 2 vols. (*Sefer Tagin* is found in volume 2, pp. 674–683). This is given below as **LMV**. It is also worth noting that this volume also formed the basis of C.D. Ginsburg's listing under תאגים pp. 680–701 after his treatment of *tav*,[32] so his listing is of limited value in any comparison. He lists his view of the special letters again by *parasha*, and whilst he generally follows the London *Maḥzor Vitry*, this is not always the case.[33]

3. The ***Sefer Tagi*** that occurs in the *Tanakh* of Rabbi Shem Tov Ibn Ga'on ben 'Avraham after the end of the *Torah* section. This was written in 1312 by a key authority, the *Badey ha-'Aron* himself.[34] Formerly Sassoon 82,[35] I first encountered it in 2017 through a scan of the images on microfilm held by the National Library of Israel.[36] The listing occurs on folios 177–179, however, the scan was particularly difficult to read. This was particularly pronounced on folio 177, the first page of the listings where a large

31 Available to view at: http://www.bl.uk/manuscripts/FullDisplay.aspx?index=9&ref=Add_MS_27201 (first accessed 1/9/16).

32 Ginsburg, Christian D., *The Massorah, Vol. II*, London 1880.

33 Ginzburg also takes issues with decisions made by Dr. S. Baer over his choice of instances for the letter *'alef*, see *Vol IV VI*, p. 1a.

34 As noted by Olszowy-Schlanger 'the Sefer Tagei and the tradition of modified letters is also transmitted in North Iberian kabbalistic circles, notably by Shem Tov ben Abraham ibn Gaon (1283–c. 1330), native of the Castilian town of Soria, who included the tagin and modified letters in a beautifully illuminated Pentateuch codex he copied in Soria in 1312' (Olszowy-Schlanger, J., *The Making of the Bologna Scroll* from from *The Ancient Torah of Bolognia: features and history*, Brill, Leiden, 2019, p. 131).

35 See Sassoon, D.S., *Ohel David. Descriptive Catalogue of the Hebrew and Samaritan Manuscripts in the Sassoon Library, vol. 1, London, 1932*, pp. 2–5, n° 82.

36 First accessed 6/10/17. JNUL kindly gave me permission to reproduce the scanned images, for which I thank them, even though I have subsequently replaced them with the new enhanced colour images.

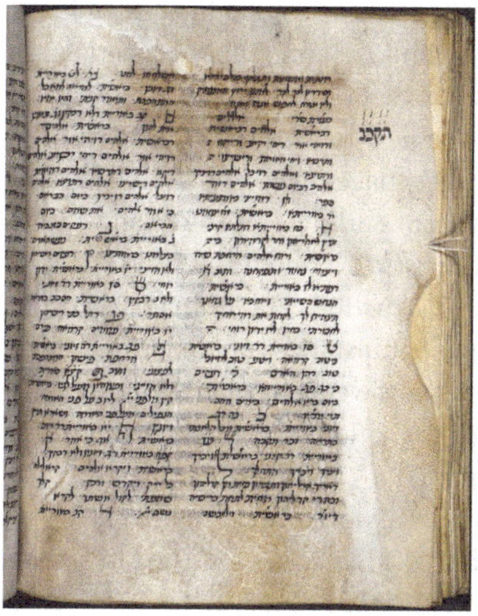

FIGURE 6 Add. MS 27201, 209v, the first page of instances after the introduction to *Sefer Tagin* found on 209r.

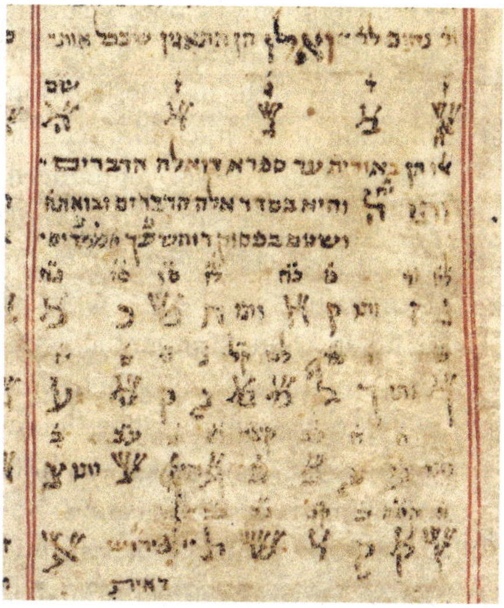

FIGURE 7 The forms of the letters from Sassoon 82 (JUD. 002), above which are shown the number of instances. From the introductory section.

section of the listings at the bottom of the columns affecting letters *he*, *vav*, *zayin* and *ḥet* was very faded. Moreover, Shem Tov appeared to have then skipped straight to *lamed* on folio 178 from the *ḥet* at the base of the previous page. Shem Tov clearly recognised his omission later as the omitted letters *ṭet*, *yod*, *kaf* and *kaf sofit* were written in the top, sides and bottom margins. However, it is in these marginal listings where the most fading and damage has occurred and whilst they can be seen, much of the ink residue present is not obviously visible in the microfilm version.[37] However, through the welcome approach of a colleague detailed

37 Having completed this monograph and submitted it for peer review, I commenced my PhD and in my first session with my joint supervisor Dr Ben Outhwaite, I explained that is was this manuscript—Sassoon 82—which I would very much like to have better quality imagery. However, as noted recently by Isserles 'in 1990, this manuscript was in the Floersheim Trust collection, see *The Image of the World: Jewish tradition in Manuscripts and Printed Books. Catalogue of an Exhibition Held at the Jewish Historical Museum*, Amsterdam (14 Sept.–25 Nov. 1990), Amsterdam 1990' (Isserles, Oesch and Hubmann, op. cit.,

in the footnotes below, I secured new enhanced digital images and permissions from the current owner Mr. Jaqui E. Safra. The manuscript has also received the new designation JUD. 022. I have therefore used a combination of the microfilm scan and the new images to assess better the listing, and I have also reproduced the key pages in appendix 2. Additionally, having access to the full *Tanakh* that Shem Tov wrote often allows one to clarify what his intention was in the listing.[38] Shem Tov also brings an introductory section that repeats the instructions and numbers (written in full in Aramaic rather than numerals) of instances of the letters which serves as a double check of his intentions as well as having the number of the instances written above a form of the letter, as shown above. To this manuscript I have assigned the siglum **ST**.

Allowing us to triangulate R. Shem Tov's views, there is also a separate listing of the instructions together with images of the letters in the ***Badey ha-'Aron uMigdal Ḥanan'el*** written in Recueil de commentaires cabalistiques—Hébreu 840 copied in the 14th–15th Century and residing in the Bibliothèque Nationale de France. The instructions being on f103.[39] This is given below as **BH**.[40] Chapter 6 on the subject of the *tagin* is also reproduced in the printed *Sefer Tagin* (see below). Finally, it is **ST** that Basser uses as the basis of his his excellent 2010 Hebrew book, ספר תגי, though also drawing on other sources as cross references.[41]

---

p. 213). However, the location of this key manuscript thereafter was unknown and this was confirmed by the JNUL. A colleague Nehemia Gordon who had recently interviewed me about my scribal practice (see www.nehemiaswall.com/scribe-toolbox and www.sofer.co.uk) was in a private collection in Geneva photographing a different manuscript and he was asked to also photograph the key three folios from Sassoon 82 that present Shem Tov's version of *Sefer Tagin*. Recognising the document from reading a draft of this monograph, Nehemia contacted me to let me know and also ask if there were any areas he should concentrate on. I gave him a guide to the marginal and faded areas on folio 177, explaining they were part of the listing and not marginal notes. Nehemia took many valuable close up images, both standard and infrared, to see if would highlight any remainder of ink traces on the faded areas to see if it would reveal any other elements of the listings and passed them to me in late October 2019. I therefore obtained permission from the current owner to utilise these enhanced images to revise the monograph and also use the images of the letters to replace those I had been using from the microfilm scan.

38 Though on occasion what he lists, he does not decorate, and vice versa.

39 Viewable at: http://gallica.bnf.fr/ark:/12148/btv1b10720531s/f103.image and http://gallica.bnf.fr/ark:/12148/btv1b10720531s/f104.image (first accessed 17/9/16).

40 The work is a kabbalistic work in five parts, finished in the month of *Iyyar*, 1325, and named by Shem Tov after his traveling companion, Ḥanan'el b. 'Azkara, who died before reaching his destination.

41 Basser, Y., *Sefer Tagi*, Israel, 2010. However, this book is not entirely an academic work, as

4. Paris, Bibliothèque Nationale, **Ms Hébreu 837**, ff. 148r–159r. This manuscript, originally designated 285 finds *Sefer Tagin* amongst a selection of other texts. It is dated 15th C. by Gallica, and Justine Isserles[42] confirms that the manuscript has variety of 15th c. Italian book-hand scripts on paper.[43] It is given below as **H**. It is however a very flawed text, and has some sixty instances missing for the letter *he* between *parashat Va-yeshev* and *parashat Va-yera'*.[44]
   It was also used as the base for the most commonly known version of *Sefer Tagin* (mentioned above), the printed *Editio princeps* of *Sepher Taghin* (ספר תגין), *Liber Coronularum*, (ed.) J.J.L. BARGES, Paris, 1866, pp. 1–28 (with a Hebrew preface by Senior (Shneur) Sachs). That printed text is shown below as **EPST**.
5. Kreuzenstein, Sammlung Graf Wilczek, Inv.—**Nr.** 5667, HDSHDS. This single page fragment is a *Sefer Tagin* listing showing the end of *ḥet* part way through to *kaf*. It is dated to 14th–15th Century and has been rescued through the Books Within Books project,[45] and is held within the Austrian repository, where it is listed as a *Tiqqun Sofrim*.[46] The number of instances are given alongside the listing, but not the descriptions of the letters. The letters forms are drawn into the text at each instance. It is a very useful fragment, as it tends to give a much more expanded listing with more use of phrases rather than single words. This helps clarify the intention of the instance. Moreover, it perhaps suggests that, rather than slavishly copying his *Vorlage* of *Sefer Tagin*, the scribe here has taken the trouble to check

---

when there are disagreements between the sources, Basser will follow Shem Tov purely on the basis of his rabbinic authority. Additionally, as Basser notes, he only had access to the microfilm scans, which would have prevented seeing some instances. Nonetheless, his book is excellent and was very helpful, and particularly added the *Ben Mesheq* to my considerations.

42 Email exchange dated 27/11/17.

43 Viewable at http://gallica.bnf.fr/ark:/12148/btv1b10546339r/f306.item (first accessed 11/8/17).

44 Ephraim Caspi holds that H was copied directly from P (personal correspondence) and there are indeed much similarity in them, in which case H would have less standing in the corpus. However, there are enough examples brought in this monograph to show there are significant and differences between the texts in terms of orthography and some instances (added words etc.), which suggests that this is not the case, and rather they seem to be from the same family of tradition/common *Vorlagen*.

45 Details at http://www.hebrewmanuscript.com/.

46 Accessible through http://hebraica.at/hebraica/hebraica1/Bibliothek/?l=&s=236 (first accessed 25/2/18).

the references against the *Torah* verses and expand on the listing to clarify.[47] It is given below as K.

6. Similar to BH is **Ms. Guenzburg. 481** a manuscript from the end 12th–early 13th century manuscript held in the Russian State Library. A liturgical-halachic compendium/*Maḥzor Vitry*, following the *Nusaḥ Tsarfat*. However, it is also of limited use as it only has drawings of the forms of the letters, not the descriptions or the list of instances.[48]

Secondary sources:

There are other works that can be considered parallels to *Sefer Tagin* in that they contain similar listings of these instances but are **not** prefaced by the introduction to *Sefer Tagin*, nor do they include specific letter descriptions, numbers and instructions. Whilst some grant these texts almost equal authority to the main corpus of actual listing of *Sefer Tagin*, it is, I believe, worth making a specific distinction. Since these listings are generally mixed in with other instructions such as *petuḥot* and *setumot* (open and closed sections), large and small letters, dotted letters and reversed letters, and instructions regarding orthography, it is possible that some of these were not copied from a listing of *Sefer Tagin* but rather assembled from *Sifrey Torah* that these sages had access to. Hence the variances, omissions and additions to the—for the want of a better word—'official' listings are more pronounced. However, they are valuable as secondary witnesses to the tradition to assist where there are disagreements between the core texts.

For this monograph, I will be drawing on the following manuscripts as secondary sources:

1. **Add. MS 27201** *Maḥzor Vitry*—this is indeed the same manuscript as quoted above. However, before the core *Sefer Tagin* introduction and listing that begins on folio 209r, there are twenty folios commencing on

47 K, in this respect is perhaps like **ST**, in that whilst 'the average hired scribe would have been consciously more loyal to his model, probably would have avoided critical and deliberate intervention in the transmission, yet would have been more fallible and vulnerable to the involuntary changes and mistakes conditioned by the mechanics of copying ... the scholar-copyist might intentionally interfere in the transmission, revise his exemplar, emend and reconstruct the text, add to it and modify it according to his knowledge, memory, conjecture or other exemplars, and indeed regard copying as a critical editing and not merely as duplicating. Moreover, logic suggests that scribes would tend to repeat obvious mistakes in their models, while copyists would correct the corrupted text. Indeed, these assumptions can be substantiated and verified by the scribes' and copyists' own statements in their colophons.' Beit Arié, M., *Transmission of Texts by Scribes and Copyists: Unconscious and Critical Interferences*, John Ryland University Bulletin, Vol. 75, Issue 3, 1993, pp. 39–40.

48 Original image kindly supplied to me by Justine Isserles, which I have drawn out for reproduction here.

folio 199v that list an **alternative version** that is more akin to a secondary source, in that it is mixed together with other scribal instructions such as large, small and dotted letters and the positions of the *petuḥot* and *setumot*. Indeed, the scribe writes והלין תגי וספר תורה ופתוחות וסתומות וסדרות על פי קבלה מסורות (and these are the *tagin* [in] the *Sefer Torah* and open and closed sections and sequences according to received tradition). This may be combined from the source already in this manuscript (which would lessen its value) or may have been copied from a different tradition. Certainly some of the letter forms brought are a little different to how they appear in the main *Sefer Tagin* listing (though in that itself the letters are not always consistent) so it is possible that it has been copied from a different source. Although it precedes the main listing, this has been assigned the siglum **MV2**.[49]

2. **Parma 2427**. A similar variant of *Sefer Tagin* brought as part of a תקון סופרים (scribe's copyists guide). It is held by the Palatina Library, Parma, Italy, and was formerly Catalogue De-Rossi, Parma, Italy 578. It is dated to the 15th Century.[50]
3. **תגין וזיונין** *Tagin veZiyyunin* **Q651–652**. This is found as a two part listing in a codex of the *Torah, Haftorot* and *Megillot* in a German manuscript from Weimar and held in the Thuringsche Landesbibliothek. it is dated approximately 1150–1217.[51]
4. **Add. MS 11639**. Dated 1277–1324, it contains a miscellany of biblical and other texts (known as 'The Northern French Miscellany' or earlier 'the British Museum Miscellany'): including 'the Pentateuch, *Haftarot, Tikkun Soferim*, Five Scrolls, prayer book for the entire year with *Hagadah*, legal texts, poetry, and the book of Tobit in Hebrew'. Our interest lies from folio 123v to 168v where in the margins of the other texts is similar attempt to edit *Sefer Tagin* into a larger work in a faded brown script which often goes around the page in decorative steps pages with listings in spiralled patterns. It is held by the British Library. Since the work mostly weaves round the page, it is quite difficult to read.[52]

---

49 It is certainly odd that this alternative version is never referenced. However, this may be because after two folios where the *tagin* are demonstrated on the words listed, the copyist seems to 'give up' and thereafter only randomly adds the odd decoration on each page even though the words themselves continue to be listed.

50 Available to view at: http://web.nli.org.il/sites/NLI/English/digitallibrary/pages/viewer.aspx?&presentorid=MANUSCRIPTS&docid=PNX_MANUSCRIPTS000084123-1#|FL16542748 (first accessed 12/11/16).

51 Available through Hebrewbooks.org (Part 1 = 45999 and Part 2 = 45699).

52 Available to view at http://www.bl.uk/manuscripts/Viewer.aspx?ref=add_ms_11639 (first accessed 20/10/17).

5. **Parma 1959**. Folios 184v to 195r. Also held by the Palatina Library, Parma, Italy under the title of האותיות המלופפות ושאר אותיות משונות שבתורה (the curled letters and the rest of the strange letters that are in the *Torah*) and written by 'Avraham ben Yehudah 'Ibn Ḥayyim in 1462. This manuscript is treated in detail in Débora Marques de Matos, *The MS. Parma 1959 in the Context of Portuguese Hebrew Illumination*, Universidade De Lisboa, Faculdade De Letres Insituto De História Da Arte, 2011. The section containing the 'List of oddly shaped letter found in an accurate Torah Scroll' is detailed on pp. 77–80. The comment by the author suggests he constructed the text himself from a specific *Sefer Torah*, rather than combining lists he had in his possession, as he writes, כמו שמצאתים בס"ת המדוייק ובעבור שלא מצאתים אלא בס"ת זה ראיתי שהוא טוב לתופשם הנה ואלו הן האותיות הנאמרות לעיל (as I found within in an accurate *Sefer Torah* and because one does not find it except in the this *Torah* that I saw, that it is good to record them (lit. catch them) here, and these are the letters mentioned above).[53]
6. **Add. MS 27167**. This beautifully decorated manuscript is held by the British Library and also has a variant on *Sefer Tagin*. It was formerly Catalogue Margoliouth, London, England 83 and The British Library, London, England ALM 277 and is dated to the 14th/15th Century. It seems to have an affinity with Parma 1959, given the naming conventions of the *parashiyyot* employed, so may be drawing on the same *Vorlage*. Certainly the texts match very closely with very few differences. It has no introductory section and sadly the manuscript only covers the special letters in Genesis in folios 455v–461r before it moves to listing the small letters, so unfortunately, is of limited use.

Three other 'authoritative' texts worthy of mention, to help settle disagreements, that were employed for this paper were:

1. ***Qiryat Sefer*** by the Me'iri—R. Menaḥem ben Shelomo (1249–1316), Provençal scholar and commentator of the *Talmud*.[54]
2. The ***Ben Mesheq***. *Tiqqun Sofrim ve'Iṭur Sofrim* written by 'Eli'ezer ben 'Eved-el Yitsḥaq, printed in Prague in 1658/9. This *tiqqun* also lists all of the special letters by *parasha*. However, it is worth noting that the author

53 Available to view at: http://web.nli.org.il/sites/NLI/English/digitallibrary/pages/viewer.aspx?&presentorid=MANUSCRIPTS&docid=PNX_MANUSCRIPTS000080690-1#|FL49206813.

54 I accessed several printed versions of this work. The most useful was the Part 2, printed in Izmir 1881, which contains his listing of the special letters by *parasha* pp. 24–99. Available at http://www.hebrewbooks.org/49533 (first accessed 22/8/17).

tends to add additional instances when faced with a choice between alternative options.

3. The ***Ba'al ha-Ṭurim*** by R. Jacob ben Asher, known as the Ba'al ha-Ṭurim (probably born in Cologne c. 1269 and probably died at Toledo c. 1343). Not a listing as such, the Ba'al ha-Ṭurim may have had access to some form of *Sefer Tagin* or had seen many scrolls that followed it, as peppered through his commentary on the *Torah* he brings many *midrashim* explaining the special *tagin*. He only comments on a fraction of entries, however, which suggest he was only working from scrolls that he had seen. I have translated the entries from the Hebrew, but *The Davis Edition*, published by Mesorah Publications (1999–2004) is a particularly useful source as the author R. Avie Gold annotates each occasion such an instance is brought in the translation by R. Eliyahu Touger.

There are also many other manuscripts and books with listings[55] that I have located along with a large number of *Sifrey Torah* and *Tanakh* codices that employ

55 Razhabi's listing in *Torah Shelemah* Vol. 29, already mentioned above is a part of the huge multi-volumed work. This volume contains a very unique collection of visual *midrash* with examples of special letters found throughout many scrolls, however, not all are actually related to *Sefer Tagin*. He describes many of these scribal oddities and brings the opinions of many sources and commentators on their history and form. Additionally, there is the listing brought by Dr S. Baer in תקון הסופר והקורא (*Copyist Guide for the Scribe and the Reader*), Frankfurt a. M (früher Rödelheim), Druck and Verlag von M. Lehrberger & Co., 1900. However, he starts only at the letter *vav* (mentioning *'alef* only in the footnotes) and tends to conflate the traditions found in Yemenite *Sifrey Torah* with those from *Sefer Tagin*. Also that of the Ḥatam Sofer found in *Keneset Sofrim* originally written in Pressburg and reprinted in Jerusalem by *Makhon Benei Moshe*, 2005. Other quite partial listings, where sages bring *midrashim* on the letters, include *Sefer Tagi leRabbeynu 'Eliezar miGermazia* (this sage is commonly known as the Roqeaḥ). However, he only lists those in the early parts of Genesis up to Gen. 18:21. These are brought in Basser's book (op. cit., pp. 271–384). There are also entries in *Peirush ha-Roqeaḥ al ha-Torah* by the same sage, *Sefer Paneaḥ Razeh uPeirush Rabbeynu Ḥayyim Palṭiel al ha-Torah, Sefer Parparot la-Torah leRabbeynu Avigdor Tsarfati* and *Sefer Ramzey Yo'el*. The halachic test for scribes, *Me'ir 'Eyney Sofrim* also gives a partial listing of letters with extra *tagin* as part of its description of all the special letters and open and closed sections. Whilst the *derashot* brought by these sages are interesting, given their partial nature, again these traditions may not have been derived from a *Sefer Tagin* listing and may have been collated from examples of usage in *Sifrey Torah* that they had personally witnessed, and thus, I would argue, of slightly less value. It is important to note that what is stated in an halakhic text may never have actually been practiced by scribes *in toto* or at all. It should also be stated that even usage in a codex is no guarantee of scribal practice. A codex is not a *Torah* and so something preserved in a codex may never have been used in an actual *Torah*—the most famous being Gaster's *Tittled Bible*, which has many more *tagin* that any of the sources testify to, and, as a result,

Sefer Tagin.[56] I have not brought all of these in this particular monograph, but the footnotes give details of sources should the reader wish to explore them further. Whilst I will be concerned with establishing the likely original or most accurate reading through a comparison of the available manuscript sources, this monograph does not treat in any detail the possible reasons behind the listings of particular instances. There are many midrashic reasons offered by various authorities for individual words chosen for decoration, however, there is no guarantee that any of these reflect the original intention for their inclusion by the author or authors of *Sefer Tagin*. This is a subject for wider consideration and study.

5 Some Example Uses in *Sifrey Torah*

However, for comparison with the halakhic texts, I have also brought a few example illustrations of how the letter forms have been used in *Sifrey Torah* over time, from the many examples I have located in various digital repositories.[57] The first is drawn from images of the oldest complete *Sefer Torah* to employ *Sefer Tagin*, **Il Rotolo 2**.[58] The second is one of the oldest, a *Torah* dated to the 12–13th century and held by the Biblioteca Apostolica Vaticana. **Vat. ebr. 1** which has 212 columns and is written on *gevil* parchment.[59] The third is a particularly fine and consistent example of how the forms are used. **Or. 1463** was written in 1500–1599, but unfortunately, is only partially preserved consisting of the whole

I have discounted it from this investigation. Indeed many of the forms in the Gaster *Tittled Bible* would be immediately considered *pasul*—even under the looser halakhic opinions of the past.

56 At the time of writing, I have located some seventy-six full or partial manuscripts that utilise some form of *Sefer Tagin*. R. Ephraim Caspi, in his correspondence with me, notes that he has found some 500. These are part of my wider studies into options for the forms of the letters.

57 Far too many to bring within this monograph but, again, part of my wider analysis of the forms. Hence the choice of a mere handful of examples here to illustrate the letter forms against the halakhic texts.

58 Drawings made from photos within the power-point presentation, Perani, M., *The Rediscovery of the most ancient entire Sefer Torah at the Bologna University Library (12th Century) A Rare Witness of the Masoretic Babylonian Graphic and Textual Tradition*, University of Bologna, 2016. Further detail is also available in the pamphlet, Antonio, B., De Tata, R. and Perani, M., *Il Rotolo 2 dela Biblioteca Universitaria de Bologna, il Pentateuco piÙ antica del mondo*, BUB, 2015.

59 Viewable at https://digi.vatlib.it/view/MSS_Vat.ebr.1 (first accessed 15/10/16).

of Genesis and Exodus as far as 38:19.[60] The fourth is from a much later 'modern' period and is a beautifully decorated and historically special *Torah*. **The Alexander *Torah*** was written in 1790 and was saved from the *Sho'ah*. I had the honour of restoring it, during which I photographed it extensively.[61] These are just a selection, however, for there are many more available images in other available manuscripts and countless different views of how the forms of the letters and the *tagin* could be drawn.

6 Adding to the Core Corpus, Oxford Bodleian MS. Heb. d. 33/3 (fol. 9), a Known Fragment from the Cairo *Genizah*

As part of my research, to expand on this corpus, as well as highlighting **MV2**, I had located one partial manuscript of *Sefer Tagin* that is not widely known or referenced. It consists of two sides of an undated listing on vellum bought by the Rev. G.J. Chester in 1891 from the Cairo *Genizah* described incorrectly as a 'fragment of a grammatical treatise in Arabic' and listed as part of the 'Masora finalis' under entry 2755 'Masorah, Grammar and Lexicography'.[62]

This section covers the end of the listing for most of *mem sofit* though *nun*, *nun sofit*, *samekh* and the start of *'ayin*. Helpfully, the scribe has added dots over the letters to indicate which he means and thus avoid confusion. However, it only brings drawings of the letters and the number of instances and omits the actual descriptions. It is a great shame that no further pages are available as this source is very clear and well presented and the script suggests it is quite an old witness, possibly 11th century from the land of Israel.[63]

---

60 Viewable at: http://www.bl.uk/manuscripts/FullDisplay.aspx?ref=Or_1463 (first accessed 30/8/16).

61 The history of the travels of the *Torah* throughout Germany to London and the story of its restoration, including a large section on the special *tagin* are chronicled in my book, Michaels, M., *The Torah in the Wardrobe*, Kulmus Publishing, London, 2017.

62 Neubauer, Adolf, Cowley, Arthur Ernest, *Catalogue of the Hebrew Manuscripts in the Bodleian Library*, Oxford Clarendon Press, 1906, p. 173.

63 Sharing them with Justine Isserles, her initial view was that it looked very much like 'an old Italian square script of the late 11th or early 12th century from Southern Italy. The [rare] square folio format [used] is ... typical from this region and was used during the 11th and later until 12th century'. However, Prof. Judith Olszowy-Schlanger with whom she shared this manuscript, feels that it is '11th century, West Oriental Palestinian'. A similar assessment was also given independently by Dr Ben Outhwaite of the Cambridge *Genizah* who stated that 'it's a rather lovely old fragment on parchment. It's of Palestinian character (look at the *'alef*s—the way the left leg comes all the way from the top of the letter, rather than midway through the stroke is a clear sign of Palestinian heritage). It's early 11th c.

Held by the Bodleian, I have assigned **Oxford MS. Heb. d. 33/3 (fol. 9)** the siglum **OB.**[64] For me, this raised the possibility that other pages from this manuscript were scattered through the Cairo *Genizah* collections, similarly mislabeled and not fully recognised for what they are. I therefore started to make some attempts to locate other sections of this particular manuscript. I have not succeeded in that venture as yet.

at the latest, and probably 100 years or more earlier than that. There are very clear serifs on most of the letters, which again points to an earlier rather than a later date.' Either assessment would have made this the oldest extant, albeit partial, version of *Sefer Tagin*.

64 Available through the Friedberg *Genizah* Project and also at: http://genizah.bodleian.ox.ac.uk/fragment/MS_Heb_d_33/9a and http://genizah.bodleian.ox.ac.uk/fragment/MS_Heb_d_33/9b (first accessed 15/10/17). I was subsequently informed by Benjamin Caspi (personal correspondence) that the existence of **OB** as being from *Sefer Tagin* was known to others, though not widely publicised as such. I had identified one of the sheets in the Friedberg *Genizah* site and the other had been identified by Rabbi Mordechai Weintroyb.

CHAPTER 2

A New (Partial) Witness

1 T-S D1.42—Two New Pages from a Version of *Sefer Tagin* Identified from the Cairo *Genizah*

On reviewing some 119 manuscripts listed under *Masorah* in the Cambridge *Genizah* collection, at the suggestion of Dr Ben Outhwaite, I initially located a **further set of two pages from yet another manuscript version of *Sefer Tagin*—T-S D1.42.**[1] This had also been partially mislabelled, described as a 'Lexicography [containing a] list of biblical words and phrases containing a particular letter in the front, middle or end. Letters *he* to *ṭet* are preserved.'[2]

It is, in fact, another example of a listing of *Sefer Tagin* which gives the numbers of instances and description but apparently with no example forms, though it later transpired that this is because the forms were written at the end of the work only, as can be seen on the joined fragment **T-S NS 287.11-F** (see below). Our scribe often adds (but sadly, not consistently) a single straight-line *tag* to indicate where the special letters occur in a word. Before some of the sections in marginal or line space in smaller writing, there is the word שער (gate) and then the letter, as if the author is opening up and revealing a secret to the reader. It is possible these may have been added by a later scribe.[3]

These two sides written on ruled lines on vellum (leaf height 17.8 cm × 14.5 cm width) cover the end of the first version of the letter *he* through the second version of the *he* form, the letter *vav*, two forms of *zayin*, two forms of *ḥet* and most of the listing for *ṭet*. Unfortunately, the manuscript has suffered some water damage, it is slightly torn and there are a few holes in the parchment and, as a

1 This is viewable at https://cudl.lib.cam.ac.uk/view/MS-TS-D-00001-00042/1 (first accessed 14/12/17). The manuscript was donated by Dr Solomon Schechter (1847–1915) and his patron Dr Charles Taylor (1840–1908) in 1898 as part of the Taylor-Schechter *Genizah* Collection.

2 As described on the Cambridge site in note 1 above.

3 שערי (gates of) as titles for section dividers are often used in halakhic texts and this may just be a synonym for section. For example the halakhic scribal text *Mishnat 'Avraham* refers to his sections as gates. However, the use of the specific word does also feel that the writer is opening up a world to you and revealing some esoteric knowledge. The use of this word may stem from the kabbalistic idea of the fifty gates of wisdom/understanding and that Moses was only able to penetrate the secrets of forty-nine of these. Based on the comparison with the other core sources, this does not belong to the original text of *Sefer Tagin*, which is why it may be the author or later scribe adding it.

 | DOI:10.1163/9789004426368_003

FIGURE 8 CUL T-S D1.42 1v

FIGURE 9 CUL T-S D1.42 1r

result, some of the wording is obscured or faded. Both have 26 lines, 1v is written on the hair side and 1r on the flesh side.[4]

2 Dating and Locating T-S D1.42

Having identified the fragment as an early witness, I sought paleographical confirmation of dating and geographical location of the manuscript, since this was not given in the catalogue data. This was done largely through drawing on examples from the online database of dated Hebrew manuscripts Sfardata, looking at script types in manuscripts that are dated through colophons.[5] As these manuscripts are not generally available for reproduction, I have drawn out some example lines in the table below to show the similarities between these and the script of our Cambridge *Genizah* fragments. Two key letters here were *ʾalef* and *shin*. The *ʾalef* has a left leg that curves in and then turns out.[6] The *shin* is very straightforward with the middle branch no more than a line. The *yod* is also quite short in terms of its tail. No scripts match this, but some are quite similar. Indeed, one sees immediate similarities with the Oriental square script and more likely that of the land of Israel (and indeed specific examples from Jerusalem are shown in the table below) dated largely to the 11th Century. Were that the case, our fragments would certainly then rival **OB** for the position of oldest (partial) copy of *Sefer Tagin*.

There are definite similarities with (1) MS Cairo, from the Karaite Synagogue, once considered the earliest dated colophon in a Hebrew codex, but now regarded as a copy made in the 11th century. According to the colophon the manuscript was written by Moshe ben 'Asher in Tiberius in 894/5 C.E., but Beit Arié states it is in fact about 1000.[7] There are also similarities with St. Petersburg

4 This became more obvious when I was able to see the fragments in actuality at the Cambridge *Genizah* on the first day of my PhD studies on 4/10/19, where they were shown to me by my joint supervisor Dr Ben Outhwaite, who pointed this out.

5 A brief statement by the scribe, containing information about the scribe, the place of writing, the date of completion, whom the work was for and other biographical details.

6 According to Judith Olszowy-Schlanger, the direction of the left leg of the *ʾalef* (inward or outward) is a difference between southwestern (land of Israel) and northeastern (Iraq) Oriental script. This is a distinction not recognized by Beit-Arie and Engel (personal correspondence from Nehemia Gordon, November 2019).

7 Brought by Malachi Beit Arié in *Hebrew Codicology* (Preprint internet version 0.9—Hebrew), April 2018, p. 1. Also source: 0M001 in Sfardata. Also see Beit Arié, M., (in collaboration with Engel E. and Yardeni, A.), אסופות כתבים עבריים מימי—הביניים כרך א: כתב מזרחי וכתב תימני, (*Specimens of Medieval Hebrew Scripts, Part 1; Oriental and Yemenite Scripts*), The Israel Academy of Sciences and Humanities, Jerusalem, 1987, p. 1.

TABLE 1 Sample scripts for comparison with our Cambridge *Genizah* fragments CG

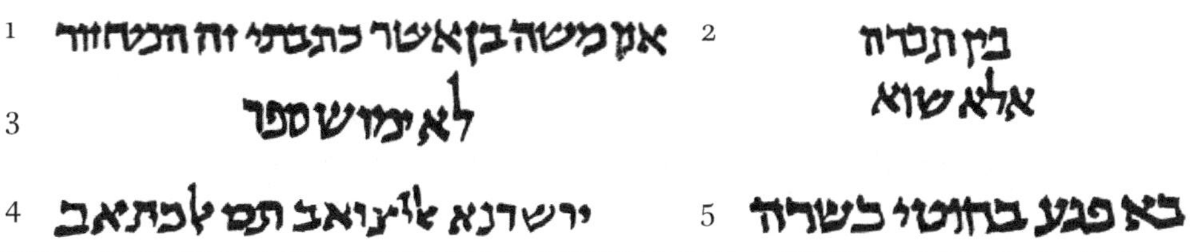

NLR Evr.II B 39 written by Yosef ben Ya'akov *ha-Ma'aravi* in 988/989 C.E.[8] in Jerusalem (2). (3) St. Petersburg NLR Evr. II B 8 is dated to 1020/21 and written in the land of Israel by *ha-Sofer* (the scribe), Zechariah ben 'Anan *ha-Melamed* (the teacher) similarly.[9] Though the scan shows quite damaged letters, British Library Or. 5565 E fol. 15, written in Jerusalem in 1030 by a Karaite, Kalef ben 'Alon, also has considerable similarities. This shows good examples of the the turned outwards *'alef* leg and the simplified *shin*.[10] Indeed it seems to be after this date that we start to see some simplification of the *shin* in other manuscripts in the wider Orient (see below). (4) CUL T-S Misc 35.108 also written in Jerusalem, in 1035, has similarities with our fragments, though slightly more sophisticated.[11] Conversely, whilst it is by no means as sophisticated a script, and is quite spindly in nature, we do see some simplification of the letters forms (particularly the *shin*) in CUL T-S 8.234 written in Ashkelon in 1060/1 by 'Azaryah ben David.[12] It is worth noting that there are also manuscripts from the Orient generally that are also similar, so the geographical location it is not entirely certain, though the dating seems fairly likely.[13] Over-

8 Source: oR007 in Sfardata. Also ... אסופות כתבים, op. cit., p. 19.

9 Source: oR013 in Sfardata.

10 Source: oC727 in Sfardata.

11 Source: oC727 in Sfardata. Also ... אסופות כתבים, op. cit., p. 24.

12 Source: oC689 in Sfardata. Also ... אסופות כתבים, op. cit., p. 31.

13 For example, St. Petersburg NLR Evr.-Ar.1 1811 written in the Orient in 1034 (Source: oR012 in Sfardata) is indeed quite similar across many of the letter forms. and St. Petersburg NLR Evr.-Ar.1 831 (Source: oR093 in Sfardata) written in the Orient, in 1043, has a similar simplified *shin* although the *'alef* lacks its turned out foot. Though much thinner scripts, there are also similarities with CUL T-S NS 243.20 (Source: oY005 in Sfardata) written in the Orient, in 1061/62 and also with Sassoon 1044 (Source: oY122 in Sfardata) held in Israel in Jerusalem, written in the Orient, in 1066. Additionally, MS Heb 8°2238, held in the JNUL is a complete small manuscript of *parashat Shelaḥ-Lekha* and written in Egypt in 1106/7 (discussed in detail in Narkiss, B., *Hebrew Illuminated Manuscripts*, Macmillan/Keter Publishing House, Jerusalem, 1969, p. 46/47) has some similarities with our fragments. There

all I would tend to favour the view that our fragments are most likely Oriental and specifically from land of Israel, possibly even Jerusalem, likely written in the 11th Century.[14]

3 Identifying Additional Joins, T-S AS 139.152, T-S NS 287.11 and T-S AS 139.144

After completing most of the initial work in transcribing and commenting on **T-S D1.42**, I discovered that this particular fragment is clearly joined to three other fragments of the same edition of *Sefer Tagin* from the Cairo *Genizah*, that are also not widely known.[15] They are also held by Cambridge University Library.

T-S AS 139.152-B and **T-S AS 139.152-F** carry on directly from the end of **T-S D1.42** continuing the listing of letter *ṭet* and go on through the two sides up to *yod, kaf* and *kaf sofit* and the start of *lamed.* It is much more fragmentary with only one half of the portrait page existing and a small part of the next page.[16] Halfway down the folios we see **T-S AS 139.158-B** and **T-S AS 139.158-F** which cover *mem* and *mem sofit* respectively. Next are **T-S AS 139.144-B** and **T-S AS 139.144-F**, which constitutes the smallest fragment, and covers some instances from *kaf, kaf sofit, mem sofit* and *nun*. These cover the base of two folios.[17] Finally is **T-S NS 287.11-F** where the head of the page shows the end of *Sefer Tagin* and gives the instances connected to *tav* followed by images of this scribes' view of the different letters forms.[2] This, as previously mentioned in part 1, explains why **T-S D1.42** and our other fragments do not give such images within the text. As we will see below, our scribe's *tagin* are more like lines or forks rather than the line with a blob on top, that we are more familiar with. I have added these images of the letter forms from **T-S NS 287.11-F**, when a letter is discussed.

---

are no doubt others that could be brought but this seems a fair sample to show the likely origin of our fragments.

14 This assessment was also given independently by Justine Isserles in an email exchange *motsei Shabbat* 24/2/18. She concluded it was likely Judea/Samaria, 11th–12th century.

15 T-S AS 139.152 and T-S NS 287.11 are briefly referenced in footnote 40 in Caspi, E., מקורות דרשניים לאותיות המתויגות והמשונות בתורה (*Interpretive Sources for the Tittled and Strange letter in the Torah*), from קובץ חצי גבורים—פליטת סופרים, מאסף תורני, ח, עלול תשע"ה, so these two, at least, were previously known, but these have not been subjected to critical review, reconstruction and commentary, as undertaken in part 2 of this monograph.

16 First accessed 18/2/18 though the Friedberg *Genizah* Project.

17 Alert to the script and format, I discovered this join 18/2/18 scrolling through the AS manuscripts on the Friedberg *Genizah* Project.

FIGURE 10 CUL T-S AS 139.152-B

FIGURE 11 CUL T-S AS 139.152-F

FIGURE 12 CUL T-S AS 139.158-B

FIGURE 13 CUL T-S AS 139.158-F

FIGURE 14 CUL T-S AS 139.144-B

FIGURE 15 CUL T-S AS 139.144-F

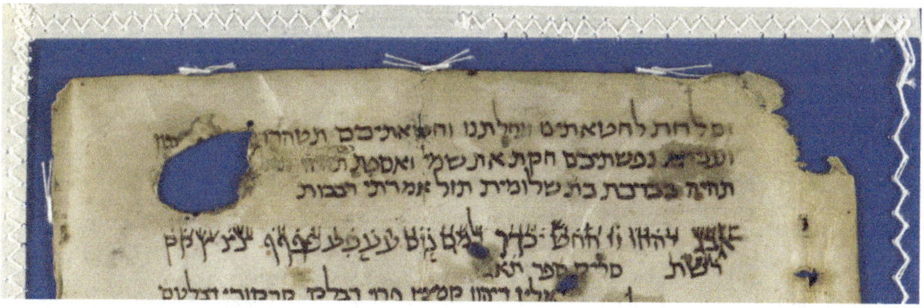

FIGURE 16 Top section of T-S NS 287.11-F

Collectively these additional fragments to **T-S D1.42** are from a volume that clearly contained the whole of *Sefer Tagin*. I have thus assigned them collectively the siglum **CG**, however, I will reference them independently as each section is treated in turn.

It is also interesting to note that the scribe of **CG** does not include the section on ביה שמו at the end of the section on the letter *tav*. So perhaps this early witness suggests that this element was not part of *Sefer Tagin* originally, after all.

For the sake of completeness, in part 3, I have also transcribed and provided a critical commentary on the Oxford fragment **MS. Heb d. 33/9 (OB)**, since it represents a very early witness, also likely from the land of Israel dated to 10th/11th centuries. I have detailed the additional instances it brings over and above those listed in **CG**.

4 An Additional Find, a Secondary Source T-S Misc. 24.182 from the Cairo *Genizah*

On 14th May 2019, Dr Kim Phillips of the Cambridge *Genizah* Unit, spotted **T-S Misc. 24.182**, and shared it with me. These were four leaves that were described as 'Bible: Genesis 30:40–50:26 [in shorthand giving keywords only]; Exodus 1:1–2:11 [in shorthand giving keywords only]; 23:22–40:38 [in shorthand giving keywords only]; Leviticus 1:1–4:27 [in shorthand giving keywords only]' and 'that many of the letters are decorated.'[18]

On examination, I identified them as remnants from a composite secondary source of *Sefer Tagin* (i.e. combined with dotted and other *ʾotiyot meshunot, petuḥot and setumot*)[19] ordered by *parasha* similar to other secondary sources described above. However, unlike our other parchment *Genizah* finds, these leaves are on paper, 18.2 × 13.3 cms, 1 column of text with 21–23 lines per sheet. Some of the leaves have some damaged letters, but most of it is quite clear.

18 Davis, M.C., *Catalogue I, Hebrew Bible MSS*, Cambridge University Press, 1978.

19 We can see this initially, for example, from the inclusion of וַיִּשָּׁקֵהוּ ('and he kissed him') from Gen. 32:4 on line 7 of **T-S Misc. 24.182** P2-B.

5 Dating T-S Misc. 24.182

It is on paper and thus more likely 11/12/13th century. Examining the fragments with Dr Ben Outhwaite in November 2019, confirmed that it is rag paper with no woodpulp content and has no visible laid lines.[20]

Looking at the base script of the manuscript and ignoring the additional decoration pertaining to *Sefer Tagin*, we see what resembles we see what has been variously termed *Mashait*, rabbinical, book-hand, and medial script.[21]

One distinguishing feature of *Mashait* scripts such as those early ones from the Orient, Egypt or Babylonia, is an *ʾalef* shaped like a 'k', but here the *ʾalef* is more like a roman 'N', which we can see in the later Judean or Parsic scripts Additionally, the *mem* is often without a base or has a very short base. Here there is a fairly pronounced base. As with the core manuscript **T-S D1.42**, I have not managed to find an exact match in terms of scripts, but some dated manuscripts do display some similarities to the alphabet above.

CUL T-S 13J11.5 written in Jerusalem c. 1035 by one Shelomo ben Yehudah Ga'on has similarities with the *shin, mem, tsade,* though other letters are not quite as simple, *ʾalef* being the prime example.[22] Also similarities with many letters can be seen in CUL T-S F3.29 written in 1089/90 in Lebanon by ʾAvraham

20 Dr Outhwaite's opinion, 'if I had to say, then 12th–13th [Century]. It does not have obvious 13th c.+ features (such as diagonal line endings). The paper is still the cruder classical period paper, though we do get it being used deep into the Mamluk period too' (personal correspondence 15/5/19). For more on paper production, see chapter 2 *Paper* pp. 239–263 from Beit Arié, M., *Hebrew Codicology* (Preprint internet version 0.9 Hebrew and 0.2 English (April 2018)). This is also covered in detail in Sirat C., *Hebrew Manuscripts of the Middle Ages*, Cambridge University Press, 2002, pp. 106–109.

21 'Whilst book hand and cursive styles in the Hebrew scripts diverged, sometimes cursive was used for non-Biblical literary texts, but in such cases it was written carefully and regularly. This finally led in its turn to the rise of a special book-hand which we call Mashait.' From Birbaum, S., *The Development of the Hebrew Scripts* (a previously unpublished lecture given in 1966) in Timm, E., Birnbaum E., and Birnbaum D., *Solomon A. Birnbaum: Ein Leben fur die Wissenschaft, A Lifetime of Achievement*, Vol. II, Palaeography, De Gruyter, Germany, 2011, p. 94. Also see p. 729 from *Alphabet, Hebrew, Encyclopaedia Judaica* Vol. 2, Keter Publishing House, Jerusalem, 1971, 'cursive was sometimes used as a book hand when, of course, more care was taken with the writing' and p. 731, in particular, for relevant examples. Yardeni refers to these as 'semi-cursive hands, called 'half-a-calamus or Meshita' in contemporary literary sources' Yardeni, A., *The Book of Hebrew Script: History, Palaeography, Script Styles, Calligraphy & Design.*, Carta, Jerusalem, 2010, p. 97. In the first and subsequent volumes of *Specimens of Mediaeval Hebrew Scripts*, Jerusalem, Israel Academy of Science and Humanities, Beit Arié (ed.) refers to this script as בינוני (lit. in between), i.e. semi-cursive.

22 ... אסופות כתבים, op. cit. p. 25.

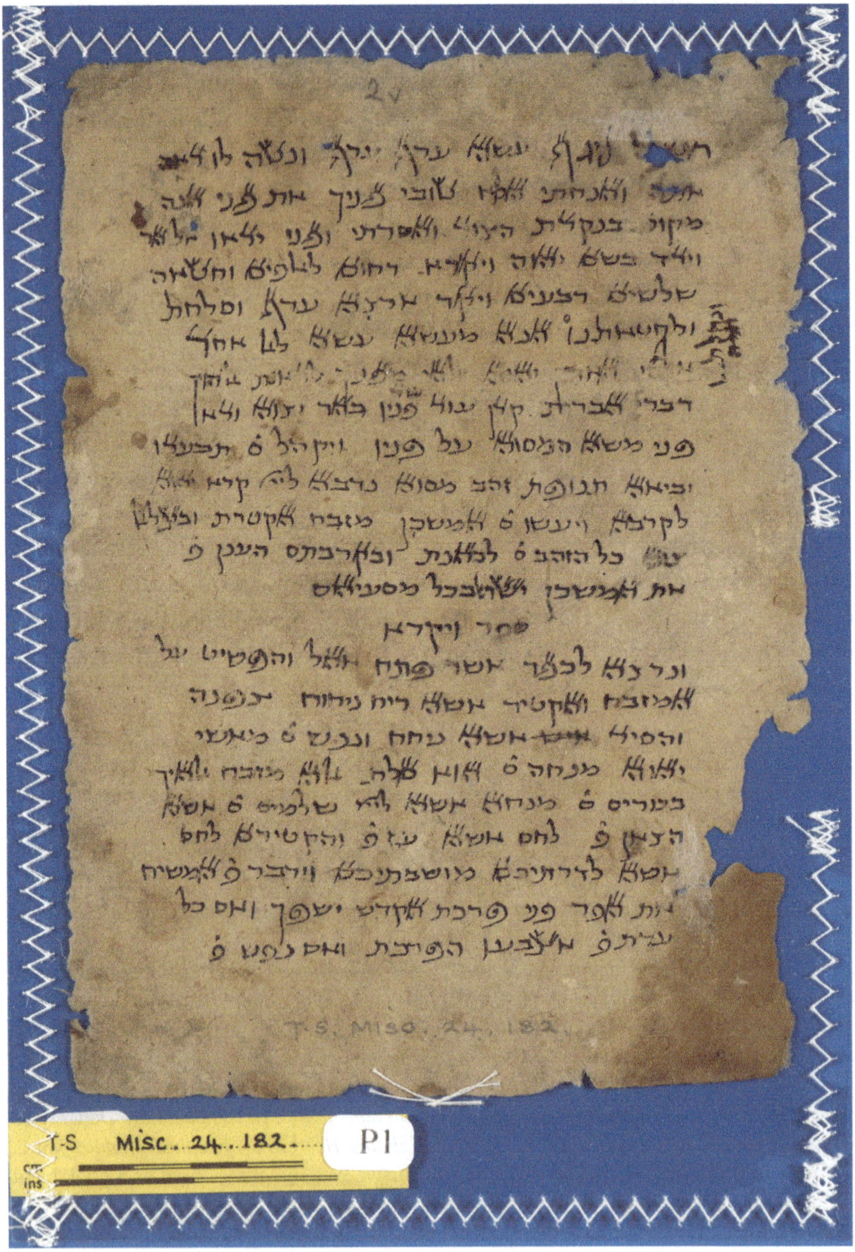

FIGURE 17 CUL T-S Misc. 24.182 P1-B

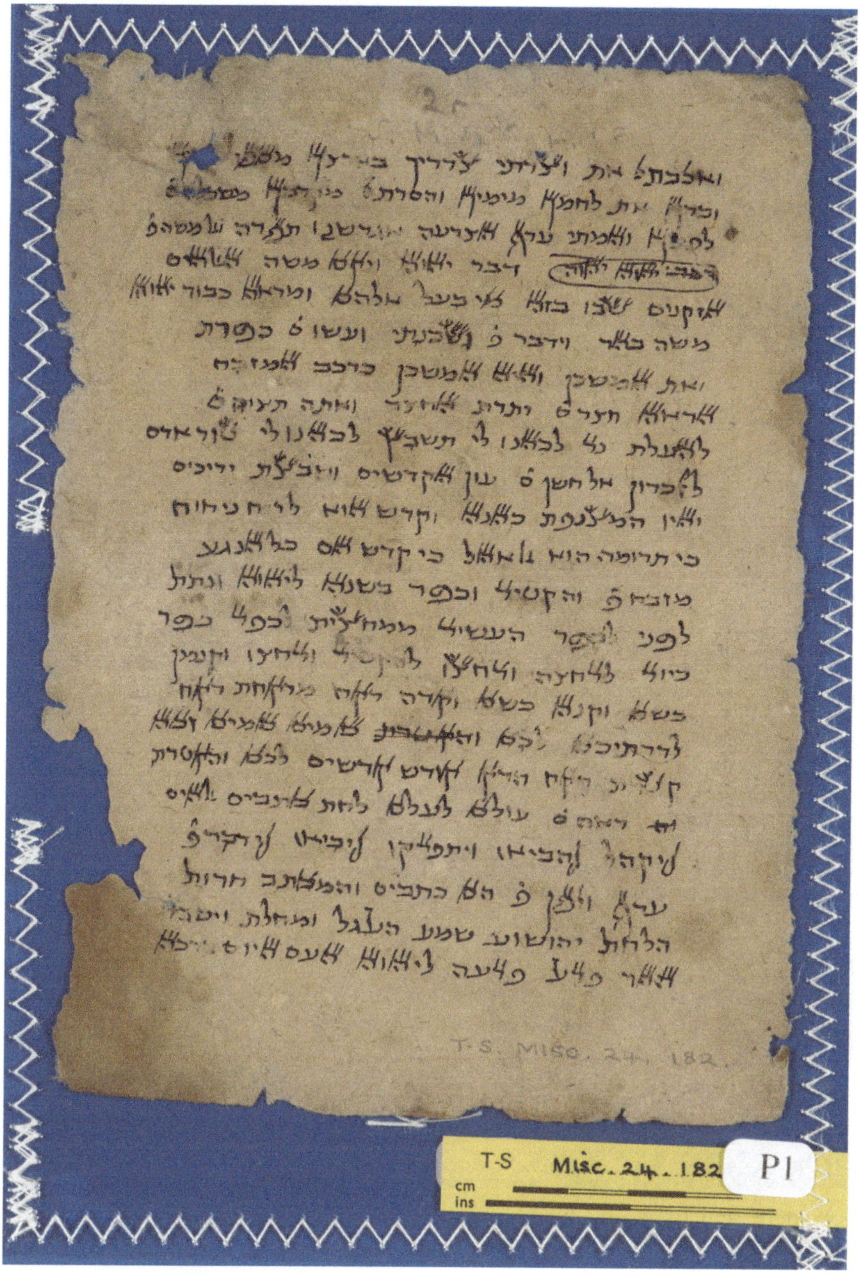

FIGURE 18 CUL T-S Misc. 24.182 P1-F

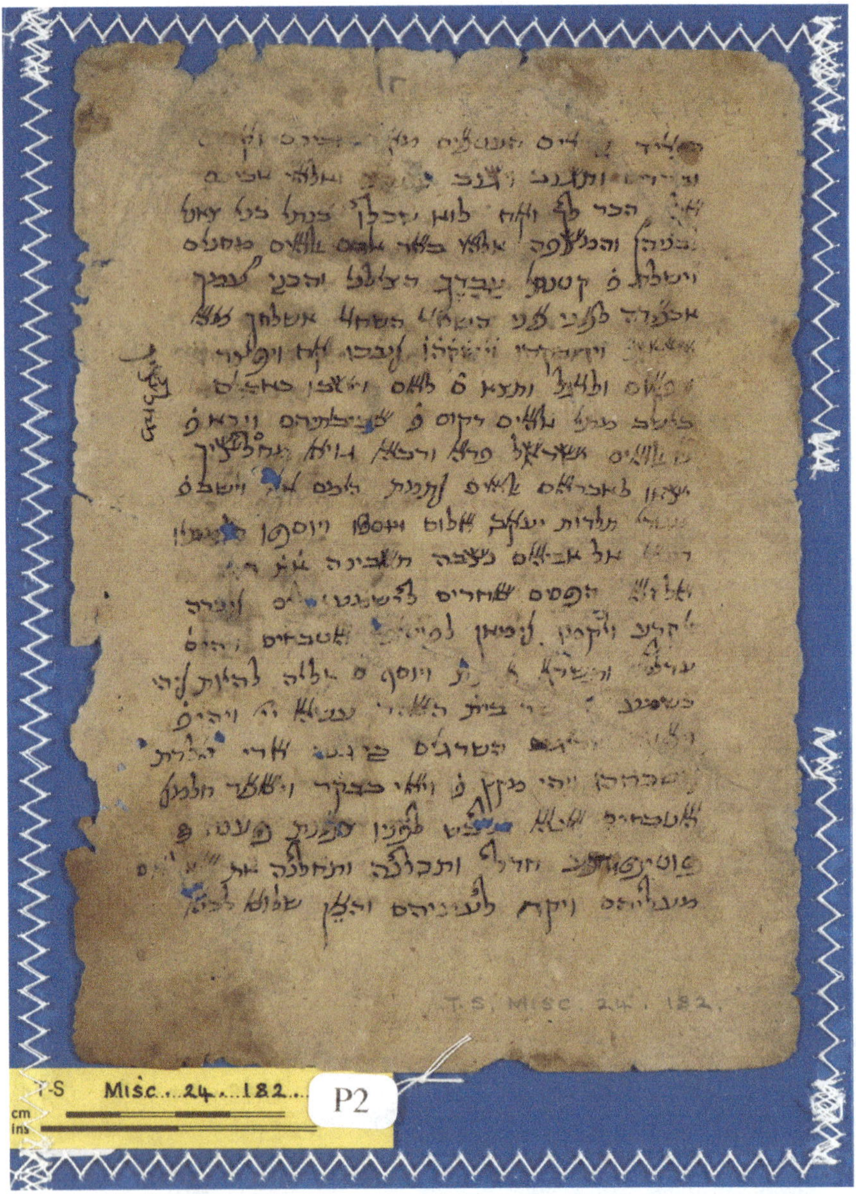

FIGURE 19 CUL T-S Misc. 24.182 P2-B

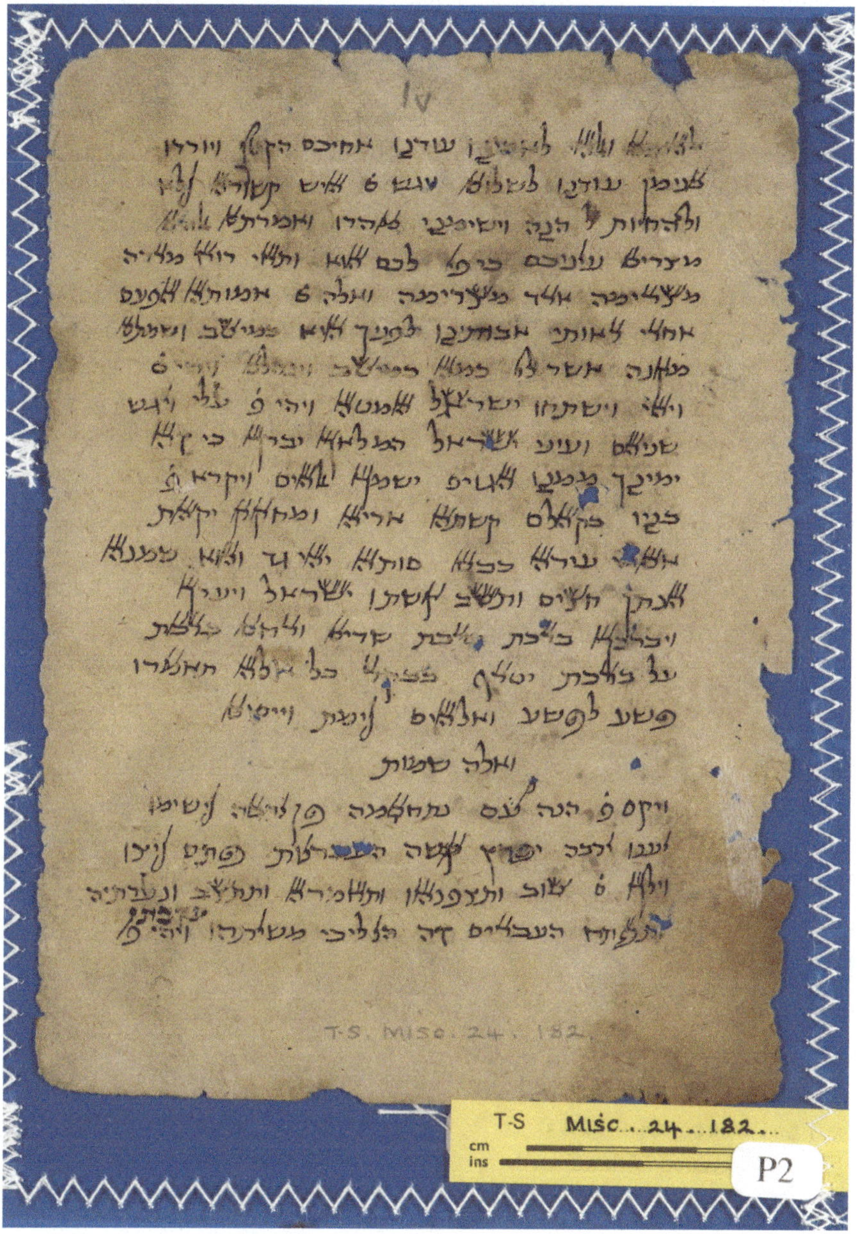

FIGURE 20 CUL T-S Misc. 24.182 P2-F

ben Shabbtai.[23] Again whilst many letters are very similar, the *ʾalef* differs. A fairly good match can also be seen with the much later manuscript Oxford BL Hunt. 166 written in 1375 in Syria by Tsedaqa be ʿOvadyah.[24] However, arguably none of these are quite near enough to be sure of the dating.

It is a partial secondary source, though obviously a very important and new one. Thus for the sections it covers, I drew on it specifically when there were disagreements amongst the core sources, as with the other secondary sources listed.

Since it is a new *Genizah* discovery, I have also added the full folio images above. It does also occasionally bring unique instances that are not seen elsewhere, and these have been noted for information, even though they are not pertinent to the core texts. Finally, I have fully transcribed, annotated and, where necessary, reconstructed damaged sections in appendix 1, added after the three main parts.

23 Ibid., p. 34.
24 Ibid., p. 97.

CHAPTER 3

Transcription and Analysis

1 Diacritical Conventions

In the transcriptions below, the following diacritical conventions apply:

א is a letter that is clear or obvious.

[א] is the likely reading in a section that has been blotted out or torn, based on the other manuscripts, or when it is not at all clear [ ] is given.

{א} is when there is a disagreement between the sources where out manuscript may have added this based on available space. Often this is where words are *ma-le'* (full)[1] in some sources but not others or in 𝔐. Alternatively they may be extensions to the instance with a word that precedes or follow. In the reconstruction image these letters are shown in grey outline.

א in blue is where a letter has faded, blotted out or is otherwise unclear/questionable.[2]

אאא is where there has been an extra word written in a much smaller script between the lines. these interlinear superscript additions are usually where a word has been omitted or corrected. Occasionally there are also smaller words written in the margins. These are also noted.

א̊ indicates where the special letters occur, often marked in the manuscript with a single *tag*-like line. Not all the letters that should be so marked have this, however, as our scribe is inconsistent in his usage. This transcription decision follows the convention of the Shem Tov *Sefer Tagi*, that similarly places a hollow circle over the letter that he believes constitutes the instance.

א̇ usually indicating letters where there are abbreviations (including numerals) are marked with a dot above. Sometimes these dots are cancellation marks that are used instead of erasing the letters, or indicating some error such as a metathesis.

//// indicates an area of the manuscript left deliberately blank.

1 I prefer to use the terms *ma-le'* (full) and *ḥaser* (missing) rather than the terms plene and defective as the latter suggests something negative, when actually the *ḥaser* orthography is the older textual tradition.

2 There is only one word in **CG** where there has been deliberate erasure (noted below), so I have not specifically distinguished between fading and erasure.

 | DOI:10.1163/9789004426368_004

To add clarity to each individual instance I have added a • as a separator, which is a usual convention on most variants of *Sefer Tagin* and the Paris printed version, though this is not employed in **CG**. I have added a number for each instance of a special letter form and line by line translated it, added the *parasha* it appears in, chapter and verse, and then commented on each instance accordingly.

However, where the fragments are so damaged that there are many missing instances, I have indicated what the missing words might be using Parma 2574 (**P**) as the default, but taking into account any possible variants in the core sources, and drawing on the secondary sources where there is still disagreement.

2 Digital Composition and Font Construction

Since the additional fragments of **CG** are only parts of pages, to reconstruct the pages from which they came, element, I cut out the fragments digitally and matched them up, placing them into position on a blanked out folio sized from **T-S D1.42**. I then developed a typeface from the script used so as to see what might fit in the space provided. However, it should be noted that our scribe is not entirely consistent with the size of his script and so the font size I have employed varies a little between lines (around 10 % variance on font size), based on the size of the script that is preserved on that particular line. Letters shown in black outline were most likely present in the manuscript. Those in grey denote differences amongst the sources, often matters of orthography, or where the reconstruction is less certain.

The full font of the *ʾalef-bet* which I have named Cambridge *Genizah Sefer Tagin* is shown below:

PART 1

CHAPTER 4

Critical Analysis of T-S D.142

1 End of Listing of Instances for the First Special Letter *He* Form

Covering 360 different instances,[1] the first entry for the letter *he* represents some 19.2 % of the total instances in *Sefer Tagin*. Our manuscript begins its listing towards the end of that letter. Prior to this we would have read about the special form of *he* having four *tagin* and not being joined. However, this is not extant in our CG manuscript fragments. Nonetheless, because it such a long section, the form of this letter is repeated at the end of the listing, together with extra information, as a reminder and, as such, this will be treated when we reach that.

CUL T-S D1.42 1v—26 Lines

Line 1: [1][ה̊אד]ם למעל • [2]ה̊כיפורים • [3]אל ה̊מים • [4]אזכרתה̊ • [5]ירכה̊ •

1. (*Parashat Naso'*) '[sin] **that men commit**' (Num. 5:6). 2. '[ram] **of atonement**' (Num. 5:8). 3. **'to the water'** (Num. 5:17). 4. **'the memorial part** [of the meal offering]' (Num. 5:26). 5. **'her thigh'** (Num. 5:27).

Whilst this is the first line in our fragment, it is not the first instance of what constitutes the 360 occurrences of the special *he* that is described earlier in *Sefer Tagin*.

1. The first word of this instance in the top right corner is obscured by both a rip in the parchment and a large stain. P, MV and H clearly bring האדם.[2] ST is faded but is likely also ה̊אדם based on the enhanced images.
2. P, MV and H all agree bringing הכיפורים. ST is *ḥaser yod* הכפורים. However, none of the core sources accords with how it is written in the Masoretic Text of the *Torah* 𝔐,[3] as it is *ḥaser vav* הכפרים.

1 All our core sources are in accord with this number.

2 Though this is incorrectly transcribed in LMV as האדם. למעל הכפורים., with incorrect use of separator dots.

3 Using the Jewish Publication Society edition.

 | DOI:10.1163/9789004426368_005

3. P, MV and H agree bringing אל המים. ST brings just המים.
4. P, MV, ST (though faded) and H all agree bringing אזכרתה.

Prior to the fifth instance listed in our manuscript, ST brings two additional instances היתה ('and it will come to pass') which does not appear until Num. 5:27, which would put it out of sequence. Additionally, it then has המשכן ('the Tabernacle') from Num. 5:17, which would be in sequence. Both would be in *parashat Naso'*. However, our manuscript, P, MV and H do not bring these additional insertions and there is little support from the secondary sources.[4] H does add in אל ה to fill the line space and then repeats this on the next page.

5. P, MV, ST and H all agree bringing ירכה.

Line 2: [4ב]אזכרתה • [6]ונזרעה • [7]ועשה לה • [8]ונקה • [9]להזיר • [10]הזירו • [11]אלהי •
4b. **'the memorial part'** 6. **'and she will conceive'** (Num. 5:28). 7. **'and he** [the priest] **will do to her'** (Num. 5:30). 8. **'and he will be clean'** (Num. 5:31). 9. **'to consecrate** [himself]' (Num. 6:2). 10 **'of his consecration'** (Num. 6:6). 11. '[his] **God'** (Num. 6:7).

The first instance on this line appears to be an example of dittography. This word has just been brought in instance 4 and does not appear again within Num 5:27–28 which, by means of its positioning in the list, it would have to. P, MV and H do not bring this. ST is, unfortunately, too faded in any of the available images. The scribe of CG simply appears to have erred.[5]

6. P, MV and H agree, bringing ונזרעה. ST is too faded, with possible water damage.
7. P, MV and H present ועשה לה as one instance with no divider between the two words, in which case there would be difficulty in knowing which *he* takes the special form. Given the general convention employed by *Sefer Tagin*, such an occurrence would normally then be followed by the word תרויהון (both of them) if that was the intention.[6] Our scribe has only indicated the *he* of ועשה, but since he is not consistent elsewhere, we cannot necessarily take this as meaning that for him they represent one instance only, though it seems likely. ST is faded, but לה can be made out and there

4 Q651–652 does bring המשכן in support of ST, but otherwise no other secondary source brings either additional instance suggested by ST.
5 No secondary source has this dittography, indeed a few omit this instance entirely.
6 Or indeed קדמאה (first) or בתראה (last) if these were the intention. See introduction.

are two hollow circles in the spaces where they would be expected, which suggests that there were two instances here, i.e. ועשה̊ and לה̊.[7]

8. P, MV and H agree, bringing ונקה. ST is faded but reads ונקה̊ האי[ש] ('and the man will be clean') as further clarification of the instance.[8]
9. P, MV, ST and H all agree, bringing להזיר.
10. P and MV agree, bringing הזירו. ST is too faded in any available image. H omits, possibly because it is similar to the previous instance.
11. Our scribe adds no indicator on the letter *he*. P and H give אלהיו על ראשו ('his God is upon his head'). ST is faded, but reads similarly אלה̊יו על ראשו. MV brings just אלהיו. Our manuscript appears to be missing the *vav* at the end of אלהיו, as well as omitting the two additional words that would have helped clarify the instance.

Line 3: [12]כן יעשה̊ • [13]לה̊קים • [14]מזבח דויאמר • [15]המזבח דזאת • [16]הקהל/הקול •

12. **'so must he do'** (Num 6:21). 13. **'to set up'** (Num 7:1). 14. '[the] **altar' of** [the verse beginning] **'and He said'** (Num 7:11). 15. **'the altar' of** [the verse beginning] **'this is the** [dedication]' (Num. 7.84). 16. 'the congregation' OR **'the voice'** (likely Num. 7:89).

12. P, MV, ST and H all agree, bringing כן יעשה.
13. P, MV and H agree, bringing להקים. ST brings a longer entry להקים את המשכן ('to set up the Tabernacle'), which could confuse as it does not add the circle over either *he* in the phrase.

---

7 The Shem Tov *Tanakh* does show both letters *he* decorated, which would accord with this view. Basser, who whilst bringing variants, largely follows Shem Tov in his version of *Sefer Tagi*, certainly reads this and therefore lists two separate instances (op. cit., p. 87). Both Parma 2427 and Q651–652 do decorate both letters, *Ben Mesheq*'s listing for *parashat Naso'* reads ההי"ן דועשה לה (the [letters] *he* of 'and he will do' [and] 'to her') and that of the Me'iri in his *Qiryat Sefer* reads ועשה לה ונקה הה"א בשלשתם מתוייגות שלש ('and he will do', 'to her' 'and he will be clean' the *he* in all three of them has three *tagin*). Add. MS 11639 brings only on לה̊. MV2 does list ועשה לה הכהן ('and the priest will do to her') and also ונקה הב האיש מעון ('and he will be clean from iniquity') but adds no decoration on any of the letters. Parma 1959 omits either of the possible instances from Num. 5:30. As noted, whilst these works are not examples of *Sefer Tagin*, they clearly draw on variants of the *Sefer Tagin* tradition and so there is evidence here that both these instances should be decorated. Ginsburg (op. cit. p. 695) also lists both instances even though he normally follows MV. Our new secondary source **T-S Misc. 24.182** is not extant for Numbers.

8 It is also worth noting that the *Ba'al ha-Ṭurim* comments on this particular instance. It states, ''and he will be clean'—3 *tagin* on the *he*, to say to you that he will be absolved from five sins [*he* = 5]—the sin of adultery, the sin of being with an unmarried woman, the sin that he should not come to her [after being accused of being a *soṭah*], the sin of his sons and the sin of his daughters.'

14. Our scribe has omitted an important letter here—the actual *he* of המזבח, which is the one supposed to carry the decoration. **P** and **H** are clearer bringing the *he*. Again **ST** brings a slightly longer entry to clarify לחנכת המזבח̊ דויאמר this time marking the *he* and also explicitly linking this instance to the next instance, both containing references to 'dedication'.

15. Our text is missing a key word. **P**, **MV** and **H** all bring המזבח דזאת חנוכת whilst **ST** gives this as המזבח̊ דזאת חנכת with the last word *ḥaser vav* which accords with how it is written in 𝔐. This phrase, זאת חנכת המזבח, could present a problem as it occurs in close proximity in both Num. 7:84 and 7:88. However, the latter occurs at the end of the verse and as detailed above, the convention established in *Sefer Tagin* is that when a specific instruction, such as דזאת חנכת here, this generally (though not always) refers to the words at the beginning of a verse. Thus, this would be Num. 7.84.

16. This entry is particularly fascinating, as it gets to the root of a conflict over this particular instance. Our **CG** scribe appears to have originally written הקהל ('the congregation') but the left leg of the the second *he* has been partially erased and the roof bend of the *lamed* extended leaving the second letter as a *vav*, albeit with too wide a *rosh* (head), so that it reads instead הקול. There is clearly some disagreement here. **P** and **H** bring הקהל but **MV** gives הקול and **ST** omits this instance entirely, presumably unsure. By convention, this instance has to lie between Num. 7.84 and Num. 7:89 and, as such, can only be וישמע את ה̊קול (and he [Moses] heard the voice [God's]), presumably why this has been corrected in our manuscript by the original scribe or a later hand.[9]

Line 4: [17]הכרובים • [18]לטה̊רם • [19]בגדיה̊ם • [20]רחוקה̊ • [21]ילדתיה̊ו • [22]האמן • [23]ואל

17. **'the cherubim'** (Num. 7:89). (*Parashat Beha'alotkha*) 18. **'to cleanse them'** (Num. 8:7). 19. **'their clothes'** (Num. 8:7). 20. **'far off'** (Num. 9:10). 21. **'birthed them'** (Num. 11:12). 22. **'the nursing father'** (Num 11:12). 23. **'do not …**

17. The word הכרובים *ma-le' vav* does not appear in *Torah*,[10] so it is odd that our scribe should use a fuller orthography here. **P**, **MV** and **H** are *ḥaser vav*

---

9 Q651–652 specifically brings וישמע את ה̊קול in full. Parma 2427 lists the word הקול, but does not decorate the *he*. **MV2**, Parma 1959 and Add. MS 11639 omit. *Ben Mesheq* only references the *qof* as being decorated in that word, whilst *Qiryat Sefer* just notes the word is *ma-le' vav*.

10 Though does so in the *Tanakh*, its first use with the fuller orthography being 1Kings 6:27.

הכרבים. ST brings a longer entry הכרבים דוידבר אליו (the *cherubim* of [the verse beginning] 'and He spoke to him').

18. P, MV, ST and H all agree, bringing לטהרם.
19. P, MV, ST and H all agree, bringing בגדיהם.
20. Once again our scribe has chosen a fuller orthography as does ST bringing רחוקה, whereas 𝔐 is *ḥaser*. P, MV and H are *ḥaser vav*.[11]
21. P, MV, ST (though faded) and H all agree, bringing ילדתיהו .
22. The final *nun* is much shorter here than is usual in this manuscript, thus resembling a *zayin*. However, the other manuscripts are clearer; P, MV[12] and H give האמן as 𝔐, whereas ST writes it *ma-le' vav* האומן.[13]
23. P, MV, ST and H all agree, bringing ואל אראה.

Line 5: **אראה • 24אספה לי • 25זקני העם • 26התקדשו • 27ומיצא להם בבת •**
... let me look' (Num. 11:15). 24. **'gather to me'** (Num. 11:16). 25. **'the elders of the people'** (Num. 11:16). 26. **'sanctify yourselves'** (Num. 11:18) 27. **the last 'will they suffice them'** (Num. 11:22).

24. ST agrees. MV adds an extra word אספה לי ~~שבעים~~ (gather me seventy) clarifying the instance further, but has then crossed a line through the added word, whereas P and H both just bring אספה.[14]
25. P, MV and ST agree, bringing זקני העם. However, H gives here two separate entries זקניה // העם, This is incorrect, since there is no word זקניה in Numbers.[15]
26. P, MV, ST and H all agree, bringing התקדשו.
27. בבת is an odd abbreviation here and the first letter *bet* is not required. It is likely that the scribe of **CG** recognised this and has added a cancellation dot over that first *bet* instead of erasing. The full verse reads, הצאן ובקר ישחט להם ומצא להם אם את כל דגי הים יאסף להם ומצא להם, and our scribe appears to be suggesting that only the last occurrence should be adorned, though he has not marked the *he*. In this, he is in accord with ST which gives ומצא להם בתרא. This presents a disagreement, as P and H

11 This word is also known for having a dot (*puncta extraordinaria*) over the letter *he*. One of ten such dotted letters in the *Torah*.

12 Incorrectly transcribed in LMV as דאמן.

13 The *Ba'al ha-Ṭurim* also comments on the extra *tagin* on האמן explaining that 'through five things a father benefits his sons, and they are: looks, strength, wealth, wisdom, years [of life]' and then proceeds to bring verses from *Tanakh* in support of each.

14 The *Ba'al ha-Ṭurim* also comments on אספה explaining that the elders chosen by Moses 'must be experts and careful [in observance] of the five books of the *Torah*'.

15 The Paris printed version EPST does not follow this and transcribes instead זקני העם.

read ומצה להם תר' and תרווי' respectively. **MV** writes in full תרויהון (both of them).[16] These three manuscripts suggest that the decoration should apply on both instances of להם that follow ומצא in the verse.[17]

Line 6: [28]היד • [29]היקרך • [30]השלו • [31]רבה • [32]המתאוים • [33]נאמן הוא • [34]ומראה • [35]ויהס •

28. **'the hand'** (Num. 11:23). 29. **'will come to pass'** (Num. 11:23). 30. **'the quail'** (Num. 11:32). 31. **'great [plague]'** (Num. 11:33). 32. **'that lusted'** (Num. 11.34). 33. **'he** [Moses] **is trusted'** (Num. 12:7). 34. **'manifestly'** (Num. 12:8). (*Parashat Shelaḥ-Lekha*) 35. **'and he** [Caleb] **stilled'** (Num. 13:30).

28. **P**, **MV** and **H** agree as does **ST**, bringing היד, but there is another faded word in **ST**, which may have added clarification, but which is not clear in any available image.
29. **P**, **MV**, **ST** and **H** all agree, bringing היקרך.
30. **P**, **ST** and **H** agree, bringing השלו. **MV** reads השליו adding a *yod*.[18]
31. **P**, **MV** and **H** agree, bringing רבה.[19] **ST** omits this instance.[20]
32. **P**, **MV** and **ST** agree, bringing המתאוים, though **MV** has the *yod* suspended over the *vav* having omitted it originally. **H** appears to read המתאונים adding a superfluous *nun*.
33. **P**, **MV**, **ST** and **H** all agree, bringing נאמן הוא.
34. **P**, **MV**, **ST** and **H** all agree, bringing ומראה. However, in **MV** the *resh* of the word is poorly formed resembling a *yod*.[21]
35. **P**, **MV**, **ST** and **H** all agree, bringing ויהס, though **MV** has written ~~ויהס~~ and crossed out before writing the correct word.[22]

Line 7: [36]למה֯ • [37]למה זה֯ • [38]חלה • [39]אלה֯יכם דאני • [40]ה֯אם תמנו • [41]ברית ה֯כה֯ונת •

16 Incorrectly transcribed in **LMV** as a separate entry .תרויהון.
17 Q651–652 and Add. MS 11639 just gives one instance of ומצה לה֯ם agreeing with our **CG** scribe. *Ben Mesheq* writes כב ב' היהן דלהם להם ([verse] 22, two *hes* of 'to them' 'to them'). *Qiryat Sefer* goes a little further suggesting that להם ארבע בפסוק אחד ובכלם הה"א מתוייגת ('to them' [occurs] four times in one verse and on all of them the *he* has *tagin*). **MV2** does list ישחט להם ומצא and then לה֯ם, but with no decoration on any of the letters. Parma 2427 and Parma 1959 both omit any reference to either instance.
18 The extra *yod* is ignored in the **LMV** transcription, but kept by Ginsburg.
19 Though **EPST** incorrectly transcribes as דבה.
20 Additionally, Shem Tov does not bring this instance in his *Tanakh*.
21 This is a common issue with this manuscript. It is transcribed correctly in **LMV**.
22 In the Yemenite tradition and in some other *Sifrey Torah* the *samekh* of this word ויהס is one of those written large.

36. **'why'** (poss. Num. 14:3). 37. **'why do [you]'** (Num. 14:41) 38. **'*challah* [portion]'** (Num. 15:20). 39. **the 'your God' of [the verse beginning] 'I'** (Num. 15:41). (*Parashat Qoraḥ*) 40. **'shall we completely** [perish?]' (Num 17:28). (*Parashat Pinḥas*) 41. **'covenant of** [everlasting] **priesthood'** (Num 25:13).

36 and 37. Our scribe has written למה twice, however, his intention is that they are different entries, as one is marked on the *he* of the first לְמָה and the second is on the *he* of זה. The other manuscripts disagree. **P, MV, ST** and H all read למה זה אתם with **ST** marking only the *he* of למה. There is only one occurrence of למה between Num. 13:30 and 14:41 but this is rather ולמה ('and why') in Num. 14:3 where the people complain that God has brought them to the desert to die. In Num. 41:41, Moses is instead asking the people why they transgress God's commandments. Alternatively, if the two instances brought by our scribe are included to balance each other, one might have expected that he should have written ולמה and placed the second ornamentation on that and not on זה, which does have some support in the secondary sources.[23]

38. Our scribe originally omitted this instance, but this was subsequently added in superscript in the space between entries. **P, MV, H** and **ST** all agree, bringing חלה.[24]

39. **P** and **MV** agree, bringing אלהיכם דאני. **ST** reads instead אני ייי אלהיכם בתרא (the last 'I am the Lord Your God'). **H** incorrectly breaks this into two separate instances דאני // אלהיכם. This presents a problem as the full verse reads, אני יהוה אלהיכם אשר הוצאתי אתכם מארץ מצרים להיות לכם לאלהים אני יהוה אלהיכם giving two possibilities. **ST** is clear it is the last one only but the entries given by all the others leaves us with a choice of two, since both are in the verse beginning 'I'.[25]

---

23 *Ben Mesheq* gives ב היהן דלמה זה (two *he*s in 'why this') *Qiryat Sefer* explains that למה זה הה"א בשניהם מתוייגת ('why this' the *he* in both of them is decorated). Thus there is certainly a tradition to mark both. Q651–652 gives למה זה אתם with both decorated. MV2 lists למה זה אתם but decorates none of the letters. Parma 2427 and Parma 1959 both omit any reference to either instance.

24 The *Ba'al ha-Ṭurim* also comments on this instance, explaining that the extra *tagin* allude to the 'five grains one must take *challah* from and that one is [also] obligated regarding five *reva'im* of flour'.

25 MV2 lists this as אני ייי אלהיכם which suggests the last part of the verse, but decorates no letter. Q651–652 brings אלהיכם אשר הוצאתי which clearly refers to the first instance in the verse. Once again, Parma 2427 and Parma 1959 both omit any reference to either instance. *Qiryat Sefer* also believes both should be decorated explaining that אלהיכם הה"א מתויגת ('your God', the *he* is decorated) and then lists הוצאתי as *ma-le'* and then adds אלהיכם גם הוא הה"א מתויגת (('your God', also this [one] the *he* is decorated). *Ben Mesheq*'s entry is a

40. P, MV, ST and H all agree, bringing האם תמנו.
41. Our scribe originally had a *he* in front of the word which he marked as having a decoration, but this may have been erased deliberately rather than faded. He also writes כהונת *ma-le' vav*. P does not have the *he* reading ברית כהונת. MV brings ברית כהנת and ST is likely the same but only ברית is legible in the enhanced images. The scribe of H brings a metathesis בתׄרׄי כהנת with the incorrect letters dotted, presumably to point out the error.[26]

Line 8: **[42]זה האשׄה תרוייהו • זה האשה • [43]יעשה ונסכו • [44]ונסכיהם דויום**

42. **'this is the fire offering'** [on] **both of them** (Num. 28:3). **'this is the fire offering'.** 43. **'and its drink offering** shall be made**'** (Num. 28.15). 44. **'and their drink offerings'** of [the section] **'and on the day ...**

42. Our scribe perhaps appears to be a little confused. He has written that both letters *he* should carry the extra *tagin*, but only marks one of the letters. He then repeats the phrase, even though this does not occur again in Numbers. P **gives** זה האשה תר׳, and H similarly states זה האשה תרוייהו. ST leaves out the instruction תרוייהו instead indicating which letters it feels should be adorned, זה הׄאשׄה. MV brings האשה תרויהון which takes זה out of consideration, but adds the further problem that this could then refer to the האשה in Num. 25:15. Something has been erased under תרויהון which may have clarified the intention, but this is not visible. ST seems to give the clearest instruction.[27]
43. P, MV and H all agree, bringing יעשה. ST clarifies the instance on יעשׄה ונסכו. יעשה has been added subsequently in superscript in CG.
44. P and MV give נסכיהם דוביום הבכורים, ST is faded but seems to be נסכיהׄם דוביום הבכורים too, H gives נסכיהם דביום הבכורי׳׳ missing a *vav* and abbre-

---

little confused, ב׳ היהן דלאלהיכם אלהיכם ה״א דאלהיכם (two [letters] *he* of 'to your God', 'your God' *he* of 'their God'). So this may mean both instances.

26 It is transcribed correctly in EPST.

27 Q651–652 and Parma 1959 bring decoration on both words, זׄה הׄאשׄה. *Ben Mesheq* with a tendency to add where it is unsure brings ג׳ ההין מזה האשה ([all] three [letters] *he* from 'this is the woman'). *Qiryat Sefer* explains, זה הה״א מתוייגת ('this' the *he* is decorated). The *Ba'al ha-Ṭurim* disagrees and states that 'there should be three *tagin* on the last *he* [only] of האשה to tell you that I [God] gave you five types of sacrifices, and the burnt offering is the most cherished of all of them. And if you study the five books of *Torah*, I will accord it as if you had brought the five types of sacrifices'. Add. MS 11639 lists this instance with regard to a *petuḥa* but does not decorate either letters *he*. Similarly MV2 lists זה האשה but does not decorate any *he*. Parma 2427 omits. There is clearly a lot of disagreement over this instance.

viating the final word. Our **CG** scribe has transcribed particularly poorly. This instance is interesting as it breaks with convention and instead of giving the reference in relation to the verse it is in, it instead refers to the section beginning in verse 25, but our instance is not in fact till verse 31.

Line 9: הבכורים • [45]ונסכיהם דויום השבת • [46]ונסכיה • [47]אלה תעשו • ////[??]השני

... **of the first fruits'**. (Num. 28:31). 45. **'their drink offering'** of the section **'and the day of the sabbath'**. 46. **'and its drink offerings'** (Num. 29:31). 47. **'these you will make** [as an offering]' (Num. 29:39). //// [??] **'the second'** (Num. 29:19).

45. Our scribe brings a very different tradition here. **P** and **MV** give ונסכיהם דיום שיני and **H** similarly with ונסכיהם דביום שיני, **ST** brings דוביום השני • ונסכיה̊ם and ignoring the superfluous separator, only this matches 𝔐. Whilst the wording is slightly different in each, they are all concerned with the 'drink offerings of the second day' which occurs in Num. 29:19, the section beginning two verses earlier in 29:17. There is no section with *Shabbat* specifically mentioned, only וביום השביעי ('and on the seventh day') and this section shows both ונסכהם *ḥaser yod* or the singular ונסכה ('the drink offering')— i.e. Num. 29:32–34. Our scribe seems to have erred and השני is marked in the margin.[28] It is perhaps odd that these four occurrences only, that involve the drink offering (plural and singular), are singled out for the special decoration, when the concept appears numerous times in the discussion of the daily sacrifices.
46. **P**, **MV**, **ST** and **H** all agree, bringing ונסכיה.
47. **P**, **MV**, **ST** and **H** all agree, bringing אלה תעשו. The *tav* in **ST** is not written clearly in any of the images.

Line 10: [48]אלה החקים • [49]לעריה • [50]וילכדה • [51]הראבוני • [52]והגדי • [53]המטות •

48. **'these are the laws'** (Num. 30:17). (*Parashat Maṭot*) 49. **'to its cities'** (Num 32:33). (*Parashat Mase'ei*) 50. **'and captured it'** (Num. 32:39) 51. **'the Reubenites'** (Num. 34:14). 52. **'the Gaddites'** (Num. 34:14). 53. **'the tribes'** (Num. 34:15).

---

28 There is an unclear marking added above, likely indicating the marginal correction. There is an earlier reference to sacrifices וביום שבת in Num. 28:9, but that would be out of sequence and it only mentions ונסכו in the singular in the verse. שבת and ונסכיהם do not occur in close proximity in the *Torah*. *Ben Mesheq* reads as **P** and **MV**, ונסכיהם דיום שיני and *Qiryat Sefer* also agrees that ונסכיהם הה"א מתויגת ('and their drink offerings' the *he* is decorated) in the section on the second day. **MV2** lists וביום השיני ונסכיהם but does not decorate the letter. Parma 2427 brings ונסכהם (*ḥaser yod*) and also does not decorate it. Add. MS 11639 and Parma 1959 omit.

Before instance 48 here, ST brings an additional listing ראשי ה֯מטות ('the heads of the tribes') from Num. 30:2 from *parashat Maṭot*, but no other core witness brings this.[29]

48. P, ST and H agree, bringing אלה החקים. Only ST makes it clear which *he* is to be decorated with the circular mark over the intended letter אלה ה֯חקים. Our scribe has neglected to add his indicator. MV gives החוקים *ma-le' vav* which does not match 𝔐. It then adds two additional words before concluding the listing, בתראה דמטות (the last in [*parashat*] *Maṭot*). It is likely that the scribe of MV has realised that the copy he is using as his *Vorlage* is incorrect, as this listing has been placed amongst those for *parashat Pinḥas*[30] and such a phrase is not present in this section, thus perhaps he is noting here that it should be listed later.
49. P, MV, ST and H all agree, bringing לעריה.
50. MV and ST agree, bringing וילכדה. P and H differ, since they see this as one entry וילכדה דהראובני ('and captured it' of the [verse beginning] 'the Reubenites') and H gives וילכדיה with an extra *yod*.[31] This cannot be the case as וילכדה appears only once in the whole book of Numbers and this is related to the *Bene Makhir ben Menashe* not the Reubenites. Thus our CG manuscript, without the superfluous joining ד, likely reflects a more accurate listing, as MV and ST.
51. MV and ST agree, bringing הראובני. Our scribe, however, brings a metathesis הראבוני but the *vav* has been rubbed away subsequently, as the error was noticed.
52. P, MV, and H agree, bringing והגדי.[32] ST appears to omit four instances and indeed Shem Tov may have skipped a line from his *Vorlage* but he did notice this later and added these vertically in the margin, in this case [ו]ה֯גדי.
53. P, MV and H agree. ST also brings ה֯מ[טות] in the margin.

Line 11: [54]יפנ֯ה • [55]עמיה֯וד • [56]אלף אמ֯ה • [57]לה֯ם דומדתם • [58]והערים בת֯ • [59]תהיינה בת֯ •

54. '[sons of] **Yefuneh** (Num. 34:19). 55. '[son of] **Amihud'** (Num. 34:20). 56. **'a thousand cubits'** (Num. 35:4). 57. **'to them' of** [the verse beginning] **'and you will measure them'** (Num. 35:5). 58. **the last 'and the cities'** (Num. 35:13). 59. **the last 'shall be'** (Num. 35:13).

29 No other secondary source supports this.

30 LMV transcribes as part of the listing for *Pinḥas* and again lists these as if they are separate entries .בתראה. דמטות

31 However, despite this, EPST transcribes as two separate instances · וילכדיה · הראובני.

32 Though EPST transcribes as הגדי, missing the *vav*.

54. **P**, **MV** and **H** agree. **ST** brings יפנ֯ה in the margin.
55. **P**, **MV** and **H** agree. **ST** brings ע[מי]ה֯וד in the margin.
56. **P**, **MV**, **ST** and **H** all agree, bringing אלף אמה.
57. **P**, **MV**, **ST** and **H** all agree, bringing להם דודתם. **ST** adds further clarification with additional words from the verse, giving לה֯ם דומדתם מחוץ לעיר ('to them' of [the verse beginning] 'and you will measure them from outside the city').
58. **ST** gives בתר֯, **P** and **H** give בתרא and **MV** in full בתראה but otherwise agree with והערים.
59. Our scribe has originally omitted this instance, but it is written in small faded letters in the margin but has omitted the *vav*, as all the others bring ותהינה. **P** adds בת֯, **ST** בתרא, **H** בתר׳ and once again **MV** in full בתראה.

Line 12: **[60]והצילו • [61]והשיבו • [62]הגדול • [63]הגדול • [64]לא יענה בת֯ • [65]ותיבה֯ • [66]ה֯אבות •**

60. **'and they** [the congregation] **shall deliver'** (Num. 35:25). 61. **'and they** [the congregation] **shall restore'** (Num. 35:25). 62. **'the High** [Priest]' (Num. 35:25 or 28). 63. **'the High** [Priest]' (Num. 35:28). 64. **the last 'will not testify'** (Num. 35:30). 65. **'and** [the] **ark'** 66. **'the fathers'** (Num. 36:1).

60. **P**, **MV**, **ST** and **H** all agree, bringing והצילו.
61. **P**, **MV**, **ST** and **H** all agree, bringing והשיבו.

62 and 63. **P** and **MV** agree, bringing הגדול twice. **ST** brings an instance which could, on first appearances, be an extension of one of these, bringing הכהן ה֯גדול ('the High Priest') and that Shem Tov has omitted the second. However, this is in fact an additional instance from Num. 35:25, for in the margins **ST** brings ה֯גדל, and then repeats ה֯גדל, which makes three instances, with these two from Num 35:28 as the others. However, in the Shem Tov *Tanakh*, the instance in verse 25 and only the first one from verse 28 is decorated, making two.[33] **ST**, having originally omitted them,

33 Q651–652 brings a listing עד מות הכהן הגדול · שמן ה֯קדש · ואחר מות הכהן ה֯גדול ('until the death of the High Priest'. 'Your holy Name'. 'the holy oil'. 'and after the death of the High Priest') which suggests that there is one instance in Num. 35:25 and one Num. 35:28, as the Shem Tov *Tanakh*, though does not decorate the first. **MV2** lists הכהן הגדול · ואחר מות הכהן הגדול but does not decorate any of the letters, so this could indicate either option. Parma 2427 brings הכהן ה֯גדל הגדל לדרתיכם ('the High Priest' 'High' 'throughout your generations') as one listing decorating only the one letter, but could be either option. Add. MS 11639 brings only one listing הכהן ה֯גדול. Parma 1959 list both instances as מות הכהן ה֯גדל · ה֯גדל but this could also be either option. This is echoed by *Qiryat Sefer* who explains, הגדל הגדל חסרים וה״א בשניהם מתוייגת ('High' 'High' are [written] *ḥaser*

is also the only core source to present as 𝔐, *ḥaser vav*, i.e הגדל. H omits the second instance of הגדול.

64. P, MV, ST and H all bring just לא יענה without the reference to it being ב̇ת (the last). This makes sense, since it is the only occurrence of this phrase and there is only one *he*, so would not need this distinction.

65. Our CG scribe has added a word here that appears in no other witness—ותיבה—and indeed does not appear in the book of Numbers. This fact seems to have been noticed as the word has a hollow circle drawn above the *yod* of the word, possibly to cancel the word from the list.[34] Instead P, MV, ST and H all bring בתוכה̊ (in the midst) from Num. 35:34. It is possible that in our scribe's *Vorlage* the word was unclear or badly faded, the base of the *bet* faded and so leaving a *vav*, the *vav* too short leaving a *yod* and the *kaf* not rounded sufficiently so resembling a *bet*, though this is quite a few errors in one word. He clearly did not check the reference.

66. P, MV, ST and H all agree, bringing האבות.

Line 13: [67]ה̊נשיאים • [68/69]ביה̊וה̊ תרויהו • [70]ותה̊יינה קדמ̇ • [71]ה̊מצות • [72]וה̊משפטים •

67. **'the princes'** (Num. 36:1). 68. and 69. **'by God' on both of them** (Num. 36:2). 70. **'they were married'**[35] [on] **the first** [*he*] (Num. 36:11). 71. **'the commandments'** (Num. 36:13). 72. **'and the judgements'** (Num. 36:13)

67. P, MV and H agree, bringing הנשיאים. ST too, but adds the next word in the verse for clarification, giving ה̊נשיאים ראשי ('the princes, heads of').

68 and 69. Unlike our manuscript, P and H avoid writing the Tetragrammaton in full, bringing ביי̇ תר̇ and ביי תרווי׳ respectively. MV omits these two instances. It is ST that brings the clearest instruction, locating the instance as אדני צוה ביה̊וה̊ ('and my lord was commanded by God') and showing which of the letters *he* should be decorated.

70. P abbreviates as קד̇, ST קדמ̇ and H קדמא׳. MV gives in full קדמאה, but all agree with ותהיינה. ST then appears to have a further word, but this

---

[without a *vav*] and the *he* in both of them is decorated). *Ben Mesheq* reads instead כח ג היהן הכהן ה״א קדמאה הגדל הגדל ([verse] 28, three [letters] *he*, 'the Priest' [on] the first *he*, 'the High', 'the High'), but since there are only two in verse 28, perhaps the earlier one in verse 25 is also included here, but the verse not indicated correctly. There is certainly considerable disagreement here and it is not clear whether two or three are intended and if two, which two.

34 Though elsewhere our CG scribe has employed cancellation dots.

35 Lit. 'became'.

is too faded and not identifiable in any of the available images. Our **CG** scribe does not seem to have an issue with writing God's Holy Name into this non-sacred manuscript, which may be a further sign of antiquity, but equally recognising that in this case where both letters *he* are decorated using the ייי form would potentially confuse. Interestingly, the scribe of our new secondary source **T-S Misc. 24.182** similarly has no compunction about writing the Tetragrammaton either.[36]

71 and 72. **P**, **MV**, **ST** and **H** all agree, bringing המצות and והמשפטים.

2 Description and Example Forms of the First Special Letter *He*

Line 14: **אלין ד[אר]בע קרני ולא דביקין /////// תוב דחד קרנא ודבקין**
These [are the letters *he*] **that have four horns and are not joined.** /////// **Also** [letters *he*] **that have one horn and are joined ...**

We come to the end of the longest section of *Sefer Tagin* which is on the first special *he*. However, the original writing on **CG** has been erased and written over with a much smaller script. It is difficult to assess what the original said. We are then introduced to the next letter form, another special *he*. As mentioned, our **CG** scribe does not bring his image of either of the form when he addresses the letter, as do other witnesses and only has these at the end on fragment **T-S NS 287.11**. He does not even mention the letter *he* by name at this point.

36 Alternatives such as ייי stem from the prohibition of accidentally erasing the written Name of God and the fact that a non-sacred text containing God's Holy Names may not be treated with appropriate sanctity/care and cound fall into 'a place of destruction'. This is derived from a reading of Deut 12:1–7, the key phrases being ונתצתם את מזבחתם ושברתם את מצבתם ואשריהם תשרפון באש ופסילי אלהיהם תגדעון ואבדתם את שמם מן המקום ההוא: לא תעשון כן ליהוה אלהיכם (and you shall shatter their altars, and break their pillars, and burn their *ʾasherim* with fire, and cut down the statues of their gods, and destroy their name from that place. You shall not do thus to the Lord your God). For more information on the practical application of this see my papers *Adventures in Practical Halachah no. 3: Neither Clever nor a Simpleton*, Kulmus Publishing, 2019 and *Adventures in Practical Halachah no. 4: To a Place Destruction*, Kulmus Publishing, 2019 (both available through www.kulmus.co.uk) and Bloom, A., ספר אור המלך (*The Book of the Light of the King*), Jerusalem, 2000, a slim halakhic volume devoted to scribal issues around God's Holy Names. Of necessity this monograph also contains the Holy Names of God, so please treat it with care.

The most familiar version of the first he *form is seen in the printed* Maḥzor Vitry (*LMV*)*—shown top right. However, this is merely one possibility amongst many that are found in the manuscripts.*

Right, our **CG** *scribe brings two forms from* ***T-S NS 287.11-F****, that supposedly represent his description in the listing here. However, the first which is supposed to have four* tagin, *has none and merely a dot above the* he, *but the leg is indeed not joined. It is possible that the dot means that he was unsure of the form—certainly we see this on some other letters that he has drawn. The letter* he *that is supposed to have one* tag *has two, the right one having a flag shape, but the left leg does correctly join on this letter* (*though barely*) *as per the description. Our scribe seems to be somewhat confused as to the forms of these letters.*

Our new secondary source from the Cambridge Genizah ***T-S Misc. 24.182*** (*see right*) *brings a different variant of the* he *with four* tagin, *where three sit on the roof and the fourth points downwards from the left corner of the roof, which we see in a number of the other sources. Indeed, as we see in Table 2 below, it is the core distinction between the various sources and some choose only to have three* tagin, *presumably to avoid the downward pointing* tag, *even though the instruction calls for four.*

P reads instead הלין דארבעה קרני ולא דבקין, **ST** הדין אלין דארבע קרנין ולא דבקין and H הלין דארבע קרני ולא דבקין. Because it follows the *parasha* format, **MV** does not bring an end statement about the letter form. The main difference is the use of אלין or הלין. Both mean the same 'these' but the form with *ʾalef* is an older biblical Aramaic form. Our **CG** manuscript subscribes to this.

3 Description and Example Forms of the Second Special Letter *He*

Regarding our second *he* form, P reads תוב דחדא קרנא ודבקין with an extra *ʾalef* in דחדא, H gives חד without the first *dalet*. Both spell באורייתא with a second *yod*, a later development. **MV** in its *parasha* format ignores the תוב (also) but otherwise matches our manuscript, bringing ה דחד קרנא ודבקין. **ST** brings similar within the listing, ותו ה דחד קרנא ודבקין יֹחֹ באוריתֹ /// וסימנהון ברבֹ (and also *he* with one horn and joined—18 in the Torah ////// and their signs [???]). The last word is not clear. In the extra introductory section in **ST**, this is expanded on with additional information, which no other version presents. This specifically comments on how these are not spread out through the *Torah*, but instead very concentrated within a few sections. It brings ותו׳ ה דכתיב בחד קרנא ודבק בנהא במעהא תמניא עשר והיא בסדר אלה הדברים ובאתחנן ושנים בפסוק אחד דוהשיבך

TABLE 2 Forms for the first special letter *he*, as brought by the halakhic texts to which we have compared our manuscript, along with some other examples.

 *Maḥzor Vitry* Parma 2574 (P)	 *Maḥzor Vitry* Add. MS 27201 (MV)	 Shem Tov *Tanakh* *Sefer Tagi* (ST)	 *Badey ha-'Aron* Heb. 840 (BH)	 *Sefer Tagi* Heb. 837 (H)
Not extant Nr. 5667 (K)	 Parma 2427	 Parma 1959	 Q651–652	 MS Geunz. 481
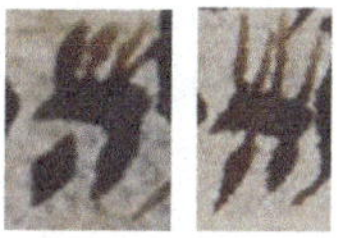 *Maḥzor Vitry* Add. MS 27201 (MV2)	 Add. MS 11639	 Add. MS 27167	 Bologna *Torah*	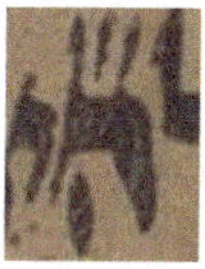 Vat. ebr. 1
 Or. 1463	 Alexander *Torah*			

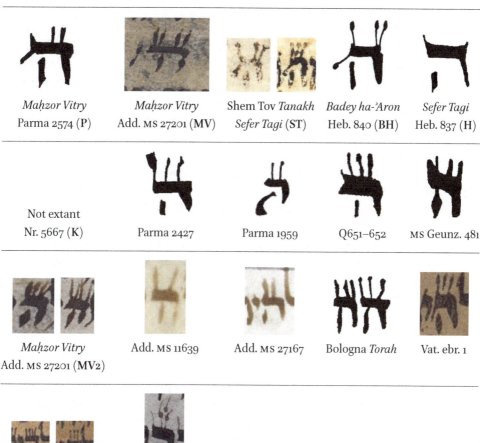

Maḥzor Vitry Add. MS 27201, Or. 1463, Add. MS 11639 and Add. MS 27167 are all free to reproduce for academic use and © The British Library Board. Shem Tov *Sefer Tagi* used with permission of Jaqui E. Safra. *Vat. ebr.1* © *Biblioteca Apostolica Vaticana reproduced with kind permission of the Vatican.* Alexander *Torah* images © Marc Michaels. Other images were not available for reproduction, so I have drawn them from the manuscript images accessed.

ה' מצרים (and also *he* that is written with one horn and its leg is joined inside[37] [there are] eighteen and they are in the sections *ʾEleh Ha-Devarim*, and in *Va-ʾetḥanan* and two are in one verse, that [begins] 'and God will bring you back to Egypt'). This explanation of where the instances occur seems an addition by Shem Tov, likely not in the original text. In **BH** we find more simply ותו' ה דכתיבא בחד קרנא ודבקין (and also a *he* that is written with one horn and joined) which uses the Aramaic ותרין instead of the Hebrew ושנים. It is worth noting here that the list of eighteen instances is only eighteen in actuality, if one follows the instruction in instance 4/5 to have both the letters *he* on הלה embellished.

Again the most familiar version of the second he *form is seen in the printed* Maḥzor Vitry (*LMV*)*—shown right—but there is much variance. It should be noted that many of our sources simply do not bring an example of this form. The form in our manuscript* ***T-S NS 287.11-F*** *is shown above with the other* he *form, but, as mentioned, has two* tagin *instead of the normal one similar to MS Geunz. 481. Unfortunately, because our secondary source* ***T-S Misc. 24.182*** *is not extant for Deuteronomy, we do not have an image of the second* he *form as all of the instances concerning this form occur within* parashat Devarim, parashat Va-ʾetḥanan *and* parashat Ki Tavoʾ, *as* ***ST*** *mentions.*

4 Listing of Instances for the Second Special Letter *He*

Line 15: **יֹחֹ באוריתא [1]ותהינו • [2]ולא האזין • [3]העוים • [4/5]הלא דכי רק בֹמֹ בֹ**

... 18 [instances] **in the *Torah.*** (*Parashat Devarim*) 1. **'and deemed it'** (Deut. 1:41). 2. **'and did not give ear'** (Deut. 1:45). 3. **'and the 'Avvim'** (Deut 2:23). 4/5. **'is it not' of the** [verse beginning] **'for only** [Og]**' twice ...** (Deut. 3:11).

1. **P**, **MV**, **ST** and **H** all agree, bringing ותהינו. However, our scribe has his *yod* too close to the *he*, so is difficult to read.
2. **P**, **MV**, and **ST** just give האזין but our scribe has added in ולא, making the instance clearer. **H**, however, gives this as הארץ in error, as perhaps the *Vorlage* the scribe copied from had the the *yod* and *nun sofit* too close together, resembling a *tsade sofit*.[38]

---

37 A difficult phrase. These words would literally translate as 'her sons are in her womb'. Here it seems the 'sons' are the legs of the letter and are joined inside—i.e. away from the edge, which is exactly how a joined *he* in old manuscripts would be differentiated from a *ḥet* where the left leg was at the end of the roof.

38 This error is faithfully transcribed in the Paris printed version ESPT.

TABLE 3 Forms for the second special letter *he*. Often no distinction is made with the previous *he* form and it is seldom used in any *Torah* since it looks like a current *he* except that it is supposed to join, which is not permitted. As we can see above, only our scribe in **CG**, Add. MS 11639 and **MV** brings a letter form where the leg actually joins, though the former and latter with a very thin stroke.

 *Maḥzor Vitry* Parma 2574 (**P**)	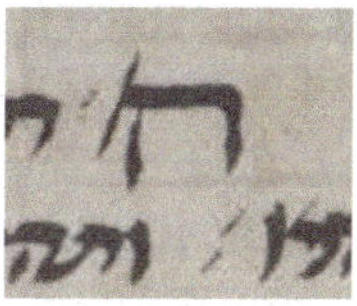 *Maḥzor Vitry* Add. MS 27201 (**MV**)	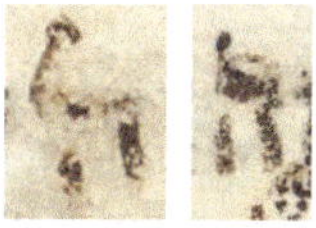 Shem Tov Tanakh *Sefer Tagi* (**ST**)	Not present *Badey ha-ʾAron* Heb. 840 (**BH**)	 *Sefer Tagin* Heb. 837 (**H**)
Not extant Nr. 5667 (**K**)	Employs the same form as the previous *he* Parma 2427	Employs the same form as the previous *he* Parma 1959	Employs the same form as the previous *he* Q651–652	 MS Geunz. 481
Not present *Maḥzor Vitry* Add. MS 27201 (**MV2**)	 Add. MS 11639	Not present Add. MS 27167	Image not available Bologna *Torah*	Not present Vat. ebr. 1
Not extant Or. 1463	Not present Alexander *Torah*			

3. **P**, **MV** and **H** correctly give והעוים as it appears in 𝔐. Our **CG** text, like that of **ST**, misses the first *vav*.

4 and 5. The fourth instance appears to have a serious error differing from the other core sources. **P** reads הלה דכי רק עוג תר and **MV** similarly הלה ב דכי רק עוג תרויהון. **ST** just reads הלה תרו, the assumption of all of these witnesses is that it is both letters *he* in the first word. However, whilst our text does suggest it is both too (even though the abbreviations are not clear), the spelling of הלה as הלא would prevent that. **H** too has the same issue, reading הלא היא דכי רק עוג תרוו׳. This is an example of קרי *qeri* (it is

read as) with an *'alef* but כתיב *ketiv* (it is written) with a *he*. Our scribe, as that of H, has used the *qeri* in error.[39]

Line 16: בו • [6]הארגוב דויותר • [7]הממלכות • [8]עלה ראש הפסגה • [9]וראה

... in it.[40] 6. **'the 'Argov' of the** [verse beginning] **'and the rest'** (Deut. 3:13). 7. **'the kingdoms'** (Deut. 3:21). (*Parashat Va-'etḥanan*) 8. **'go up to the top of Pisgah'** (Deut 3:27). 9. **'and see ...'**

6. P, MV, ST and H bring דויתר, as 𝔐 which is *ḥaser vav*. Our manuscript is *ma-le'*. ST is the only core source to also brings הארגב *ḥaser vav*, as 𝔐.
7. P, MV, ST and H all agree, bringing הממלכות.
8. As P and H, our manuscript adds הפסגה, whereas MV and ST bring only עלה ראש. However, this could cause confusion, since it brings an extra pair of letters *he* that could be potential candidates. Fortunately, our scribe has added a mark above the *he* of עלה. ST also brings the circular mark on עלה.
9. All but the tops of the letters *vav* and *resh* have faded, but in all likelihood our manuscript accords with ST that gives וראה בעיניך. P, MV and H do not bring this instance going straight to תראה. Possibly, at some stage, it dropped out of the list because of confusion over two similar words וראה and תראה and the former was omitted by several sources.

Line 17: בעיניך • [10]אשר תראה • [11]והשחתם • [12]להכעיסו • [13]העדותי • [14]השמר •

... with your eyes' (Deut 3:27). 10. **'which you will see'** (Deut. 3:28). 11. **'and you will deal corruptly'** (Deut. 4:25). 12. **'to provoke Him'** (Deut. 4:25). 13. **'destroyed'** (Deut. 4:26).

10. P, MV, ST and H read only תראה. Our manuscript adds אשר clarifying the instance.
11. P, MV, ST and H all agree, bringing והשחתם.

---

39 Parma 1959 brings the word in context, listing ערש ברזל הלה ('a bedstead of iron, is it not'). Add. MS 11639 also brings הלה with both decorated. *Ben Mesheq* brings ב׳ הי״הן דהלה (two [letters] *he* of 'it is not'). *Qiryat Sefer* states הלה בה״א במקום אלף ושני ההה״ן מוזרקת בצד הימני ('is it not' with a *he* in place of *'alef*, and the two [letters] *he* are curved on the right side). Parma 2427 lists but does not decorate either letter, and similarly the scan of Q651–652 is unclear but הלה is listed though neither *he* appears to be decorated. MV2 similarly lists the word, but does not decorate it.

40 This is a similar mechanism to that used by ST extensively where Shem Tov often adds remarks בֿ בה or בֿ בו (two in it [the verse]). This appears to be used only here in our fragment.

12. **P**, **MV**, **ST** and **H** all agree, bringing להכעיסו.
13. העידתי is, in fact, the first word of this verse in the *Torah* and this is reflected correctly only in **H**. **P** omits the *yod*, bringing העדתי. Our manuscript omits the first *yod* and adds a *vav*, which reflects the spelling in both **MV** and **ST** (though the latter is a little unclear because of fading).
14. This instance is subject to some debate, since the following instance והפיץ occurs in the very next verse, Deut. 4:26. Our instance is therefore likely to be השמד from Deut. 4:25 and the *resh* should be a *dalet*; two very close forms, so easily confused.[41] However, it is not faded and either our **CG** scribe has introduced this error or copied it from his *Vorlage* with the same error. This same error is present in **MV** and **P** is probably השמר' too, but there is a small dash after the *resh* and also a little way under the *resh* and so it could be taken for a ה. Unfortunately, **ST** is also faded, but also appears to be השמר as the last letter shape appears rounded on the corner. **H** reads instead השמה and there is clearly confusion here; since no core witness appears to bring the correct reading.[42]

Line 18: **[15]והפיץ • [16]מעשה ידי אדם • [17]והתמכרתם שם • [18]ואין קנה •**

15. **'and** [God] **will scatter'** (Deut. 4:25). 16. **'the work of men's hands'** (Deut. 4:28). (*Parashat Ki Tavo'*) 17. **'and you will sell yourselves there'** (Deut. 28:68). 18. **'and no one will buy** [you there]' (Deut. 28:68).

15. **P**, **MV** and **ST** agree, as does **H** but its final *tsade* is so curved round, it resembles a long medial one והפיצ.
16. **P**, **MV**, **ST** and **H** all agree, bringing מעשה ידי אדם.
17. **P**, **MV**, **ST**, **H** all omit the word שם, bringing just והתמכרתם.
18. **MV** agrees. **P** and **H** just give קנה as 𝔐, and **ST** brings קוֹנה *ma-le' vav*.

41 For example, *Qeset ha-Sofer* 5:2 explains 'One must be very careful with the heel protrusion behind squaring [the letter] so that it doesn't look like a *resh* and it be invalidated through the reading of a child.'

42 Unfortunately, the Shem Tov *Tanakh* is not extant for much of *Devarim* and *Va-'etḥanan* including this example. Q651–652 brings כי הֿשמד helping to clarify the instance. *Qiryat Sefer* does suggest there is some form of decoration on this word, bringing this השמד הה"א מעגלת ('destroyed'—the *he* is curled). MV2 lists השמד תשמדון ('shall be utterly destroyed') but does not decorate the *he*, which actually resembles a *tav*, so may be a transcription error. Parma 2427, Parma 1959, Add. MS 11639 and *Ben Mesheq* all omit.

5 Description and Example Forms of the Special Letter *Vav*

Line 19: **ושארה דתלתה קרני ///// דמידלי רישיהון ואיקום מר׳**

and the rest [of the letters *he*] have two horns. ///// [*Vav*] where their heads are extended and are standing up/raised …

After having brought the two special *he* forms, and before we learn about the *vav*, we are informed that all the rest of the letters *he* in the *Torah* should have two horn *tagin* and not one *tag*, as is the convention today on the letter *he*, according to normative scribal practice. **P**, **ST**, and **H** spell **ושארא דתלתא** and **ST** also gives the plural in full **קרנין**. **MV** does not bring this additional information, since it follows the *parasha* format.

In the left margin by line 20, in small letters is written **שער ו** (the gate of *vav*), presumably since the letter is not mentioned in the description. Nonetheless, our scribe brings his description of the special *vav*. As regards the start of the description **P** and **MV** bring, **דמדלי רישיהון ואקים** (that their heads are elevated[43] and [their legs/knees] **stand up/raised**[44] [to their fronts]) omitting the first *yod*, **H** similarly brings, **דמידלי רישיהון ואקים**, instead of **ואיקום** brought by our **CG** scribe.[45] **ST** is quite different, bringing **דמידלי רישיהון ועקים** (their heads are elevated and **bent/crooked**[46] [to their fronts]) in the introduction. In the listing, we find **ו דמידלי ועקים** (*vav* that are extended and [their legs/knees] are bent to their front). **BH** brings similarly **ו דמדלי רישיהון ועקים**. The legs or knees are thus either raised or bent.

The vav in the printed Maḥzor Vitry (*LMV*)*—shown right—is probably the most 'normal' looking. Many variants are much more extreme.*

The vav *form brought by our scribe in* ***T-S NS 287.11-F*** *(right) has an additional small* vav *on its head as its extension but no real significant raising or bending of the form below.*

T-S Misc. 24.182 *(right) brings a very curled cursive form which resembles a J with an additional line above. This curl is very common in other forms as seen below and it is what would invalidate the form as a* kasher vav *in normative scribal practice, as it just does not look like a* vav.

---

43 Melamed, E.Z., *Aramaic Hebrew English Dictionary of the Babylonian Talmud*, Feldheim Publishers, Jerusalem, 2005, p. 260.

44 Ibid. p. 61.

45 It is this spelling **איקום**, that is specifically brought by Melamed (see previous footnote).

46 Jastrow, op. cit., p. 1106.

Line 20: מורעיהון לקדמיהון ח̇ל̇ באוריתא [1]והרגו אתי • [2]ואנכי
their appearances to their front, [there are] 38 in the Torah. (*Parashat Lekh Lekha*) 1. **'and they** [the Egyptians] **will kill me** [Abram]' (Gen. 12:12). 2. **'and I ...**

It is in line 20, where the last part of the description of the *vav* is written, that there is perhaps the most significant departure for **CG** against all of the existing core witnesses, as regards what in the letter is either raised or bent. **P**, **MV**, **ST**, **H** and **BH** all state כרעיהון לקדמיהון (its legs/knees[47] forwards). Our manuscript reads instead מורעיהון. Is it perhaps a transcription error where כרע has been written as מורע? However, since the previous line ends with a space filler מר̇ this is more likely to suggest that this word is being copied from a *Vorlage* rather than our **CG** scribe introducing this error, and that this is a deliberate inclusion. מורעיהון itself is a difficult word to translate here as it literally means 'their pastures'[48] which is not at all relevant in this context. Jastrow suggests it is linked to מאורע which signifies an 'event' or 'occasion'.[49] מרע, however, is to 'make weak, sick or afflict'.[50] Rabbi Dr Charles Middlesborough suggests that the answer is somewhat simpler. He suggests since 'the *'ayin* in Aramaic sometimes replaces the *'alef* in Hebrew, if you substitute the one for the other then you have a word, מוראיהון, most likely meaning 'appearances', which would appear to fit the context ... well'.[51] Hence the translation adopted above to reflect our scribe's variant text. Regardless, this does seem to be some corruption of the more likely original text, כרעיהון.

Whereas other manuscripts give the number as ל̇ח̇ (38), including **ST** in the listing which also adds וסימ̇ (and their signs), it is given in full in the **ST** introduction and in **BH** as תלתין ותמניא (thirty-eight). Our scribe deliberately reverses this to read ח̇ל̇ signifying the word *ḥol* (profane/ordinary). Such 'playfulness' with numbers can often be seen with certain numeric combinations in book page numbers which can be reversed to spell a short Hebrew word.[52]

The scribe in our fragment has also generally failed to indicate the *vav* with a line mark and this can be a problem in some words where the letter occurs more than once. However, with one exception, as we will see through the listing, the *vav* in question is the first, which is often the *vav* conversive on a verb.

---

47 Jastrow, M., *Dictionary of the Targumim, Talmud Babli, Yerushalmi and Midrashic Literature*, Judaica Press, New York, 1989, p. 673.

48 See *Targum* Pseudo-Jonathan Gen: 13:7 where it is spelt *ḥaser vav* מרעיהון.

49 Jastrow, op. cit., p. 722.

50 Ibid. p. 845.

51 In an email exchange 18/12/17.

52 The most common is י̇ח̇ (18) which is reversed to spell חי (life).

TABLE 4 Forms for the special letter *vav*. As explained above, many of the forms one sees would be considered *pasul* (invalid) in normative scribal practice, as they have little resemblance to an actual *vav* and can resemble a *nun* or *pe sofit* instead. It is certainly telling that *Qiryat Sefer* consistently refers to this form as רע (bad).

 *Maḥzor Vitry* Parma 2574 (**P**)	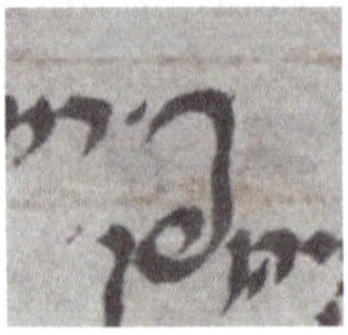 *Maḥzor Vitry* Add. MS 27201 (**MV**)	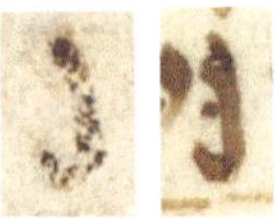 Shem Tov *Tanakh* *Sefer Tagi* (**ST**)	 *Badey ha-ʾAron* Heb. 840 (**BH**)	 *Sefer Tagin* Heb. 837 (**H**)
Not extant Nr. 5667 (**K**)	 Parma 2427	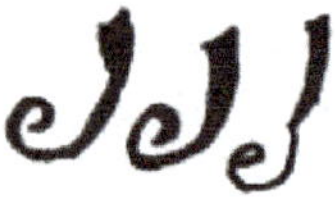 Parma 1959	 Q651–652	 MS Geunz. 481
 *Maḥzor Vitry* Add MS 27201 (**MV2**)	 Add. MS 11639	 Add MS. 27167	Image not available Bologna *Torah*	 Vat. ebr. 1
 Or. 1463	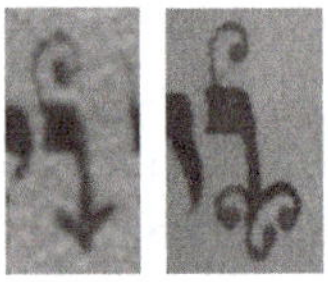 Alexander *Torah*			

6 Listing of Instances for the Special Letter *Vav*

1. The first instance has an immediate issue, since we are unsure of which *vav* to adorn. **P** and **MV** agree and **P** places a dot on the first *vav*, והרגו אתי. **ST** and **H** both bring והרגו אותי *ma-le'vav* in the second word, which would add further to the options, but **ST** places the circular mark on the first *vav* too, giving והרגו̊. 𝔐 is *ḥaser vav* אתי, so it has to be the first word.[53]
2. **P**, **MV**, **ST** and **H** all agree. Again, in theory, there is a second *vav* in this phrase, but **ST** is clear that the decoration is in ואנכי̊, and though the last part has faded seems to also give הולך ע[רירי].

Line 21: **הולך ערירי • [3]ותמת שרה • [4]ותמת רחל • [5]ויכירה ויאמר •**

… go childless' (Gen. 15:2). (*Parashat Ḥayyei Sarah*) 3. **'and Sarah died'** (Gen. 23:2). 4. (*Parashat Va-yishlaḥ*) **'and Rachel died'** (Gen 35:19). (*Parashat Va-yeshev*) 5. **'and he** [Jacob] **knew it and he said'** (Gen. 37:33).

3. **P**, **MV**, and **H** agree, bringing ותמת שרה. **ST** is very faded, but likely the same.[54]
4. **P**, **MV**, **ST** and **H** all agree, bringing ותמת רחל.[55]
5. **P**, **MV** and **H** all bring just ויכירה. **ST** seems to bring ו̊יכירהו with a extra *vav* at the end of the word. **H** then lists it again as the scribe has clearly forgotten that he had already written it on the end of the previous page.[56] None of the other manuscript witnesses bring ויאמר presumably because this would just lead to confusion as to which *vav* was intended.[57]

---

53 Interestingly both Q651–652 and Parma 2427 bring an additional instance, ו̊ינגע ייי את פרעה ('and the LORD plagued Pharaoh') from Gen. 12:17. *Qiryat Sefer* also indicates וינגע הוא'ו מוזרקת וצורתה רע ('and He plagued' the *vav* is curled and its form is bad). *Ben Mesheq* too gives ס י"ב ז' וינגע הוי"ו כעין וי"ו של וימח דפ' נח (chapter 12 [verse] 7 'and He plagued' the *vav* is like the *vav* in 'and He blotted' (Gen 7:23) in *parashat Noaḥ*).[2] Add. MS 11639, Add. MS 27167 and Parma 1959 omit. This is unusual level of agreement on an instance that is missing from all the core sources. That said **MV2** brings וי̊נגע ייי את פרעה decorating only the *yod* and this is the core sources as an instance (see below) in the listing for the special *yod*, so may be the source of confusion.

54 Unfortunately, this instance in the Shem Tov *Tanakh* is not extant. Add. MS 27167 oddly brings the decoration on the first *tav*.

55 Prior to this instance our *Genizah* secondary source **T-S Misc. 24.182** brings ו̊יבכו (and they [Jacob and Esau] wept) from Gen. 33:4 and is unique in doing so, as none of the core or secondary sources bring this.

56 **EPST** only transcribes one.

57 As our fragment, Q651–652 does also bring ו̊יכירה ויאמר but is clear which *vav* is decor-

Line 22: [6]וימאן להתנחם • [7]ויהי כשמע אדניו • [8]ולא יכל יוסף • [9]וימת

6. **‘but he** [Jacob] **refused to be comforted’** (Gen. 37:35). 7. **‘and it came to pass that when his** [Joseph’s] **master** [Potiphar] **heard’** (Gen. 39:19). 8. **‘and Joseph could not** [refrain]’ (Gen. 45:1). (*Parashat Va-yeḥi*) 9. **‘and he died** …

6. P, MV, ST and H all agree, bringing וימאן להתנחם.
7. MV agrees. P and H give כשמוע *ma-le’ vav* even though 𝔐 is *ḥaser*. ST is very faded but likely agrees bringing ויהי כשמע א[דׄ].[58]
8. P, ST and H agree, bringing ולא יכל יוסף. MV omits.

ST lists an additional two instances between instances 8 and 9, which the other core witnesses do not bring. However, it is very faded and difficult to make out from the manuscript image available. A close inspection shows the first seems to have the words, ו̊[ ]ו את יוסף. This is problematic as the instance Shem Tov brings in his *Tanakh* has אל and not את. It gives instead ו̊יצוו אל יוסף (‘and they sent a message to Joseph’) in Gen. 50:16. The second extra listing is clearer being ו̊יאמר יוסף (‘and Joseph said’) in Gen. 50:24. However, ST enjoys no support from any of the secondary sources for either additional instance.

9. Our scribe brings וימת יוסף, but this could be either Gen. 50:26 or Ex. 1:6. However, all the other core texts are clear that it should be the first occurrence only. P brings וימת יוסף קדׄ, and H gives קמא׳ omitting the *dalet*. MV writes in full קדמאה. ST is unclear on the scan, but the enhanced images show ו̊ימת יוסף קדׄ, and only the first is decorated in the Shem Tov *Tanakh*.[59]

---

ated. **MV2** lists ויכירה ויאמר but does not decorate either. Parma 2427 brings just ו̊יכירה. Add. MS 11639 lists ויכירה ויו גדול (‘and he knew it’ a large *vav*). **T-S Misc. 24.182** lists ו̊יכרה *ḥaser vav*. 𝔐 is *ma-le’* as is brought by the other sources. Add. MS 27167 and Parma 1959 omit. *Qiryat Sefer* and *Ben Mesheq* do not list in this manner.

58 After this instance our **T-S Misc. 24.182** brings חלמ̊ו (his dream) from Gen. 40:4 and is again unique in doing so, as none of the core or secondary sources bring this. Given the general pattern of the first letter *vav* in the word being decorated, however, this instance is unlikely.

59 Q651–652, **MV2** (whose scribe decorates ו̊ימת elaborately and differently from the form brought in **MV**) and Add. MS 11639 bring only the instance in *Va-yeḥi* and *Qiryat Sefer* similarly in *Va-yeḥi* brings וימת הוא״ו מאותן שצורתן רע ומוזרקת (‘and he died’ the *vav* from it has a bad form and is curled). **T-S Misc. 24.182** also brings ו̊ימת only in *parashat Va-yeḥi*. Parma 2427, Parma 1959 and *Ben Mesheq* omit either.

Line 23: יוסף • [10]וישימו עליו • [11]ויצו פרעה • [12]ויך את המצרי • [13]ויבקש
... **Joseph**' (Gen. 50:26). (*Parashat Shemot*) 10. '**and they** [the Egyptians] **set** [taskmasters] **upon him** [Israel]' (Ex. 1:11). 11 '**and** [Pharoah] **commanded**' (Ex. 1:22). 12. '**and he** [Moses] **slew the Egyptian**' (Ex. 2:12). 13. '**and he** [Pharoah] **sought ...**

10. **P**, **MV**, **H** all just bring וישימו. Our manuscript adds the next word in the verse עליו bringing yet another *vav* into contention. **ST** though faded also brings just וׄישימו.
11. **P**, **MV**, and **H** all just bring ויצו. Our manuscript clarifies by adding the next word in the verse פרעה. The enhanced images show that **ST** does list ויצב and the first *vav* may have some residue of a circle. However, the Shem Tov *Tanakh* does not decorate either *vav*. As mentioned above, since most of the other instances are on the *vav* conversive in the verb forms, it is likely it is the first and this is confirmed in the secondary sources.[60]
12. **P**, **MV**, and **H** all just bring ויך. Our manuscript again clarifies by adding additional words from the verse, את המצרי, and this is echoed by **ST** this time who also brings וׄיך את המצרי. These last three examples are very interesting as this listing from our fragment seems to be more extensive and this has been the occasion in a few other instances.
13. **MV** just brings ויבקש. **P** and **H** bring ויבקש להרוג *ma-le' vav*, **ST** is also *ma-le'* and extends to וׄיבקש להרוג את משה ('and he sought to kill Moses) but decorates the first *vav* only. 𝔐 is *ḥaser*, להרג, which also makes it clear that it is the first (only) *vav* that takes the decoration. Our **CG** manuscript is the only one to bring this accurately.

Line 24: להרג • [14]ויאנחו • [15]ויזעקו • [16]ויחר אף יהוה במשה • [17]ומאז באתי
... **to kill** [Moses]' (Ex. 2:15). 14. '**and** [the children of Israel] **sighed**' (Ex. 2:23). 15. '**and they cried out**' (Ex. 2:23) 16. '**and God's anger was kindled against Moses**' (Ex. 4:14). 17. '**and since I** [Moses] **came ...**

14. **P**, **MV**, **ST** and **H** all agree. **ST** decorates only the first *vav*, וׄיאנחו.
15. **P**, **MV**, **ST** and **H** all agree. **ST** decorates only the first *vav*, וׄיזעקו.

---

60 Q651–652 and Add. MS 11639 bring וׄיצו פרעה agreeing with our fragment in extending the reference. **MV2** lists ויצו פרעה, but does not decorate any letter. Parma 2427 extends even further bringing וׄיצו פרעה לכל עׄמו ('and Pharaoh commanded all his people'). *Qiryat Sefer* does not give a clear instruction as to which, stating ויצו הוא׳ו בצורה רע ומוזרקת ('and he commanded' the *vav* form is bad and curled). Parma 1959 and *Ben Mesheq* omit.

16. **P**, **ST** and **H** all agree, and once again avoid writing the Tetragrammaton by having three letters *yod* as previously. **MV** also brings ייי, but omits the word משה. Our scribe, once again has no issue with writing God's Holy Name in full.

ST adds a further instance ו̊יאמן העם ('and the people believed') from Ex. 4:31 in *parashat Shemot*, which is missing from our manuscript and the other core sources. This is also decorated in the Shem Tov *Tanakh*.[61]

17. **P**, **MV** and **H** just bring ומאז באתי, **ST** is very faded, but the enhanced images reveal ו̊מאז. Again our manuscript is fuller.

Line 25: **אל פרעה • [18]ולא שמעו אל משה • [19]ומת כל בכור • [20]וילן העם •**
... to Pharoah' (Ex. 5:23). (*Parashat Va-ʾeraʾ*) 18. **'and they** [the Israelites] **did not listen to Moses'** (Ex. 6:9). (*Parashat Boʾ*) 19. **'and all the first born** [Egyptians] **will die'** (Ex. 11:5). (*Parashat Be-shallaḥ*) 20. **'and the people thirsted'** (Ex. 17:3).

18. There is some debate over what constitutes the next instance. **P** brings ולא שמעו אלי ('and they did not listen to me') and **H** similarly brings ולא שמעו אליו ('and they did not listen to him'). However, there are no such phrases in the *Torah*. **MV** just brings ולא שמעו. However, our manuscript and **ST** are very clear that this instance is Ex. 6:9, **ST** bringing ו̊לא שמעו אל משה.[62]

---

61 Parma 2427 does not bring this but does bring ו̊יהי בימים הרבים ('and it was in the course of many days') earlier in Ex. 2:23 and Q651–652 does similarly shortening to ו̊יהי בימים. *Qiryat Sefer* also notes that ויהי הוא'ו בצורה רעה ומוזרקת בימים הרבים שניהם ביו'ד הרבים ('and it was' the *vav* has a bad form and is curled, 'in the course of many days' both of them have lots of [letters] *yod*). *Ben Mesheq* also brings ו̊יהי but apparently related to ס"ב ו' but the word is not in this verse. **MV2** also lists ויהי בימים but offers no decoration. Add. MS 11639 has ויהי בימים הרבים פתו̇ indicating the *petuḥa* but does not decorate the *vav*. There seems general agreement amongst the secondary sources that there is an instance that apparently has dropped from the core sources, but there is no support for ST's inclusion. Add. MS 11639 also brings ו̊ירא ('and looked'), however, this word appears in several places in that section, twice in Ex. 2:11, once in verse 12 and again after in verse 25 and finds no support elsewhere. Additionally, Q51–652 also brings ו̊תעל ('rose up') in Ex. 2:23 which would group well with the other two from that verse that are in the core sources, but finds no other support. Q651–652 also brings and ו̊יוציאה מחיקו ('when he took it from his chest') at Ex. 4:7 and *Ben Mesheq* accords with this listing וס"ד ז' ויוציאה (chapter 4, [verse] 7 'when he took it') in his listing for the special *vav*. Parma 1959 lists none of these options. There is indeed a great deal of disagreement amongst the sources.

62 Q651–652 also agrees bringing ו̊לא שמעו אל משה. Parma 2427 brings only ו̊לא שמעו. *Qiryat Sefer* also brings ולא הוא"ו צורתה רע ומוזרקת ('and [they] did not' the *vav* has a bad form and is curled). By its position, we assume it is referring to Ex. 6:9. **MV2** lists ולא שמעו, but

19. P adds קדׄ, ST קדמׄ, H קדמא׳ and MV in full קדמאה, which may suggest that this is the first use of this phrase, occurring in Ex. 11.5 but it does not actually appear later in Exodus, so the qualifier is referring to it being on the first *vav* in the phrase. ST places the circle on the first, bringing וֹמת כל בכור.
20. P, ST and H agree. The slight confusion that has arisen over this instance is because **LMV** has transcribed **MV** incorrectly as וילך, though the actual manuscript is clearly וילן, as confirmed by the other sources.

Line 26: [21]ועל נסותם • [22]ויבא עמלק • [23]ויחלש יהושוע • [24]ויקהל העם •
21. **'because they** [the Israelites] **incited** [God]' (Ex. 17:7). 22. **'and 'Amalek came'** (Ex. 17:8). **'and Joshua weakened** ['Amalek]' (Ex. 17:13). (*Parashat Ki Tissa'*) 24. **'and the people gathered'** (Ex. 32:1).

21. P, MV, ST and H all agree, ST marking וֹעל נסותם. However, since 𝔐 is *ḥaser vav* this also clarifies the instance to be decorated.
22. P, MV, ST and H all agree, bringing ויבא עמלק.
23. P and H bring ויחלש יהושע *ḥaser vav* as 𝔐. Our manuscript is *ma-le'*. MV just gives ויחלש and ST similarly וֹיחלש, so the *vav* in question is clearly the first.
24. P, MV, ST and H all agree.

T-S D1.42 1r—26 lines

Line 1: [25]והביאו אלי • [26/27]ויביאו אל אהרן • [28]וידבר דלך רד • [29]ויגף • [30]ויק[ח קרח] •
25. **'bring them** [the golden earrings] **to me'** (Ex. 32:2). 26. and 27. **'and they brought them** [the earrings] **to Aaron'** (Ex. 32:3). 28. **'and He said' of** [the verse beginning] **'go and go down'** (Ex. 32:7). 29. **'and** [God] **plagued'** (Ex. 32:35). (*Parashat Qoraḥ*) 30. **'and Qoraḥ took'** (Num. 16:1).

25. P, MV, ST and H all agree. It is yet another word with two letters *vav*, but ST confirms it is the first as has been our pattern, bringing וֹהביאו אלי.
26 and 27. P and MV are very clear that both letters *vav* should be marked, adding תׄר and תרויהון respectively. ST does not include that instruction

---

does not decorate a *vav*. Parma 1959, Add. MS 11639, Add. MS 27167 and *Ben Mesheq* omit. Possibly as a result of this uncertainty, Ginsburg instead lists ולא שמע (and he did not listen) in Ex. 8:15, but this is clearly an error, as it is followed by the word אלהם (to them) not אליו (to him), Ginsburg., op. cit., p. 688.

but instead adds the circular marks over both letters *vav*, bringing וֹיביאוֹ אל אהרן and both are decorated in the Shem Tov *Tanakh*. H also brings תרווי׳. All the other texts are clear, but our manuscript seems defective, in that it makes no mention of the fact that this represents two instances.[63] This is a particularly distinct instance in **CG**'s listing because of this.

28. **P, MV** and **H** agree, bringing וידבר דלך רד. **ST** omits at this point, but tacks it onto the end of the list as the penultimate entry.
29. **P, MV** and **H** agree, bringing ויגף. **ST** again omits here, but tacks it on to end of the list.
30. **P, MV** and **H** agree. **ST** expands to וֹיקח קרח בן ('and Qoraḥ, son of [Yitshar] took').

Line 2: [31]ותכס • [32]ואש יצאה • [33]וילכו • [34]ויאמרו בני ישראל • [35]וידבר העם •

31. **'and** [the ground] **closed'** (Num. 16:33). 32. **'and fire came out'** (Num. 16:35). 33. **'and they went'**. 34. **'and the children of Israel said'** (Num. 17:27). 35. **'and the people said'** (Num. 21:5).

31. **P, MV, ST** and **H** all agree, bringing ותכס.
32. **P, MV** and **H** all agree. **ST**, though faded, abbreviates to ואש יצ׳.
33. **P** and **H** agree and bring וילכו then the nearest use of this word would be Num. 16:25 which would precede the previous instance which is as 16:35. This would be outside of the normal convention for *Sefer Tagin* that does generally list in order. However, **MV** disagrees and brings וילנו ('and they murmered') which is Num. 17:6 and which fits neatly between 16:35 and 27:7. **ST** echoes this וֹילונו which is *ma-le' vav* whereas 𝔐 is *ḥaser*, וילנו. At some point there has been a simple transcription error with a כ replacing a נ or vice versa. As to which is the case, it is perhaps the list order and the secondary sources that are the deciding factors here, and our manuscript is probably defective, as is **P** and **H**.[64]

---

63 Add. MS 11639 similarly brings on both letters *vav*. *Qiryat Sefer* also remains with the majority of our manuscripts stating that ויביאו מלא ושני הווי״ן צורתן רע ומזרקות ('and they brought' is *ma-le'* and the two [letters] *vav* have a bad form and are curled). That said, Q651–652, Parma 2427 and Parma 1959 and our new *Genizah* source **T-S Misc. 24.182** bring only one *vav* indicated וֹיביאו. **MV2** lists ויביאו אל אהרן, but does not decorate either *vav*. *Ben Mesheq* omits.

64 Q651–652, Parma 2427 and Add. MS 11639 have no confusion and bring וֹילנו כל עדת from Num. 17:6. **MV2** also lists this same phrase, but does not decorate the letter *vav*. *Qiryat Sefer* too explains that וילנו הוא״ו כצורה רעה ומעגלת ('and they murmered' the *vav* is like a bad form and curled). Parma 1959 and *Ben Mesheq* omit. **T-S Misc. 24.182** is not extant.

34. **P** and **MV** and possibly **ST** (faded) abbreviate to וׄיאמרו בני ישר' (also clarifying which *vav*) and **H** similarly brings ישרא'. Our manuscript is the only to write it out in full. **MV** also adds the instruction בתראה (the last) but this seems redundant as this phrase does not appear elsewhere in Numbers, unless it meant the last letter *vav*.
35. **P**, **MV**, **ST** and **H** all agree, bringing וידבר העם.

Our manuscript, along with **P**, **H** and **MV** brings only 35 of the 38 instances. **ST** fills the gaps with three options,[65] however, none of those find support in the secondary sources who bring other options, Q651–652 in particular. Many seem to be supportive of at least one instance being וׄיהי בימים הרבים.[66] It does rather feel like the sources are trying to make up for the gaps as there are 'supposed' to be 38. However, it is possible that originally there were only 35 as לׄה could have easily been mistaken for לׄח at an early stage. This is a difficult area that will require further study for a fully satisfactory resolution.

7 Description and Example Forms of the First Special Letter *Zayin*

Our manuscript then adds in the right margin in smaller letters שערי ז (the gates of *zayin*) introducing the next letters. Our scribe has also returned to indicating which letter is intended.

In a fairly radical departure, the printed Maḥzor Vitry (***LMV***)*—shown right—brings the oddest form of this* zayin *which does not accord with any of the manuscripts. It also does not bring a second form.*

*Our **CG** scribe brings the two* zayin *forms in **T-S NS 287.11-F** (see right). The first that is to have no* tagin *has a dot above but not* tagin. *The second of which is supposed to have a bent head, has instead a line straight up from the left side of its head.*

Whilst sections that would contain the first form of zayin *are extant in **T-S Misc. 24.182**, it is simply omitted by the scribe. Thus we have no image of the form or any evidence to bring on questionable instances from this source. The second form of* zayin *is not extant in this source.*

---

65 Which Basser includes, op. cit., pp. 81–82, even though he recognises elsewhere that none other of his sources supports these.

66 Baer does includes this in his shorter listing of 30 instances for the *vav*, op. cit., p. 21. However, there are several other variants in this list and is not an entirely trustworthy source, as it is seems a compilation from *Sefer Tagin* as used in *Sifrey Torah* and the Yemenite tradition, as mentioned previously.

Line 3: ז דלא מזאינא באמצעיתה יד̇ באוריתא [1]ז̊ה ינחמנו • [2]ויז̊כר

***Zayin* that has no *zayin* type decoration in its centre** [of the roof of the letter, there are] **14 in the Torah.** (*Parashat Bere'shit*) 1. **'this** [one] **will comfort us'** (Gen. 5:29). (*Parashat Va-yetse'*) 2. **'and God remembered …**

P similarly states דלא מזייני באמצעא יד̇ באוריית̇ but brings a form at the end of the listings that has a massive curled *tag* that comes from the centre. **H** brings דלא מזייני באמצע יד̇ באוריי' and then brings a couple of example forms which have *tagin* coming from each of the four corners of the roof of the letter like spikes. It is **MV** where we see the most radical variant; as it states דמזייני באמצעיתיו יד באוריתא (that **has** a *zayin* type decoration in its centre)—the complete opposite of the other witnesses. It then brings an extremely odd drawing of the form it intends, that does not resemble a *zayin* at all and another that has three *tagin* and curves from the roof. Indeed, it brings other variants each time the listing appears. **ST** also differs greatly bringing בחד יד̇ באוריתדלא מזיינין אלא ([*zayin*] that is not decorated [with *zayin* type decorations] except with one, 14 in the *Torah*), which it clarifies in the earlier introductory listing as בחד זיונא (with one *zayin* type decoration). In effect this is also giving the complete reverse of the intention of **P**, **H** and our manuscript. **ST** also adds a further word before beginning the listing—מנהון[ ]ו—but the second (and possibly a third) letter is obscured. **BH** similar to **ST** brings ז דלא מזיינין אלא בחד זיונא ארבע עשרה באוריתא with the number in Hebrew. מזאינא that is employed by our manuscript is a fuller Aramaic form.

8 Listing of Instances for the First Special Letter *Zayin*

1. **P**, **MV**, and **ST** agree, bringing זה ינחמנו as 𝔐. **H** spells *ma-le' yod* ינחמינו.
2. **P**, **MV**, and **ST** agree, bringing ויזכר אלהים את רחל. **H** abbreviates using the *'alef-lamed* ligature. Our **CG** scribe has employed a glyph that represents *'alef-lamed-he*. Elsewhere through **CG** sometimes the scribe omits the *he* and sometimes includes it, such that the same symbol is just *'alef-lamed*.[67]

Line 4: אלהים את רחל • [3]כי ז̊ה הבכור • [4]ויעז̊רך • [5]בנימין ז̊אב • [6]מילדי העב̇

… Rachel' (Gen. 30:22). (*Parashat Va-yeḥi*) 3. **'for this is the firstborn'** (Gen. 48:18) **'who will help you'** (Gen. 49:25). 5. **'Benjamin is a wolf'** (Gen. 49:27). (*Parashat Shemot*) 6. **'one of the Hebrews' children …**

---

67 Whilst I have not used this in the transcription, I have preserved the form in the reconstruction, creating an additional glyph.

TABLE 5 Forms for the first special letter *zayin*. MV brings many versions of the letter form (see right and below) and is not at all consistent. If they use the form at all, many listings, *Sifrey Torah* and codices do not show any difference between the first and the second *zayin* forms. Additionally, the order in listings does not always make it clear which is which.

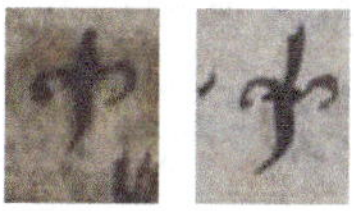

 *Maḥzor Vitry* Parma 2574 (**P**)	 *Maḥzor Vitry* Add. MS 27201 (**MV**)	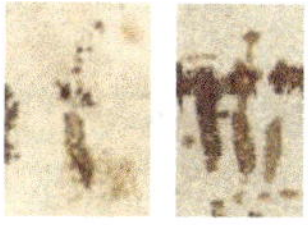 Shem Tov *Tanakh* *Sefer Tagi* (**ST**)	 *Badey ha-ʾAron* Heb. 840 (**BH**)	 *Sefer Tagin* Heb. 837 (**H**)
Not extant Nr. 5667 (**K**)	 Parma 2427	 Parma 1959	 Q651–652	 MS Geunz. 481
Not present *Maḥzor Vitry* Add. MS 27201 (**MV2**)	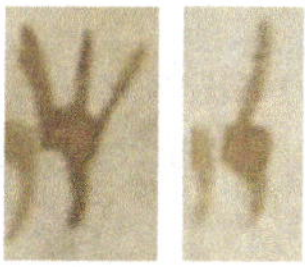 Add. MS 11639	Not present Add. MS 27167	 Bologna *Torah*	 Vat. ebr. 1
 Or 1463	 Alexander *Torah*			

3. P, MV and H agree כי זה הבכור, bringing. ST omits כי.
4. P, MV, ST and H all agree, bringing ויעזרך.
5. P, MV and H just bring זאב. ST brings ז֯אב יטרף ('a wolf that tears'). Our manuscript is the only core source to mention Benjamin specifically.
6. P, MV, ST (though faded) and H all bring העברים זה. Our manuscript is quite faded here but extends to מילדי העבֹ זה, which helps clarify, though abbreviates the second word at the end of the line.

Line 5: ז֯ה • 7למה ז֯ה עז֯בתן • 8ואת המטה הז֯ה • 9ז֯ה אלי ואנוהו • 10לעיני ז֯קני ישראל •
... this is' (Ex. 2:6). 7. **'why have you left** [the man]' (Ex. 2:20). 8. **'and this rod'** (Ex. 4:17). 9. (*Parashat Yitro*) **'this is my God and I will glorify Him'** (Ex. 15:2). 10. **'in the eyes of the elders of Israel'** (Ex. 17:6).

7. Our scribe indicates two instances here marking both ז֯ה and עז֯בתן. However, P, MV and H only bring the word עזבתן, so clearly intend only one instance. ST brings both זה עז֯בתן but only places the circular mark over the last word. However, as we will see, if this second instance is included here, that will give 15 instances and we are informed there are only 14. Our scribe is possibly mistaken, likely because he has just indicated the word ז֯ה in the previous instance.[68]
8. P, MV, ST and H just bring המטה הז֯ה. Our manuscript is again fuller.
9. Our manuscript has omitted this instance, however, it has been written in very small letters above the next instance. P, MV and H just bring זה אלי, ST employing the *'alef-lamed* ligature.
10. ST abbreviates as יש׳. P and MV abbreviate as ישר׳ and H employs the *'alef-lamed* ligature, but all agree on לעיני זקני.

Line 6: 11אז֯כיר את שמי • 12מעט מז֯בחי • 13וז֯ה יהיה לך • 14מגן עז֯רך • ז דלא
11. **'cause My Name to be mentioned'** (Ex. 20:21). 12. **'small' 'My altar'** (Ex. 20:23). (*Parashat Shofetim*) 13. **'and this will be to you'** (Deut. 18:3). (*Parashat Ve-zo't Ha-berakhah*) 14. **'the shield of your help'** (Deut. 33:29). ***Zayin* that has no ...**

68 Q651–652 brings למה זה עז֯בתן with a very odd form for the decorated *zayin*. However, in support of our scribe Parma 2427 also brings למה ז֯ה עז֯בתן decorating both. Similarly *Qiryat Sefer* states זה עזבתן הזי״ן בשניהם מוזרקת ('[why] have you left' the *zayin* in both of them is bent). MV2 just lists עזבתן, but with no decoration. Parma 1959, Add. MS 11639 omit and *Ben Mesheq* seems to, as well (though Basser notes that he includes both, op. cit., p. 196, note 282).

11. P gives just אזכיר. H too, but it looks like אזכור with a carelessly written *yod* resembling a *vav*. The improved images of **ST** reveal that it expands slightly, but abbreviates, bringing אזֿכיר את שׁ. **MV** omits.
12. Our manuscript brings an extra word before this instance which is not in 𝔐 but which appears to be מעט. **P**, **ST** (though faded) and **H** only bring מזבחי. **MV** omits. It is not at all clear what our scribe intended by his insertion.
13. **P**, and **H** agree. **MV** shortens, bringing וזה יהיה ⌗ and **ST** similarly וזֿה יה[יה].
14. **P**, **MV**, **ST** (though the first word is faded in all the images) and **H** all agree, bringing מגן עזרך.

9 Description and Example Forms of the Second Special Letter *Zayin*

Our manuscript begins the description of our next letter, another variant of *zayin*, on this line.

Line 7: **מזאינא ועקים ראשיהון ט֗ באוריתא [1]זֿמה הוא • [2]ואת זֿכר •**
… ***zayin type decoration*** **and their heads are bent** [there are] **9 in the *Torah*.** (*Parashat ʾAḥarey Mot*) 1. **'it is a depravity'** (Lev. 18:17). 2. **'and with a man'** (Lev. 18:22).

P and **H** both read תוב ז דלא מזייני ואקים רישיהון (also *zayin* that has no *zayin* type decoration and their heads stand up/are raised). **ST** adds a further instruction by stating that ותוב דלא מזייני ואקים רישׁ לבתריהון (also [*zayin*] that has no *zayin* type decoration and their heads stand up/are raised to their backs [i.e. behind them]). In **ST**'s introduction and also **BH** there is a longer descriptor, ותו ז דלא מזייני ואקים רישיהון לבתריהון תשעה באוריתא והיא מסדר אחרי וקדושים עד אם בחקתי (and also a *zayin* where their heads stand up/are raised behind them, nine in the *Torah* and they are from the sections *ʾAḥarey* [*Mot*] and *Qedoshim* until *Im Be-ḥuqotai*). **ST** abbreviates תשעֿ באוריתֿ. This explanation of where the instances occur seems an addition from Shem Tov, likely not in the original text. **MV** does not appear to distinguish between the two forms as when the first instances are introduced it is not proceeded by any description and the forms that are brought are the same as we had in the previous special *zayin* form. Our **CG** scribe is the only core source to describe this form as עקים (bent). Thus, once again, as we have seen with the *vav* above, we have a disagreement over whether this is אקים (raised) or עקים (bent), and this time our manuscript goes with the latter reading.

TABLE 6 Forms for the second special letter *zayin*. P brings some options. MV seems to make no distinction between this form and the previous one. H may not be drawing a form, but it certainly has no *tagin*. Sometimes the listing order is not clear as to which form goes with which type of *zayin*.

 *Maḥzor Vitry* Parma 2574 (**P**)	 *Maḥzor Vitry* Add. MS 27201 (**MV**)	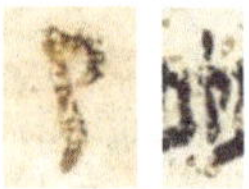 Shem Tov *Tanakh* *Sefer Tagi* (**ST**)	 *Badey ha-'Aron* Heb. 840 (**BH**)	 *Sefer Tagin* Heb. 837 (**H**)
Not extant Nr. 5667 (**K**)	 Parma 2427	Employs the same form as the previous *zayin* Parma 1959	Employs the same form as the previous *zayin* Q651–652	 MS Geunz. 481
Not present *Maḥzor Vitry* Add. MS 27201 (**MV2**)	 Add. MS 11639	Not present Add. MS 27167	Image not available Bologna *Torah*	 Vat. ebr. 1
Not available Or. 1463	Employs the same form as the previous *zayin* Alexander *Torah*			

10 Listing of Instances for the Second Special Letter *Zayin*

The listing begins on this line and all of the nine of the list occur only in the later half of the book of Leviticus and nowhere else.

1. P and MV agree. ST brings just זמה and H brings זימה היא *ma-le' yod*. 𝔐 is זמה הוא. It is possible there is a faded leg of a *vav* brought by our manuscript.
2. P, MV, ST (though very faded) and H all agree, bringing ואת זכר.

Line 8: [3]לא תהיה זמה • [4]אשה זונה • [5]וזרעתם לריק • [6]זרעכם • [7]אזרה • [8]ואז
(*Parashat Qedoshim*) 3. **'and there not be depravity amongst you'** (Lev. 20:14). (*Parashat 'Emor*) 4. **'a women [who is] a harlot'** (Lev. 21:7) (*Parashat Be-ḥukotai*) 5. **'and you will sew** [your seeds] **in vain'** (Lev. 26:16). 6. **'your seeds'** (Lev. 26:16). 7. **'I will scatter'** (Lev. 26:33). 8. **'and then ...**

3. P, MV and H agree, ST brings correctly ולא תהיה זמה reflecting 𝔐 with the *vav* of ולא.
4. P agrees. H gives אשה זנה *ḥaser vav*. MV brings a fuller entry אשה זנה וחללה ('a woman who is a harlot and profaned') and is *ḥaser vav*. ST gives similarly אשה זונה וחללה but is *ma-le' vav*. 𝔐 is *ḥaser*.
5. P, MV, and H agree. The enhanced images reveal that ST also brings וזרעתם לריק.
6. Our scribe here departs dramatically from the other available core *Sefer Tagin* witnesses bringing a different listing that is 3 verses earlier and seemingly related to the previous instance. P, MV and H all bring instead עזכם ('of your power') from Lev. 26:19. ST is too faded in any available image, but that same instance is present in the Shem Tov *Tanakh*.[69]
7. MV agrees. P and H bring אזרה אתכם ('I will scatter you'). ST is too faded, but the instance is present in the Shem Tov *Tanakh*. 𝔐 reads ואתכם אזרה ('and you I will scatter').[70]

---

69 In support of our scribe, Q651–Q652, Add. MS 11639 and Parma 1959 bring this instance זרעכם and MV2 also lists זרעכם but with no decoration. *Qiryat Sefer* and *Ben Mesheq* bring instead עזכם as the other core *Sefer Tagin* manuscripts.

70 This is further supported by the *Ba'al ha-Ṭurim* which states that 'the *zayin* [of אזרה is a ז עקמה (bent *zayin*) to tell you that I [God] gave you the land of seven peoples, that you should establish the *Torah* there, as it says 'she [wisdom] carved out seven pillars' (Prov. 9:1) but you had seven abominations in your hearts so 'I will scatter you [amongst the nations]''.

8. **P, MV, ST** (though faded) and **H** all bring only ואז ירצו, and our scribe adds an additional two words from the verse to clarify.

There are supposed to be nine entries in this section and our manuscript brings only eight. He is missing the last which is brought by the other witnesses. **P, MV** and **H** bring תעזב and **ST** expands to תעזב̊ מהם ('[the land] will be forsaken from them') from Lev. 26:43. Our manuscript is seemingly deficient.

11 Description and Example Forms of the First Special Letter *Ḥet*

Line 9: **ירצו את עונם • שער ח כׄחׄ באוריתא דתלתה קרני תרתיה**
... they will gain appeasement for their iniquity' (Lev. 26:41). **Gate of *ḥet.* 28** [letters *ḥet*] **in the *Torah* with three horns, two at its ...**

Our manuscript adds שער ח in the gap between the letters and then proceeds to describe the first special *ḥet* form. **P** brings כׄחׄ באוריי דתלת קרני תרין לאחוריהון וחד לקדמיהון. **MV** reads similarly כח באורייתא דתלתא קרני תרין לאחוריהון וחד לקדמיהון adding an *ʾalef* to תלתא and this particular spelling is also echoed by **H** which gives כׄחׄ באוריית׳ דתלתא קרני תרין לאחוריהון וחד לקדמהון. Unfortunately, the **ST** listing is too damaged to determine the text, but in the introduction it gives, ח דלה תלתא זיוני תרי לבתריהון וחד לקדמי׳ עשרין ותמנא באוריתא, which is echoed by the instruction in **BH**, ח דלה תלתא זיוני תרין לבתריהון וחד לקדמיהון עשרים ותמנא באוריתא. ([letters] *ḥet* that have three *zayin* type decorations, two towards their backs and one to their front, twenty eight in the *Torah*) referring specifically to *ziyyuney* rather than *qarnayim* and giving the numbers in full. Thus we have general agreement on the number of instances and only a slight variance on the form between the halakhic texts in terms of the descriptor used for the *tagin.*

Whilst the description brought is similar, our manuscript spells the numerals with a final *he*, and writes 'the two of it' as a feminine, תרתיה and, unlike other letters, brings the description of the first *ḥet* in the singular.

The printed Maḥzor Vitry (***LMV***) *brings the form right, with two of the* tagin *towards the right end of the roof and one on the end of the left side.*

Despite having stated that the two tagin *should be on the right side, our scribe in* ***T-S NS 287.11-F*** (*right*) *oddly brings instead only one on that side and on the the left side has a sort of crossed* tag *which is possibly representing two. Indeed, it is the placement of the* tagin *on the roof and in some cases the number* (*with some only showing two*) *that provides the main difference between the sources.*

T-S Misc. 24.182 (*right*) *brings three* tagin *on the roof and like many of the other sources places two to the right and one to the left.*

TABLE 7 Forms for the first special letter *ḥet*. Again some *Sifrey Torah* and codices make no distinction between the first and second form for the *ḥet* and often mix them up, despite the clarity of the descriptions.

 *Maḥzor Vitry* Parma 2574 (P)	 *Maḥzor Vitry* Add. MS 27201 (MV)	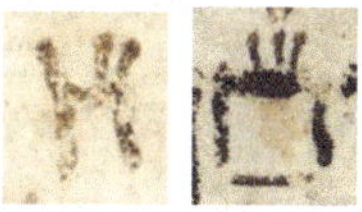 Shem Tov *Tanakh* *Sefer Tagi* (ST)	 *Badey ha-ʾAron* Heb. 840 (BH)	 *Sefer Tagin* Heb. 837 (H)
Not extant Nr. 5667 (K)	 Parma 2427	 Parma 1959	 Q651–652	 MS Geunz. 481
 *Maḥzor Vitry* Add. MS 27201 (MV2)	 Add. MS 11639	 Add. MS 27167	 Bologna *Torah*	Not present Vat ebr. 1
 Or. 1463	 Alexander *Torah*			

12 Listing of Instances for the First Special Letter *Ḥet*

Line 10: לאחוריה וחד לקדמיה [1]ורוח אלהים • [2]מרחפת • [3]שיח • [4]ויצמח •
back and one in its front (*Parashat Bere'shit*) 1. **'and the spirit of God'** (Gen. 1:2). 2. **'hovered'** (Gen. 1:2). 3. **'shrubs** [of the field]' (Gen. 2:5). 4. **'and He made it grow'** (Gen. 2:9).

The microfilm scan of **ST** is very faded in this section with very few words visible and, unfortunately, the enhanced images add relatively little clarification.[71] Fortunately, there is relatively little disagreement in this section between the various witnesses, and our manuscript is similarly consistent.

1. **P**, **MV**, and **ST** (though faded) agree, bringing ורוח אלהים. **H** gives instance 1 and 2 as one section without a divider, ורוח אלהים מרחפת.
2. **P**, **MV** and **ST** agree, bringing מרחפת.
3. **P** and **MV** agree. **H** gives כל שיח ('all the shrubs'). **ST** is not legible.
4. **P**, **MV** and **H** all agree, bringing ויצמח. **ST** is not legible. The *ḥet* on our manuscript is partly faded resembling a *vav*. A small *ḥet* has been written by the side, possibly by a later scribe.

Line 11: [5]נחמד • [6]ותפקחנה • [7]ויפקח • [8]ותחי • [9]רוח • [10]ירחים • [11]ותחמרה • [12]חרבה •
5. '[every] **nice** [tree]' (Gen 2:9). 6. **'and** [the eyes of both of them] **were opened'** (Gen. 3:7). (*Parashat Va-yera'*) 7. **'and He opened** [Hagar's eyes]' (Gen. 21:19). (*Parashat Va-yiggash*) 8. **'revived'** (Gen. 45:27). 9. **'and the spirit** [of Jacob]' (Gen 45:27). (*Parashat Shemot*) 10. **'months'** (Ex. 2:2). 11. **'she daubed it'** (Ex. 2:3). 12. **'towards** [mount] **Horeb'** (Ex. 3:1).

5. **P**, **MV** and **H** all agree, bringing נחמד.

ST then adds ונחמד העץ ('and the tree was nice') from Gen 3:6, though no other witness brings this, core or secondary.

6 to 7. **P**, **MV** and **H** all agree, bringing ותפקחנה and ויפקח. One can just make out ותפ in the **ST** images, but nothing else is legible.

8 and 9. Our manuscript brings 8 and 9 as two separate instances, though רוח is quite blotted out and difficult to read, whereas **P** lists as ותחי רוח תר' ('and the spirit [of Jacob] revived' on both of them) and **H** similarly ותחי

71 Additionally, these early parts of Genesis are not extant in Shem Tov's *Tanakh*.

רוח תרוונהון. **ST** probably lists both as רוח ב בה ('spirit' 2 in it [the verse]) is just legible. **MV** omits both instances. **P**, **ST** and **H** agree. **MV** omits.

10, 11 and 12. **P** and **H** agree, bringing ירחים, ותחמרה and חרבה. **ST** agrees with instances 10 and 12 in the enhanced images, but the middle one is not legible in any available image. **MV** omits all three.

Line 12: חלום [13]ורחבה • [14]ברוחך • [15]נחית • [16]יאחזמו • [17]ופחד • [18]כצפיחית • [19]בתחתית—בר •

'dream' 13. **'and broad'** (Ex. 3:8). (*Parashat Be-shallaḥ*) 14. **'with Your wind'** (Ex. 15:10). 15. **'You have led'** (Ex. 15:13). 16. '[trembling] **takes hold of them'** (Ex. 15:15). 17. **'and dread'** (Ex. 15:16). 18. **'like wafers'** (Ex. 16:31). (*Parashat Yitro*) 19. **'underneath'** (Ex. 19:17).

Before the main list, a hand has written in small letters the word חלום ('dream'). However, this word does not appear between Ex. 3:1 and 3:8. הלם ('hither') does in Ex. 3:5, but this word has no *ḥet*. However, our *Genizah* secondary source **T-S Misc. 24.182** does bring חלום too, but much earlier. From its positioning in the listing it is Gen. 37:5, referring to Joseph's first dream in *parashat Va-yeshev*.[72] It is possible this has been added by a subsequent hand to our core fragment in a convenient, but incorrect space.

T-S Misc. 24.182 also brings חרי ('white bread') from Gen. 40:16, but only Parma 2427 lists סלי חרי (baskets of white bread), but with no decoration.

13. **P** and **H** agree, bringing ורחבה. **MV** omits and **ST** is not legible.
14. **P**, **MV**, **ST** and **H** all agree, bringing ברוחך.
15. **P**, **MV** and **H** agree, bringing נחית. **ST** is not legible.

16 and 17. **P**, **MV**, **ST** and **H** all agree, bringing יאחזמו and ופחד.

18. **P**, **MV** and **H** agree, bringing כצפיחית. **ST** is very faded, but does show the first two letters כצ.
19. **P**, **MV** (slightly water damaged; so blurred) and **H** agree, bringing בתחתית. **ST** is not legible.

Our **CG** manuscript ends this line with בר. It is not clear what is meant by this.

Line 13: [20]הולך וחזק • [21]ויחרד בת • [22]לבלתי תחטאו • [23]מזבח אדמה • [24]ושמרת

20. '[the shofar] **grew louder'** (Ex. 19:19). 21. **the last 'and trembled'** (Ex. 19:18). 22. **'that you sin not'** (Ex. 20:16). 23. **'altar of earth'** (Ex. 20:20). (*Parashat Va-'etḥanan*) 24. **'And keep ...**

72 Of the other secondary sources, Basser states that only *Ben Mesheq* brings this (op. cit., p. 175), but I cannot see this in the listing.

ST is not at all legible in this section in the scan and, unfortunately, the enhanced images also add little.

20. P and H agree bringing הולך וחזק. MV has this instead as instance 21 having swapped round the order.
21. P and H agree. MV has this instead as instance 20 giving ויחרד בתראה in full.
22. P, MV and H all agree, bringing לבלתי תחטאו. ST does show לבלתי in the enhanced imagery.
23. P, MV and H all agree, bringing מזבח אדמה.
24. P and H agree. MV omits. This presents an issue, since this phrase does not appear in the *Torah*. Instead, this has to be ושמרת את חקיו which appears in Deut 4:40. This is confirmed by the Shem Tov *Tanakh*, but enjoys only limited support in the secondary sources. Our manuscript, as others, is defective, missing את.[73]

Line 14: חקיו • [25]ועדותיו וחקיו • [26]לא תחסר • [27]ולחיתך • ח דפתוח לו׳
… his commandments' (Deut. 4:40). 25. **'and his witnesses and his commandments'** (Deut. 6:17). (*Parashat 'Eqev*) 26. **'you will not lack'** (Deut. 8:9). 27. **'and to your animals'. *Ḥet* that is open,** [there are] **36 …**

Again ST is hardly legible in this section in any of the available imagery.

25. P and H agree, bringing ועדותיו וחקיו. MV omits.
26. P, MV and H all agree, bringing לא תחסר.
27. P and H agree, bringing ולחיתך. MV omits. This is another difficult area as whilst three of our witnesses, including our manuscript, bring this word, again it does not appear in the *Torah*. In his footnotes, Basser suggests that the intention might have been לחיתנו ('preserve us alive') in Deut. 6:24, but that would be out of sequence. However, he lists והחמה ('and the

73 Turning to our secondary sources, Basser states that Q615–652 brings this. The scan is damaged, but it may appear to be the case. **MV2** lists the phrase ושמרת את חקיו but gives no decoration. Add. MS 11639 brings את חקיו. *Ben Mesheq* brings ח״ק דחקיו (*ḥet* [and] *qof* of 'His commandments'). *Qiryat Sefer* only refers to the *qof* being decorated חקיו הקו״ף מתוייגת שנים ('His commandments' the *qof* is decorated with two [*tagin*]), though Basser states that the *ḥet* is also decorated in *Qiryat Sefer*, (op. cit., p. 263). Parma 2427 and Parma 1959 omit.

hot displeasure') in Deut. 9:19 as Shem Tov adds the extra three *tagin* to this word in his *Tanakh* (though also spreads the letter's legs apart, as per the next sections form description—see above right).[74] There is definitely some indication from the secondary sources that this word should be decorated, but the form is up for debate as most suggest it is the spread form only. Moreover, the word also bears no relationship to that listed by **P**, **H** and our **CG** text.[75] It is also listed under the next from of *ḥet* (see below) suggesting it should only be the spread form.

As well as the confusion on this last instance, whilst all the texts agree there are 28 instances, the three consistent texts here, **P**, **H** and our **CG** manuscript, only bring 27. **ST** does add one based on his *Tanakh* usage (ונחמד העץ from Gen 3:6), but it gains no secondary support. Our manuscript tries to add חלום, but that is not present in the *Torah*, so there is a clear omission here that will need further investigation.

13 Description and Example Forms of the Second Special Letter *Ḥet*

At the end of the line we are now introduced to the second version of the *ḥet* and that there are 36, which disagrees with the other core sources. Our manuscript also misses the normal introductory word ותוב (and also).

Right: The printed Maḥzor Vitry (*LMV*) *brings a fairly simple spread* ḥet *with one* tag *on the left side.*

*Right: even though our **CG** scribe has stated in the description that the letter should be wide open, the letter form he brings in **T-S NS 287.11-F** is just a normal* ḥet *though with a dot on the top. This is further evidence that the use of the dots on the letter are down to this scribe not knowing how to form the letter and avoiding committing to a form.*

T-S Misc. 24.182 *(right) brings the second form as well and it is a fairly straightforward stretched letter with the more prominent angle on the left leg which matches a number of the other sources where the left leg is more prominent, Here, however, it is subtle.*

---

74 As brought by Basser, op. cit., p. 85. Because this is the last entry this could be anywhere after Deut 8:9 to the end of the *Torah*.

75 Turning to our secondary sources, Q651–652 does bring והחמה, but this is the spread form, not the form with three *tagin*, so does not necessarily support **ST** here. Parma 2427 and Add. MS 11639 also bring the spread form on והחמה. **MV2** lists the word, but with no decoration. *Qiryat Sefer* only refers to the word to mention it has no *yod*. Parma 1959 omits.

P states that ותוב ח דפתי׳ לז׳ באוריית׳ (and also a *ḥet* that is wide open [there] are 37 in the *Torah*). **MV** also brings 37 reading, ותוב ח דפתיא לז באוריית׳ and the description is in full as פתיא. This seems to be echoed by **H** which also appears to give 37 instances, though admittedly the letter is not clear. It reads: ותוֹב ח דפתי׳ ל׳ז באוריי׳.[76] The description in the main list **ST** is not legible and indeed, unfortunately, the **ST** listing is not available for this entire letter form. However, in the introductory summary and also in **BH** we read a qualification to the description, that its leg/knee (singular) is what is wide open and reads, ותו ח׳ דפתיין כרעיהו תלתין ושבעה באוריתא.

There seems to be general agreement in the core sources that the number of instances should be thirty-seven and our **CG** manuscript may be in error here. Alternatively, this may just be a poorly formed *zayin*, and the intention was thirty-seven and not thirty-six. That aside, the key word here is given in Hebrew in our manuscript as פתוח, but in Aramaic in the other sources as פתיין or פתיא but still means being open wide or accessible.[77] **BH**, as we have seen, also adds the word כרעיהו, meaning its leg or knee[78] and it is this that perhaps is responsible for some of the disagreement over the form over time, as the description without that qualification suggests that both legs would be splayed open. However, since this could be leg or knee, we do not know of the whole leg would be bent, or only part way down from the knee. Indeed, these variant forms do materialise in the forms brought by the halakhic texts and later developments in *Sifrey Torah* or codices which add curves extending from the knee of the letter (see examples below).[79] However, these are later developments and our core and secondary halakhic texts generally just spread one (the left) or both legs.

---

76 However, because it is not clear the **EPST** printed version states that there are 36 instances.

77 Jastrow, op. cit., pp. 1252–1253.

78 Jastrow, op. cit., p. 673.

79 This particular form is a little more well known as it is used in the *Shema* in *Tefillin* or *Mezuzot* where there is a fairly established 'kabbalistic' tradition of writing this oddly expanded or spread *ḥet* in וחרה ('anger') in Deut. 11:16 in the very negative context of God destroying the land if the Israelites do not keep the commandments. One *sofer* I know felt that the *ḥet* is spread so that the *ḥaron 'af* should apply only to the *resha'im* (wicked ones) supposedly sourced from *'Ittur Sofrim* (commentary to *Me'ir 'Eyney Sofrim*) but I cannot locate the reference to support this, in the section it would be. The *Da'at Qedoshim* also says it spread so that it in some way reduces God's potential anger. This is particularly apt given the instances that are listed which often show God's anger. It has become known as משוך *meshokh* (spread/stretched/pulled) and it has developed a number of forms. A clearly related, but alternative, form is also present in Yemenite *Sifrey Torah*, where it is instead known as עקום *'aqum* (bent) with the left leg a slightly longer straight line at an angle.

TABLE 8 Forms for the second special letter *ḥet*, most often a spreading of the legs. Sometimes only only the left leg is lengthened and on an angle. Others add decorative curls at the knee or bottom of the legs to widen the letter.

 *Maḥzor Vitry*, Parma 2574 (**P**)	 *Maḥzor Vitry* Add. MS 27201 (**MV**)	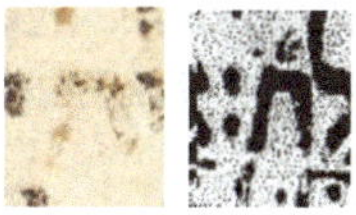 Shem Tov *Tanakh Sefer Tagi* (**ST**)	 *Badey ha-ʾAron* Heb. 840 (**BH**)	 *Sefer Tagin* Heb. 837 (**H**)
 Nr. 5667 (**K**)	 Parma 2427	Not present Parma 1959	 Q651–652	 MS Geunz. 481
 *Maḥzor Vitry* Add. MS 27201 (**MV2**)	 Add. MS 11639	Not present Add. MS 27167	 Bologna *Torah*	Not present Vat. ebr. 1
 Or. 1463	 Alexander *Torah*			

14 Listing of Instances for the Second Special Letter *Ḥet*

Line 15: [באוריתֿ] [1]הנחש השיאני • [2]ואחבא • [3]גחונך • [4]תצמיח לך • [5]לקחת •
... [in the *Torah*] (*Parashat Bere'shit*) 1. **'the serpent beguiled me'** (Gen. 3:13, out of sequence). 2. **'and I hid myself'** (Gen. 3:10). 3. **'your belly'** (Gen. 3:14). 4. '[thorns and thistles] **will be brought forth for you'** (Gen 3:18). 5. **'to take'** (Gen. 4:11).

1. P, **MV** and H agree, bringing הנחש השיאני, however, this instance should really be second and the next should be first; as it precedes it in the *Torah*. All of the core manuscripts make this error in ordering.
2. P, **MV** and H all agree, bringing ואחבא.
3. P, **MV** and H all extend to על גחונך ('upon your belly').
4. P, **MV** and H all agree, bringing תצמיח לך.
5. P adds a dot after לקחת as it intends this to be a separate instance to 6 that follows. In our manuscript it is difficult to tell, but our scribe certainly indicates the *ḥet* here, and it looks like he does on the next instance too, but this is badly water stained. That he omits the את also suggests our scribe is seeing two separate instances here. **MV** and H, however, gives לקחת את דמי אחיך as one instance only, but neither indicates which *ḥet*. In his *Tanakh*, Shem Tov decorates only the *ḥet* in לקחת.

Line 16: וַיִּמַ?? [6]דמי אחיך • [7]לחבורתי • [8]בחרו • [9]ידון רוחי • [10]נפתחו • [11]וימחו • [12]ויחדלו •
מש
and he blotted? 6. **'the bloods of your brother'** (Gen 4:11). 7. **'for bruising me'** (Gen. 4:23). (*Parashat Noaḥ*) 8. **'they chose'** (Gen. 6:2). 9. **'My spirit shall** [not] **abide'** (Gen. 6:3). 10. **'were opened'** (Gen. 7:11). 11. **'and He blotted out'** (Gen. 7:23). 12. **'and they left off'** (Gen. 11:8).

Our manuscript brings what may be an additional instance, but only the first few letters are legible because of water staining. It is, however, smaller, pointed and given the vowels, may be וַיִּמַח which is the singular verb present in Gen. 7:23 and may be an addition. However, why is it written in the margin and not before that instance is not clear, and the water stained letter looks a bit more like a *tsade* than a *ḥet*. Additionally, this is not brought by any other witness.

At this point, lacking much input from **ST**, we are, however, able to access fragment Kreuzenstein, Sammlung Graf Wilczek, Inv.-Nr. 5667, HDSHDS (**K**) as an additional core witness.

6. P, **MV** and H extend to את דמי אחיך. K is damaged, but the letters חיך are present with a splayed *ḥet* form, suggesting this also agrees.

7. **MV** and **ST** (though very faint) agree, bringing לחבורתי. **K** is similarly *ma-le᾽ vav* and also adds וילד ('and a young man') beforehand in clarification. **P** and **H** spell *ḥaser vav* לחברתי, as is the case in 𝔐.
8. **P** and **MV** agree, bringing בחרו. **K** again adds clarification, bringing מכל אשר בח֯רו ('from whoever they chose'). One can just make out אשר in **ST**. **H** reads incorrectly בחרן, having extended the *vav* into a *nun sofit*.[80]
9. **P** agrees, bringing ידון רוחי. **MV** and **H** extend to לא ידון רוחי which is more appropriate to the sense of the instance. **K** is damaged in this area but preserves the additional words רובות השמי, which do not appear in Genesis.

10 and 11. **P**, **MV**, **H** and **K** all agree, bringing נפתחו and וימחו. On instance 11 **K** adds מן הארץ ('from the earth'). **ST** is not visible.

12. **P**, **MV**, **H** agree and **ST** though very faint also seems to give וי֯חדלו. **K** is damaged, but given the clarification words that follow are [לב]נות העיר ('to build the city')—though 𝔐 is *ḥaser vav* לבנת—it also likely lists this instance in the torn space. Our manuscript then takes two letters from the next instance as a line filler.

Line 17: 13מש֯חיתם • 14לש֯חתה • 15מא֯חריו • 16ויח֯בקהו • [17ח֯יה רעה] קדמׄ • 18ויח֯ר אף
(*Parashat Va-yera᾽*) 13. **'for we will destroy this place'** (Gen. 19:13). 14. **'to destroy it'** (Gen. 19:13) 15. **'from behind him'** (Gen. 19:26). 16. **'and he** [Esau] **embraced him** [Jacob]' (Gen. 33:4). (*Parashat Va-yishlaḥ*) 17. **the first** ['evil beast'] (Gen. 37:20). (*Parashat Ki Tissa᾽*) 18. **'and angry was ...**

13. **P**, **MV** and **ST** agree, bringing משחיתם. **K** again provides a longer context with כי מש֯חיתים אנחנו ('for we will destroy') and like **H** gives משחיתים *ma-le᾽yod*. All of the witnesses differ from 𝔐 which is משחתים.
14. **P**, **MV**, **ST** and **H** all agree, bringing לשחתה. **K** is torn, but probably agrees since the last two letters shown are תה and are likely from this word.
15. **MV** and **H** agree, bringing מאחריו. **P** incorrectly adds an extra letter bringing מאחרינו. **K** extends again bringing ותבט אשתו מא֯חריו ('but his wife looked back from behind him').
16. **P** and **MV** agree, bringing ויחבקהו as 𝔐. **H** is *ma-le᾽yod*, ויחבקיהו. **K** is damaged but extends again, bringing וירץ עשב ל[קראתו ויח֯]בקהו ('and Esau ran to greet him and they embraced').
17. **P** gives חיה רעה קדׄ, **MV** gives חיה רעה קדמאה in full and **H** is incorrectly *ma-le᾽yod* bringing חייה רעה קדמ׳. **K** adds an additional word to provide the context rather than saying it is the first, ואמרנו ח֯יה רעה ('and we will

80 Which EPST faithfully and incorrectly transcribes.

say an evil beast'). On the enhanced images of ST one can just make out ח̊יה and קדמ̇. Our manuscript is badly damaged with a hole here, but is probably bringing the same instance given the inclusion of קדמ̇.

18. P, MV, H and K all agree. ST likely is the same bringing [ויח̊ר] אף מש[ה]

Line 18: משה • [19]ח̊טאה גדולה • [20]וישח̊טם • [21]תצלח̊ • [22][ל]זב[ח̊י] • [23][ויח̊]ר אף דויצמד •

... **Moses'** (Ex. 32:19) 19. **'a great sin'** (Ex. 32:30). (*Parashat Shelaḥ-Lekha*) 20. **'and He has slain them'** (Num. 14:16). 21 '[it will not] **succeed'** (Num. 14:41). (*Parashat Balaq*) 22. **'to the sacrifices [of their gods]'** (Num. 25:2). 23. **'and He was angry' of** [the verse beginning] **'and** [Israel] **joined'** (Num 25.3).

19. P, MV and H all agree, bringing חטאה גדולה *ma-le' vav*, and one can see ח̊טאה ג[דלה] on ST, however, none of these, or our manuscript, deal with the fact that this exact phrase appears in both Ex. 32:30 and 31. K is damaged, but it appears to read את[ם חטא]תם ח̊טאה גדלה ('you have sinned a great sin') which would locate this as specifically from Ex. 32:30. We do not know if ST spells *ḥaser*, but K does spell גדלה *ḥaser vav* which accords with 𝔐.[81]

T-S Misc. 24.182 brings ו̊יקח (and he took), which, from its positioning in the list, is from Gen. 42:24 and is unique in that no other core or secondary source brings this.

20. P, MV and H all agree, bringing וישחטם. K extends to וישח̊טם במדבר ('and He has slain them in the desert'). ST is not visible.
21. P and MV agree, bringing תצלח. H omits. K, slightly damaged, extends to [ו]היא לא תצלח̊ ('it will not succeed'). ST is not visible.
22. P gives לזבחי and this seems to be echoed in our damaged manuscript. K once again extends to ותקראן לעם זבח̊י ('and they called the people to the sacrifices'). MV and H both omit.
23. P and K agree, bringing ויחר אף דויצמד and though it is very faint ST does bring דויצמד, so likely agrees. MV and H omit.

There is considerable disagreement in the last few instances, but our **CG** manuscript echoes **P**, which is generally the most consistent and possibly reliable of the available witnesses. In this, it is supported by the **K** fragment, which brings extended readings to clarify the instances.

81 Basser, however, places this at Gen. 32:31 op. cit., pp. 85 and 224.

Line 19: [24]ויחר אף דויניעם • [25]אנשים חטאים • [26]ושחתם וישחטם • [27]החמה • [28]וחרה [אף]

(*Parashat Maṭot*) 24. **'and He was angry'** of [the verse beginning] **'he made them wander'** (Num. 32:13). 25. **'sinful men'** (Num. 32:14). 26. **'and destroyed them' 'and slaughtered them'** (Num. 32:15). (*Parashat 'Eqev*) 27. **'the hot displeasure'** (Deut. 9:19). 28. **'and the anger …**

24. **P** and **MV** both bring ויחר דויניעם. One can just make out ויחר אף in **ST**. Having followed the standard format, quoting the start of the verse in which the instance occurs, this time **K** gives a different approach listing in full, ויחר אף ייי בישר' ויניעם במדבר ('And God's anger was kindled against Israel and He made them wander in the desert'). **H** omits.
25. **P** and **MV** both just bring חטאים. **K** brings תרבות אנשים חטאי' ('a brood of sinful men'). **H** omits.
26. Our manuscript has originally brought וישחטם and **P** agrees. **MV** spells as וישחם omitting the *ṭet*. **H** and **K** omit completely. However, this would be out of order and above this word in smaller writing we have ושחתם ('and you will destroy') in Num. 32:15, written as a correction by our scribe or a later scribe recognising that this is the intention. Basser makes this suggestion,[82] but our manuscript confirms this is likely the intention.[83] **ST** is not visible.
27. **P** and **H** agree, bringing החמה, both also omitting the *vav* at the start of the word as it occurs in 𝔐. **K** agrees, but extends to יגרתי מפני האף והחמה ('I was in dread because of the hot displeasure') correctly adding the *vav*.[84] **ST** is not visible.
28. Our manuscript is damaged and it is difficult to assess whether there is a word missing at the end of line 19 but possibly not given the margin width—in which case our manuscript may be missing a key word, אף. Additionally, the water damage has made it difficult to see the first word on line 20, but this looks like it may be the abbreviation for the Tetragrammaton, even though elsewhere it has been written in full, though that was possibly because it was a specific instance rather than additional locat-

82 *Op. cit.*, p. 86.

83 Supporting Num. 14:16 the *Ba'al ha-Ṭurim* explains that the *ḥet* of the word וישחטם is to be written as a ח שבורה (broken letter *ḥet*) 'to say that they transgressed against the *Torah* which He had established through eight covenants of a general nature and eight of a particular nature'. Gold suggests that this is drawn from *Peirush ha-Roqeaḥ* who describes this letter as פתוחה ושבורה רגלה (its leg is open and broken) which echoes פתיין (*Ba'al haTurim Chumash-Vayikra*, Davis Edition, op. cit., p. 1526). The Shem Tov *Tanakh* is not extant for Num. 32:15 and none of the secondary sources support **CG** in including this.

84 This word was discussed above as a possible last instance in the previous *ḥet* form.

ing words. P brings וחרה אף ייי, MV seems to brings וחרה אף החיוה to avoid writing God's name, but this may instead be an error and should read הויה, which is a known permutation of the Name to avoid writing it.[85] K brings וחרה אף ייי בכם ('and God's anger is against you'). H brings, incorrectly, ויחר אף ייי. ST is not visible.

Line 20: יי • [[29]תח̊]ת • [30]בשמ̊חה • [31]ישל̊חנו • [32]ובח̊סר כל • [33]ובח̊מתו • [34]ח̊רי • [35]ובח̊מה •

... **of God'** (Deut. 11:17). (*Parashat Ki Tavo'*) 29. **'because'** (Deut. 28:47). 30. **'in gladness'** (Deut. 28:47). 31. **'shall send against you'** (Deut. 28:48). 32. **'in want of all** [things]' (Deut. 28:48). (*Parashat Nitsavim*) 33. **'and in His hot wrath'** (Deut. 29:22). 34. **'the heat** [of anger]' (Deut. 29:23). 35. **'and in hot wrath'** (Deut. 29:27).

After much confusion in the previous lines, we now come to a section with almost complete agreement between our core witnesses.

29 to 35. P, MV and H all agree. From the enhanced imagery, one can see that ST has instance 31, ישל̊ח[נו] 32, ובח̊סר כל, 34, ח̊רי and 35, ובח̊מה in the margin under a border flourish. K, as usual, extends its listing to phrases bringing in turn, תח̊ת [א]שר עבדת וג׳ • בשמ̊חה • ועבדת את איביך • אשר ישל̊חנו ייי בך • ובחסר כל • אשר הפך ייי באפו ובח̊מתו • ('because you did [not] serve' etc.[86] 'in gladness'. 'and you will serve your enemy whom God shall send against you'. 'in want of all [things]'. 'which God overturned in His anger and in His hot wrath'). However, it appears to omit instance 34, חרי. It continues [ב]אף ובח̊מה ובקצף ('[in] anger and wrath and indignation').

Line 21: [36]ח̊מת תנינם • [37]ח̊תום • ט̇ דערבעה זיאני ס̇ז̇ באור׳ [1]כי ט̊וב

(*Parashat Ha-'azinu*) 36. **'the venom of serpents'** (Deut. 32:33). 37. **'sealed'** (Deut. 32:34). ***Ṭet*** **with four** ***zayin*** type decorations, [there are] **67 in the** ***Torah.*** (*Parashat Bere'shit*) 1. **'it was good'** ...

36. P and MV give חמת תנינים and H abbreviates to חמת תניני׳ but both are still *ma-le' yod*. Our manuscript, like K, which shows ח̊מת תנינם is *ḥaser yod* as is the case with 𝔐. ST is not clear.

85 See Ginzburgh, Y., *The Art of Education: Internalizing Ever-new Horizons*, Gal Einai Publication Society, 2005, pp. 265–267.

86 𝔐 is תחת אשר לא עבדת. K omits the word לא in error.

37. P, MV and H all agree, bringing חתום. K extends to ח֯תום באצרותי ('sealed in My treasuries'). ST is not clear.

Having omitted instance 34, K compensates its listing by adding a further instance not seen in the other core sources, [אש]כי֯ר חצי ('My arrows drunk with blood') from Deut. 32:42.[87]

15 Description and Example Forms of the Special Letter *Ṭet*

Our manuscript now turns to the special letter *ṭet*. **P and** H both give instead a different count of the instances and the number of *tagin*, ט סו באוריי' דה זיוני (*ṭet*, 66 in the *Torah* with **five** *zayin* type decorations). **MV** agrees with our manuscript in terms of the number of *tagin*, bringing ט סׄזׄ באורייתׄ דדׄ זיוני and ST in the introductory section gives ט דאת לה ארבעא זיוני שיתין ושבע באור' (*ṭet* which have four *zayin* type decorations, sixty-seven in the *Torah*) which is echoed by the entry in BH which reads similarly, ט דאת לה ארבעה זיוני שיתין ושבעה באוריתא. However, the reading in the marginal listing itself in ST is very faded indeed, but appears to start ט דארבא' קרנין (*ṭet* that has four horns …) but the number is not visible. K also gives סׄזׄ (67). Whilst most sources show four *tagin*, there is clearly some debate as to the number of *tagin*, and also where they should be placed.

Right: The more familiar form from the printed Maḥzor Vitry (*LMV*) *showing four* tagin, *three in the normal place and one on the right head.*

Our scribe brings a very interesting form for his ṭet *in T-S NS 287.11-F* (*right*) *which does look like it has five* tagin, *one thick one on the right head, one thin one descending into the body of the letter* (*see curled* ṭet *below*) *and the three* tagin *on the left head resemble a sort of pitchfork shape.*

T-S Misc. 24.182 (*right*) *also brings four* tagin, *three in the normal position and one on the right roof. This is not constant throughout the sources and, as we shall see, there is a basic disagreement as the number of* tagin.

---

87 In support of this Q651–652 does bring אשכי֯ר חצי. MV2 **and** Parma 2427 list this, but do not decorate the *ḥet*. Add. MS 11639, Parma 1959, *Qiryat Sefer* and *Ben Mesheq* omit. Interestingly Baer brings this as the last entry in his list of 39 quite different words with a חי"ת עקום (bent *ḥet*), op. cit., p. 23.

TABLE 9 Forms for the special letter *ṭet*. Quite a few sport the 'extra' fifth *tag* in the form of the curlicue in the body of the letter. Some even have six or seven.

		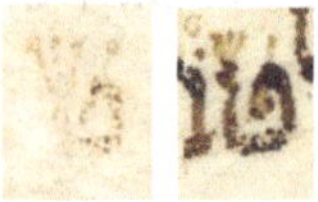		
Maḥzor Vitry Parma 2574 (**P**)	*Maḥzor Vitry* Add. MS 27201 (**MV**)	Shem Tov *Tanakh* *Sefer Tagi* (**ST**)	*Badey ha-'Aron* Heb. 840 (**BH**)	*Sefer Tagin* Heb. 837 (**H**)

Nr. 5667 (**K**)	Parma 2427	Parma 1959	Q651–652	MS Geunz. 481

Maḥzor Vitry Add. MS 27201 (**MV2**)	Add. MS 11639	Add. MS 27167	Bologna *Torah*	Vat. ebr. 1

Or. 1463	Alexander *Torah*			

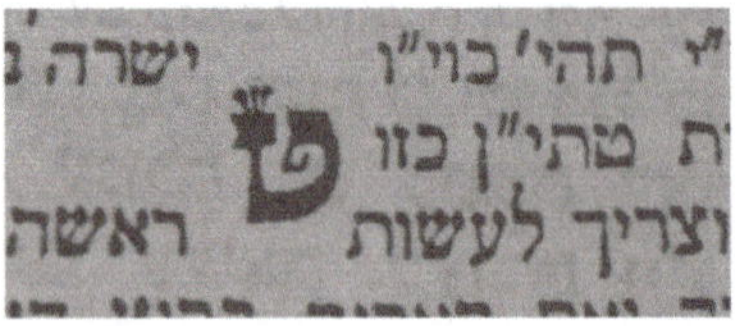

It is possible that the fifth *tag* is in fact the curlicue that descends into the body of the letter which has become known as the ט מלופפת (curled *ṭet*) which echoes the more well known פ מלופפת (curled *pe*). For example *Dikdukei ha-Sofer* Section 7 (above right) explains that a *ṭet melufefet* should be used if a scribe is also wont to use the *pe melufefet*.

In support of this, this same issue features in Shlomo Zucker's assessment of a 13th C. *Torah* Scroll from Northern Spain that follows *Sefer Tagin* and in particular the opinion of Ibn Gaon.[88] He notes that in this particular scroll, 'in addition to the four ornamental strokes or tittles, the right bent downward arm of the Teth is spiral.' Moreover, 'the same shape have these Teths (*sic.*) in ben Gaon's Bible', although they deviate from [the] shape of the same 'anomalous Teth in Gaon's own copy of the Sefer Tagey in his Bible, in which the downward line is strait! (*sic.*)'[89]

Indeed, this is the case (see drawing from the 13th C. *Torah* right and again from Shem Tov's *Tanakh* (see table above)), thus the *Badey ha-ʾAron* is unsure of how many *tagin* should be there, and whether this includes the spiral one.

16 Listing of Instances for the Special Letter *Ṭet*

The listing then begins.

1. P and H abbreviate to קדׄ and קדמא respectively. MV gives in full קדמאה. But otherwise they agree, bringing כי טוב. K extends to את האור כי טוב קדמאה ('the light that it was good' the first [good]). ST is very faded but appears to agree, reading כי טׄוב קדמׄ.

Line 22: **קדמׄ • [2]והנה טׄוב מאד • [3]ויטׄע • [4]טׄוב למאכל • [5]טׄוב הן האדם •**

... **the first** [occurrence] (Gen. 1:4). 2. **'and behold it it was very good'** (Gen. 1:31). 3. **'and He planted'** (Gen 2:8). 4. **'and good to eat'** (Gen. 2:9) 5. [the] **'good'** [that occurs in the verse beginning] **'of the man'** (Gen. 3:22).

2. Our manuscript is **unique, being the only core source to bring this instance.**[90]
3. **P, MV** and H all agree, bringing ויטע. K is damaged, but extends to [וי]טע ייי ('and God planted'). **ST** is very faded but brings ויטׄע too.

---

88 Zucker, Shlomo, *A Torah-Scroll from Northern Spain Following the Tradition of Curved Letters, from a Circle of 13th Century Kabbalists*, Jewish National and University Library, 2013 (accessed 26/3/17). Details for this *Torah* can also be viewed at: http://www.sothebys.com/en/auctions/ecatalogue/2009/important-judaica-n08606/lot.142.html (accessed 26/3/17).

89 Zucker, S., op cit., p. 5.

90 Of our secondary sources, only *Qiryat Sefer* brings this. At the end of section 6 on *parashat Bere'shit* it reads טוב הטי"ת לפופה ומתוייגת בשלשה ('good' the *ṭet* is curled and is decorated with three [*tagin*]). Indeed, there is a tradition amongst some scribes to have a *ṭet melufefet* on every occurrence of טוב (good) in the creation story.

4. **P**, **MV**, **ST**, **H** and **K** all agree, bringing טוב למאכל. However, 𝔐 is וטוב למאכל, and all the core sources have omitted a *vav*.[91]

Though very faded, the enhanced imagery suggests that **ST** now brings a further instance that does not appear in the other core sources, ט̊וב ה[ע]ץ ('the tree is good')[92] from Gen. 3:6, and this is present in the Shem Tov *Tanakh*. However, this extra instance finds no support amongst the secondary sources.

5. **P**, **MV** and **H** all bring דהן. **ST** is faded but brings ט̊וב דהן האדם. Our manuscript has omitted a letter. **K** lists the same instance, but as a longer phrase from the verse היה כאחד ממנו לדעת [ט̊]וב ('has become like one of us, knowing good'). However, prior to this instance there is a damaged section ending with what could be [וי]צמח from Gen. 2:9. However, this word has already been listed under the previous *ḥet* form with three *tagin*. **K** has likely erred.

Line 23: **[6]ויט̊ע כרם • [7]ויט דויעתק • [8]היט̊יב בעבורה • [9]ט̊ובת מראה • [10]רק ט̊וב •**
(*Parashat Noaḥ*) 6. **'and he** [Noah] **planted a vineyard'** (Gen. 9:20). (*Parashat Lekh Lekha*) 7. [the] **'and he** [Abram] **pitched** [his tent]' **of** [the verse beginning] **'and he moved on'** (Gen. 12:8) 8. **'and because of her** [Sarai] **it went well'** (Gen. 12:16) (*Parashat Ḥayyei Sarah*) 9. **'goodly appearance'** (Gen. 24:16). (*Parashat Toledot*) 10. **'only good'** (Gen 26:29).

6. **P**, **MV**, **H** and **K** all agree, bringing ויטע כרם. **ST** is not visible on the microfilmscan, but the enhanced imagery shows that it too agrees.
7. **P**, **MV** and **H** agree, bringing ויט דויעתק. Our scribe originally omitted the first word. **K** brings the same instance, but phrases as ויט̊ אהלה ('and pitched his tent'). **ST** seems to bring ויט̊ [אהל]ה, so likely agrees with **K**.
8. **P**, **MV** and **H** agree. **ST** though faded badly also seems to bring [היט̊י]ב בעבודה. **K** disagrees and brings instead ויאמ̊ ה[ב]ט̊ נא השמימה ('and He said look to the heavens') from Gen. 15:5.[93]
9. **P** and **H** agree, bringing טובת מראה. **MV** brings טובת מראה מאד (very goodly appearance) which would fix the instance as Gen. 24:16 and not 26:7,

91 However, the secondary sources do preserve this correctly. **MV2**, Parma 2427, Q651–652, Add. MS 27167 Parma 1959, *Qiryat Sefer* and *Ben Mesheq* all give וטוב. Add. MS 11639 omits.

92 Which Basser lists as טוב העץ למאכל, though the last word is possibly not included, op. cit., p. 86.

93 However, **K** finds no support amongst any secondary source.

which could also have been a possibility. These three witnesses bring טובת *ma-le' vav* when 𝔐 at Gen. 24:16 is טבת *ḥaser vav*. ST, though very difficult to make out also brings ט֯ובת מ[ר]א[ה]. K, in keeping with our view that its scribe has not merely copied the list in front of him, but checked and reworded entries, does bring the word as *ḥaser* and states [והנ]ער ט֯בת מראה ('and the young girl was of goodly appearance') also confirming this as Gen. 24:16.

10. P, MV, ST and H all agree, bringing רק טוב. K extends to [עש]ינו עמך רק ט֯וב ('we have done with you only good').

Line 24: **[11]וייט֯בו דבריהם • [12]וייט֯ב הדבר בעיני פרעה • [13]במיט֯ב הארץ הושב •**
(*Parashat Va-yishlaḥ*) 11. **'and their words were good'** (Gen. 34:18). (*Parashat Miqqets*) 12. **'and the thing was good** in the eyes of **Pharaoh'** (Gen. 41:37). (*Parashat Va-yiggash*) 13. **'the good part of the land to dwell'** (Gen. 47:6).

11. P and ST agree, bringing ויטבו דבריהם. ST has the last word written vertically upwards as he has run out of line space (see right). H and K do not match 𝔐 as they are *ḥaser yod* in the first word ויטבו. H abbreviates to דבריה׳. MV omits this instance completely.

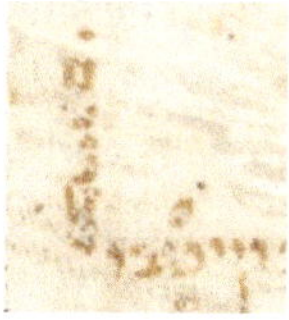

12. P, ST (though very faded), H and K (though damaged) agree, bringing וייטב הדבר בעיני פרעה and once again MV omits. Our scribe had originally omitted a word, which he adds in smaller script.
13. P and K give במיטב הארץ. ST is faded but certainly brings במיט֯ב הארץ. H too but abbreviates to במיט׳ and MV omits. This instance presents a problem as it could be in Gen. 47:6 or Gen. 47:11. Our manuscript has added an additional word which is a little difficult to read but is likely הושב ('dwell') which makes it clear that the intention is in fact Gen. 47:6 and again makes our manuscript unique in our core corpus of *Sefer Tagin* in bringing this clarification.[94] However, it is worth noting that whist it is very faded, ST may bring another instance which is not sufficiently legible

94 Parma 2427 almost lists as our manuscript bringing הוא • במיט֯ב • הושב adding הוא but separating out הושב with a dot as if it were separate instance. T-S Misc. 24.182 brings הו֯א במיט֯ב similarly but also then brings במיט֯ב again which from its positioning is Gen. 47:11, thus supporting ST. Q651–652 and Add. MS 11639 bring only במיט֯ב הארץ. Add. MS 27167 just brings במיט֯ב, so in theory could be either. *Qiryat Sefer* states that במיטב הטי"ת לפופה ומתוייגת ששה ('the good part' the *ṭet* is curled and is decorated [with] six [*tagin*]) and then brings הושב מלא ('to dwell' is written full), so is clearly referencing Gen. 47:6. *Ben Mesheq* lists ט"ת במיטב. Parma 1959 and MV2 omit.

or possibly is bringing the word הושב as our scribe and then repeats במיטב הא[ר]ץ clearly intending both verses to be listed.[95]

Line 25: [14]חשבה לטובה • [15]כי טוב הוא • [16]המטה הזה • [17]טוב לנו • [18]ויט • [19]ויט •
(*Parashat Va-yeḥi*) 14. **'thought to do him good'** (Gen. 50:20). (*Parashat Shemot*) 15. **'for he** [Moses] **was good'** (Ex. 2:2). 16. **'this staff'** (Ex. 4:17). (*Parashat Be-shallaḥ*) 17. **'better for us'** (Ex. 14:12) 18. **'and he stretched** [out his arm]' (Ex. 14:21). 19. **'and he stretched** [out his arm]' (Ex. 14:27).

14. P, MV and H all agree but are all *ma-le' vav* in לטובה. ST though faded brings something before חשבה לטובה which seems to be צ֯, but is otherwise unclear. K extends to אלהים חשבה [ל]טבה ('God thought to do him good') and is the only source to reflect 𝔐 which is *ḥaser vav*.
15. P and H agree. ST is again very faded but appears to agree with כי טוב הוא. K has the same instance, but phrases differently as ותרא אותו כי טוב ('and she saw that he was good') אותו is *ma-le' vav* whereas 𝔐 is *ḥaser* אתו. MV omits.[96]
16. P and H agree, K adds את. ST almost certainly gives המטה הזה too. MV omits.
17. P, MV and H all agree and ST, though very faint, seems to have טוב לנו too. K extends to כי טוב לנו [ע]בד את ('better for us to serve [the Egyptians]').
18. P, ST, MV and H all agree. P, however, does not have a dot dividing the two instances of ויט. K extends to ויט משה את ידו על הים ('and Moses stretched out his hand to the sea'), however, only brings one instance of this and does not repeat, moving next to instance 20.
19. P, MV and H all agree. The enhanced images reveal ST also brings a second instance of ויט. K, as we have already noted, omits.

Line 26: [20]נטית • [21]ממטיר לכם • [22]תלקטהו • [23]על כל הטובה • [24]ושפטתי •
20. **'You** [God] **stretch out** [Your right hand]' (Ex. 15:12). 21. **'I** [God] **will rain down to you** [bread]' (Ex. 16:4). 22. **'you shall gather it** [the manna]' (Ex. 16:26). (*Parashat Yitro*) 23. **'over all the good'** (Ex. 18:9). 24. **'and I** [Moses] **judge'** (Ex. 18:16).

---

95 Basser thus gives both in his listing, op. cit., p. 87.

96 The *Ba'al ha-Ṭurim* explains that 'there are five [extra] *tagin* on טוב, two [extra] on the *ṭet* [making five], one on the *vav*, two [extra] on the *bet*, to say that in the future he [Moses] would receive the five books of the *Torah*'.

20. **P**, **MV** and **H** all agree and **ST** appears to also bring just נט֯ית. **K** extends to נט֯ית ימינך ('You stretch our Your right hand').
21. **P** and **H** agree, bringing ממטיר לכם. **MV** just brings ממטיר and whilst very faint **ST** accords also bringing just ממט֯יר. **K** extends to הנני ממט֯יר לכם ('behold I will rain down to you').
22. **P**, **MV** and **H** all agree, bringing תלקטהו as 𝔐. **ST** brings תלקט֯והו *ma-le'vav*. **K** extends to ששת ימים תלקט֯הו ('six days you will gather it').
23. **P**, **MV** and **H** all agree. **ST** though faded similarly seem to give על כל ט֯ובה. **K** extends to ויחד יתרו על כל הט֯בה ('and Jethro rejoiced over all the good') but spells the last word *ḥaser vav* when 𝔐 is *ma-le'* as in our other witnesses.
24. **P** and **H** agree and though very faint **ST** does too, bringing ושפט֯תי **MV** spells incorrectly ושפתי omitting the key letter—the *ṭet*. **K** extends slightly to read [וש]פט֯תי בין ('and I will judge between').

Listings for the letter *ṭet* continue on in T-S AS 139.152, but our first **CG** manuscript fragments end here.

17 Summary—T-S D1.42

Overall **T-S D1.42** presents an excellent core witness to *Sefer Tagin* and is closest perhaps to *Maḥzor Vitry* Parma 2574 (**P**). It is largely accurate with only relatively few errors and some of these have been corrected with small added letters in margins or between lines. In this, it adds to the evidence of the other witnesses to help dispel some of the queries around specific instances. Our manuscript often brings additional words that clarify the instance further solving some problems around which instance is meant. Occasionally it, like others, brings fuller orthography which does not match 𝔐 and, occasionally, it does match the Masoretic text when others do not. It also has a small number of unique additions.

Its letter forms, as shown in **T-S NS 287.11-F**, are certainly a little different to the sorts of forms that we mostly encounter in other manuscripts, and some letters are adorned with a dot and do not seem to conform to the form described at all. The scribe may have been unsure what to draw, or the dot may have another meaning that is not clear.

As a general point, the amount of differences and also the occasional listing of words that do not appear in all of the witnesses is interesting, since this suggests scribes were often copyists of pre-existing lists that came into their hands and when anything was not clear they just wrote what they thought rather than actually checking whether the references made sense. Our **CG** scribe seems no different here (unlike that of **K** (and perhaps **ST**) where we can see that some effort was made to add to the listing to add greater clarification). Thus, it seems that they perpetuated or created new errors. Over time this served to be problematic for scribes wishing to adhere to this tradition, as no source preserves a fully reliable record or agree fully on the forms of the letters to be employed, even this potentially oldest extant source from the Cairo *Genizah*. Nonetheless, comparison of the texts certainly clarifies a number of those issues and lends much stronger support to particular readings. **T-S D1.42** plays a valuable role in that.

T-S Misc. 24.182 as a new composite secondary source also from the *Genizah*, has also helped contribute to our understanding. Whilst it omits quite a few instances that are found in many other sources, it occasionally brings some unique instances that are also not seen elsewhere.

These manuscript fragments certainly add a great deal to the study of *Sefer Tagin* and the additional fragments that join to the the two sides of **T-S D1.42** and follow below, yield yet more clarifications and surprises.

PART 2

CHAPTER 5

Analysis and Reconstruction of Joined Fragments

1 Reconstruction of Additional Pages of Our New Core Source

As mentioned above in Part 1, there are additional joins to the **T-S D1.42** fragment and these add to the listings of specially formed letters that are to be adorned with *tagin* and/or other decorative elements. These are all similarly to be found in the Cambridge *Genizah* collection and thus collectively termed **CG**. This part of the monograph treats those additional fragments and, additionally, **attempts to reconstruct them, digitally joining them and filling in the lacunae using the font I have developed.** This is similarly done through comparison against the core corpus of *Sefer Tagin* and again the secondary listings where some form of *Sefer Tagin* has been preserved within a wider text of rules for writing *Torah*, or lists that has been amassed from witnessing *Sifrey Torah* that preserve these traditions.

However, whilst we are on fairly secure ground when parts of lines are preserved, there are some lines where there are no existing words at all, and so reconstruction is, of necessity, a little more speculative.

T-S AS 139.152-B (left side)—21 lines preserved

2 Continuing the Listing for the Special Letter *Ṭet*

As mentioned previously, this fragment is particularly damaged and only the right side of the page is extant. Thus only a few words are shown on each line. Continuing the listing from the previous fragment, covered in part 1, we immediately see disagreement between the core sources.

Line 1: [1]**ושפטו** [קדמ • ישפוטו הם • {לבלתי} תחטאו • {ואלה} המשפטים •]
(*Parashat Yitro*) [the first] **'and let them judge'** (Ex. 18.22). [the last 'and they judged' (Ex. 18:26). '{that you} sin not' (Ex. 20:17). (*Parashat Mishpaṭim*) '{and these are} the judgements' (Ex. 21:1).]

1. **P**, **MV** and **H** agree with the instance from Ex. 18:22, and, for them, this is followed by the second use of that word in Ex. 18:26, though **MV** makes

 DOI:10.1163/9789004426368_006

no mention of קד or בת on either. ST is too faded in any available imagery to see what is brought clearly but the word קדמ׳ appears to be there. The Shem Tov *Tanakh* also brings the decoration on ושפטו ('and let them judge') in Ex. 18:22, supporting this reading. Nonetheless, whilst **P**, **MV** and **H** having both entries as ושפטו brings a neat symmetry, we cannot assume that this is the simplest explanation. **K** does agree with the first instance bringing ושפטו קדמ, however, disagrees with the second instance, bringing instead ישפוטו הם ('and they judged themselves') which is also in Ex. 18:26. However, there is also ישפטו הם (*ḥaser vav*) in Ex. 18:22, so **K** having the extra *vav* is significant in this case. Basser suggests that the instance is ישפוטו בתראה (the last 'they judged themselves') which would also mean Ex 18:26,[1] but **ST** is inconclusive, reading [   ]טו בתרא[ה]. However, it is worth noting that the Shem Tov *Tanakh* brings the decoration on neither word in Ex. 18:26. Unfortunately, our manuscript does not offer any assistance, though our secondary sources (shown in the note below) seem largely to support **K**, so I have elected to use this in the reconstruction.[2]

In terms of the rest of the reconstructed line. **P**, **MV** and **H** bring תחטאו and **ST**, though faded, similarly תחטאו. **K** typically extends to לבלתי תחטאו ('that you sin not').

P and **H** then bring המשפטים. **ST** appears to bring [וא]ל[ה המ]ש[פ]טים ('and these are the judgements') which is echoed by **K** who also extends to [וא]לה המשפטים. Shem Tov does also decorate המשפטים in his *Tanakh* in this verse, thus supporting this reading. **MV** omits. In the reconstruction, using the font I developed, it would lead to quite a short line if we followed **P** alone, so it is possible that our fragment also extended as **ST** and **K**. Alternatively he wrote out קדמאה and בתראה in full, however, from the previous folios covered our scribe generally tends to abbreviate these modifiers. I have

1 Basser, op. cit., p. 87.

2 Turning to our secondary sources, Q651–652 brings both ושפטו and ישפטו הם (*ḥaser vav*) and by positioning agrees with K, as does Parma 1959 who brings וטפטו and ישפוטו. MV2 also lists ושפטו and ישפטו הם but does not decorate the letters. Parma 2427 does not bring the first instance, but does bring הקטן ישפוטו ('small [matter] they judged') from Ex. 18:26. Add. MS 11639, in a quite decorative page, brings וטפטו עד ישפטו ישפטו הם decorating only the first two but the first is barely decorated whilst the second has five *tagin* as expected. It then follows with the five *tagin* on a second ישפטו הם which, whilst *ḥaser vav*, is meant to be Ex. 18:26. *Ben Mesheq* typically avoids the issue by bringing all four instances across the two verses and reads כב ט״ט דושפטו ישפטו כו טית דושפטו ... טית [ב]ישפטו ([verse] 22 *ṭet* of 'and let them judge' 'they will judge' [verse] 26 *ṭet* of 'and let them judge' … *ṭet* [in] 'they will judge'). *Qiryat Sefer* similarly expands the number and brings ושפטו ישפטו שלשתם הטי״ת לפופה ומתוייגת ששה ('and let them judge' 'they will judge' 'they will judge' the three of them, the *ṭet* is curled and is decorated with six *tagin*). The *Ba'al ha-Ṭurim* makes no comment on any of these possibilities. Add. MS 27167 has only listings for Genesis.

therefore chosen to follow the former option for the reconstruction as they clarify and give more context to the instances.

Line 2: [2]ולא תט̊ה • [ט̊ור אד{ו}ם • פט̊דה • קט̊רת רקח • ונט̊ה לו • כל ט̊ובי •]
2. 'and you shall not wrest' (Ex. 23.6). (*Parashat Tetsavveh*) ['a row of ruby' (Ex. 28:17). 'topaz' (Ex. 28:17). (*Parashat Ki Tissa'*) 'a perfumed incense' (Ex. 30:35). 'and pitch it' (Ex. 33:7). 'all My goodness' (Ex. 33:19).

2. P, ST (though very faded) and H agree with our scribe, adding an additional *vav*. MV and K give instead לא תטה, which is as 𝔐.

Reconstructing the rest of the line, P and MV bring טור אדם and improved imagery for ST also yields ט̊ור אדם. H is similar, but brings אדום *ma-le' vav*, though 𝔐 is *ḥaser*. In terms of positioning in the listing, this would be Ex. 28:17, rather than its later appearance in Ex. 35:10.

For the next instance P brings the next word in that verse פטדה, which H and MV both omit. Whilst only the *ṭet* itself in the word is clear on the microfilm scan the enhanced imagery for ST shows פט̊דה more clearly and there is space for an additional word before the next instance, possibly וברקת ('and emerald') which follows in the verse. K omits both of these instances that are focussed on the stones in the High Priest's breastplate. It brings instead משפט̊ אבינך ('the judgement of your poor') which follows on immediately after לא תטה in Ex. 23:6. However, K is the only core source that does this.[3]

P, MV and H then bring קטרת רקח from Ex. 30:35 *ḥaser* as 𝔐 and ST, though faded, does also show this but *ma-le' vav* קט̊רת רוקח. K extends to ועשית אותה [ק]טרת ('and you will make it an incense').

P, MV and H bring ונטה לו from Ex. 33:7. ST is very faint, though ונט̊[ה] seems to be there and Shem Tov does decorate ונט̊ה in his *Tanakh* in this verse, thus supporting this reading. K extends and brings instead ומשה יקח ונט̊ה ('and Moses would take ... and pitch it').

Finally P, MV and H bring כל טובי which K extends considerably to ויאמ̊ אני אעביר כל ט̊ובי ('and He said, I will make all My goodness pass'). טו[ב]י is very faint in ST and Shem Tov does decorate ט̊ובי in his *Tanakh* in this verse, thus supporting this reading.

---

3 Turning to our secondary sources Parma 2427 does have this phrase in its listing, but only to indicate it is a *setuma* (closed section). *Qiryat Sefer* brings תטה משפט הטיתי״ן לפופות ומתוייגות ששה ('wrest' [and] 'judgement' the [letters] *ṭet* are curled and have six *tagin*), supporting K. MV2 lists the two together לא תטה משפט but does not decorate the letters so we do not know if either or both are intended. T-S Misc. 24.182, Q621–652, Add. MS 11639, Parma 1959 and *Ben Mesheq* do not bring this. However, it is possible that there has been confusion as this instance of the word משפט does generally take a *pe melufefet* (curled *pe*) in most sources.

Line 3: [3]וחט֯אה • [4]ולח[ט֯את{י}נו • וייט֯ב {בעיניו} • דבר ט֯וב {על ישראל} •]
3. **'and sin'** (Ex. 34.7). 4. **'and for** [our sin' (Ex. 34.9). (*Parashat Shemini*) ['and it was good {in his eyes}' (Lev. 10:20). 'spoke good {about Israel}' (Num. 10:29).]

3. **P, MV, H** and **ST** (though very faded) all agree. **K** extends to ופשע [ו]חט֯אה ('and transgression and sin').
4. Given the surviving characters, it would seem likely that **P, MV, H** and **ST** all agree. Interestingly, all the core comparators are *ma-le'yod* when 𝔐 is *ḥaser* ולחטאתנו. **K** is also *ma-le'yod* and extends to וסלחת לעונינו ולחט֯אתינו ('and pardon us for our iniquity and for our sin'). Unfortunately, we cannot see what our scribe brought.

P and H bring וייטב הדבר ('and the thing was good') but there is no such phrase in Exodus or Leviticus, so this cannot be correct. **MV** and **ST** disagree, bringing instead וייטב בעיניו from Lev. 10:20 which **K** agrees with, extending to וישמע משה וייט֯ב ('and Moses heard and it was good'). From the enhanced images we can see that that **ST** extends, probably intending ד[ו]יש[מ]ע (of [the verse beginning] 'and he heard') but may have omitted a letter or two.[4] Shem Tov also decorates וייט֯ב in his *Tanakh* in this verse, thus supporting this reading. Our scribe may well have followed P and H in error, but I have added the most likely instance into the reconstruction.

P, MV and H then bring דבר טוב from Num. 10:29, which ST extends out to דבר ט֯וב על ישראל ('spoke good about Israel') and K brings כי ייי דבר טוב על ('for God spoke good about'). Given the length of the line and the next instance our fragment brings, it is likely our scribe also brought an extended version of this instance that may be similar to ST given most start דבר טוב.

Line 4: [5]הט֯וב הוא • א[{שר} י{י}ט֯יב {ייי} • והט֯בנו לך {בתׄ} • ויט֯ש על המחנה •]
5. (*Parashat Beha'alotkha*) **'whatever good'** (Num. 10.32). ['{that God} does good' (Num. 10:32). the last 'we do that good {to you}' (Num 10:32). 'cast down on the camp' (Num. 11:31).]

5. **P, MV, H** and **ST** all read הטוב ההוא, **K** extends to והיה הט֯וב ההוא ('and it will that whatever good') and does not bring a separator as just carries on with the other two instances in the verse (see below). Our scribe has erred omitting a *he*.

4 It is possible that this reads ד[וישמע משה] (of [the verse beginning] 'and Moses heard') but that is quite speculative, as only a *dalet* seems clear from the scan.

P, MV and H bring ייטיב ייי. ST appears to bring ייטב *ḥaser yod*. K brings two instances together indicating each *ṭet* separately אשר יטיב ייי עמנו והטבנו ('that God does good to us, we do that good [to you]') omitting a different *yod* in the first instance. 𝔐 is ייטיב. There seems to be a faded *ʾalef* after the first instance on this line of our fragment but very close to the previous word, so I have added אשר to the reconstruction following K. I have, however, confined this to grey characters in the reconstruction, as it is questionable.

P and H then bring והטבנו לך בתו׳ implying Num. 10:32, as opposed to the usage of that phrase earlier in Num. 10:29. By its position in the list, this is fairly obvious, thus ST (though faded) seems to bring והטבנו לך[5] only. K's entry is shown above. MV clearly intends this too but because he adds separator dots in the wrong place, it looks like it brings instead two instances • והטבנו • בתראה •.

The last instance on the line has general agreement as P, H and K all bring ויטש על המחנה from Num 11:31. K, somewhat unnecessarily, given available space, abbreviates the last word to המחנ׳. MV just brings ויטש. ST is not visible, however, Shem Tov does not appear to decorate ויטש in his *Tanakh* in this verse.[6]

Line 5: [6]וישטחו להם • [7]ש[טוח • {ותמ{ו}נת ייי} יביט • שבט אביך {הקרב} •]

6. **'and they spread themselves'** (Num. 11:32). 7. 's[preading'] (Num. 11:32). ['{and the similitude of God} he beholds' (Num. 12:8). (*Parashat Qoraḥ*) 'the tribe of your father, {bring near}' (Num. 18:2).]

6. P, MV, and H only give וישטחו whereas our scribe, like K, clarifies the instance further by adding להם. ST is not visible, though Shem Tov does decorate וישטחו in his *Tanakh* in this verse, thus supporting this reading.
7. Given the surviving character it would seem likely that P, MV, H and K all agree, bringing the next word in the verse as a separate instance, though K has no separator. ST is not visible, though Shem Tov does decorate שטוח in his *Tanakh* in this verse, thus supporting this reading.

In line 5, if we follow P solely, we would see a very short line from the instances that it brings. P, MV and H bring יביט whereas K extends to ותמונת ייי יביט ('and the similitude of God he beholds'), though *ma-leʾ vav* in the first word, whereas 𝔐 is *ḥaser*. ST is not visible, though Shem Tov does decorate יביט in his *Tanakh* in this verse, thus supporting this reading.

Similarly whilst P, H bring only שבט אביך, MV also brings this, but wrote שבט אפ^ב^יך with a corrective *bet* above the *pe*. K extends to שבט אביך הקרב ('the tribe of your father

5 Basser, nonetheless, adds בתראה, op. cit., p. 88.

6 Basser, nonetheless, includes this in his listing, op. cit., p. 88.

[bring] near'). ST is not visible, though Shem Tov does decorate שבט̊ in his *Tanakh* in this verse, thus supporting this reading. Given our scribe extended instance 6, as K, perhaps he did similar with these two instances, which would certainly fill out the line.

Line 6: [8]משפט̊ן • [9]לחקת [משפט • במשפט̊ האורים • {כמשפט̊ם קדמ̊}]

8. (*Parashat Pinḥas*) **'their judgement'** (Num. 27:5). 9. **'a statute of** [judgement]' (Num. 27:11). ['in the judgement of the Urim' (Num. 27:21). {the first 'after their judgment' (Num. 29:6).}]

8. **P**, **MV** and **H** agree. **ST** is not visible, though Shem Tov does decorate משפט̊ן in his *Tanakh* in this verse, thus supporting this reading. **K**, however, brings a very different instance משפט̊ אחד יהיה ('one judgement will there be') from Num. 15:16, though 𝔐 reads ומשפט ('and judgement'). Regardless, that would be very out of sequence given its previous listings, so this seems inaccurate.[7]
9. **P**, **MV** and **H** agree bringing לקחת משפט. **K** extends to [ואם א]ין אחים וג̇ לקחת משפט̊ ('and if there are no brothers' etc. 'to appoint a judgement') quoting the beginning of the verse. **ST** is not visible and, unfortunately, the Shem Tov *Tanakh* is not extant.

Once again, following **P** alone would leave us with a short line. It is, however, unlikely that our scribe followed **K** in bringing the extended reference we saw in instance 9 as he has not employed that format elsewhere. Given the Aramaic forms employed previously, it would more likely be something akin to לקחת משפט דואם (the 'appoint a judgement' of [the verse beginning] 'and if'). This would certainly differentiate it from the use of the phrase לקחת משפט in Num 35:29, but the sequence itself would account for that.

P, **MV**, **H** and **K** are all in agreement about the next instance as they bring במשפט̊ האורים from Num. 27:21, so it is unlikely our fragment differs. However, it may be that our fragment did have an additional entry, perhaps that of **K**, dealt with in instance 10 (see below), such as כמשפטים קדמ̊ (the first 'after their judgement'). **ST** is not visible and, unfortunately, the Shem Tov *Tanakh* is not extant for this section.[8]

---

7 No other core sources bring this and, unfortunately, the Shem Tov *Tanakh* is not extant for this verse. Turning to our secondary sources, none from Q651–652, Parma 2427, Add. MS 11639, **MV2**, Parma 1959, *Qiryat Sefer* or *Ben Mesheq* bring this instance. **K** enjoys no other support for this suggested instance.

8 Basser thus omits this from his listing, op. cit., p. 88.

Line 7: [10]כמשפטם בת • [{ו}לא תטמא • כי המשפט • {ו}{י}יטב בעיני} • ייטב]
10. the last **'after their judgement'** (Num. 29.33). (*Parashat Mase'ei*) ['{and} you will not defile' (Num. 35:34). (*Parashat Devarim*) 'for the judgment' (Deut. 1:17). (*Parashat Va-'etḥanan*) {'and it was pleasing in my eyes'} (Deut. 1:23). [the] 'it was good' ...]

10. **P**, **H** and **MV** agree, bringing an instance from Num. 29:33. **H** brings בתר׳ and **MV** again potentially misleads separating the two words as if they are two instances • כמשפטם • בתראה •. **ST**, though very faint, also seems to give [כמ]שפטם בתרא. However, **K** does not agree and instead brings • ונסכיהם [כ]משפטם דבחדש השביעי ('and their drink offerings' from 'the seventh month'. This would be from Num. 29:6), though the reference to the seventh month is in fact in the next verse 29:7 and 𝔐 reads לחדש השביעי ('of the seventh month'). The separator in **K** also serves to confuse. It is possible that that both instances of כמשפטם were originally intended and listed.[9] It would certainly fill out the space in line 6, as mentioned above.

There is then a bit of an open space in our fragment before the next instance, whereas one would have expected to see a letter a bit closer to the בת.

P, **MV** and **H** then give לא תטמא from Num. 35:34, but 𝔐 is ולא. **K** extends to ולא תטמא את הארץ ('and you will not defile the land'). **ST** is virtually invisible, but the faintest traces show ולא תטמא.

The enhanced imagery reveals that **ST** then seems to bring an additional instance which appears to be ויט ממסעי which is not present in any other of the core sources, but there is no such word in Num. 33:1 where *parashat Mase'ei* begins, nor even a word with a *ṭet* in it, so it is not clear what was intended here.

---

9 Turning to our secondary sources, there is considerable disagreement here. Q651–652 brings ונסכיהם כמשפטם referencing a number of special decorated letters. Its positioning falling between a reference from Num. 28:25 and Num. 29:15, suggests he agrees with **K** and it should be Num. 29:6 (Basser incorrectly records this as Num 29:33, *op. cit.*, p. 256). Similarly, *Qiryat Sefer* brings כמשפטם ... והטי״ת לפופה ומתוייגת משני צדדיה ('after their judgements' ... and the *ṭet* is curled and adorned with *tagin* on both sides) in the section concerning *Rosh Hashanah*, thus Num 29:6. On the other hand Parma 2427 brings its entry כמשפטם sandwiched between Num. 29:32 and 29:35, thus agreeing with the other core sources. Add. MS 11639 also appears to specify Num. 29:33 as it brings וביום השביעי עד כמשפטן ('and on the seventh day' until 'after their judgement') but errs ending the word with a *nun sofit*. *Ben Mesheq* typically brings both possibilities ו ... ב׳ט דכמשפטם and לג ב׳ט דכמשפטם. MV2 brings ובום השביעי • עד כמשפטם • פ • but this seems merely to be indicating a *petuḥa* section. Parma 1959 brings neither.

P, MV and H then bring only כי המשפט from Deut. 1:17, whereas K extends to כי [ה]משפ̊ט לאלהים ('for the judgement is God's'). ST is not visible, however, Shem Tov does decorate המשפ̊ט in his *Tanakh*, thus supporting this reading.

K then brings an additional instance ויטב בעיני הדבר ואקח ('and the thing was pleasing in my eyes and I took') which is Deut. 1:23 though 𝔐 is וייטב, *ma-le' yod*. This is certainly in sequence, however, again none of the other core sources bring this, though all of the secondary sources do.[10] Additionally, Shem Tov does seem to partly support K as in his *Tanakh* he brings a decoration on the *ṭet* of וייט̊ב in Deut 1:23, however, only the *lefufa* (curled) element (above right) and not the other *tagin*, so he may have been unsure. It is possible that our fragment has some variant of K's instance as there is some available space and given the repetition of the key word ייטב this does not seem an unreasonable assertion. Also, given that repetition, this may have fallen out at some point in the other core sources.[11]

Line 8: [11]דושמרת את [חקיו • ייט̊יב דכבד • ייט̊ב להם • {לטט̊פת {קדמ̇}} •]

11. ... of [the verse beginning] **'and you will keep** [His statues' (Deut. 4:40). [the] 'it was good' of [the verse beginning] 'honour' (Deut. 5:16). 'be well with them' (Deut. 5:26). {the first 'as reminders' (Deut. 6:8)}.]

11. P agrees. H gives וייטב בדושמרת את חקיו with an additional *dalet* written above the *bet* of the second word, by way of correction, but without deleting the *bet*. K brings the same but phrases as ושמרת את [ח]קיו וג' אשר ייטב לך ('and you will keep His statutes' etc. 'which is good for you'). MV omits. ST is not visible and, unfortunately, the Shem Tov *Tanakh* is not extant.

In terms of the reconstruction, once again we would have a short line following P alone. To begin, P brings ייטיב דכבד from Deut. 5:16. MV brings ייטב דכבד *ḥaser yod* as 𝔐, and

10 ויט̊ב *ḥaser yod* as K sandwiched between Deut. 1:19 and Deut 1:41, which can only be Deut 1.23. Add. MS 11639 and Parma 1959 also brings וייט̊ב. *Qiryat Sefer* brings וייטב (בשני יודי"ן) והטי"ת לפופה ('and it was pleasing' (with two [letters] *yod*) and the *ṭet* is curled). This perhaps suggests some thought it should have one *yod* like K. *Ben Mesheq* just gives כג טית דוייטב (23 [the] *ṭet* of 'and it was pleasing') but no explanation as to what is special about it. Parma 2427 does bring וייטב in the listing, but does not decorate it, though one assumes it is there for that reason. Similarly, MV2 brings ויטב בעיני הדבר but does not decorate. K enjoys a great deal of support amongst the secondary sources for this additional instance.

11 Though many, but not all, instances of ייטב or וייטב are decorated through the *Torah* and so it would be interesting to assess why some are and others not. This may be contextual and is something for wider study.

H brings יטיב דכבד. K stays with its current framing approach, bringing כבד את אביך וג' למען ייטב לך ('honour your father' etc. 'so that it will be well for you').[12]

Unfortunately, this is where we lose reference to K as no more entries for *ṭet* are present. This is a shame as it has consistently provided clarifications, and also preserved instances the other core sources have not.

P, MV and H continue the next instance with ייטב להם from Deut. 5:26. ST is not visible and, unfortunately, the Shem Tov *Tanakh* is not extant. Once again we have an unexplained space in our fragment and so this may have been filled with a further instance, such as לטטפת קדמ̇, as described below, which would bring our fragment into line with the other sources.

Line 9: [12]**לט̊וט̊פת** • [13][רו הט̊וב • ט̊נאך • עליך לט̊וב • תזל כט̊ל • אוצ[14]דרכיו]

12. **'As reminders'** (Deut. 6:8). (*Parashat Ki Tavo'*) **'His** [good] **treasure'** (Deut. 28:12). ['your basket' (Deut. 28:17). (*Parashat Nitsavim*) 'for good' (Deut. 30:9). (*Parashat Ha'azinu*) 'flow as dew' (Deut. 32:2). 14. 'His ways ...]

12. Our scribe spells לטוטפת *ma-le' vav* which may imply that this is referring to Deut. 11:18, which is *ma-le' vav* in 𝔐. With the marking above the second letter *ṭet* only, he suggests only one instance is present and so may also have only marked the second *ṭet* on the previous instance, if he included it. P gives לטטפת קד̇ ובתר̇ ('as reminders', the first and last). H is similar abbreviating as קדמ̇. MV with an inconvenient separator dot and similarly *ma-le' vav* gives לטוטפות • קדמאה ובתרא:. ST is very faint, but the enhanced images show לט̊וט̊פת קד̇ also *ma-le' vav* which suggests the first occasion of the word but marking both letters *ṭet*. ST then brings [ל]טוטפת בתרא still *ma-le' vav*, but marks neither *ṭet*. Unfortunately, the Shem Tov *Tanakh* is not extant.[13] Our core sources seem in agreement that there is more than one instance here, though it

12 The *Ba'al ha-Ṭurim* notes against the instance in Deut. 5:16 that '[there are] *tagin* on the *ṭet* for a mother carries him for nine months and his father and mother were careful about the nine attributes spoken of in [tractate] *Nedarim*'. He then brings an acronym formed from these and lists the specifics of children born of undesirable circumstances.

13 Turning to the secondary sources, Parma 2427 and Parma 1959 bring both לט̊ט̊פת and לט̊וט̊פת implying all four are decorated. *Qiryat Sefer* also hold that all four are decorated לטטפת כלו חסר והטטין לפופות ומתוייגות שלש בכל ענף ('as reminders' completely *ḥaser* and the [letters] *ṭet* are curled and decorated with three *tagin* on each wing) and then לטוטפת חסר הוא"ו השניה ומלא בראשנה והטטי"ן לפופות ומתוייגות שנים בצד הימני ושלש בשמאלי ('as reminders' missing the second *vav* but full with the first and the [letters] *ṭet* are curled and decorated with two *tagin* on the right and three on the left). Q651–652 brings just that of Deut 11:18 but decorates both letters *ṭet* לט̊וט̊פת. Conversely, Add. MS

is not clear whether the intention is for both letters *ṭet* in one word, or for both words in the two verses Deut. 6:8 and Deut. 11:18. In the latter, we would be left with the problem of which *ṭet* on each? One would assume that if both letters *ṭet* were intended then the normal phrasing employed would have been תרויהון (both of them), but this is not used anywhere in the sources. Given the short line and that all our sources are in agreement that we have multiple instances here, it is highly likely that there was another reference to לטטפת (*ḥaser vav* as 𝔐) which was on the end of line 8 from Deut 6:8 and the instance on line 9 perhaps should have been followed with בת̊. However, our scribe has perhaps omitted this possibly in error, but possibly because one was doubly *ḥaser* and one had one *vav*, and this was considered sufficient distinction in his *Vorlage*.

13. P, MV and H agree. ST is very faint but also brings [או]צרו הט̊וב.

P and MV then bring טנאך from Deut. 28:17. H is similar, but originally omitted the *ʾalef* bringing טנ^אך. Basser states that ST extends to ארור ט̊אנך ('cursed by your basket') but this is not clear on any available images. Shem Tov does decorate ט̊נאך in his *Tanakh* in this verse, so does agree with this instance.

P, MV and H then bring עליך לטוב. ST has only לט̊וב visible, but then follows with what be another instance as there is a faint circle, but this is not discernable.

P, MV and H all bring תזל כטל from Deut. 32:2. ST definitely has ת[ז]ל visible and Shem Tov does decorate כט̊ל in his *Tanakh* in this verse, thus supporting this reading.

14. P, MV and H all bring דרכיו משפט ('His ways are justice'). ST though faded certainly brings משפט̊, so likely has the preceding word too.

11639 brings only Deut 6:8 with both letters decorated לט̊ט̊פת. *Ben Mesheq* brings ח ט' דלטטפת (8 *ṭet* of 'as reminders'), which suggests only one is decorated in Deut 6:8, but does not say which and also ט'ט מלטוטפת (*ṭet* from 'as reminders') which also suggests one from Deut 11:19 but again, we do not know which. MV2 lists only לטוטפת בין עיניך ('as reminders between your eyes') without decoration and likely in relation to it being a *setumah*. Of the instance in Deut. 6:8 the *Baʿal ha-Ṭurim* suggests that ''as reminders'—9 *tagin* corresponding to nine organs of the head', however, to get to nine the extra three *tagin* are on the *pe* (which is consistent with the listing for *pe* in *Sefer Tagin*) and the letters *ṭet* would therefore be normal. He makes no mention of any extra *tagin* in the instance at Deut. 11:19. As much disagreement prevails amongst our secondary sources as our core ones, but decorating all four letters *ṭet* would generally take the total listing over the anticipated 66 or 67 required, so it seems less likely that all should be included.

Line 10: משפת • 15בטח [בדד • יערפו טל שער י דאוקים כי כף תמנין]
… **are justice'** (Deut. 32:4). (*Ve-zo't Ha-berakhah*) 15. **'safety'** (Deut. 33:28). ['drop down dew' (Deut 33:28). Gate of *yod*. [*Yod*] that is bent like a *kaf*, eighty …]

15. Our fragment preserves only one word in the next instance, whereas our other sources provide more context. **P** and **MV** give ישׂ׳ בטח ('Israel in safety') which **H** gives in full as ישראל. **ST** instead gives [בטח] בדד ('in safety dwelt') but which is the same instance and it is possible our scribe has recorded it as **ST**.

We assume that our fragment's listing for *ṭet* ends with Deut. 33:28 as **P**, **MV** and **H** bring יערפו טל. Basser states that **ST** extends to [אף שמיו יע]רפו טל ('even His heavens, drop down dew') and the imagery does suggest this.[14] However, though he lists it here, in Shem Tov's *Tanakh*, he does not decorate the letter in טל.

Together with those on the previous folio detailed in the first section above, the Cambridge *Genizah* fragments have preserved 39 of the possible 66 or 67. Based on the reconstruction, the additions from **K** above our other core sources that are largely confirmed by the secondary sources and that our fragments preserve—likely two instances concerning לטטפת/לטוטפות rather than four from some secondary sources—I have identified 67 specific instances.[15]

3 Description and Example Forms of the Special Letter *Yod*

We now turn to a new letter listing, that of the *yod*. However, the start of the description is not extant in **CG** and we are left with very little information. **P** explains that this דאוקים כי כף (that is raised like a [letter] *kaf*) and this presents a great deal of problems for scribes who try to put a form to this letter without making it *pasul*. Since it is a the smallest letter and a specific instruction to make it look like another letter goes completely against the scribal *halakha* which has developed very strict rules to avoid one letter resembling another.[16]

14 Basser, op. cit., p. 89.

15 Drawing particularly on **K** and which I believe are more likely given the wider sources I have referenced, these do differ from Basser's listing of 67 (op. cit., pp. 86–89) which is very skewed towards **ST**.

16 For example, *Mishneh Torah Hilkhot Tefillin* 1:19 reads 'therefore one must be careful with the forms of the letters so that a *yod* does not look like a *vav* or a *vav* like a *yod*; a *kaf*

ST in the introduction gives דקאים ככף. This is probably merely a metathesis error rather than a substantive difference, and he meant to write דאקים. That this is the case is revealed by the enhanced imagery for the listing where ST brings דאקים כ̈כף. However this metathesis is, nonetheless, repeated in BH. MV writes instead דעקים כי כף (bent like a *kaf*). K brings no description, just a drawing of the form.

Right: Our printed Maḥzor Vitry (*LMV*) *top left is quite conservative in its form, unlike many others, adding only an enlarged* qots (*thorn*).

Given the difficulties faced by scribes in using this form, it is interesting to see that our scribe has rather ducked the issue in his rendition of the form in T-S NS 287.11-F (*right*). *He brings instead a* yod *form with a dot above it, suggesting he is not sure how to make the form and perhaps too concerned to make an attempt. This does not stop other scribes bringing forms that would certainly be considered* pasul (*invalid*) *following current or even past* halakha *for* sofrut. *Some forms brought resemble small letters* kaf, ḥet *or even a* nun *or* mem.

T-S Misc. 24.182 (*right*) *brings a fairly straightforward but very long line on the roof of the small letter, making it resemble a small* lamed.

Line 11: **ותלת באור** • [1]בי]ום ברא אלהים • בימים ההם תר • הרי אררט • [2]חרבו]

... **three in the *Torah*.** (*Parashat Bere'shit*) 1. **'On the day** [God created' (Gen. 5:1). 'in those days' (Gen. 6:4). (*Parashat Noaḥ*) 'the mountains of Ararat' (Gen. 8:4). 2. 'dried up ...]

Missing the full description, we again have to rely on other sources to find out how many letters *yod* are to be decorated. P explains that there are פג באוריית (83 in the *Torah*). **MV**, **K** and **H** similarly agree with this number. Our **CG** scribe has written the three in full rather than using the Hebrew letters as numerals. Thus we presume the number was also 83, and it is likely that the end of the previous line read תמנין (eighty), similar to **ST** who brings תמנין ותלתא in the introduction and in the descriptor in **BH**, and though faded, also gives פג באורית just before the listing itself. **H** then repeats באוריי' in error at the top of the next folio.

should not resemble a *bet* or a *bet* a *kaf*; and a *dalet* a *resh*, or a *resh* a *dalet* and other similar instances, so all who read them may so so easily [lit. swiftly]'.

TABLE 10 Forms for the special letter *yod*, as brought by the halakhic texts to which we have compared our manuscript, along with some other examples. Very few would be considered *kasher* by modern standards since they resemble different letters, as explained above.

		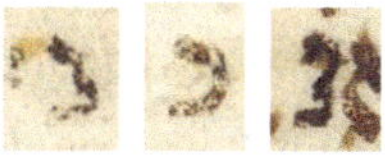		
Maḥzor Vitry Parma 2574 (P)	*Maḥzor Vitry* Add. MS 27201 (MV)	Shem Tov *Tanakh* *Sefer Tagi* (ST)	*Badey ha-'Aron* Heb. 840 (BH)	*Sefer Tagin* Heb. 837 (H)

Nr. 5667 (K)	Parma 2427	Parma 1959	Q651–652	MS Geunz. 481
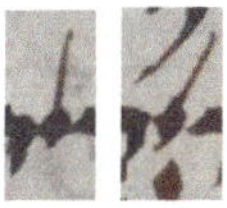				
Maḥzor Vitry Add. MS 27201 (MV2)	Add. MS 11639	Add. MS 27167	Bologna *Torah*	Vat. ebr. 1
	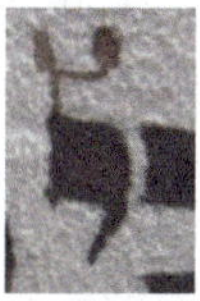			
Or. 1463	Alexander *Torah*			

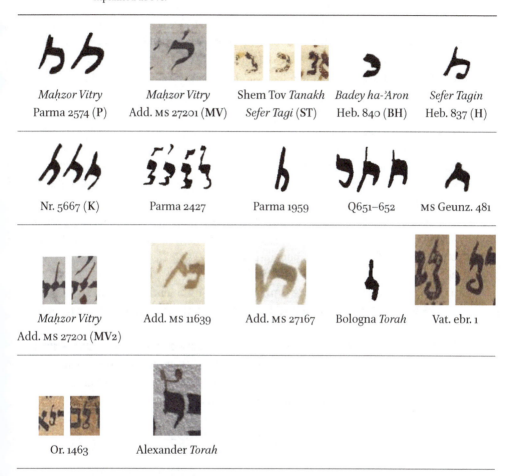

4 Listing of Instances for the Special Letter *Yod*

1. The two remaining letters on this line suggest that the first instance is as per our other sources. P and MV bring ביום ברא אלהים ('on the day God created'), H abbreviates the last word to אלהי׳. K appears to be the same but the last word is damaged and not legible. ST is very faded but also appears to give ביום ברא אל[הי]ם.

Turning to the reconstruction, P brings בימים ההם תר׳ which is Gen. 6:4. H separates the reference bringing // בימים ההם // תרווי // as if they were different instances. K starts the phrase earlier bringing ארץ בי֯מי֯ם הה[ם] ('in the earth in those days') indicating both letters *yod*. ST, though difficult to see, brings an additional entry before this instance, namely לא י֯דון ('shall not abide') from Gen 6:3. Given this is not present in the other core sources, this may not have been originally an instance, and instead I would argue that this is a misreading of his *Vorlage*. MV brings בימים ההם תרי יודין ('in those days' two [letters] *yod*). I suspect that Shem Tov's *Vorlage* may have been similar and he misread תרי (two) as תר׳ (both) in abbreviated form. Left with יודין possibly written *ḥaser* as ידין he misread as ידון and assigned it to Gen. 6:3, which even though slightly out of order was close enough for him to think this an easy error for a previous scribe to make. He likely then inserted it into his list as a separate instance, in what would be the right order. Unfortunately, the Shem Tov *Tanakh* is not extant for this instance.[17] ST then brings בי֯מי֯ם ההם ב̇ בה i.e. that both letters *yod* in that phrase should be decorated and, unfortunately, the Shem Tov *Tanakh* is not extant.

P then brings הרי אררט from Gen. 8:4 with which MV, and H all accord. ST, though faint, seems to put the decoration on the *he* in error, ה֯רי אררט K is damaged with only אררט surviving from the listing, but presumably agrees.

2. The start of the instance is presumably on the end of this line as P, MV, ST (though faded), H and K that all bring חרבו המים ('the water dried up').

Line 12: המי֯ם • [3] י֯בשה הארץ • [אחדי֯ם • י֯בצר מהם • י֯זמו • הפי֯צם • וי֯נגע •]
... the water' (Gen. 8:13). 3. **'the earth dried up'** (Gen. 8:14). ['one' (Gen. 11.1). 'withheld from them' (Gen. 11:6). 'they plan' (Gen. 11:6). 'He scattered them' (Gen. 11:9). (*Parashat Lekh Lekha*) 'and He plagued' (Gen. 12:17).]

3. P, MV, ST, H and K all agree bringing יבשה הארץ.

Reconstructing the rest of the line P, MV and H bring אחדים from Gen. 11.1. However, ST and K extend and by doing so add potential confusion. ST brings [דברי]ם אחדי֯ם ('one speech') thus giving us two possible candidates for the *yod*, but does appear to mark only the second.[18] Similarly K, though damaged, brings ודברים א[חדים] adding a *vav* to the first word in accordance with 𝔐.

17 This word is listed as being decorated elsewhere in *Sefer Tagin* but it is on the letter *nun sofit*. From our secondary sources Q651–652, Parma 2427, Add. 27167, MV2 and Parma 1959 all only decorate the *nun sofit* and not the *yod*. *Qiryat Sefer* just notes that ידון מלה ('abide' is *ma-le*'). Add. MS 11639 and *Ben Mesheq* omit entirely. Basser, in my view incorrectly, includes it in his listing (op. cit., p. 89) but does note that EPST and P do not include it.

18 Leading Basser to note 'the *yod* of 'one' only', op. cit., p. 89.

P then brings יבצר מהם from Gen. 11:6 as does MV (though separating them, as if two instances יבצר • מהם), ST and H also agree.

All also agree with the next instance from the same verse יזמו. K does reference both these letters *yod*, but in a single long instance since they are from the same verse. He brings instead, ועתה לא יׄבצר מהם כל אשר יׄזמו ('and now nothing will be withheld from them, all which they plan [to do'].)

P, MV, ST and H then all bring הפיצם from Gen 11:9. K is again damaged, but clearly in agreement, bringing ו[מש]ם הפיׄ[צם] ('and from there scattered them').

The last instance on this line is likely וינגע from Gen. 12:17, as brought by all the core sources though the word itself in K is not extant, it does appear to extend its listing to [ויׄנגע] ייי את פרעׄ ('and God plagued Pharaoh').

Line 13: [4]ויׄחלק • [5]יׄשפט • [6]להמיׄת [צדיק • ונשאתיׄ • נציׄב • אמריׄ לי • [7]ויׄרע]

4. **'and he divided'** (Gen. 14:15). 5. **'will judge'** (Gen 16:5). (*Parashat Va-yera'*) 6. **'to slay** [the righteous' (Gen. 18:25). 'and I will raise up'[19] (Gen. 18:26). 'pillar' (Gen. 19:26). 'say of me' (Gen. 20:13). 7. 'and evil ...]

4. P, MV, ST and H agree, bringing ויחלק. K extends to ויׄחלק עליהם ('and he divided himself against them').
5. P and H agree. K brings ישפט ייי ביניׄ ('God will judge between me') from the same verse, but places the decoration instead on the second *yod* of a different word. The enhanced imagery shows that ST, though faint does also bring יׄשפט and Shem Tov does decorate יׄשפט in his *Tanakh* in this verse, thus supporting this reading.[20] MV omits.
6. P, MV and H bring להמית צדיק, however, they do not indicate which letter *yod* is intended. ST brings להמיׄת צדיק which clarifies. K also appears to agree with the instance, though only לה of the word is fully extant. Unfortunately, our manuscript is partially faded, but it certainly looks like there is an additional small *tag* on the roof of the *yod* indicating that it is this letter, which serves to clarify the instance intended along with ST.[21]

19 In the sense of forgiveness.

20 Turning to our secondary sources, Parma 2427 lists ישפט ייי but does not decorate the *yod*. Q651–652 and Add. MS 11639 both list the phrase ישפט יי ביני ובינ֗יך but do not decorate any *yod*, instead bringing it only because of Masoretic dot (*puncta extraordinaria*). MV2 is similar, bringing ישפט ייי ביני ובינ֗יך. Parma 1959 and Add. MS 27167 omit ישפט and also only brings the reference to the Masoretic dot. *Qiryat Sefer* just notes that ישפט מלא ('will judge' is *ma-le'*) and then talks of the Masoretic dot separately. *Ben Mesheq* omits ישפט in his section on *tagin*. K seems out of step with the general opinion.

21 Interestingly out of all the possibilities within Genesis, Add. MS 27167 brings only one example of the decorated *yod* form and that is in להמיׄת, hence the available image above.

Reconstructing the rest of the line we see MV, ST and H all bring ונשאתי from Gen. 18:26 and K extends this to ונשאתי לכל המקום ('and I will raise up all the places'). P oddly spells this incorrectly as ונאשתני.

P then brings the single word נציב from Gen. 19:26, which MV and ST extend to נציב מלח and K extends further to ותהי נציב מלח ('and she became a pillar of salt'). H completely omits. Our scribe probably does not have room to extend.

The next two words could constitute one or two instances. P, MV and H bring אמרי לי from Gen. 20:13 as one instance but do not indicate which *yod* should be decorated. ST potentially complicates it further bringing אמרי לי אחי ('say of me [he is] my brother'), which presents us with three options, but fortunately the circle is marked only above the first. Shem Tov decorates only אמרי in his *Tanakh* in this verse, thus supporting this reading. K does similar, bringing אמרי לי also marking only the first *yod*.[22]

7. The end of this instance is on the following line, but **P, MV, ST, H** and **K** all agree, bringing וירע הדבר.

Line 14: **הדבר • [8]ופיכל שר צ**[באוו • ויתרצצו • נזיד • עיף • [9]ויחרד]

... was the thing' (Gen. 21:11). 8. **'and Phichol the captain of his host'** (Gen. 21:32). [(*Parashat Toledot*) 'and they struggled' (Gen. 25:22) 'pottage' (Gen. 25:29). 'tired' (Gen. 25:29). 9. 'and he trembled ...]

K adds an additional instance before instance 8, indeed bringing the words immediately before that instance ויקם אבימלך ('and 'Avimelekh arose') from Gen. 21:32. However, no other core source brings this, including our fragment.[23]

8. **P, MV, H** and **K** only give ופיכל as 𝔐. **ST** brings ופיכול, *ma-le' vav*. Our scribe adds a little further context to the instance adding שר but also likely צבאו even though very faded since the remaining letter form is certainly not from the next instance.

MV, H and K agree with 𝔐 bringing ויתרצצו from Gen. 25:22. P and ST bring instead ויתרוצצו *ma-le' vav*.

22 Q651–652 also brings only one *yod* אמרי לי. *Qiryat Sefer*, however, suggests the decoration is on both words, bringing אמרי לי היוד׳ין מוזרקות למעלה ולמטה ('say of me' the [letters] *yod* are curled above and below). MV2 does list אמרי לי but adds no decoration, so does not help the debate. Parma 2427, Add. MS 11639, Parma 1959, Add. MS 27167 and *Ben Mesheq* omit.

23 None of our secondary sources bring this either.

P, **MV**, **ST** (though very faded) and **H** then all bring נזיד from Gen. 25:29. **K** does bring this too, but with an instance before this. However, only two letters remain ו֯י. In the seven verses that separate the two given instances, there are no less than 11 possibilities with words that begin with these two letters. Given the grouping, I'm inclined to favour וי֯זד ('boiled') from the same verse, however, no other core source brings an instance in this position.[24] It is possible that our scribe has brought this as there could be space, given it is a small word. However, the general disagreement (see note below) suggests this is unlikely.

P, **MV** and **ST** (though again very faded) then bring עיף from Gen. 25:29, which **K** extends to כי עי֯ף אנכי ('for I am tired). The scribe of **H** probably misread the ף in his *Vorlage*, for he brings עיני.[25]

9. Once again, the start of the instance is not preserved from the previous line but is likely ויחרד יצחק as brought by **P** and **H**. **ST** is not visible, though Shem Tov only decorates וי֯חרד in his *Tanakh* in this verse. **K** also confirms, bringing וי֯חרד יצחק. **MV** only brings ויחרד, avoiding the possibility for confusion entirely. However, our scribe has decorated the *yod* in י֯צחק. He may have intended only this, or both, or perhaps erred and added the indicator accidentally.

Line 15: **י֯צחק • [10]ו[י֯שט]ם • [11]קצת[י֯ • נפתלת֯י • באשר֯י • אשרונ֯י • דודא֯ים •]**

... [i.e] **Isaac**' (Gen. 27:33). 10. **'and he hated'** (Gen. 27:41). 11. **'I am weary'** (Gen. 27:46). ['I have wrestled' (Gen. 30:8). 'I am happy' (Gen. 30:13). '[will call] me happy' (Gen. 30:13). (*Parashat Va-yetse'*) 'mandrakes'.

10. **P**, **MV**, and **H** agree. **K** extends to וישטם עש[ו] ('and Esau hated'). **ST** is not visible, though Shem Tov decorates וי֯שתם in his *Tanakh* in this verse, thus supporting this reading.
11. **P**, **MV** and **H** agree, bringing קצתי.[26] **K** is damaged, but likely extends to [קצת֯י] בחיי ('I am weary of my life') adding more possible letters *yod*, but

24 From our secondary sources, only Parma 1959 supports this suggestion and would potentially agree with K, as it brings וי֯זד יעקב. Q651–652 brings the next instance that our core sources do ויזד יעקב נז֯יד ('and Jacob boiled soup') only decorating one. *Qiryat Sefer* also seems to agree and brings נזיד מלא והיו'ד מוזרקת למעלה וכן היו"ד של עיף ('soup' is *ma-le'* and the *yod* is curled above and so is the *yod* of 'tired') as does *Ben Mesheq* כ"ט י"ד מן נזיד (29. [the] *yod* from 'soup'). **MV2** brings נזיד but does not decorate the letter. Parma 2427, Add. MS 11639, Add. 27167 omits either.

25 Which is corrected to עיף in the printed version EPST.

26 This word is also famous for the small ק (*'ot ze'ira*) that it traditionally takes in another scribal tradition.

he does not mark them. ST is not visible, but Shem Tov decorates קצת֯י in his *Tanakh* in this verse, thus supporting this reading.

P, MV, ST and H then bring נפתלתי from Gen. 30:8. K typically extends to נפתולי אלהים נפתלת֯י ('with mighty wrestling I have wrestled').

Similarly P, MV, ST and H all bring באשרי and אשרוני, as separate instances both from Gen. 30:13, which K likely brings together as באשר֯י כי אשרו[נ֯י] ('I am happy for [the daughters will call me] happy'), though the second *yod* is damaged, so we do not know if it was indicated. Given both are listed, it is perhaps odd that נפתולי from the previous instance is not similarly decorated. ST is not visible, but Shem Tov decorates נפתלת֯י and both באשר֯י and אשרונ֯י in his *Tanakh*, thus supporting the generally agreed reading.

P, MV, ST and H all then bring דודאים from Gen. 30:14. K is not extant.

Line 16: [12]דודא֯י • [13]בני • [14][יז]בלני • [15]נשי • [ילד֯י • בנת֯י • בנ֯י • צאנ֯י • מחנ֯ים • [16]הצי֯לני]

12. **'mandrakes'** (Gen. 30:15). 13. **'my son's'** (Gen. 30:15). 14. **'will dwell with me'** (Gen. 30:20). 15. **'my wives'** (Gen. 30:26). ['my children' (Gen. 30:26). 'my daughters' (Gen. 31:43). 'my children' (Gen. 31:43). 'my flocks' (Gen. 31:43). 'Maḥanayim'[27] (Gen. 32:3). (*Parashat Va-yishlaḥ*) 16. 'Deliver me' ...]

12. Because of the word that follows, בני, this is obviously the first occurrence of דודאי in this verse. P collapses instance 12 and 13 together by stating דודאי בני תר֗ ('my son's mandrakes', both of them) and H similar writing תרווי׳ fuller. K also brings both together and indicates each *yod* giving דודא֯י בנ֯י. MV separates the two instances, but also indicates it is both (though confusingly showing that word as a separate instance) giving דודאי • בני • תרויהון •. ST is perhaps clearest, bringing דודא֯י בנ֯י תרויהו[ן] marking both instances with the circle and stating that both are intended.
13. See the previous instance. Our scribe has not indicated the *yod* but, given previous examples, this is likely an error of omission rather than a view that it is just a word appended to the previous instance. Additionally, the *nun* and *yod* have merged together because of damage.
14. The next instances presents a problem since there are two letters *yod* in the word brought by P, MV, ST and H. ST marks only one יזבלנ֯י, which he confirms in his *Tanakh* decorating only יזבלני; however K indicates both, bringing י֯זבלנ֯י.[28] Unfortunately, the entry in our fragment is damaged with

27 Lit. camps.
28 Turning to our secondary sources, Q651–652 and Add. MS 11639 bring only the last *yod*

the first *yod* under a large stain and the *nun* and *yod* merging at the end, so it is not clear whether either or both instances are marked by our scribe.

15. P, MV, ST and H agree. K extends to את נשי.

P, MV and H all bring ילדי from Gen. 30:26, but it is not clear which *yod* should be decorated. ST is clear that it is only the second, bringing ילדי. K seems confused bringing ואת ילדי • תר • only indicating the second, but then stating that it is on both.[29]

The next three entries are a clearer grouping with P, MV, ST and H all bringing בנתי then בני and finally צאני, all from Gen. 31:42. Recognising this, K elects to quote the three as a group bringing הב[נות בנתי] והבנים בני והצאן צאני ('The daughters are my daughters, and the children are my children, and the flocks are my flocks').

P, MV, ST and H follow up with מחנים from Gen. 32:3, which K extends to ההוא מחנים ('that [place] Maḥanayim').

16. The entry that begins on this line and ends on the next is likely הצילני קדמ. MV writes קדמאה in full, H abbreviates as our CG scribe, and P gives קד. In this case, the first seems to be referring to the letter *yod* in the word הצילני, as opposed to the first occurrence of the word; since this appears only once during the whole of Genesis. ST, though faded, clearly decorates only the first *yod*, bringing הצילני קדמ. However, K disagrees, bringing instead הצילני תר ('deliver me' both [letters *yod*]) and indeed decorates both in the word.[30] It is shame that our fragment is not extant as there is much disagreement here and in the secondary sources (see note below).[31] Additionally, this instance is apparently out of sequence; as the next instance 17 actually occurs in the previous verse. All our core sources err.

יזבלני. Supporting K, *Qiryat Sefer* brings יזבלני היודי״ן מתוייגות שנים שנים ('will dwell with me' the letters *yod* are decorated with two [*tagin*] twice) and similarly *Ben Mesheq* brings ך ב׳ יודי״ן מיזבלני (20. two [letters] *yod* in 'will dwell with me'). MV2 lists יזבלני but does not decorate either *yod*. Parma 2427, Parma 1959 and Add. MS 27167 omit.

29 Q651–652, Parma 2427 and Parma 1959 bring ואת ילדי. Similarly *Ben Mesheq* reads כ״ח יוד בתרא מילדי (28. the last *yod* from 'my children'). *Qiryat Sefer*, however, seems to want to add to both, bringing נשי ילדי היודי״ן מוזרקת בעגול קצר ('my wives', 'my children' the [letters] *yod* are curled with a slight curl). Add. MS 11639, MV2 and Add. MS 27167 omit.

30 *Ben Mesheq* is clear there is only one but for him it is the last one, bringing י״א יו״ד בתרא מהצילני (11. the last *yod* from 'deliver me'). T-S Misc. 24.182 brings הצילני decorating both letters *yod* and supporting K. The scan of Q651–652 is difficult to read, but may also be bringing both, הצילני, supporting K. Parma 2427, Parma 1959, Add. MS 11639, Add. MS 27167 and *Qiryat Sefer* all omit.

31 Basser makes no reference to the fact that ST also brings this instance in the incorrect order (op. cit., p. 90).

Line 17: קדמֹ • [17]**קטנתי** • [18]**כאיבי**[ם] • [חילם • בי{ו}שב הארץ • מתי מספר • את הימ{י}ם]

... **the first** [*yod*]' (Gen. 32:12). 17. **'I am not worthy'**[32] (Gen. 32:11). 18. **'in pain'** (Gen. 34:25). ['their wealth' (Gen. 34:29). 'amongst the inhabitants of the land' (Gen. 34:30). 'few in number' (Gen. 34:30). 'hot springs' (Gen. 36:24).]

17. **P**, **MV** and **H** agree and though **ST** is very faded, appears to read קט[נתי].[33] **K** extends to קטנתי מכל.

MV and **ST** (though faded) then bring an instance that is out of sequence, listing חילם ('their wealth') from Gen. 34:29, even though this is four verses earlier. **K** brings an additional entry linked to instance 18, but clearly meant it to have a decorated *yod* of its own, listing בהיותם ('when they were') from Gen. 34:29.[34]

18. **P**, **MV**, and **H** bring כאבים agreeing with 𝔐. Our fragment is *ma-le' yod*. As we have seen **K** brings בהיותם כאבים ('when they were in pain') as two linked instances. **ST** is not visible, and the Shem Tov *Tanakh* for this verse is not extant.

P and **H** then bring חילם from Gen. 34:29 which **MV** and **ST** had bought earlier, out of sequence. **K** instead brings [ ]באו על החלי which presumably is intended to be באו על החללים ('came upon the slain') from Gen. 34:27, but does not indicate the *yod* and the word is missing a *lamed*. It is likely that **ST** brings this as well, for though faded, it reads החללים. It is possible that חילם may have become חלים in K's *Vorlage*, and he assumed Gen. 34:27 instead of verse 29. Basser notes that although **ST** also brings החללים, he also suspects there is an error here, because of the confusion between the two similar words.[35]

Following on, **P** and **H** bring ביושב הארץ from Gen. 34:30. **MV** brings just ביושב though both letters *bet* resemble letters *kaf*. **K** is *ḥaser vav* according with 𝔐 and extends to

---

32 In the sense of being small and diminished, of no importance.

33 On קטנתי in Gen. 32:11, the *Ba'al ha-Ṭurim* explains that 'the *yod* is bent—for even though I [Jacob] have been blessed with ten blessings, I am afraid that perhaps my sins will cause me [to lose those blessings]'.

34 No secondary sources support this additional instance brought by **K**.

35 Basser op. cit., p. 90. Turning to our secondary sources, Q651–652 is clear that it is חילם. Also listed is החללים דאת כל, but this is because of the decorated letters *lamed*. Parma 2427 does similar though marks only one *lamed* על החללים but omits חילם. *Qiryat Sefer* agrees with **K** and perhaps **ST** and brings החללים היו״ד מוזרקת ('the slain' the *yod* is curled). **MV2** lists באו על החללים but decorates none of the letters. **T-S Misc. 24.182**, Add. MS 11639, Parma 1959, Add. MS 27167 and *Ben Mesheq* omit either possibility.

להבאישני בישב הארץ ('make me odious amongst the inhabitants of the land'). ST is not visible and, unfortunately, the Shem Tov *Tanakh* is not extant.

P, MV and H all bring מתי מספר from the same verse Gen. 34:30. K extends to אני מתי֯ מספר ('I, being few in number'). ST is not visible and again the Shem Tov *Tanakh* is not extant.

P and H bring את הימים *ma-le'yod*, but 𝔐 in Gen. 36:24 is את הימם, as we see brought in MV. Only את remains legible in ST and, unfortunately, the Shem Tov *Tanakh* is not extant, but the instance is likely the same. The scribe of K departs from his normal practice and adds [incorrect] pointing, bringing הַיַּמִם before the damaged end of the line, possibly because the pointing is quite a rare form, הַיֵּמִם. I would be inclined to think that our scribe has most likely followed 𝔐, as space is crowded and adding the additional *vav* and *yod* into the instances pushes the line even further into the margin, but I have added them in grey.

Line 18: [19]בת מי֯ זהב • [20]מגורי֯ • [וי֯קרע • וי֯קמו • לפוטי֯פר {ד{ו}המדינים} • [21]{וי֯ט]
19. **'the daughter of Mey-Zahav'**[36] (Gen. 36:39). (*Parashat Va-yeshev*) 20. **'sojournings'** (Gen. 37:1). ['and he rent' (Gen. 37:34). 'and they arose' (Gen. 37:35). 'to Potiphar' of [the verse beginning 'the Midianites' (Gen. 37:36). {'and he turned ...}]

19. P, MV and H give just מי זהב. Our manuscript adds בת ('daughter'). K may have similarly added, but the section on the previous line is not extant. ST is not visible and the Shem Tov *Tanakh* is not extant.
20. P, MV (though with a short *vav* so it resembles מגירי) and H agree. K extends this to בארץ מגורי ('in the land of the sojournings of [his father]'). ST is not visible and the Shem Tov *Tanakh* is not extant.[37]

Out of sequence in the listing and damaged, T-S Misc. 24.182 appears to bring another instance [ח]למתי֯ו (for his dreams) from Gen. 37:8, but this is not present in any other source.

According to Basser,[38] ST then brings an instance that is not in any of the other core sources or indeed any of our secondary ones. This is אנכי מבקש ('I seek') from Gen. 37:16,

36 Lit. 'water of gold'.

37 On Gen 37:1, the *Ba'al ha-Ṭurim* remarks that 'the *yod* is bent like a *kaf* for he [Jacob] said 'just as Esau merited all this honour—because of honouring [our father], even though my father blessed me with ten blessings, I had to send ten [different] things, as it is written, 'two hundred she-goats ... etc. [ten types of animals are listed in Gen. 32:15–16]'—I will therefore go and bend myself and honour my father in Hebron''.

38 Basser, op. cit., p. 91.

but this is not visible in the available images, nor is this extant in the Shem Tov *Tanakh*. Indeed, ST is no longer visible for quite some considerable part of this marginal column, even in the enhanced imagery.

P, MV and H all bring ויקרע from Gen. 37:34. K, however, omits this instance. ST is not visible and the Shem Tov *Tanakh* is not extant.

P, MV and H all then bring ויקמו from Gen. 37:35. K extends to ויקמו כל בניו ('and all his brothers arose'). ST is still not visible and the Shem Tov *Tanakh* is not extant.

P and MV then bring לפוטיפר. Basser claims that ST then brings לפוטיפר דהמדינים ('to Potiphar' of [the verse beginning] 'the Midianites'). So this is Gen. 37:36, which, according to 𝔐, begins והמדינים, but again this is not visible and the Shem Tov *Tanakh* is not extant.[39] Unfortunately, K is damaged, but it looks like a part of the *samekh* of the next word סריס is present. H omits. Given the short length of the line if we follow P and MV, it is likely our CG scribe also clarified the instance by extending.

21. This next instance is problematic. Our scribe has brought only אליה at the start of the next line and in this may agree with MV which also brings just אליה. P and H bring אליה לשכב from Gen. 39:10. ST is not visible, however, Shem Tov decorates אליה in his *Tanakh* in this verse i.e. Gen. 39:10, thus supporting this reading. Either way, the assumption is that the *yod* is in that word. K differs, decorating a word in close proximity to another אליה, bringing instead ויט אליה אל הדרך ('and he turned towards her along the way') from Gen. 38:16. We do not know if our scribe added ויט on this line. There is some space. If he did, we certainly cannot say which *yod* he decorated, as the area is heavily stained. Magnifying this a great deal, it is still difficult to say whether there is a line on the *yod* of אליה, but I would say not, in which case he may have supported the reading in K.[40] Thematically we have seen two previous instances where the word ויט has been decorated, but this was with regard to the letter *ṭet*.[41]

---

39 Basser, op. cit., p. 91.

40 My wife, Avielah Barclay-Michaels, is a tetrachromat able to perceive many more colours than the average person, and she also feels that there is no indicating line present on the the *yod* of אליה. Turning to our secondary sources, K also gains some support from Q651–652 which brings ויט and Add. MS 11639 which brings ויט אליה and also *Qiryat Sefer* which brings ויט אליה היוד״ין מוזרקות ('and he turned towards her' [both letters] *yod* are curled). MV2 lists ויט אליה but does not decorate the letters. T-S Misc. 24.182 does, however, bring just אליה with a decorated *yod*. Parma 2427 Parma 1959, Add. MS 27167 and *Ben Mesheq* bring neither option.

41 See the listing above.

Line 19: **אליה • [22]להיות עמה** • [שריגם • השרגים • וישחכהו • {והנה עיניכם} •] ...} **towards her'** (Gen. 39:10 {or Gen. 38:16}). 22. **'to be with her'** (Gen. 39:10). ['branches' (Gen, 40:10), 'the branches' (Gen. 40:12). 'but forgot him' (Gen. 40:23). (*Parashat Va-yiggash*) 'your eyes' (Gen. 45:12).]

22. P, MV and H agree as 𝔐. K extends to לשכב אצלה ולהיות עמה ('to lie beside her and be with her') bringing a superfluous *vav* at the start of the key word להיות. ST is not visible, though Shem Tov decorates להיות in his *Tanakh* in this verse, thus supporting this reading.

P and H have a metathesis, bringing שרגים, MV is *ma-le' yod*, bringing שריגים The reading from Gen. 40:10 in 𝔐 is שריגם. ST is not visible, so we do not know what spelling was brought in the listing, though Shem Tov decorates שריגם in his *Tanakh* in this verse. K is not extant, but presumably this is present in the damaged area.

P, MV and H all then bring השרגים from Gen. 40:12. K appears to spell the key word incorrectly bringing השריגם. ST is not visible, though Shem Tov decorates השרגים in his *Tanakh* in this verse, thus supporting this reading.

K then brings a related instance that is not in any other core witness. Having referenced the three branches of the cupbearer's vine, it then adds שלשת הסלים ('the three baskets') of the baker's dream from Gen. 40:18. It is a shame our fragment is not extant at this point, as this extra instance displays a certain symmetry, and it would have been valuable to see what our scribe brought. Given available space, however, it is likely that he omitted this.[42]

Instead, P, MV, ST and H all bring וישחכהו from Gen. 40:23, which K also brings this after the extra entry noted above.

P and H then bring ועיניכם, but this word does not appear in Genesis, as it appears to have a superfluous *yod*. MV brings instead ועינכם ('and do not regard') from Gen. 45:20, but this should be listed after the instance that appears first on line 20 and MV lists it prior. This would mean these three are listing out of sequence. ST is not visible, however, in his *Tanakh* Shem Tov does not decorate either *yod* in והנה עיניכם in Gen. 45:12, though he does decorate ועינכם from Gen. 45:20 thus supporting MV. K brings instead והנה עיני[כם] ('and behold your eyes') from Gen. 45:12 indicating both letters *yod*. This would indeed occur before פי המדבר in the same verse and removing the *vav*

42 Shem Tov does not decorate הסלים in his *Tanakh*. From our secondary sources, K's reading is supported by by Add. MS 11639 who brings שלשת הסלים ('the three baskets'). Q651–652 does bring שלשת הסלים but decorates the *samekh*. *Ben Mesheq* also references the *samekh*, י"ח סמ"ך מן הסלים (18. *samekh* from 'the baskets'). MV2 lists שלשת הסלים but does not decorate any letters. It is possible that K has confused this with the *yod*. **T-S Misc. 24.182**, Parma 2427, Parma 1959, Add. MS 27167 and *Qiryat Sefer* make no reference to this.

from P and H would give us this. It is possible that the *vav* from והנה has been attached to the word and הנה omitted.[43] However, if one was to follow **K**, and both letters *yod* were originally intended, there might have been a reference such as תרוויהון (both of them) in the other sources, which is not the case. Given that the secondary sources mostly bring both, it is indeed unfortunate that we do not know what our scribe brought in this space. Whilst I do not normally support the minority reading, I am inclined towards **K**, given it is in sequence and given the extra *yod* in **P** and **H**, so have added this to our reconstruction here. This is a difficult area and investigations into the sources have so far proven inconclusive. Nonetheless, it seems that our fragment still only brings one of the possible two instances, unless it follows פי המדבר, but then one would have thought the addition of ישבו בארץ in superscript would have been placed elsewhere, since it is after Gen. 45:20.

It should also be noted that our *Genizah* secondary source, **T-S Misc. 24.182**, brings another suggested instance for this section ויהי בבקר ('and it was in the morning') from Gen. 41:8 in *parashat Miqqets* but this finds no support elsewhere.[44]

Line 20: [23]פי המד[בר] [24]ישבו בארץ • [{ועינכם} • אשר נתן לי • ויגש אתם • פן ירבה • יענו אתו • העבריות תנינא •]

23. **'mouth of the desert'** (Gen 45:12). [{'and your eyes'} (Gen. 45:20)] **'dwell in the land'** (Gen. 47:6). (*Parashat Va-yeḥi*) ['whom [God] has given me' (Gen 48:9). 'and brought them' (Gen. 48:10). (*Parashat Shemot*) 'lest they multiply' (Ex. 1:10). 'they afflicted them' (Ex. 1:12). **the second 'the Hebrew women'** (Ex. 1:16).

---

43 Turning to our secondary sources, Add. MS 11639 partly supports **K**, bringing והנה עינכם from Gen. 45:12 with the first *yod* decorated only, but also follows up with ועינכם אל ('and your eyes do not') from Gen. 45:20. Parma 2427 brings עיניכם ראות ('your eyes see') also partly supporting **K** also decorating the first *yod*, but similarly also brings ועינכם אל תחס ('and your eyes should not regard'). Q651–652 also brings עיניכם ראות and whilst the scan is blurred the decoration appears to be only on the second *yod* instead and then brings ועינכם אל תחוס *ma-le' vav* on the last word. *Qiryat Sefer* gives עיניכם ביו׳ד הרבים והיו׳ד הראשונה מוזרקת ראות חסר ('your eyes' with an extra *yod* and the first *yod* is curled, 'see' is *ḥaser*) and then later brings ועינכם היו״ד מוזרקת תחס חסר ('and your eyes' the *yod* is curled, 'regard' is *ḥaser*). *Ben Mesheq*, however, brings only one ך׳ יוד מעינכם (20. *yod* from 'and your eyes'). Four secondary sources have both, and in the right sequence, though **T-S Misc. 24.182** brings only one, עינכם with the first *yod* decorated. Parma 1959, **MV2** and Add. MS 27617 omit reference to either option. Interestingly, **MV** appears to continue the listing with לישמאלים ('to the Ishmaelites') but this is in fact the listing for the letter *lamed*, since the large letter showing this has been omitted.

44 This is likely an error, since this is generally listed only as the *he* in the word ויהי in the core and secondary sources.

23. **P**, **MV**, **ST** and **H** agree, bringing פי המדבר. Uncharacteristically, **K** shortens and brings only פ̊י.[45]
24. **P**, **ST and H** agree, bringing ישבו בארץ. **MV** has extended to ישבו בארץ גשן ('dwell in the land of Goshen'). Indeed, our scribe has omitted this initially but it has been added in afterwards above the line. **K** differs, bringing instead the same word but in an earlier verse ועתה י̊שבו נא עבדיך ('and now, please let your servants dwell') from Gen 47:4.[46]

Unlike many of the lines where we have had additional space, here we just have far too many entries competing for the available space. As we saw above, we may have וע̊ינכם from Gen. 45:20, though I'm less inclined to support its inclusion.

Reconstructing the rest of the line, **P**, **MV**, **ST** and **H** all bring אשר נתן לי from Gen. 48:9 and **K** extends אשר נתן ל̊י אלהים בז[ה] ('whom God has given me here').

P then reads וישג אתם which is a metathesis. This is clearly incorrect as **MV**, **ST** and **H** all give correctly ויגש אתם from Gen. 48:10. **K** is damaged, but most likely gives [ו̊יגש] אתם אליו ('and he brought them near to him'). Thus I have corrected the word in the reconstruction to accord with this, as our scribe most likely recorded it correctly.

P, **MV**, **ST** and **H** then bring פן ירבה from Ex. 1:10. **K** extends to פן י̊רבה והיה כ̊י ('lest they multiply and it come to pass that') and in doing so, adds a further instance which no other core witness brings.[47]

45 Though a few secondary sources also bring shortened versions. **T-S Misc. 24.182**, Parma 2427 and Q651–652 bring כי פ̊י ('for the mouth'). *Qiryat Sefer* brings פי היו״ד מוזרקת ('mouth' the *yod* is curled) and *Ben Mesheq* gives י״ב יוד מפי (12. *yod* from 'mouth'). Add. MS 11639, Parma 1959, Add. MS 27167 and **MV2** all omit.

46 Turning to our secondary sources, Parma 2427 brings ישבו בארץ גשן as **MV**. Q651–652 brings במי̊טב הארץ ישבו ('in the best of the land ... dwell') so by positioning also implies Gen. 47:6. *Qiryat Sefer* also brings ישבו מוזרקת היו״ד ('dwell' the *yod* is curled) and by its position it is also Gen. 47:6. **T-S Misc. 24.182**, Parma 1959, Add. MS 27167, **MV2** and *Ben Mesheq* omit. **K** does not seem to enjoy any support amongst the secondary sources. It should also be noted that prior to this, Q651–652 brings אחר̊י ראות̊י ('since I have seen') from Gen. 46:30 and this latter additional instance is echoed by Add. MS 11639 bringing ראות̊י though *Qiryat Sefer* states אחרי הרי״ש מוזרקת ראותי מלא והרי״ש מוזרקת אמרי ('since' the *resh* is curled, 'I have seen' is *ma-le'* and the *resh* is curled) and *Ben Mesheq* notes רי״ש דראותי (the *resh* of 'I have seen') that is decorated, so perhaps this is where confusion may have arisen.

47 From our secondary sources, Q651–652 brings פן י̊רבה only. **T-S Misc. 24.182** brings just י̊רבה. *Qiryat Sefer* notes that ירבה היו״ד מוזרקת למעלה ולמטה ('multiply' the *yod* is curled above and below). **MV2** lists פן ירבה without a decorated letter. Parma 2427, Parma 1959, Add. MS 27167 and Add. MS 11639 all omit. *Ben Mesheq* also omits, though does bring a number of other letters *yod* that it states should be decorated that do not appear elsewhere. **K**'s second instance enjoys no other support from our secondary sources.

P, MV, ST and H then all bring יענו אותו from Ex. 1:12. However, all are *ma-le'vav* when 𝔐 is יענו אתו which only K echoes, also extending to וכאשר י֯ענו אתו ('and when they [the Egyptians] afflicted them [Israel]').

Given the next line begins with the instance from Ex. 2:10, based on the impressions remaining of the damaged letters and the sequence, we would also need to fit onto this line the instance העבריות תנינא from Ex. 1:16,[48] which is brought by P, MV ST, H and K (who abbreviates to תני֯), but there just does not appear to be enough space to do so. So it is possible that something has been omitted or possibly written in superscript, as we have seen already in this line.

T-S Misc. 24.182 brings another instance הי֯ליכי 'take away' from Ex. 2:9, not seen decorated in other sources.[49]

Line 21: 25מש[י֯תהו] • [אין בי֯ת • להי֯{ו}ת עד • ואי֯בתי֯ • והס{י}ר{ו}תי֯ • {מושב{ו}תי֯כם
דוכל דם} • בקרבי֯ •]

25. **'I drew him'** (Ex. 2:10). (*Parashat Bo'*) ['there was no house' (Ex. 12:30). (*Parashat Mishpaṭim*) 'to be a witness' (Ex. 23:1). 'I will hate' (Ex. 23:22). 'I will take away' (Ex. 23:25). (*Parashat Tsav*) 'in all your dwellings' of [the verse beginning] 'and all blood' (Lev. 7:26) 'near to me' (Lev. 10:3).]

25. Our fragment has only two letters surviving on this line but they begin the instance brought by **P, MV, H** and **K** from Ex. 2:10. **ST** is not visible, though Shem Tov decorates משי֯תהו in his *Tanakh* in this verse, thus supporting this reading.

In terms of the reconstruction of the rest of the line, P and H bring אין בית from Ex. 12:30. However, each word contains a *yod*. ST is faint, but also gives [א]ין בי֯ת and Shem Tov's *Tanakh* only gives the *yod* in בי֯ת, thus further supporting that positioning of the embellishment. K extends the instance, giving three possible letters *yod* כי אין בי֯ת אשר ('for there was no house which') but also only marks the one. MV omits.

P, MV and H then bring להיות עד from Ex. 23:1. The enhanced imagery reveals ST brings להי֯ת עד, *ḥaser vav*, as 𝔐. K also brings להי֯ת *ḥaser vav* and it is likely that עד followed, but that part of the fragment is not extant.

P, MV and H then brings ואיבתי from Ex. 23:22. However, again, it is not clear which *yod* in the word is to be decorated. ST is not visible, but Shem Tov's *Tanakh* (though

48 Which in this second instance is *ma-le' vav* as opposed to the previous verse where the word is *ḥaser*.

49 Parma 2427 lists the word, but brings no decoration.

difficult to read) only decorates the first *yod*. K brings ואיבתי את איביך ('and I will hate your enemies') and of the four letters *yod* available decorates two from the first word.[50]

P and H then brings והסרתי from Ex. 23:25 as 𝔐. MV is *ma-le' vav* והסרותי. K brings והסירתי מחלה ('I will take sickness away') *ma-le' yod* and decorates the last *yod* which is fortunate given 𝔐 only has that *yod*.[51]

We then have some level of disagreement. P reads incorrectly מושבותיכם • ואכל דם • as if it were two instances, but of course there is no letter *yod* in the second. H brings מושבותיכם דאכל דם, however, there is no phrase אכל דם in either Exodus or Leviticus. K is doubly *ḥaser vav* and extends the phrase to וכל דם לא ת[אכלו] בכל משבתיכם ('and you will not eat any blood in any of your dwellings') situating the instance firmly as Lev. 7:26[52] where 𝔐 is מושבתיכם. So it is likely that P should have joined the two instances and H has substituted an *'alef* for a *vav* and it should read מושבותיכם דוכל דם. MV omits and ST is not visible, and this is not brought in Shem Tov's *Tanakh*, possibly because of this confusion. It is a shame our fragment is not extant as this would have helped clarify.[53] That said, based on the entries where there is general agreement there would simply not be enough space in the line for this particular instance, and given this confusion it is a likely candidate for omission or perhaps insertion in small characters having been originally missed.

Finally, P and H bring בקרובי *ma-le' vav* in from Lev. 10:3. MV brings as 𝔐, בקרבי, and ST, though very faint in the enhanced imagery extends to בקרבי [א]קד[ש] as does K, בקרבי אקדש ('through those near to me I will be sanctified').

We now switch to the left side of **T-S AS 139.144-B**, where the fragment continues with the listing for *yod*.

---

50 From our secondary sources, **T-S Misc. 24.182** and Q651–652 decorate both letters *yod* ואיבתי supporting K. *Qiryat Sefer* also seems to support K, bringing [וא]יביתי היודי"ן דפתיות ומזרקות ('and I will hate' the [letters] *yod* are open and curled). Parma 2427 and Add. MS 11639 bring the decoration only on the first *yod* ואיבתי. **MV2** lists ואיבתי but decorates neither letter *yod*. Parma 1959 and *Ben Mesheq* omit.

51 From our secondary sources, **T-S Misc. 24.182** brings only one decorated letter, the second, as the word is written *ḥaser yod* והסרתי. Q651–652 decorates two letters *yod* והסירתי מחלה, even though 𝔐 has only the last *yod*. Parma 2427 does list והסירתי מחלה *ma-le' yod* but decorates neither letter. Similarly Add. MS 11639 brings והסרתי with no obvious decoration. Parma 1959 omits. *Ben Mesheq* brings ה"א דוהסרתי (the *he* of 'I will take away') and *Qiryat Sefer* notes the word, but only to remark it is *ḥaser*.

52 Though it is worth noting that ואכל דם and מושבותיכם also appear in close proximity, but not in the right sequence, in Lev. 3:17.

53 From our secondary sources, Parma 2427 does list the word מושבתיכם but does not indicate a letter to decorate. *Qiryat Sefer* also mentions the word, but only in relation to other letters. Q651–652, Parma 1959, Add. MS 11639, **MV2** and *Ben Mesheq* omit any reference. **T-S Misc. 24.182** is not extant for this instance onwards.

T-S AS 139.144-B (left side)—5 lines preserved

Line 22: [26]פני֯מה • [27]נזרי֯ה • [28]לצ]מי֯ת{ו}ת בת • ונפלה י֯רכה • כפי֯ נדרו • [29]מצאתי֯[
(*Parashat Shemini*) 26. **'within'** (Lev. 10:18) (*Parashat Be-har*) 27. **'undressed vines'** (Lev. 25:11) 28. [the last] **'in perpetuity'** (Lev. 25:23). [(*Parashat Naso'*) 'and her thigh will fall away' (Num 5:27). 'according to his vow' (Num. 6:21). 29. (*Parashat Be-ha'alotekha*) 'I have found …]

26. P, MV and H agree. ST is very faint, bringing, פ[ני֯מ]ה. K extends to אל הקדש פני֯[מה] ('into the Sanctuary within').

MV only then brings מושבותיכם לדורתיכם דיין, which may be a misplaced reference back to the מושבותיכם that we saw in the earlier line which MV omitted, but is likely a misordering with this instance actually belonging to the entry on *mem sofit* that follows (see that section below).

27. Our fragment is very damaged, which is unfortunate, as this next instance sees some disagreement. P appears to read טירך, but this is partly because the two first letters have joined together and it is likely נזירך. H reads נזירך ('your undressed vine') which is either a transcription error from his *Vorlage*, or could be instead a reference to its occurrence in Lev. 25:5.[54] MV also gives נזירך, but in the listing for the letter *zayin* in *parashat Be-har*. ST is not visible and this is not decorated in the Shem Tov *Tanakh*. It thus falls is K who, despite an initial error, corrects and clarifies the instance bringing תבצרו את ~~נייר~~ נזרי֯ה ('[do not] gather [grapes] from its undressed vines') from Lev. 25:11. It is difficult to know if our fragment has spelt the word correctly, but it certainly seems that this is the intention of the instance here, supporting K and reflecting some of the secondary sources that also bring this.[55] However, Shem Tov does not decorate נזריה either, in his *Tanakh*.
28. Our fragment only has a couple of letters that appear to be לצ, but P likely agrees bringing לצמיתות בת. H brings the fuller לצמיתות בתרא. MV does bring לצמיתות בתראה, but this is shown under the listing for *lamed*. All

---

54 Duly transcribed as נזירך in EPST.

55 Slightly difficult to spot as the *nun* resembles a *bet*, but Q651–652 brings נזי֯ריה with the first *yod* decorated when there is not one in 𝔐. Parma 2427 lists נזריה, but does not decorate any letter. *Qiryat Sefer* brings both options, but only in relation as to where one should place the *yod* and not with regard to decoration. Parma 1959, Add. MS 11639, MV2 and *Ben Mesheq* omit.

these sources are *ma-le' vav* but 𝔐 is *ḥaser vav*, לצמיתת. The qualifier 'last' as well as the presence of a *yod* means that this is referring to Lev. 25:36 as opposed to Lev. 25:23 where it is also *ḥaser yod* לצמתת. That said, **K** appears to bring לצמ̊יתית בתו̇ר, which does have a second *yod* in error, but still decorates the first. **ST** is not visible and Shem Tov's *Tanakh* omits this instance completely.[56]

Reconstructing the rest of the line, we see **P** and **H** brings ונפלה ירכה from Num. 5:27, as mentioned above. **ST** also likely brings ונפלה י̊ר[כה] and Shem Tov decorates י̊רכה in his *Tanakh*, thus supporting this reading. **K** also likely brings the same ונפלה י̊[רכה], but the key word is not extant. **MV** brings just ירכה.

P and **MV** then bring כפי נדרו from Num. 6:21. **K** only has נדרו extant, but presumably the previous word was present at the end of the previous line. The scribe of **H** perhaps copies his *Vorlage* incorrectly as כפי נזרו confusing the *dalet* form with a *zayin*.[57] **ST** is not visible, though Shem Tov decorates כפ̊י in his *Tanakh*, thus supporting this reading.

29. The line likely ends with מצאתי ('I have found') given the next line begins חן as **P** and **MV**. **H** appears to bring מצאתיהן in error, joining the two words and changing the *ḥet* to a *he*.[58] **K** extends to הרגני נא הרוג ואם מצאתי חן, which is not quite accurate, since 𝔐 reads הרגני נא הרג אם מצאת̊י חן ('kill me, I pray, out of hand, if I have found favour'). **ST** is not visible and the Shem Tov *Tanakh* omits this instance; possibly he saw something similar to **H** and rejected it. Additionally, some secondary sources bring an alternative possibility, the מצתי חן in Num 11:11 instead. The presence of the *'alef* in the word, in our core sources, may be significant.[59]

---

56 As a result, Basser rejects it from his listing, (arguably incorrectly), though noting its existence in a footnote (op. cit., p. 92). Turning to our secondary sources, Q651–652 lists לצמיתת, but does not seem to decorate the *yod*. Parma 2427 brings לצמתת, omitting the letter *yod* entirely. **MV2**, Add. MS 11639, Parma 1959, *Qiryat Sefer* and *Ben Mesheq* omit.

57 Duly transcribed as כפי נזרו in EPST.

58 Transcribed as מצאתיהן in EPST.

59 Again, as a result, Basser rejects it from his listing (arguably incorrectly), though noting its existence in a footnote (op. cit., p. 92). Turning to our secondary sources, only *Qiryat Sefer* supports our core sources, bringing הרג חסר מצאתי היו״ד מעגלת ('killed' is *ḥaser*, 'I have found' the *yod* is curled), which from the positioning is Num. 11:15. Parma 2427 lists מצתי without the *'alef* and, by its positioning, is suggesting Num. 11:11 instead. **MV2** lists ולמה לא מצאתי חן ('and why have I not found favour') also from Num. 11:11 and Add. MS 11639 brings even fuller ולמה לא מצאתי חן בעיניך ('and why have I not found favour in your eyes'). However, none of these three decorate the *yod* and two have the *'alef* in מצאתי. Q651–652 and Parma 1959 omit.

Line 23: חן • [30]עמוד עמדי̊ • [31]מי̊סרך • [{אשר לא} י̊שא פנים • {{ו}לא} י̊דבק • בי̊דך •]
… favour' (Num. 11:15). (*Parashat Va-'ethạnan*) 30. **'stand by Me'** (Deut. 5:28). (*Parashat 'Eqev*) 31. **'chastises you'** (Deut. 8:5). ['{who does not} favour persons' (Deut. 10:17). (*Parashat Re'eh*) '{will not} cleave' (Deut. 13:18). 'in your hand' (Deut. 13:18).]

30. P and H and our fragment all bring עמוד *ma-le' vav* and only **MV** brings instead עמד, matching 𝔐 which is *ḥaser vav*. **ST**, though partly faded, does bring עמדי̊. Unfortunately, **K** only has the two words that precede this phrase ואתה פה ('but as for you here') extant and we cannot see the orthography of the next word or the actual decorated word that follows, but the instance intended is clearly the same.
31. P and H agree as 𝔐. **MV** brings מיסרך *ma-le' vav*. **K** extends to ייי אלהיך מי̊סרך ('The Lord, your God chastises you'). **ST** is very faded, but the ך of the word does seem to be present and, unfortunately, the Shem Tov *Tanakh* is not extant.[60]

P, MV and H then bring ישא פנים from Deut. 10:17. K extends to אשר לא י̊שא פנים ('who favours no persons'). ST is very faint, but suggests י̊ש[א] and the next line may have פנים. Shem Tov decorates י̊שא in his *Tanakh*, supporting this reading.

The list continues with ידבק, according to P, MV and H and ST (though faint) from Deut. 13:18. K brings לא י̊דב[ק]. However, 𝔐 is actually ולא ידבק.

Finally on this line P, MV, H and ST (though faint) bring בידך that follows on in the same verse Deut. 13:18. K is not extant. Contrary to issues seen above, where there was not enough space to put all of the likely instances in, here we have the opposite where the instances from the core sources would simply not fill the line before the next line down. It is possible that our scribe has expanded the references beyond the single words, similar to K, possibly bringing the word לא on a couple of them as he does below with instance 32 since they describe the instance better and there is a slight faded line that might be the remains of a *lamed* of לא and not the *yod* of ישא.

Line 24: [32]לא י̊חדל • [33]לא תשי̊ג [//// דתלתא זיוני חמשין ותמניא באור̇]
32. **'will never cease'** (Deut. 15:11). 33. **'you will not remove'** (Deut. 19:14). [//// [*Kaf*] with three *zayin* type decorations, fifty eight in the *Torah*]

32. P, MV and H bring just יחדל. ST, though faded, does bring י̊חדל. K expands further to כי לא י̊חדל אביון ('for the poor will never cease'). Basser

60 Commenting on the word in Deut 5:8 the *Ba'al ha-Ṭurim* notes that 'the *yod* is bent [as if God is telling Moses] that you will stand in awe before Me—bent over'.

notes[61] that **ST** adds an additional instance decorating the *yod* of אביון from the same verse (Deut. 15:11) and the images, though very faded, do seem to support this. However, no other core source agrees and **K** has specifically not added a decoration on that *yod* even though it lists the word.[62]

33. **P**, **MV**, **H** and **K** agree. **ST**, though very faded, also brings לא תשיג. The enhanced imagery suggests that ST then adds כֹּא, though it is not clear what this represents.

This concludes the listing for *yod*—the extant parts of our manuscript likely supplying 33 of the 83 listed and these are in general agreement with the primary sources, though occasionally adds additional contextual words to further clarify the instance meant and this is particularly important for נזריה. Summing all of the instances where we have general agreement from multiple sources, and not just one source bringing an additional instance, does indeed gives us 83 if עיניכם from Gen. 45:12 has only the one decorated *yod*, but 84, if there are two.

5 Description and Example Forms of the Special Letter *Kaf*

We now move to *kaf*, however, the description for the letter form and number of instances is missing. The gap we do have is quite large, but the smaller words שער כ (gate of *kaf*), as we have seen previously for other letters, do not appear to have been added in that space, unless they are closer to the start of the entries for *kaf* and not centred in the space. Given the spacing available, it is likely that our scribe wrote the numbers in full, as he did with the *yod*, rather than the numerals used in other sources. **ST** moves to the right hand margin for the listing of *kaf*.

One of the main issues we encounter is the number of instances that are listed regarding the letter *kaf*. Unfortunately, our fragment is not able to add to the debate. **P** brings כ נה דג זיוני באורייתא (*kaf*—55 that have 3 *zayin* type decorations

61 Basser, op. cit., p. 92.

62 Turning to our secondary sources, Parma 2427 brings only יחדל. *Qiryat Sefer* brings יחדל היו״ד דפתית ('will cease' the *yod* that is broken) and though Basser claims he brings אביון too, in support of **ST**, this is not listed, (op. cit., p. 269). *Ben Mesheq* brings two instances י״א ב׳ יודי״ן מכי יחדל (11. two letters *yod* from 'for there will not cease'). **MV2** lists כי לא יחדל but decorates not letter in the phrase. Q651–652, Add. MS 11639, and Parma 1959 omit either option. **ST**'s proposed additional instance enjoys no support amongst core or our secondary sources, though Basser does include אביון too, in support of **ST**, pushing his list to 84 (op. cit., p. 92).

in the *Torah*). **MV** states דג׳ זיוני but does not bring a number of instances, as usual. **H** brings the same information in a slight re-order כ נ׳ה באורייתא דג׳ זייניין (*kaf*—55 in the *Torah* that have 3 *zayin* type decorations).[63] The complication is brought by **ST**, which in the introduction and also in **BH** brings כ דאית לה תלתא זיוני חמשין ותמניא באורייתא (*kaf*—that it has three *zayin* type decorations, fifty-eight in the *Torah*). Though very faded, **ST** also brings כ דתלתא זינין נ̇ח̇ באוריתא in the actual listing itself. This is likely because ח and ה are similar looking letters, and may have been confused at some point. Sadly with the damage to the our fragment, we cannot get to an accurate count to see which might be correct. Fortunately, we do have **K** which has clearly encountered a similar confusion, this time between כ and נ which can be also mistaken for each other, and as such this scribe wrote כ ~~כ̇ח̇~~ נ̇ח̇ (kaf—~~28~~ 58). K's scribe is very clear there are 58 instances having seemingly deliberately corrected subsequently.

The printed Maḥzor Vitry (*LMV*) *places two* tagin *above and one centred below, but this does not quite tie up with the actual manuscript it was transcribed from* (*right*).

In his rendition of the form in T-S NS 287.11-F (right), *our scribe brings only two* tagin *with a dot above in the centre. Given previous usage, this might suggest our scribe is unsure of the position of the third* tag. As *we see below from other forms given by the other sources there is some considerable disagreement as to the placing of this third* tag *as scribes do not like placing it hanging from the roof as it could resemble a* pe, *which could invalidate the letter form.*

T-S **Misc. 24.182** (*right*) *brings the form with two* tagin *on the roof and one extremely long* tag *descending from the underside of the roof on the left side. This is very thick and pronounced making the letter almost resemble a* mem. *However, it also brings a form that has a fourth* tag *below. Perhaps one of the more extreme forms against those seen below.*

With the exception of a few instances at the very start, the available images for **ST** for this particular section concerning *kaf* are very very faint, comprising a thin column of words that have been written in the right hand margin of the folio. Where I could, I have pieced together a few additional instances by magnifying the images, assessing where the instances would likely fall, and matching that to surviving letters.

63 However, because of this, **EPST** has an incorrect transcription with נ shown as a כ and so states there are twenty-five and not fifty-five. It does, however, list the fifty-six from H; another pointer to 58 being the more likely number.

TABLE 11 Forms for the special letter *kaf*. Some have three *tagin* above but some have two *tagin* above and one descending from the roof on the left side. However, as noted, since this can make the letter resemble a *pe*, we see scribes often only having two *tagin* on the form—avoiding the third. P brings one form with four. Some place the third *tag* on the bottom in various positions to avoid the problem, for example **MV**, **MV2** and Vat ebr. 1.

Maḥzor Vitry
Parma 2574 (**P**)

Maḥzor Vitry
Add. MS 27201 (**MV**)

Shem Tov *Tanakh*
Sefer Tagi (**ST**)

Badey ha-ʾAron
Heb. 840 (**BH**)

Sefer Tagin
Heb. 837 (**H**)

Nr. 5667 (**K**)

Parma 2427

Parma 1959

Q651–652

MS Geunz. 481

Maḥzor Vitry
Add. MS 27201 (**MV2**)

Add. MS 11639

Add. MS 26167

Bologna *Torah*

Vat. ebr. 1

Or. 1463

Alexander *Torah*

6 Listing of Instances for the Special Letter *Kaf*

Line 25: **ויכל אלהים • מלאכתו בת̊**[1] • [2] [זכ̊ר ונקבה • {ויזכ̊ר אלהים את רחל} •]
(*Parashat Bere'shit*) **'and God completed'** (Gen. 2:2). 2. **the last 'His work'** (Gen 2:3). ['male and female' (Gen. 5:2). (*Parashat Va-yetse'—out of sequence*) 'and God remembered Rachel' (Gen. 30:22).]

1. P, MV, ST and H just bring ויכל. K only has אלהים surviving from the phrase.
2. P agrees. MV brings מלאכתו בתרא and ST מלאכ̊תו בתראה. H misspells as מלכתו בתרא and K brings מכ̊ל מלאכ̊תו decorating both letters *kaf*. It is possible that the בתראה in the other sources was to indicate the last *kaf* only, even though they do not include the word מכל, but much more likely based on other usage in *Sefer Tagin*, it meant the second use of the word מלאכתו in the verse, as it occurs seven words previously. Shem Tov decorates only the one *kaf* in מכל מלאכ̊תו in his *Tanakh* in this verse, thus supporting this reading.[64]

Reconstructing the line P, MV, ST, H and K all bring זכר ונקבה. This phrase first appears in *parashat Bere'shit* at 1:28, however, that would be seriously out of sequence, given we do not even begin the listing until Gen. 2:2. It then occurs at Gen. 5:2, which is the most likely position, given the order. MV brings this in the listing for *parashat Bere'shit*, since it also occurs at Gen. 6:19 in *parashat Noaḥ* which could otherwise have been a contender, since the next instance is not until Gen. 8:1.[65]

Next P and H bring ויזכר אלהים את נח from Gen. 8:1. K is slightly damaged, but likely brings the same ויזכר אלהים א[ת נח]. MV only brings ויזכר אלהים, but it is placed in the section on *parashat Noaḥ*, so it is clearly the same intention.

64 Parma 1959 and Add. MS 27167 both bring מכל מלאכ̊תו but only decorate the *kaf* in the last word. *Qiryat Sefer* brings מלאכתו שנים שבפר׳ מתוייגין שני תגין בכ׳ף ('His work' the second in the section, is decorated with two *tagin* in the *kaf*). *Ben Mesheq* gives ב"ג כ"ק מן מלאכתו ויקדש (2:3 *kaf* [and] *qof* from 'His work' [and] 'and He sanctified'). Q651–652 and MV2 are secondary sources that do support K, decorating both מכ̊ל מלאכ̊תו. MV2 also brings ביום השביעי מלאכ̊תו, (on the seventh day, from all His work'), the earlier reference. Parma 2427 and Add. MS 11639 omit either possibility.

65 This is also confirmed by our secondary sources. Q651–652, Parma 2427, Add. MS 11639 and MV2 all bring this in *parashat Bere'shit*. *Ben Mesheq* is even more specific that it is this verse ב׳ כ״ף מן זכר ([verse] 2. *kaf* from 'male'). *Qiryat Sefer* also brings this in its section on *parashat Bere'shit*, זכר מתוייג על הכ׳ף בשנים ('male' decorated on the *kaf* with two [*tagin*]). Parma 1959 and Add. MS 27167 omit. Why this instance of the possible three should be chosen for decoration requires further exploration.

The next instance is brought by **P**, **MV**, **H** and **K** ויזכר אלהים את אברהם from Gen. 19:29.

The last instance on this line brought by P and H is ויזכר דרחל from Gen. 30:22 which MV and K prefer to show as ויזכר אלהים את רחל which certainly fits in with the format of the previous two instances better. However, supporting the alternative way of presenting these three instances by using ד (of) is perhaps ST. For though they are very faint, the enhanced images reveal ויזכ֯ר • דנח, but with a superfluous separator, followed by ויז[כ֯]ר דאברהם, with a blot on the key letter *kaf* and then ויזכ֯ר דרחל. Whilst all are agreed on the instances, given the number of instances between the two extant instances we have in our fragment, it is likely that our scribe has erred. He simply does not have the room on the sheet to list all of these in their correct order given the size of the writing. Also, given the repetition of ויזכר three times, it would be a quite easy error to make. This becomes more evident as we look at the next two lines where there are two large unexplained gaps. I therefore would argue our **CG** scribe's eye skipped out the two instances concerning Noah and Abraham and went straight to the one concerning Rachel and then realised his error on the next line, adding the ones he missed there instead.

Line 26: [3]**ברכ֯ת אביך** • [4]**וילכ֯ו גם א]חיו** • נתחכ֯מה לו • {ויזכ֯ר אלהים את נח} •
3. (*Parashat Va-yeḥi*) **'the blessing of your father'** (Gen. 49:26). 4. **'and his brothers also went'** (Gen. 50:1). [(*Parashat Shemot*) 'let us deal cleverly with him [Israel]' (Ex. 1:10). [(*Parashat Noaḥ—out of sequence*) 'and God remembered Noah (Gen. 8:1)]

3. **P**, **MV**, **H** and **K** all agree. **ST**, though faint also gives ברכ֯ת אב[יך].
4. **MV** and **H** agree, bringing וילכו גם אחיו. **P** brings just וילכו גם. **K** is damaged on the key word but we can see there גם אחיו, so presumably agrees. וילכ֯ו can be made out on **ST**.

P, **MV** and **H** then bring נתחכמה לו from Ex. 1:10. **K** omits לו. **ST** is not visible, but נתחכ֯מה is decorated in the Shem Tov *Tanakh*, supporting the reading.

However, in terms of continuing our reconstruction, as we mentioned above, there simply are not enough words on this line and the one that follows on the next folio fragment **T-S AS 139.152-F**. It is possible that our manuscript had other listings between Ex. 1:10 and Ex. 2:24 but no other source brings additional entries. Thus it is more likely that having omitted the couple of instances involving Noah and Abraham, our scribe has suddenly realised this half way through line 4 and chose instead to insert them at the end of line 26 and the start of line 1 on the next folio, even though they would be out of sequence. This certainly fits our reconstruction, particularly if one follows the longer text given by **MV** and **K** for the instance concerning Rachel and not the format using ד (of) that **ST** appears to favour.

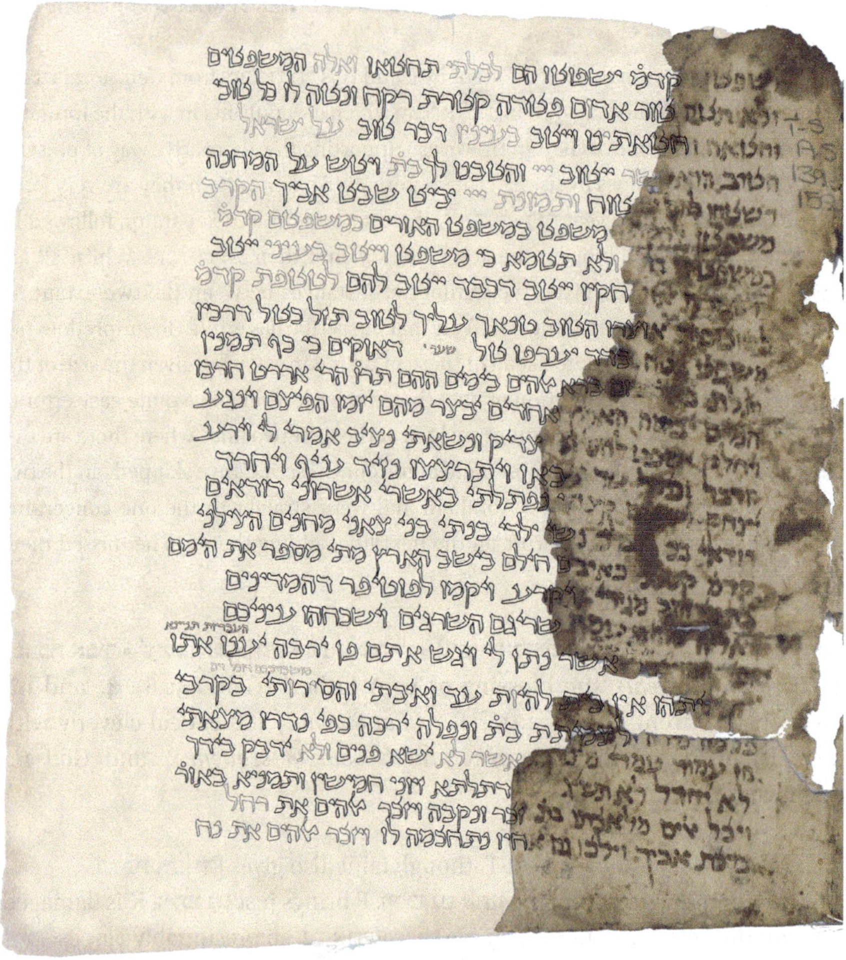

RECONSTRUCTION 1 Above is a reconstruction of the folio showing 26 lines covering the conclusion of the listing for *ṭet*, that for *yod* and the start of *kaf* that we have considered above. This covers fragments **T-S AS 139.152-B** (left side) and **T-S AS 139.144-B** (left side), though joined together they both form the right side of this reconstructed page.

Having completed this element, we are able to see above my suggested reconstruction for the fragments for one folio covering part of *ṭet* through to the start of *kaf*. As a reminder, words in black outline were most likely present, those in grey denote differences amongst the sources and where there is less certainty.

With that we then turn to a new folio which begins with the right side of **T-S AS 139.152-F**, that carries on the listing for *kaf*.

T-S AS 139.152-F (right side)—18 lines preserved

Line 1: [{ויזכ͏̊ר אלהים את אברהם} • ⁵ויזכ͏̊ר אלהים] **את בריתו**
(*Parashat Va-yera'—out of sequence*) 'and God remembered Abraham' (Gen. 19:29).] (*Parashat Shemot*) 5. '[and God remembered] **His covenant**' (Ex. 2:24).

5. **P** and **H** agree, bringing ויזכר אלהים את בריתו. **MV** brings only ו'זכר אלהים, though originally the scribe has omitted the *yod* and added it above the line. **ST**, though very faint, even on the enhanced imagery gives [ויזכ͏̊ר אל]הים את בריתו and so presumably agrees. **K** too brings ויזכר אלהים את with the last word damaged by a hole, but presumably also agrees.

Line 2: [וזה זכ͏̊רי • והכ͏̊{י}תי את מצרים • כ͏̊בד לב פרעה •] ⁶**ערב כ͏̊בד** •
['this is My memorial' (Ex. 3:15). 'and I will smite Egypt' (Ex. 3:20). (*Parashat Va-ʾera'*) 'Pharaoh's heart is hardened' (Ex. 7:14)] 6. '**heavy** [swarms of] **flies**' (Ex. 8:20).

P and **H** brings וזה זכרי from Ex. 3:15. **MV** brings וזה זכר omitting the *yod* in error, but the intention is clearly the same instance. **K** is damaged, but brings וזה [זכרי] דור which does not quite correspond with 𝔐, which reads וזה זכרי לדר דר ('this is My memorial from generation to generation'). **ST** is not visible and, unfortunately, the Shem Tov *Tanakh* is not extant for this section.

P, **MV** and **H** then bring והכתי את מצרים from Ex. 3:20, **H** abbreviating to מצרי״. **K** spells *ma-le' yod*, והכ͏̊יתי את מצרים as 𝔐. Our scribe may have brought or omitted the *yod*. **ST** is not visible and, unfortunately, the Shem Tov *Tanakh* is also not extant for this section.

Concluding the missing section, **P**, **MV**, **H** and **K** all bring כבד לב פרעה from Ex. 7:14, though the last letter is damaged on **K**. **ST** is not visible, but the Shem Tov *Tanakh* does decorate כ͏̊בד in this verse, thus supporting this reading.

6. **P**, **MV** and **H** agree. This instance on the **K** fragment is, unfortunately, not extant. **ST** is not visible, but the Shem Tov *Tanakh* does decorate כ͏̊בד in this verse, thus supporting this reading.

Line 3: [ויכ͏̊בד לב פרעה • {ו}אני הכ͏̊בדתי • יחרץ כ͏̊לב •] ⁷**מרכ͏̊בותיו** • ⁸**כ͏̊מו**
['and He hardened Paraoah's heart' (Ex. 9:7). (*Parashat Bo'*) 'I hardened' (Ex. 10:1). 'a dog whet' (Ex. 11:7).] (*Parashat Be-shallaḥ*) 7. '**their chariots** [wheels]' (Ex. 14:25). 8. '**as a …**

Reconstructing the missing section of this line **P**, **MV** and **H** bring ויכבד את לב פרעה, but there is no such phrase in 𝔐. There is a similar phrase that omits the indefinite article and arguably the intention may have been ויכבד לב פרעה from Ex. 9:7. Unfortunately, **K** is not extant here because of damage and, given the next instance and available space, may well have omitted this. ויכ̊בד לב is just visible on **ST** and the Shem Tov *Tanakh* does decorate ויכ̊בד in Ex. 9:7 thus supporting this reading.[66] Our scribe may also have added the superfluous indefinite article, but available space suggests not.

K though damaged preserves the end of an instance which he gives as את לבו (his heart) which would be Ex. 10:1 and which are the words that follow on from that which **P** and **H** bring, ואני הכבדתי from Ex. 10:1. **ST** also appears to bring ואני הכ̊בדתי. However, this has an extra *vav* and the first word in 𝔐 is just אני. **MV** correctly brings אני הכבדתי, but only out of sequence after the next instance. Our scribe may or may not have brought this superfluous *vav*.

P and **H** then bring יחרץ כלב from Ex. 11:7. **MV** had brought this one instance earlier. **K** extends the phrase to לא יחרץ כ̊לב לשונו ('a dog will not whet its tongue') though 𝔐 is *ḥaser vav* in לשנו. **ST** though very faint appears to bring יח[רץ] כ̊לב.

7. **P** agrees, **H** spells *ḥaser vav* מרכבתיו as 𝔐. However, **MV** gives מרכבות ('chariots') *ma-le' vav*, which suggests that he means instead Ex. 15:4 later. Either do fit the sequence. **K** has only the first three letters מרכ̊ surviving so may be either. **ST** brings מרכ̊בתיו לא̊, but it is not clear what the two extra letters represent. Additionally, in the Shem Tov *Tanakh* מרכ̊בתיו is decorated, whilst מרכבות is not, further supporting Ex. 14:25.[67]
8. **P**, **MV** and **H** agree and our scribe splits the instance across the line כמו נד. כ̊מו is also faintly visible in **ST**. **K** is not extant.

Line 4: **[נד • כ̊ע{ו}פרת • כ̊מכ̊ה בתרא{ה תרי} • [9]מכ̊[ון • [10]כ̊וננו • [11]אזכ̊ור •**
[**... heap**' (Ex. 15:8). 'like lead' (Ex. 15:10). the last 'like You' two [letters *kaf*] (Ex. 15:11).] 9. **'a place'** (Ex. 15:17). 10. **'have established'** (Ex. 15:17). (*Parashat Yitro*) 11. **'I will cause** [My name] **to be remembered'** (Ex. 20:21).

66 Turning to our secondary sources, Q651–652 serves to confuse a little more, bringing ויכ̊בד פרעה omitting לב. **MV2** lists ויכבד but does not decorate the letter. Parma 2427, Parma 1959, Add. MS 11639 and *Qiryat Sefer* all omit. *Ben Mesheq* actively disagrees and instead marks לד ... כ'ף דויכבד (34. ... the *kaf* of 'and he hardened') placing the decoration on the words occurrence in Ex. 9:34 instead. **T-S Misc. 24.182** is, unfortunately, not extant for this section up to Ex. 23:22.

67 From our secondary sources, Q651–652 and Parma 1959 bring מרכ̊בותיו *ma-le' vav*. Parma 2427 lists the word, but does not decorate a letter. Add. MS 11639, **MV2**, *Qiryat Sefer* and *Ben Mesheq* omit either option.

Continuing on with instances from *Shirat ha-Yam* (The Song of the Sea), **P**, **MV** and **H** then bring כעפרת from Ex. 15:10. **ST** is not visible, but the Shem Tov *Tanakh* does decorate כ֯עופרת, thus supporting this reading. **K** is not extant. The core sources all spell the word *ḥaser vav* even though 𝔐 is *ma-le'* כעופרת. Thus, our fragment may have agreed with the core sources, against 𝔐.

P then brings כמכה בת׳ and **H** similarly כמכה בתרא both as 𝔐, though **MV** spells *ma-le' vav* כמוכה בתראה. This presents a problem. Does the בתראה refer to the last *kaf* in this word, or the last occurrence of the word which is repeated twice in this verse and, if so, which *kaf* in that last occurrence? **ST** is not visible, but the Shem Tov *Tanakh* has decorated both letters *kaf* in the second occurrence of the word in Ex. 15:11 which is followed by נהדר בקדש ('glorious in holiness'). This is, in part, supported by the scribe of **K** who brings instead מי כ֯מכ֯ה ~~בתר~~ תר׳ ('who is like You', both). Clearly his *Vorlage* indicated the last *kaf* which he duly copied, but then he deliberately amended it to saying it was twice. Unfortunately, whilst he decorates both letters, we do not know which כמכה he intended; as both are preceded with מי. There is clearly some considerable disagreement, as some bring בת׳ and some תר׳. Considering this and previous examples where two of the same letters in one word are decorated, I suggest that both are partly correct and that what our text's original intention might have been instead כמכה בתראה תרי (the last 'like you' two [letters *kaf*]) and that once again (see above) תרי (two) has perhaps been mistaken along the line as the abbreviation תר׳.[68] Alternatively, it could indeed say תרוויהון (both of them) referring to each letter in the last occurrence of the word. There is no reason why both descriptors cannot be used in succession, even though the copyists of our core sources may well have considered it some kind of error. Sadly our manuscript cannot help clarify; for we do not know what our scribe brought.

9. Based on what remains of our manuscript for this instance, **P**, **MV** and **H** agree. **ST** is very faint, but also shows מכ֯ון. **K** extends to מכ֯ון לשבתך ('a place for You to dwell').
10. **P** and **MV** agree. **H** spells initially *ḥaser vav* initially, but a *vav* has been suspended כ'ננו to correct it as 𝔐. Very faint, but **ST** brings כ֯וננו too. **K** only has two letters remaining, but it is clearly intending כו[ננו]. **P**, **MV**, **H**

---

68 Our secondary sources either ignore the issue completely or add to all four rather than make a decision as to which letters *kaf* are implied. Q651–652 marks all four, כ֯מוכ֯ה כ֯מוכ֯ה both words shown as *ma-le' vav*. *Qiryat Sefer* notes כמכה שניהם חסרים ... והכפי״ן מתוייגות שנים שנים ('like You' both are *ḥaser* ... and the [letters] *kaf* are decorated, two [and] two). *Ben Mesheq* similarly gives יא כפי״ן דכמכה כמכה (11. 4 [letters] *kaf* of 'like You', 'like You'). Conversely Parma 2427 decorates none of the letters *kaf* in either כמכה. Add. MS 11639 also has both words *ma-le' vav* but marks neither with decorations. **MV2** has both *ḥaser vav* but similarly marks none of the letters *kaf*. Parma 1959 omits completely.

and K all bring אזכיר as 𝔐. Our scribe seems to have erred writing a *vav* in place of a *yod*. ST is very faint but also seems to be bringing [א]זכ̊ור, as our scribe. However, Shem Tov does not decorate אזכיר in his *Tanakh*.[69]

Line 5: [{את} תבנית המשכ̊ן • [12]{סמים} ולבנה ז]**כה** • [13]**כתובים**

[(*Parashat Terumah*) 'the pattern of the Sanctuary' (Ex. 25:9). 12. (*Parashat Ki Tissa'*) 'spices] **and pure frankincense'** (Ex. 30:34). 13. **'written ...**

P, MV and H then bring תבנית המשכן from Ex. 25:9. ST, though very faint, also appears to bring this abbreviated תב̇ המשכ̊ן. K extends to את תבנית המשכ̊ן and given available space, on what would otherwise be a very short line, our scribe may have done similar.

12. P, MV and H agree and ST, though faint also brings ולבנה [ז]כ̊ה. Our scribe has omitted to indicate the letter *kaf* as decorated. K is damaged, but seems to extend to [סמים ול]בנה זכ̊ה ('spices and pure frankincense'). Given available space and no other instances at this position, our scribe likely similarly extended.
13. Our scribe again fails to indicate the decorated letter and is *ma-le'vav*, but P, MV and H all bring כתבים *ḥaser vav*, as 𝔐. MV brings • כתבים • קדמאה ('written'—the first) divided with a superfluous dot, as if they were two separate instances, instead of being linked. P does similarly, but extends to • כתבים באצבע • קד̇ ('written with the finger'—the first.). H links and extends further to כתבים באצבע אלהי' קדמ' (the first 'written with the finger of God') which is Ex. 31:18 as opposed to the phrase occurring in Deut. 9:10, though its positioning in the list makes that obvious. ST has כ̊ת[ו]בים באצבע קדמ̇, *ma-le'vav*, that is visible so we can assume the same instance. Available space on the next line suggests our scribe may have followed H and also likely wrote קדמאה in full. At this point we lose K in our considerations.

Line 6: [באצבע אלהים קדמאה • והמכ̊תב • [14]מ]**תנותיכ̊ם** • [15]**נדריכ̊ם** •

[... by the finger of God], the first [occurrence] (Ex. 31:18). 'and the writing' (Ex. 32:16).] (*Parashat 'Emor*) 14. **'your gifts'** (Lev. 23:38). 15. **'your vows'** (Lev. 23:38).

P, MV and H all bring והמכתב from Ex. 32:16. ST also gives [ו]המכ̊תב.

69 Basser does note, however, that in the margin, Shem Tov has added נ"ח as is his normal practice when marking the presence of the special *kaf* (op. cit., p. 93).

14. MV agrees and like our scribe is *ma-le' vav* as 𝔐. P and H bring מתנתיכם *ḥaser vav*. ST is not visible, but Shem Tov decorates מנותיכ֯ם in his *Tanakh*, supporting this reading.
15. P, MV and H all agree. ST is not visible, but Shem Tov decorates נדריכ֯ם in his *Tanakh*, supporting this reading.

Line 7: [{ו}נדב{ו}תיכ֯ם {תלתיהון} • כ֯פת תמרים •] [16]**בסכ֯ות תשבו** •
['your free will offerings' (Lev. 23:38). 'branches of palm trees' (Lev. 23:40).] 16. **'in booths you will dwell'** (Lev. 23:42).

Continuing the grouping, P and H bring ונדבותיכם also from Lev. 23:38. MV is *ḥaser vav* ונדבתיכם. However, all of the sources are in error, as 𝔐 is just נדבתיכם. That said, it is possible the extra *vav* is just joining it to the previous related instance, meaning 'and'. ST is not visible for any of these three instances, but as mentioned the Shem Tov *Tanakh* does decorate all three in this verse.

P, MV and H then all bring כפת תמרים from Lev. 23:40, linked to the next instance around the festival of *Sukkot*. ST is again not visible, but the Shem Tov *Tanakh* does bring כ֯פת, supporting this reading. However, these two instances certainly do not fill the available space. Did our scribe extend the instance, err and cross through something, or did he bring an additional instance? Given none of the secondary sources bring anything here[70] and that the three instances of Lev. 23:38 are linked, we have previous evidence of the use of תלתיהון (three of them) when we have such linked instances, a word which fits quite nicely into the space.

16. P and H agree. MV is *ḥaser vav* בסכת תשבו as 𝔐. ST, very faint indeed also brings [ב]סכ֯ת ת[שבו].[71]

Line 8: [וכ֯לי הקדש • {ו}את הכ֯פ{ו}ת • יברכ֯ך • [17]ואנ]י **אברכ֯ם** •
[(*Parashat Be-midbar*) 'and the sacred vessels' (Num. 3:31). 'and the dishes' (Num. 4:7). (*Parashat Naso'*) 'may He bless you' (Num. 6:24).] 17. **'and I will bless them'** (Num. 6:27).

70 Q651–652 brings no additional instances at this point, though does extend the second of the three related instances to כל נדריכ֯ם. There are also no additions in Parma 2427, Parma 1959, Add. MS 11639, **MV2**, *Qiryat Sefer* or *Ben Mesheq*. **T-S Misc. 24.182** is, unfortunately, not extant past Lev. 4:27.

71 The *Ba'al ha-Ṭurim* brings instead בסוכות from the next verse Lev. 23:43 as the word to take the decoration, and notes that 'for until 20 cubits [*kaf* = 20] a person knows he is sitting in the shade of a *sukkah*', meaning that a *sukkah* that is over 20 cubits high is invalid.

Reconstructing the rest of the line, P, MV and H bring וכלי הקדש from Num. 3:31. P and H follow with את הכפת, from Num. 4:7. ST, though faint, is the same את הכ֯פת. MV is *ma-le' vav* את הכפות but 𝔐 is ואת הכפת, so none of the core sources are quite right in their listing.

Turning to the *Birkat ha-Kohanim* (Priestly Blessing), P, MV and H bring the first word יברכך from Num. 6:24. ST also [י]בר֯כך, very faint.

17. H agrees. P and MV omit ואני.[72] ST also appears to be just [אב]ר֯כם.

Line 9: [לחנכ֯ת • שני הכ֯ר{ו}בים • כ֯מראה • [18]לא] כ֯ן • [19]כמשפטם קדמׄ •
['the dedication of' (Num. 7:11). 'the two *cherubim*' (Num. 7:89). (*Parashat Beha'alotkha*) 'according to the pattern' (Num. 8:4). 18. 'not] **so**' (Num. 12:7). (*Parashat Pinḥas*) 20. **the first 'according to their judgements'** (Num. 29:6).

P, MV and H all bring לחנכת from Num 7:11. ST is not visible, but the Shem Tov *Tanakh* decorates לחנכ֯ת, supporting this reading.

P and H then list שני הכרובים from Num. 7:89. MV has originally omitted the *vav* and suspended it as שני הכר'בים such that the letter *resh* and *vav* joined look like a *lamed*.[73] This is an odd correction to deliberately make, as 𝔐 is *ḥaser vav*, הכרבים. ST is very faint, but does appear to give שני הכ֯רובים, and the Shem Tov *Tanakh* decorates הכ֯רבים, supporting this reading.

The final missing entry on this line is likely כמראה from Num. 8:4 as brought by P, MV and H. ST is also faint, but does appear to bring כ֯מראה. Unfortunately, the Shem Tov *Tanakh* is not extant for this instance.

18. P, MV and H agree, bringing לא כן. ST is not visible and the Shem Tov *Tanakh* is not extant.
19. H agrees, bringing כמשפטם קדמׄ. P gives קדׄ but otherwise agrees. Our scribe has omitted to indicate the letter again. ST is not visible and the Shem Tov *Tanakh* is not extant. MV, however, adds in a completely different instance in the section covering *parashat Balaq* that reads כרע שכב ('he crouched, lying [as a lion]')[74] from Num. 24:9. However, this phrase contains two letters *kaf* and no indication is given as to which should be decorated.[75] None of the other core or secondary sources bring this. ST

72 A further proof that H is not copied directly from P.
73 So that it looks like כלבים (dogs). It has been transcribed correctly *ḥaser vav* as שני הכרבים in LMV.
74 Though the *bet* is written poorly and resembles another *kaf*.
75 Q651–652, Parma 2427, Parma 1959, Add. MS 11639, MV2, *Qiryat Sefer* and *Ben Mesheq* do not bring this. MV does not appear to garner any support from our secondary sources.

is not visible and, unfortunately, the Shem Tov *Tanakh* is not extant. **MV** then brings a variant on the agreed instance, כמשפטן קדמאה, spelling the key word incorrectly with a feminine ending.

Line 10: [וכ֯בסתם • וכ֯ומז • י{ו}סף עליכ֯ם • [20]אחי]כ֯ם • [21]המלכ֯ים האלה •
[(*Parashat Maṭot*) 'and you will wash' (Num. 31:24). 'and girdles'[76] (Num. 31:50).]
(*Parashat Devarim*) 20. **'your brothers'** (Deut. 3:18). 21. **'these kings'** (Deut. 3:21).

Continuing our reconstruction, P, **MV** and H all bring וכבסתם from Num. 31:24.

P, **MV** and H then brings וכומז from Num. 31:50, though H forms the last letter poorly such that it resembles a *dalet*. ST is not visible for either of these instances and, unfortunately, the Shem Tov *Tanakh* is not extant.

Finally, P and H bring יסף עליכם as 𝔐 from Deut. 1:11. **MV** spells *ma-le' vav* יוסף עליכם. ST is not visible, but the Shem Tov *Tanakh* decorates עליכ֯ם, supporting this reading.

20. P and H extend to אחיכם בני ישר֗ and אחיכם בני ישרא' respectively. **MV** writes in full אחיכם בני ישראל ('your brothers, the children of Israel'). Our scribe is more concise. ST is not visible and the Shem Tov *Tanakh* is not extant.
21. P, **MV** and H agree, bringing המלכים האלה. H originally wrote the word without the last *he*, but this is added after a gap האל ה. ST is not visible and, unfortunately, the Shem Tov *Tanakh* is not extant.

Line 11: [חכ֯מתכ֯ם • וזכ֯רת את כ֯ל • [22]וזכ֯ר]ת את יי • [23]וזכרת כי עבד
[(*Parashat Va-'etḥanan*) 'your wisdom' (Deut. 4:6). (*Parashat 'Eqev*) 'and you will remember all' (Deut. 8:2) 22. 'and you will remember] **God'** (Deut. 8:18). (*Parashat Ki Tetse'*) 23. **'and you will remember that a slave ...**

P, **MV** and H bring חכמתכם from Deut. 4:6. ST is not visible and, unfortunately, the Shem Tov *Tanakh* is not extant.[77] However, this word has two letters *kaf* and we are unsure which of them are intended or whether it is both. The secondary sources are somewhat inconclusive in this respect.[78] None of the core sources bring a qualifier, such as first, last or both.

---

76 Possibly armlets of gold according to BDB.

77 Though Basser claims, in a footnote, that both are decorated in ST (op. cit., p. 94).

78 Turning to our secondary sources, Q651–652 marks both חכ֯מתכ֯ם, *Ben Mesheq* seem to give both too. Add. MS 11639 brings only on the first *kaf* חכ֯מתכם and *Qiryat Sefer* completely disagrees explaining חכ֯מתכם הכ"ף השנית מתוייגת ('your wisdom', the second *kaf* is decorated). Parma 2427 Parma 1959 and **MV2** omit either possibility.

P and H then bring וזכרת את כל הדרך from Deut. 8:2, but **MV** omits this instance at this point, though does bring it after the next instance, out of sequence, but only as וזכרת את כל. ST, though faint also brings וזכ̊רת את כל and the Shem Tov *Tanakh* decorates וזכ̊רת, supporting this reading and suggesting that only the first *kaf* in the phrase is decorated, though there is again disagreement within the secondary sources.[79] Given available space, it is likely our scribe similarly omitted הדרך.

22. P and **MV** agree, with both bringing the three *yod* triangle form for God's Name as does **MV** (though earlier than it should be in the listing; indeed **MV**'s ordering in this section is quite erratic). H extends adding אלהיך ('your God').[80] Very faint, ST does bring וזכ̊רת and the Shem Tov *Tanakh* decorates this instance, supporting this reading.
23. P agrees, bringing וזכרת כי עבר היתה קד׳. H brings קדמ̇. **MV** omits. Our scribe omits the indicator again. ST is not visible, but the Shem Tov *Tanakh* decorates this instance of וזכ̊רת, supporting this reading. This instance is out of sequence in the core sources and should be two instances later. It is possibly placed here in error, as it has been grouped with the other references to וזכרת.

Line 12: [היתה קדמ̇ • זכ̊ור דמרים • 24זכ̊ור ד]**את אשר לעמלק** •
[... you were' the first [occurence] (Deut. 24:18). The 'remember' of 'Miriam' (Deut. 24:9). 25. The 'remember' [of the verse including]] **'which Amalek'** (Deut 25:17).

Only one instance is left to debate in the reconstruction of this line. P, **MV** and H all bring זכור דמרים indicating that this is from Deut. 24:9. 𝔐 reads למרים but grammatically one cannot add a *dalet* to that as there is already a prefix, so the *lamed* has been dropped. ST is not visible, but the Shem Tov *Tanakh* decorates זכ̊ור in that verse, supporting this reading.

24. P, **MV** and H brings זכור דעמלק. Our **CG** scribe is more precise with the instance bringing **את אשר**, but errs by having a space between the *dalet* and

79 However, Q651–652 marks both, bringing וזכ̊רת את כ̊ל הדרך. *Ben Mesheq* also gives ב׳ כפין מוזכרת כל (the two [letters] *kaf* from 'and you will remember all') and *Qiryat Sefer* also notes וזכרת ... והכ״ף מתוייגת שנים, כל הכ״ף מתוייגת שנים ('and you will remember' ... and the *kaf* is decorated with two [*tagin*], 'all', the *kaf* is decorated with two [*tagin*]). Add. MS 11639 agrees with ST bringing וזכ̊רת את כל הדרך. Parma 2427, however, ignores the first word and instead brings only כ̊ל הדרך. MV2 also lists וזכרת את כל הדרך, but marks no letter. Parma 1959 omits either possibility.

80 A further proof that H is not copied directly from P.

the *ʾalef* of דאת and more seriously by adding a *lamed* onto עמלק which is not present in 𝔐. ST is not visible and the Shem Tov *Tanakh* does not decorate זכור in that verse.[81] H then adds an additional זכור, as if it is an additional instance, but this seems to be an error.

Line 13: [מברכֿת • ויכֿחשו • //// שער ך //// עֹז] **באוֹר דארבע קרני**
[(*Parashat Ve-zoʾt Ha-berakhah*) 'blessed of' (Deut. 33:13). 'they shall dwindle' (Deut. 33:29) //// Gate of the *kaf sofit* //// 77] **in the *Torah* with four horns.**

P, MV and H then bring מברכת from Deut. 33:13 and ST similarly [מב]רכֿת.

This is followed by P, MV and H who all bring ויכחשו from Deut. 33:29. ST is very faint, but the enhanced imagery reveals that the instance is extended to ויכֿחשו איבי (your enemies will dwindle). Given space is likely needed for the 'gate of the *kaf*' reference, our scribe likely has not extended.

With that we come to the end of the extant listings for *kaf*. Our fragment preserves 24 of the possible 55 or, more likely, 58 entries, and is largely in agreement with P, though not always. It is again a shame that sections are missing, as there are a number of disagreements between the sources that our fragment remains silent on, in particular the disagreements around כמכה.

7 Description and Example Forms of the First Special Letter *Kaf Sofit*

Turning to our next letter, unfortunately, our fragment does not preserve how many special letters *kaf sofit* there are. This is also disappointing as, again, there is considerable confusion in the sources. P appears to supply ך עֹז באוריי׳ דֹז קרני׳ (*kaf sofit*—77 in the *Torah* that have 4 horns). **MV** agrees that there דֹד קרני׳ (4 horns) but brings no number. ST gives in his introductory passage ך דאית לה ארבע קרני תלת מאה באוריתא (*kaf sofit* that has four horns, one hundred and three in the *Torah*) but in BH the same sage brings instead ך דאית לה ארבעה קרני שבעין ושיתא באוריתא (*kaf sofit* that has four horns, seventy six in the *Torah*). The descriptor in the actual listing in ST is very faint, but show קרנין עֹ[?] באוֹר, but the number is not clear. H gives instead ך עד באוריי׳ דֹד קרני׳ (*kaf sofit*—74 in the *Torah* that have 4 horns). Basser picks up on this in a footnote and also explains that 76 is what Shem Tov brings in the margin of his *Tanakh*, but that

81 Leading Basser to omit this instance from his listing, even though he notes that it is in other core sources and also *Qiryat Sefer* and *Ben Mesheq* (op. cit., p. 95).

he has found 79, but these include the three from the second form (see below) as they double up. Without these there would be 76.[82]

Fundamentally, we have little agreement on the number of instances.

The printed Maḥzor Vitry (*LMV*)*, shown right, brings a fairly standard form, but once again there are variances in the manuscripts.*

Despite the fact that our scribe has copied that there are four tagin, *in his rendition of the form in* ***T-S NS 287.11-F*** *he brings only two, one either side of the roof (right). It is possible that there is a third small* tag *on the underside of the right of the roof but this is more likely just a slip of the reed. In this, he does echo some of the other halakhic texts and* Sifrey Torah, *where only two are brought. He also seems to curl the base a little but this is possibly not deliberate, since he does bring the separate form that follows that does specifically have the curl and has no* tagin.

T-S Misc. 24.182 *shown right has three* tagin *on the roof and one descending from the underside if the left of the roof similar to the previous* kaf *form.*

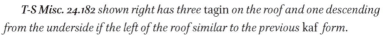

Line 14: [ויברך • ויברך • ויברך • מתהלך • אך •] 1שפך • 2לך • 3לך • 4אראך •
[(*Parashat Bere'shit*) 'and He blessed' (Gen. 1:22). 'and He blessed' (Gen. 1:28). 'and He blessed' (Gen. 2:3). 'walking about' (Gen. 3:8). (*Parashat Noaḥ*) 'only' (Gen. 9:4).] 1. **'sheds'** (Gen. 9:6). [missing 'he will shed' (Gen. 9:6)] (*Parashat Lekh Lekha*) 2 and 3. **'go for yourself'** (Gen. 12:1). 4. **'I will show you'** (Gen 12:1).

8 Listing of Instances for the First Special Letter *Kaf Sofit*

Reconstructing the missing elements of the line starts with three instances that are the same word appearing in different verses in order. P, MV and H bring ויברך three times, from Gen. 1.22, Gen. 1:28 and Gen. 2:3 respectively. ST shows at least one ויברך, and whilst the first two are not extant in the Shem Tov *Tanakh*, the third is present and decorated in the first extant folio.

P, MV and H then adds מתהלך from Gen. 3:8 and ST too מתהלך, though faint.

That is followed by אך from Gen. 9:4 as brought by P, MV and H and ST agrees, with אך just visible.

82 Basser, op. cit., p. 95.

TABLE 12 Forms for the special letter *kaf sofit*. The four *tagin* are either brought atop the roof or with one hanging from the underside on the right of the roof. As usual, many scribes are uncomfortable with this descending *tag*—presumably because it could make the letter resemble a *pe sofit*—and bring only three *tagin* despite the clear instruction. Some reduce this further to two as our CG scribe has.

 *Maḥzor Vitry* Parma 2574 (P)	 *Maḥzor Vitry* Add. MS 27201 (MV)	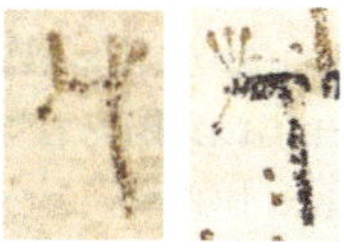 Shem Tov *Tanakh* *Sefer Tagi* (ST)	 *Badey ha-'Aron* Heb. 840 (BH)	 *Sefer Tagin* Heb. 837 (H)
Not extant Nr. 5667 (K)	 Parma 2427	 Parma 1959	 Q651–652	 MS Geunz. 481
 *Maḥzor Vitry* Add. MS 27201 (MV2)	 Add. MS 11639	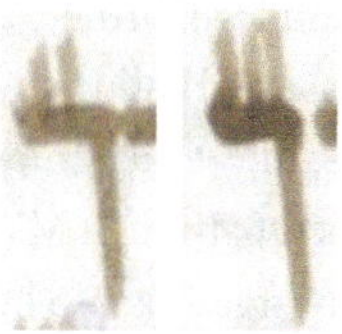 Add. MS 26167	 Bologna *Torah*	 Vat. ebr. 1
 Or. 1463	Not employed Alexander *Torah*			

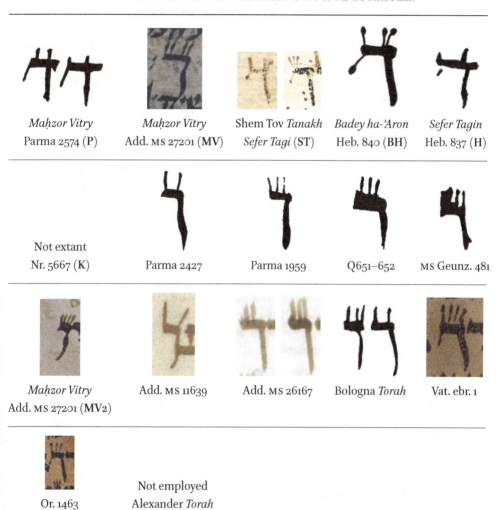

1. P, MV, ST and H bring שפך from Gen. 9:6 as our scribe. However, these three sources then follow with ישפך ('he will shed') from the same verse and ST confirms adding ב׳ בו (two in it [the verse]). However, it does look like our scribe has omitted this, probably a haplographic error where our scribe has looked up then back at his *Vorlage*, omitting the similar second word.

2 and 3. P, and H give both 2 and 3 as one instance together with no separator לך לך. ST adds a separator dot, MV omits both.

4. P, MV and H agree bringing אראך. ST is not visible and the Shem Tov *Tanakh* is not extant, but ST does add ג׳ בפ׳ (three in the verse), suggesting it is there.

Line 15: [מברכיך • וילך • זרעך • זרעך • הלך • {{ושמרו} דרך ייי • אלהים עמך •}] 5{כי}ברך אברכה • 6זרעך • 7ובזרעך

['that bless you' (Gen. 12:3) 'and he went' (Gen. 12:4). 'your seed' (Gen. 13:16). 'your seed' (Gen. 13:16). (*Parashat Va-yera*') 'went' (Gen. 18:16). {{'and keep} the way of God' (Gen. 18:19). 'God is with you' (Gen. 21:22).} 5. '{for} I will surely bless you' (Gen. 22:17). 6. **'your seed'** (Gen. 22:17). (*Parashat Va-yetse*') 7. **'and through your seed'** (Gen. 28:14).

P, MV, ST (though faint) and H all bring מברכיך from Gen. 12:3.[83]

P, MV, ST (though faint) and H all then list וילך from Gen. 12:4.

We then see two of the same word in succession as P, MV and H bring both instances of זרעך appearing in Gen. 13:16, though MV does cross one out and writes again at the end of a line after leaving a large space. ST also seems to do the same, bringing [זר]עך • זרעך.

P, MV, ST and H then bring הלך from Gen. 18:16. ST appears to extend to הלך עמם ('went with them'). This is followed by דרך ייי אלהים brought by P apparently from Gen. 18:19. H abbreviates אלהי׳. However, both have added the separator in the wrong place and the אלהים belongs with the next instance.[84]

For our final missing instance in this line P and H bring עמך from Gen. 21:22. MV divides the two instances correctly דרך ייי • אלהים עמך. ST extends to ושמרו דרך [יי] and then אלהים עמך, as the other core sources. It is possible that our fragment had these two instances written in superscript between the lines because they were omitted, along with the other small words that do remain. Otherwise there simply would not be enough space for all the instances in this line.

---

83 The *Ba'al ha-Ṭurim* notes of מברכיך that there are '3 *tagin* on the *ḥet*, for three times 20 = 60, corresponding to the 60 letters in the Priestly Blessing which begins 'may God bless', 'shine' [and] 'raise''.

84 Interestingly, this has been transcribed almost correctly in EPST as דרך • יי״ • אלהים עמך •.

5. Our scribe appears to have originally omitted this entry, possibly because of the several words זרעך listed, and this may have caused his eye to jump. It has been added later in smaller letters. However, the last letter does not appear to have been transcribed properly as he brings a *he* rather than a *kaf sofit*. Interestingly, having the *he* means that there is less confusion, as otherwise we would not know which word was to take the decoration or whether it is both. 𝔐 is clear that the phrase is ברך אברכך. **ST** extends and brings decoration on both כי ברך̊ אברכך̊ ('for you will be surely blessed') and **MV** also brings ברך אברכך, but only after a superfluous בזרעך, which seems out of place. **P** and **H** omit both. The secondary sources tend to support **ST**.[85]
6. The problem here is that the word זרעך appears twice in Gen. 22:17, and our scribe does not make it clear which is intended. **MV** also just brings one reference to זרעך, so appears to agree with our fragment. **ST** does bring זרעך̊, but it is is not entirely clear what follows in the available images, before listing [וי]רש זרעך̊ ('and your see will possess').[86] The Shem Tov *Tanakh* does decorate both instances of זרעך̊ in the verse, supporting this reading.[87] However, **P** and **H** skip both these instances moving instead to the next similar word בזרעך. **P** and **H** appear to have omitted four instances in this section. **MV** also seems confused as to the sequence of instances.

P, **MV** and **H** then bring בזרעך from Gen. 22:18. **ST** is not visible but the Shem Tov *Tanakh* brings בזרעך̊, supporting this reading. Our scribe has omitted this instance, likely because of the similarity with the next.

As referenced above, **ST** alone then brings [וי]רש זרעך̊ which Basser argues in his footnote is from Gen. 24:60, because of the large illegible gap in **ST**. Unfortunately, the enhanced imagery does not help and the Shem Tov *Tanakh* is not extant for this verse.[88]

---

85 Q651–652 also extends as **ST** and decorates both כי ברך̊ אברכך̊. Parma 2427 does similar, bringing ברך̊ אברכך̊. *Ben Mesheq* brings י״ז כ׳ף מן ברך וכ׳ף מן אברכך ([verse]17 *kaf* from 'bless' and the *kaf* from 'I will bless you'). *Qiryat Sefer* also notes for both words that הכ׳ף הכפולה מתוייגות שנים (the final *kaf* is decorated with two [*tagin*]). Conversely, Add. MS 271617 and Parma 1959 as usual agree with each other and bring כי ברך̊ אברכך, only decorating one. **MV2** lists כי ברך אברכך but does not decorate either letter even though זרעך̊ is decorated three times on the following lines. Add. MS 11639 omits.

86 Which may be from Gen. 22:17 or from Gen. 24:60. Basser assumes the latter (op. cit., p. 96), but it could be either or both.

87 Basser thus lists both זרעך̊ ככוכבי ('your seed as the stars') וירש זרעך̊ ('and your seed will possess') in that verse. (*op. cit.*, p. 96).

88 Basser, op. cit., p. 96.

7. Our scribe has brought ובזרעך. **P**, **ST** and **H** agree, but **MV** brings בזרעך again. **ST** does have a gap after this and before the next instance, but the word(s) there are not visible.

The repetition of instances involving זרעך, בזרעך and ובזרעך has caused some considerable confusion with omission or poor ordering in the sources, and our fragment seems no different. Of our primary sources, **ST** appears to be the most accurate, but with the large illegible space it is hard to confirm. Given this, it is therefore worth considering the sequences brought by the secondary sources to see if this makes matters any clearer.

Q651–652 brings וירש זרעך (Gen. 22:17), then ואת זרעך but this seems wrong as it is a) before the last instance in Gen 22:17 and b) does not have the *vav*. It then brings והתברכו בזרעך (Gen. 22:18) then ויירש זרעך (Gen. 24:60) and finally brings ובזרעך (Gen. 28:14). Parma 2427 brings זרעך near the end of its section on *parashat Va-yera'* apparently as confused as the core sources, but then ובזרעך early on in *parashat Va-yetse'*. MS 27167 and Parma 1959 bring והתברכו בזרעך and then add an instance not seen in the other sources ברך את אברהם ('blessed Abraham') from Gen. 24:1. Then both bring ובזרעך. Add MS 11639 brings אברהם • זרעך • והתברכו בזרעך and then later ובזרעך but then adds והשיבותיך but this word does not appear in Genesis. **MV2** is possibly the clearest, as it brings והרבה ארבה את זרעך ('and I will surely multiply your seed'), then וירש זרעך and then והתברכו בזרעך. **MV2** also lists ובזרעך but does not decorate the letter. *Ben Mesheq* notes ב' כפי"ן מן זרעך זרעך (two letters *kaf* from 'your seed' 'your seed') and then omits ובזרעך.[89] Finally *Qiryat Sefer* talks only of the letters *resh* in והתברכו בזרעך being decorated but does bring ובזרעך הכ'ף מתוייגת שנים ('and through your seed' the *kaf* is decorated with two [*tagin*]).

Taking all this into account, it is likely that the original intention of *Sefer Tagin* for this section was: והרבה ארבה את זרעך (Gen. 22:17), וירש זרעך (Gen. 22:17), והתברכו בזרעך (Gen. 22:18), ויירש זרעך (Gen. 24:40) and finally ובזרעך (Gen. 28:14) and no extant source has quite captured this, though **MV2** is perhaps closest.

Line 16: [ויברך א{ו}תו • מחלציך • המלאך •] [8]יברכך • [9]ישימך • [10]ויעזרך •
[(*Parashat Va-yishlaḥ*) 'and he blessed him' (Gen. 32:30). 'from your loins' (Gen. 35:11). (*Parashat Va-yeḥi*) 'the angel' (Gen. 48:16).] 8. [should be] יברך **'shall bless'** (Gen. 48:17 or 48:20). 9. **'make you'** (Gen 48:20). 10. **'and He will protect you'** (Gen. 49:25).

---

89 Basser claims that this is present, but then notes in a footnote that it relates to זרעך, op. cit., p. 96.

P and H bring ויברך אותו from Gen. 32:30. MV and ST are *ḥaser vav* ויברך אתו as 𝔐.

This is followed by מחלציך from Gen. 35:11 as brought by P, MV and H. ST is not fully visible, but seems to bring מ[חלצי]ךְ.

P, MV and H conclude the missing section with המלאך from Gen. 48:16. Faint traces in ST suggest [ה]מל[א]ךְ also. The Shem Tov *Tanakh* is not extant for this section.

8. P and MV agree with our scribe apparently adding a superfluous *kaf*, since this word does not appear between the last instance Gen. 48:16 and the next Gen. 48:20. More likely is H who brings יברך from either Gen 48:17 or 48:20, agreeing with 𝔐.[90] ST is very faint, but seems also to give [י]ברךְ. Unfortunately, the Shem Tov *Tanakh* is not extant.[91]
9. P, MV and ST agree, bringing ישימך. However, 𝔐 is *ḥaser yod* ישמך, which H brings.
10. P, MV and ST agree as 𝔐, bringing ויעזרך. It is H that adds the superfluous *yod*, bringing ויעזריך.[92]

Line 17: [ויברכךְ • וילךְ {איש} • לךְ ואספת •] [11]לךְ לשלום • [12]לךְ לקראת •
['and He will bless you' (Gen. 49:25). (*Parashat Shemot*) '{and the man} went' (Ex. 2:1). 'go and gather' (Ex. 3:16).] **11. 'go in peace'** (Ex. 4:18). 12. **'go to meet'** (Ex. 4:27).

P, ST and H bring ויברכך from Gen. 49:25. MV omits.

P and H then bring וילך from Ex. 2:1. MV and ST extend to וילך איש, and likely our scribe does too, given available space.

P, MV and H bring לך ואספת from Ex. 3:16 and ST likely does the same, even though it is difficult to read, לךְ ואספת.

11. P, MV, ST and H all agree, bringing לך לשלום. Our scribe has omitted the indicator.

---

90 Further specific proof that H is likely not copied from P.

91 From our secondary sources, T-S Misc. 24.182 brings יברךְ but we cannot say which is intended. Q651–652 does not solve our problem either and brings both יברךְ from Gen. 48:16 and בך יברךְ ('through you will be blessed') from Gen 48:20. Add. MS 11639 goes further and places a decoration on all three יברךְ and בךְ יברךְ and *Ben Mesheq* also does this, requiring all three to be decorated. Only *Qiryat Sefer* brings one instance יברך הכ'ף מתוייגת שנים ('will be blessed' the *kaf* is decorated with two [*tagin*]) and from its positioning in the list is Gen. 48:20. MV2 lists בך יברך but indicates neither. Parma 2427 omits either bringing ויברך את יוסף ('and he blessed Joseph') instead before המלאךְ. Add. MS 271617 and Parma 1959 omit either.

92 T-S Misc. 24.182 omits a letter in error, bringing ויערך.

12. P and MV agree, bringing לך לקראת. H too, though adds an *ʾalef* above the word having originally erred and written לקרת. ST extends to לך̊ לקראת מש[ה] ('go to meet Moses').

Line 18: [וילך̊ משה {ואהרן} • לך̊ אל פרעה • [13]לך מע]לי • [14]אך ביום
['and Moses went' (Ex. 4:29). (*Parashat Va-yeraʾ*) 'go to Pharoah' (Ex. 7:15). (*Parashat Boʾ*) 13. 'go from] **my presence**' (Ex. 10:28). 14. **'however, on the** [first] **day'** (Ex. 12:15).

P, ST and H bring וילך משה from Ex. 4:29. MV extends to וילך משה ואהרן ('and Moses and Aaron went') and likely our scribe does too, given available space.

This is followed by לך אל פרעה from Ex. 7:15 as brought by P, MV, ST and H.

13. P, MV, ST and H all agree, bringing לך מעלי. Our scribe likely brings this given the two extant letters.
14. The instance spans two lines. P, MV and H agree. ST is faint but also reads אך̊ ביום הראשון.

Line 19: [הראשון • {ויסע} מלאך̊ • ההלך̊ • ויל]ך̊ • [וי{ו}לך̊ {ייי} • [15]י]מינך̊
[(*Parashat Be-shallaḥ*) 'angel' (Ex. 14:19). 'who went' (Ex. 14:19). 'and he went' (Ex. 14:19). 'and {God} caused' (Ex. 14:21).] 15. **'Your right hand'** (Ex. 15:6).

P, MV, ST and H brings מלאך from Ex. 14:9.

P, ST and H then bring ההלך also from Ex. 14:19 as 𝔐. MV brings ההולך *ma-le'vav* and ST adds ב̇ בו (two in it) signifying that the last two instances come from the same verse.

This is followed by two instances of וילך according to P and H. MV also brings וילך for the first. ST extends the first to וילך̊ מאחריהם ('and he went behind them') which confirms this instance as from Ex. 14:19. My initial thought was that our scribe has extended similarly as there is certainly space, but the letters forms just do not fit the area where there are still some small traces of ink left, and instead the next instance ויולך is a better fit. There is some disagreement over the second instance as there are not two instances of the word וילך between Ex. 14:19 and Ex. 15:6. MV and ST bring instead ויולך which places this as Ex. 14:21. It is possible given space that the scribe of our fragment has extended to ויולך ייי ('and God caused') but this does still leave a small gap between this and the next instance.[93] This also still leaves a sizeable gap in the first part of the line, and no other core sources suggest extending the entries. Turning to our secondary sources, however, Q651–652, Parma 2427 and Add MS 11639 all extend to ויסע מלאך̊ ('and

93 MV2 also lists ויולך̊. Parma 2427 lists ויולך ייי but omits the decoration on the *kaf sofit*. Q651–652 lists only ויולך also omitting the decoration. Parma 1959 brings ויולך̊ only. *Ben Mesheq* lists כא כ׳ף דויולך (21. the *kaf* of 'and He caused'). *Qiryat Sefer* brings ויולך מלא

the angel travelled'). Parma 1959 brings מלאך only as the other cores sources.[94] Given this, I would contend our scribe possibly extended as these secondary sources; since this fills the space and places the almost surviving *kaf sofit* of וילך at the appropriate point in the text.

15. **P, MV, ST** and **H** agree, bringing ימינך. Indeed the sources bring this word twice, since it occurs twice in the verse and in all likelihood our scribe does the same, bringing this one at the end of this line and one on the next.

With that, we move back to the right side of **T-S AS 139.144-F** for the rest of the listing of *kaf sofit* on that page.

T-S AS 139.144-F (right side)—4 lines preserved

Line 20: **[ימינך • נחלתך • ימל{ו}ך • אלהיך • [16]הוצא]תיך • [17]לך • [18]מלאכתך**
['Your right hand' (Ex. 15:6). 'of Your inheritance' (Ex. 15:17). 'He will reign' (Ex. 15:18). 'your God' (Ex. 20:2).] (*Parashat Yitro*) 16. **'brought you'** (Ex. 20:2). 17. **'to you'** (Ex. 20:3). [likely missing 'to you' (Ex. 20:4)] 18. **'your work'** (Ex. 20:9).

Reconstructing the line, we find a further instance of ימינך also from Ex. 15:6 brought by **P, MV, ST**, and **H** as mentioned above. **ST** adds ב̇ בו: (2 in it [the verse]).

P, MV and **H** follow with נחלתך from Ex. 15:17. **ST** is very faded, but looks similar נחל[תך].

P, MV and H then bring ימלוך from Ex. 15:18. However, 𝔐 is ימלך *ḥaser vav* which is brought by **ST**, though very faded ימלך.

P, MV and H bring אלהיך from Ex. 20:2. **ST** extends to אלהיך אשר ('your God who') thus joining it to the next instance in the same verse, clearer in the enhanced imagery than the microfilm scan.[95]

16. **P, MV** and **H** agree bringing הוצאתיך. **ST** brings הוצאתיך ב בה ('brought you' 2 in it [the verse]) thus linking it to the previous instance.

והכ׳ף מתוייגת שנים ('and he caused' is *ma-le'* and the *kaf* is decorated with two [*tagin*]). Add. MS 11639 brings וילך in error, as P and H..

94 *Ben Mesheq* and *Qiryat Sefer* do not list in the same way, so cannot show any added words.

95 Basser notes that Shem Tov brings אנכי יהוה אלהיך ('I am the Lord your God'), but this seems not to be the case (op. cit., p. 97).

17. P, MV and H then bring two entries for לך. Our scribe has apparently erred, only bringing one instance. ST extends the entries for clarification. The first, though faded is לא יהיה לךׄ ('you shall not have') from Ex. 20:3. The other gives לךׄ פסל ('to you a graven image') from the next verse Ex. 20:4.[96]
18. P, MV, ST and H all agree, bringing מלאכתך.

Line 21: [ימיךׄ • ע{ו}ל{ו}תיךׄ • שלמיךׄ • אל{י}ךׄ •] [19]וברכתיך • [20]לחמךׄ • [21]מימיךׄ •
['your days' (Ex. 20:12). 'your burnt offerings' (Ex. 20:21). 'your peace offerings' (Ex. 20:21). 'to you' (Ex. 20:21).] 19. **'and I will bless you'** (Ex. 20:21). (*Parashat Mishpaṭim*) 20. **'your bread'** (Ex. 23:25). 21. **'your water'** (Ex. 23:25).

P, MV, ST and H bring ימיך from Ex. 20:12.[97]

This is followed by four instances all from Ex. 20:21. P and ST bring עולותיך doubly *ma-le' vav*,[98] H is עולתיך *ma-le' vav*, and only MV brings as 𝔐, giving עלתיך *ḥaser vav*.

All four core sources then agree on שלמיך.

P and H bring אלך, but this word only appears much earlier in chapter 3 of Exodus. These two have omitted a *yod* and MV and ST correctly bring instead אליך from the same verse Ex. 20:21, indeed the imagery reveals that ST extends to אבו[א] אליךׄ ('I will come to you'). Our scribe lacks room to extend similarly.

19. P, MV and H agree with a fifth instance from Ex. 20:21. ST is not clear, but seems to bring [וברכ]תיך בׄ בו: ('and I will bless you'—2 in it [the verse]), when one might expect 5.[99] Our scribe omitted the indicator.
20. P, MV, ST and H all agree, bringing לחמך.
21. P and H both add a superfluous *vav*, bringing ומימיך, possibly intending linking 'your bread' **and** 'your water', whereas our scribe, MV and ST are as 𝔐, bringing מימיך.

Line 22: [מקרבךׄ {תלתיהון} • בארצ{י}ךׄ •] [22]ימ]יךׄ • [23]לפניךׄ • [24]מפניךׄ דלהדף •
['from amongst you' {three of them} (Ex. 23:25). 'in your land' (Ex. 23:26).] 22. **'your days'** (Ex. 23:26). 23. **'before you'** (Ex. 23:27). (*Parashat Va-'etḥanan*) 24. **'from before you' of** [the verse beginning] **'to thrust out'** (Deut. 6:19).

---

96 Basser notes that Shem Tov brings לא תעשה לך ('you shall not make'), but this does not appear to be the case (*op. cit.*, p. 97).

97 Basser gives this as Ex. 20:11, but this word is not in that verse (op. cit., p. 97).

98 Basser only records as עולתיך (op. cit. p. 97).

99 ST does not list it, but the Shem Tov *Tanakh* also decorates צאנךׄ ('your sheep') in Ex. 20:21. This is possibly an error given it will appear twice later. Basser also excludes it from his list (op. cit., p. 97).

P, MV and H bring מקרבך, the third instance from Ex. 23:25 which ST recognises, bringing :מקרבך ג֯ בו ('from amongst you' 3 in it [the verse]).

Then P, MV and ST follow with בארצך from Ex. 23:26 as 𝔐. H is *ma-le' yod*, bringing בארציך.

Just following our core sources gives us a short line. Turning then to our secondary sources, there seems to be no other instances that they bring that would fit the gap. However, looking at the available space and the previous usage (see above) and that ST has again commented ג֯ בו, it is possible that the missing word is תלתיהון (three of them).

22. P, MV, ST and H all agree, bringing ימיך. ST adds ב֯ בו (2 in it [the verse]), referring to the two entries in Ex. 23:26.

MV then adds a further instance, עבדך ('your servant') which our scribe, P, ST and H all omit. This would need to fall between Ex. 23:26 and Ex. 23:27, but this word is not present, so this seems likely an error.

23. P, MV and H agrees, bringing לפניך. ST extends considerably to אשלח לפניך֯ [והמ]תי את ('I will send before you [My terror] and I will vex').
24. P and H give מפניך דלהדוף *ma-le' vav* whilst 𝔐 is *ḥaser vav* להדף, as our scribe. MV brings just מפניך. ST is very faint but brings מ[פני]ך֯ דהדוף, omitting the *lamed*, but the Shem Tov *Tanakh* does decorate מפניך֯ in the verse, as opposed to its occurrence in Deut. 7:1 close by, thus supporting this reading. The presence of the second word in close proximity has necessitated the use of דלהדף; hence MV is less helpful here.

ST is then not visible for the rest of its line in any imagery until ואהבך֯ on the next line, but there seems to be a much longer space that would be filled by מפניך֯ דלהדף. However, in the Shem Tov *Tanakh* no other instances are brought until ואהבך֯. This is potentially significant as our scribe has a spacing which might suggest something prior to ואהבך֯ too, but nowhere near the same amount of space.

Line 23: [ואהבך֯ • וברכך֯ • והרבך֯ • {דגנך֯} •] 25וברך • 26פרי בטנך֯ • 27אדמתך֯ •
['and He will love you' (Deut 7:13). 'and He will bless you' (Deut 7:13). 'and He will multiply you' (Deut 7:13). {'your corn'} (Deut. 7:13)] 25. **'and will bless'** (Deut. 7:13). 26. **'the fruits of your womb'** (Deut. 7:13). 27. **'and your land'** (Deut. 7:13).

The next grouping in our reconstruction, indeed all the instances in this line and the first two from the next line, all come from one verse, Deut 7:13, where the intention seems to be to decorate almost all of the letters *kaf sofit*. P, MV, ST and H bring ואהבך followed by וברכך.

P, ST and H then bring **והרבך**, but **MV** omits. Adding these into the reconstruction also brings a slightly short line.[100]

Based on the secondary sources, it is possible that there is a missing entry, but out of order, and that is דגנך ('your corn') from Deut 7:13.

25. **P**, **MV**, **ST** and **H** all agree, bringing וברך, though our scribe omitted the indicator.
26. **P** and **H** brings just בטנך. Our scribe, like **MV** and **ST** extend to פרי בטנך.
27. **P**, **MV** and **H** agree, bringing אדמתך. Difficult to read, but **ST** appears to extend to ופרי אדמתך ('and the fruits of your land') which echoes the previous instance.

An odd feature of this fragment are the two examples of vertical writing that have been added in very small letters. It seems to read מקרבך ב[ארצך] but this was already listed earlier. It is possible that our scribe originally omitted it but that would make the resultant line even shorter with additional space at the start. It is also possible that that they were originally there, but that section was damaged and then the words were added in subsequently. The longer vertical line seems to read יברכך אליך אליך לך שלום which are clearly instances from the Priestly Blessing in Num. 6:24–26. This would suggest that our scribe or a subsequent corrector is suggesting that there are four instances here. None of the other core sources bring this. The secondary sources are also silent on these instances too.

We then move to another fragment **T-S AS 139.152-F** to conclude the listing for *kaf sofit*.

T-S AS 139.152-F (left side)—7 lines preserved

Line 1: [28]אלפיך • [צאנך • ותיר{ו}שך • ויצהרך • אלפיך • צאנך • ברך •]

28. **'of your kine'** (Deut. 7:13). ['of your flock' (Deut 7:13). (*Parashat Re'eh*) 'of your wine' (Deut. 12:17). 'of your oil' (Deut. 12:17). (*Parashat Ki Tavo'*) 'of your kine' (Deut. 28:4). 'of your flock' (Deut 28:4). 'bless' (Deut. 33:11).]

100 Parma 2427 brings no other instances at the start of this line, but does add דגנך instead of אלפיך on the next line down. Q651–652 and Add. MS 11639 also add דגנך as does Parma 1959 though the *kaf sofit* is not decorated. Q651–652 also adds לאבותיך לתת לך. MV2 does also list דגנך amongst the others included here, but does not decorate any of the letters *kaf sofit*. Both *Ben Mesheq* and *Qiryat Sefer* also list a number of instances here and include דגנך in their lists. There does seem general agreement in the secondary sources that דגנך should be added to the listing.

RECONSTRUCTION 2 Above is the reconstruction of the folio showing only 23 lines, listing part of letters *kaf* and *kaf sofit* that we have covered above. This covers fragments T-S AS 139.152-F (right side) and T-S AS 139.144-F (right side), though joined together, they both form the left side of this reconstructed page.

28. **P**, **MV**, **ST** (though difficult to read) and **H** agree. This is the first listing of this word. it likely appears again later in the line.

Reconstructing the rest of the line **P**, **MV**, **ST** (though again very faded) and **H** bring another instance from Deut. 7:13, צנאך.

Revealed by the enhanced imagery, **ST** then appears to bring a further instance, not in the other core sources, but it is not at all clear. המ[?]ך֯. By its position in the list it would need to fall between Deut. 7:13 and 12:17. Possible candidates are therefore המוציאך (('who brought you') from Deut 8:13, המוליכך ('who led you') from Deut. 18:15 or המאכלך ('who fed you') from Deut. 8:16. Indeed, as a grouping these three are clearly related thematically as material blessings from God, and one could expect a decoration on all, however, Shem Tov does not decorate any of these in his *Tanakh* and **ST** enjoys no real support from any secondary sources.[101]

P and **H** then bring ותירוצך *ma-le' vav* when 𝔐 is ותירצך.

They then all bring ויצהרך from Deut. 12:17.

P and **H** then bring אלפיך again, but this time from Deut. 28:4 followed by צאנך, again from that same verse. **ST** confirms these as it seems to give ותירצך֯ ויצהרך֯ [אלפיך] דראה ה֯ :בו firmly placing these in *parashat Re'eh* and adding that there are 5 in it [the verse]. **ST** then adds צאנך֯ this time from Deut 28:4 in *parashat Ki Tavo'*. However, the enhanced imagery for **ST** then suggests that there may follow a further two entries from the next verse Deut 28.5 or 28:17, which would certainly fit in in and continue the theme of blessings from God. The first appears to be טנאך֯ ('your basket'). The second is ומשארתך֯ ('and your kneading bowl'). These are not present in our other core sources and our *Genizah* manuscript likely lacks available space given the need to start the next letter description at the end of the line, even if it was abbreviated. Shem Tov does not decorate these in his *Tanakh* and **ST** enjoys only some limited support particularly for the first additional instance from the secondary sources.[102] **MV** omits all of these instances.

Finally, all the core sources, **P**, **MV** and **H** conclude the listing with ברך from Deut. 33:11. The enhanced imagery shows that **ST** extends to ברך֯ ייי חילך ('Bless God, His valour').

---

101 Turning to our secondary sources, Parma 2427 does list המאכלך, but does not decorate it. Otherwise all other secondary sources omit.

102 Turning to our secondary sources, *Ben Mesheq* brings ה' ג' כפי"ן מברוך טאנך ומשאריך ([verse] 5–3 [letters] *kaf* from 'blessed are your baskets and your kneading bowls'). **MV2** brings the whole phrase ברוך טאנך ומשאריך, but decorates no letters. Q651–652 brings ט֯אנך֯, decorating two letters, including the *kaf sofit*. Add, MS 11639 brings ברוך֯ טאנך֯ decorating two letters *kaf sofit* in the phrase. *Qiryat Sefer* only notes that one should decorates the *ṭet* from טאנך. Parma 2427 and Parma 1959 omit.

Of the 74–79 possible entries, only 28 remain extant in our manuscript. **ST** seems to have brought three extra instances towards the ends of our listing.

9 Description and Example Forms of the Second Special Letter *Kaf Sofit*

As noted, the listing for the *kaf sofit* concludes back on **T-S AS 139.152-F** on the left hand side of that image (the right side of the folio) and appears to move to the letter *lamed*. However, one of the key issues regarding this listing is that not all the sources agree that we then move to *lamed*. Instead there is a tradition of a further *kaf sofit* form, with only three instances. However, all of these three have already been listed in the previous version of the form and this may be a reason for their omission in many sources.

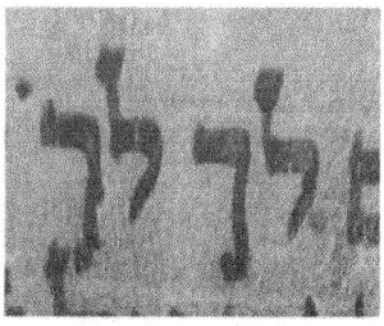

Only one word and a letter survive from the description, but reconstituting around this shows that our scribe clearly does bring this additional form and the three examples listed. This form is also interesting in that this form does appear in Yemenite *Sifrey Torah* where is is known as עקום *ʿaqum* (bent) and generally used instead of the previous form that had *tagin*.[103]

Above right: the ʿaqum *form as brought in a Yemenite* Torah *that I photographed in a synagogue in Re'ut in Israel.*

What is unclear is whether we are to treat this form as a composite. Given they already take four *tagin*, are we also to add the curl at the base of the leg? Or does this curl replace the previous form? The description offered is not specific in this regard.

P, **H** and **MV** all ignore the description of this form of the special *kaf sofit* and the three instances. Amongst our core sources, our fragment has only **ST** for company, which reads in the first section ותו ך דקאים כרעיהון לקדמיהון תלת באורית (and also a *kaf sofit* that their legs stand up/are raised to their fronts, three

103 Baer also brings only this form and not the one with four *tagin*. He describes it as a כף עקומה (bent *kaf*) and notes בשלשה מקומות כותבים את כ״ף הפשוטה עקומם וצורתה שיעקם את עוקץ רגלה מעט לשמאל כזה (in three places they write the final *kaf* bent and its form curves the point of its foot a little upwards to the left like this). However, he agrees with only one from our listing and brings instead ויברך̊ אתם אלהים ('and God blessed them') from Gen 1:28, our instance 2 and then ישפך̊ but from ישפך דם נקי בקרב ארצך ('he will shed innocent blood in the midst of your land') from Deut. 19:10. (Baer, op. cit., p. 24.)

in the *Torah*), however, this is an error with the *qof* and *ʾalef* reversed in the key word[104] and this error is repeated in BH ותו ך דקאים כרעיהון לקדמיהון תלתא באוריתא. In the actual listing the scan is unclear and appears to have דכאיף [?]הון ג באורית̇ in place of דקאים. Our scribe writes דאקים correctly, and thus is the **only core source to preserve this properly.**

The printed Maḥzor Vitry (*LMV*) *does not include this particular form, as* ***MV*** *omits it entirely. Reinforcing his inclusion in the listing of the three letters* kaf sofit *with a different form, in his rendition of the form in* ***T-S NS 287.11-F*** *our scribe has included this form* (*see right*)*, though rather poorly drawn. There is clearly an attempt to make the curl but it is not much more than a blob. The leg also seems to have gained an extra line, which is probably not a part of the form. He has chosen not to include the four* tagin, *even though the same words also appear in that listing as well. In this he is echoed by a few of the other sources shown below. Unfortunately, because these instances are grouped tightly together, the text of* ***T-S Misc. 24.182*** *in not extant for this form.*

Line 2: דאקים כ[רעיהון לקדמיהון אך̊ בשר • שפך̊ • ישפך̊ • //// שער ל //// מ̇ד̇]
that raise [their legs/knees to their fronts (and, based on **ST**, the listing that our fragment is likely to have should be) (*Parashat Noaḥ*) 'only flesh' (Gen. 9:4), 'sheds [blood]' (Gen. 9:6) and 'his [blood] will be shed' (Gen. 9:6). //// gate of *lamed* //// 64]

10 Listing of Instances for the Second Special Letter *Kaf Sofit*

However, sadly none of these instances are preserved in **CG**. The second and third instance as we have already seen come from the same verse, a key verse that displays an elegant symmetry[105] and that is particularly important in *Sefer Tagin* for other decorations on the letters *dalet*.

---

104 Which Basser faithfully and incorrectly transcribes, op. cit. p. 98.

105 See Holtz, B., *Back to the Sources*, Summit Books, 1984, p. 47. In terms of our secondary sources, Parma 2427 brings this curled form on the שפך̊, but it has the other version on ישפך̊, omitting אך completely. For both Add. MS 27167 and Parma 1959 there is a curl on שפך̊ and ישפך̊ alongside the extra *tagin*, but אך only has *tagin*. **MV2** does seem to make a distinction between the forms with the first having four *tagin* and the second only two and with a more pronounced bend in the leg. Add. MS 11639 and Q651–652 omits this curled form entirely. *Ben Mesheq* and *Qiryat Sefer* are not applicable here, as they do not illustrate the form.

TABLE 13 Forms for the second special letter *kaf sofit*. Not all of the sources bring this and there is clearly a disagreement whether they should have the extra *tagin* as well as the curl at the end of the leg of the letter. Some of the curls are quite pronounced, interfering with the form of the letter, such as in Parma 1959 and MS Geunz. 481, where they could easily be taken as large letters *nun*.

Not present *Maḥzor Vitry* Parma 2574 (P)	Not present *Maḥzor Vitry* Add. MS 27201 (MV)	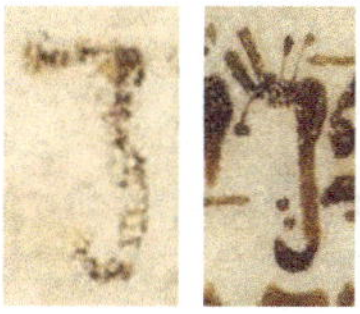 Shem Tov *Tanakh* *Sefer Tagi* (ST)	 *Badey ha-'Aron* Heb. 840 (BH)	Not present *Sefer Tagin* Heb. 837 (H)
Not extant Nr. 5667 (K)	 Parma 2427	 Parma 1959	Not present Q651–652	 MS Geunz. 481
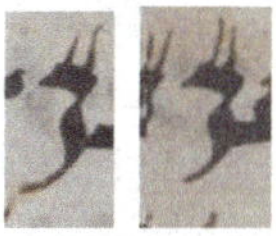 *Maḥzor Vitry* Add. MS 27201 (MV2)	Not extant Add. MS 11639	 Add. MS 26167	Not available Bologna *Torah*	 Vat. ebr. 1
 Or. 1463	Not present Alexander *Torah*			

The microfilm scan does not help, but the enhanced imagery for **ST** reveals אך̊ בשר [בנפ]שו as the first instance and then proceeds to quote the whole key verse, bringing שפך̊ דם האדם באדם דמו ישפך̊ ('he who sheds the blood of man, by man shall his blood be shed') concluding this section. It is, of course, **highly significant** that our early witness **CG** has included this listing for the second form of *kaf sofit*, given the silence of most of the other witnesses.

11 Description and Example Forms of the Special Letter *Lamed*

There is very little remaining in our fragment of the entry for *lamed* with part of the descriptor and only four instances shown across the five lines, but we can reconstruct this fairly readily.

The printed Maḥzor Vitry (*LMV*)*, shown right, brings possibly the most familiar rendition of this letter but, as mentioned, there are possibly more forms of this particular letter amongst the manuscripts than any other, with scribes trying to understand the instructions.*

Despite the description of the lamed *stating that there is a* yod *descending from the* lamed*, our scribe in **T-S NS 287.11-F** (right) has has instead placed two* tagin *on the back of the roof of the letter and elongated the the ascender.*

***T-S Misc. 24.182** (right) brings a* lamed *that is quite similar to some of the other sources below.*

At the end of line 2 it is likely that our fragment carries the small writing indicating שער ל (the gate of *lamed*) followed by the number of instances concerning the *lamed* before moving to the rest of the description in the next line. Given available space, it is likely that our scribe wrote these in abbreviated form, as **P** and **H** and not as **ST**.

P reads מׄד באורייתא דאריך קדליהון ותגיהון נחית מן קדליהון ובהדי קדליהון מחתי לתחת כרישיה דיוד. ([*lamed*] 44 in the *Torah* where their necks are longer and their *tag* descends from their neck and at the point is placed under as the head of a *yod*). **MV** is similar but brings no number of instances, as usual, but also transposes the *tav* and *yod* in מחתי reading דאריך קדליהון ותגיהון נחית מן קדליהון ובהדי קדליהון מחית לתחת כרישיה דיוד. **H** too is similar in stating מׄדׄ באורי׳ דאריך קדליהון ותאגיהון נחית מן קדליהון ובהדי קדליהון קדליהון מחתי לתחת כרישיה דיוד but breaks a page and repeats a קדליהון unnecessarily. It also adds an *ʾalef* into ותאגיהון. In the introduction concerning the *lamed*, **ST** is a little damaged with some obscured letters, but brings, דאריך קדליהון ותג[יהו]ן דנחית מן קדליהון וב[ה]די קדליהון [מ]חת[י] לתחת כרישיה דיוד א[ר]בעין וא[ר]בעה באוריתׄ. In the listing for

TABLE 14 Forms for the special letter *lamed*. Whilst the simpler examples tend to show a *yod* form descending from the top of the ascender of the *lamed*, some of the more complex forms have multiple flags, curls, forks or stirrup shapes. Indeed, these are only a selection of the vast amount of forms that have been brought by scribes over time to decorate this letter.

 *Maḥzor Vitry* Parma 2574 (P)	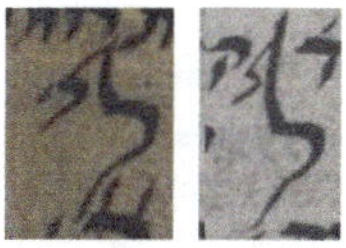 *Machzor Vitry* Add. MS 27201 (MV)	 Shem Tov *Tanakh* *Sefer Tagi* (ST)	 *Badey ha-ʾAron* Heb. 840 (BH)	 *Sefer Tagin* Heb. 837 (H)
Not extant Nr. 5667 (K)	 Parma 2427	 Parma 1959	 Q651–652	 MS Geunz. 481
 *Maḥzor Vitry* Add. MS 27201 (MV2)	Not deployed Add. MS 11639	 Add. MS 26167	 Bologna *Torah*	 Vat. ebr. 1
 Or. 1463	 Alexander *Torah*			

lamed ST shortens to דאריך קדליהוׄ ותגיהוׄ נחית מן קדליׄ מׄד באוׄר. Finally the same sage in BH brings דאריך קדליהון ותגיהון דנחית מן קדליהון ובהדי קדליהון מחתי לתחת כרישיה דיוד וארבעין וארבעה באוריתא. The sources are generally consistent in content for the descriptions, with merely a few minor spelling/order variations.

Line 3: **באורייתא ד**[אריך קדל{י}הון ות{א}גיהון {ד}נחית מן קדל{י}הון ובהדי]
in the *Torah* that [their necks are longer and their *tag* descends from their neck, and at the point …]

Line 4: **קדלהון מחתי** [לתחת כרישיה דיוד //// ויל֯ב{י}שם • וישל֯ח{י}הו]
of their necks is placed [under, as the head of a *yod* //// (*Parashat Bere'shit*) 'and clothed them' (Gen. 3:21). 'and He sent him' (Gen. 3:23)].

As we turn to the letter *lamed,* we also turn a folio for ST and the writing is clear again in all available imagery. We can therefore now see what Shem Tov fully intended in his witness to *Sefer Tagin*, and not have to rely so much on faint ink residue, or his *Tanakh.*

12 Listing of Instances for the Special Letter *Lamed*

After the letter description P and H bring וילבשם from Gen. 3:21 as 𝔐. ST brings instead ויל֯בישם *ma-le'yod.* MV has a crossing through of an extraneous *yod* ויליבשם.

The last missing instance on this line is likely וישלחהו from Gen. 3:23 as 𝔐 and as brought by MV, ST and H. P appears to be *ma-le'yod* bringing וישלחיהו.

Line 5: **[1]ל֯הם • [2]ל֯הט • [3]ל֯תב**[ה • תכל֯נה • ויכל֯א • ויתגל֯ • ל֯א ראו • עשה ל֯ו]
1. **'to them'** (possibly Gen 6:1—out of sequence?). 2. **'flaming** [sword]' (Gen. 3:24). 3. **'for the ark'** (Gen. 6:16). ['you will finish it' (Gen 6:16). 'was restrained' Gen. 8:2. 'and he was uncovered' (Gen. 9:21). 'they did not see' (Gen. 9:23). 'he had done to him' (Gen. 9:24).]

1. Our scribe appears to be bringing an entry that no other core source does starting the line with ל֯הם. Based on its position in the list and assuming that our scribe agrees with the first two instances, this entry would need to appear between Gen. 3:23 and 3.24, but this word does not occur. The word does appear in Gen. 3:7 earlier referring to Adam and Eve making themselves aprons and it is possible that this is the intention. However, this would be out of sequence. It is is worth noting that our secondary sources become of primary importance here and provide a much more

likely explanation. Parma 2427 lists ילדו להם ('were born to them') from Gen. 6:1, but does not indicate any *lamed* as special. Add. 27167 brings יל̊דו להם but decorates the *lamed* of the first word. *Ben Mesheq* agrees, explaining ס״ו א׳ ילדו הלמ״ד בראשה למטה בעוקץ תג (Chapter 6, [verse] 1 'were born' the *lamed* in its head has a thorn *tag* [going] downwards). Parma 1959 brings the most concrete support, as it marks the same *lamed* as our scribe ילדו ל̊הם. Q651–652 decorates both ובנות יל̊דו ל̊הם (and daughters were born to them).[106] This instance in our fragment would also be out of sequence, but at least is supported by many secondary sources.[107] It is possible that similarity of the next instance instance caused the confusion for our scribes ordering, if he just brought להם without ילדו and his eye had skipped forward after writing *lamed* and *he* and then wrote the *mem*. Then he realised and resumed with להט. If that is the case, even if out of sequence, then our fragment is the only core source preserving this particular instance, giving it extra credibility for inclusion in any listing.

2. **P, MV, ST** and **H** all agree, bringing להט.
3. **P, MV, ST** and **H** all agree, bringing לתבה.

P, MV, ST and **H** all bring תכלנה also from 6:16.

P, MV, ST and **H** follow with ויכלא from Gen. 8:2.

Then all the core sources similarly agree, bringing ויתגל from Gen. 9:21.

לא ראו from Gen. 9:23 follows in **P, ST** and **H**. However, **MV** omits this instance.

The line likely concludes with עשה לו from Gen. 9:24 as found in **P, MV, ST** and **H**. With the exception of one omission from **MV**, the core sources are remarkably consistent in this line and our reconstruction is fairly assured.

Line 6: [4]**ל̊א יעשה** • [5]**כאש**[ר כל̊ה • ובגד לל̊ב{ו}ש • הכר ל̊ך • שכל̊ו • ל̊ישמעאל̊ים]
(*Parashat Va-yera'*) 4. **'shall You not do** [justly]' (Gen. 18:25). (*Parashat Toledot*) 5. **'when he** [had finished' (Gen. 27:30). [(*Parashat Va-yetse'*) 'and clothes to wear' (Gen. 28:20). 'you discern' (Gen. 31:32). 'they have not miscarried' (Gen. 31:38). (*Parashat Va-yeshev*) 6/7. 'to the Ishmaelites ...]

4. **P, MV, ST** and **H** all agree, bringing לא יעשה.
5. **P, MV, ST** and **H** all agree, bringing כאשר כלה.

Reconstructing the rest of the line, **P, MV** and **H** bring ובגד ללבוש from Gen. 28:20, but since there are two letters *lamed* in the key word, we are unsure which is intended to be

---

106 Which in interesting as Add. MS 27167 and Parma 1959 generally agree and have commonalities of format.

107 Add. MS 11639 and *Ben Mesheq* omit.

special. ST brings ובגד לל֯בוש and marks both letters, and in his *Tanakh*, Shem Tov does indeed decorate both. Normally one would expect to see some reference in the other core sources as תרויהון if that was the case, which is not the case here.[108] Also, all of the core sources are *ma-le' vav*, whereas 𝔐 is *ḥaser*, ובגד ללבש. Our scribe may have spelt the word either way.

P, MV, ST and H then all bring הכר לך from Gen. 31:32.

P MV, ST and H then bring שכלו from Gen. 31:38.

The last instance (or possibly instances) connects to the first word on the next line. P brings לישמאלים בת֗. MV does list this, but there is no large *lamed* to mark the start of this grouping, giving לישמאלים ׳ בתרא, as if they are two separate instances and H also puts a separator in between לישמעאלים//בתר׳, adding to the confusion. If we assume 'the last' means the words occurrence in Gen. 37:28 as opposed to a verse earlier, then once again, we are unsure as to which *lamed* to decorate. ST brings ל֯ישמאל֯ים בתרא֗, decorating both.[109]

Line 7: **בת֗** • [6]**איש ע**[דל֯מי קדמ֗ • ל֯פניו אברך • וילבש א{ו}תו • כי חדל֯ •]
... [the] **last** [occurrence] (Gen. 37:28). 7. [the first] 'an Adullamite] **man'** (Gen. 38:1). [(*Parashat Miqqets*) 'before him *'avrekh'*[110] (Gen. 41:43). 'and he dressed him' (Gen. 41:42). 'for they left off' (Gen. 41:49).]

6. P brings עדלמי קד֗. **MV** once again adds a small dash between ׳ עדלמי קדמאה, again as if they were separate instances. **ST** brings עדל֯מי קדמא֗ and H gives עד למי קדמ׳ as if the first word were two words.[111] Our scribe is the

108 Turning to the secondary sources, Q651–652 brings ל֯לבש decorating only the first *lamed*. Conversely Parma 2427 decorates only the second *lamed* bringing לל֯בש and *Qiryat Sefer* agrees with this ללבש חסר והלמ״ד השניה מוזרקת בראשה משני צדדים ('to wear' is *ḥaser* and the second *lamed* is curled in its head from both sides). Add. MS 27167 decorates both, but Parma 1959 omits (again odd, as they usually agree). *Ben Mesheq* also brings both כ״ח ד׳ ללבוש ב׳ למד״ין (28:20 'to wear' 2 [letters] *lamed*). **MV2** lists ובגד ללבוש but decorates neither *lamed*. Add. MS 11639 omits either. Unfortunately, **T-S Misc. 24.182** is not extant until Gen. 30:40.

109 Turning to our secondary sources, **T-S Misc. 24.182** (though slightly faded) and Parma 2427 bring both, ל֯ישמאל֯ים. *Qiryat Sefer* brings לישמאלים שניהם הלמדי״ן מוזרקות ('to the Ishmaelites' both the [letters] *lamed* are curled) but based on positioning it could be the reference in either verse. *Ben Mesheq* is not clear as it brings סל״ז כ״ז לישמאלים ופכ״ח לישמאלים (chapter 36, [verse] 27, 'to the Ishmaelites' and verse 28 'to the Ishmaelites') but we are none the wiser as to which letters *lamed* should be decorated. **MV2** lists לישמאלים but decorates neither. Q651–652, Add. MS 27167, Add. MS 11639 and Parma 1959 all omit.

110 The word is generally not translated and there are midrashic comments suggesting it is a compound of *'av* (father) *rakh* (tender) or it means father to the Pharaoh, or that it is connected to *berekh* ([bending the] knee).

111 Which is transcribed incorrectly in EPST as עד למי.

only core source to add the extra איש beforehand. All also agree that this is the first instance, as opposed to when the same phrase later appears in Gen 38:12. We can assume our scribe recorded similarly.

P, MV and H then bring לפניו אברך from Gen. 41:43. ST brings only לפניו.

MV and H then bring וילבש אתו from the previous verse Gen. 41:42 as 𝔐. P and ST also brings this in this order, but spell the second word *ma-le'vav* וילבש אותו. We are not sure whether our scribe has mis-ordered, but since all of the core sources have done so, this seems likely.[112]

P, MV and H then bring כי חדל from Gen. 41:49. ST extends to כי חדל לספור ('[until] they left off numbering') the last word being *ma-le'vav* when 𝔐 is *ḥaser* לספר. Available space suggests our scribe did not extend. Adding the additional word brings another *lamed* which adds confusion, as it does not take a decoration.[113]

It is difficult to know whether this is the last instance on the line, as we now have two full lines missing. Based on line length, I would argue that we then move to the next line for the next instance. P, MV, and H then all bring ותבלענה which only appears in Genesis at Gen. 41:7 which is also out of sequence. ST does not bring it till even later. Ordering has gone seriously awry in our core sources over the last few instances. Unfortunately, we do not know whether our scribe brought the correct sequence or just echoed the others. Given all of our core sources erred, chances are our manuscript was similarly defective. The correct order of the entries should instead be:

איש עדלמי קדמֹ • ותבלענה • וילבש אתו • לפניו אברך • כי חדל.[114]

P, MV and H then bring ותחלנה from Gen. 41:54. ST differs slightly bringing the word *ma-le'yod* ותחלינה which is as 𝔐.

ST then finally brings [ותבלעג[ה, which had been omitted earlier.

P, MV, ST and H then all bring ויסב מעליהם from Gen. 42:24.

P, MV, ST and H all bring לעיניהם, also from Gen. 42:24.

P, ST, MV and H all then agree on then ולהחיות from Gen. 45:7.

---

112 T-S Misc. 24.182 also brings them in reversed order.

113 However, in support of ST, T-S Misc. 24.182 brings חדלֹ. Q651–Q652 lists כי חדל לֹט לספר. *ḥaser vav* with a line filler. Parma 2427 also brings כי חדלֹ לספר. MV2 lists כי חדל לספר, but without decoration. Add. MS 27167 and Parma 1959 bring חדלֹ לספר. Add. MS 11639 brings כי חדל, but it is not clear the *lamed* is decorated. *Qiryat Sefer* just notes that חדל הלמ"ד מוזרקת ('left off' the *lamed* is curled). *Ben Mesheq* is a case in point as it brings ופמ"ט חדל לספור, not indicating which *lamed*.

114 Basser corrects the order in his book, but makes no remarks on the fact that Shem Tov erred as our other sources, or the additional word לספור or of the *ma-le'vav*, op. cit., p. 99.

MV then brings על֯י רעה from Gen. 50:20. ST only brings על֯י and P and H omit. However, P and H do bring לרעה which occurs only once in Genesis, way back in Gen. 31:52, and, whilst we have encountered some ordering problems of late, they are not likely to be so dramatic. ST appears to give instead ל֯דעה which would be Ex. 2:4, which would make sense in the sequence. We appear to have a degree of confusion, probably because of the similarity between the word רעה and the end of לדעה.[115] Our scribe may have erred similarly, but let's assume not.

The next instance sees us back on safer ground as all the core sources bring וידע אלהים from Ex. 2:25.

P, MV and H then bring הלם from Ex. 3:5 as 𝔐. However, ST brings this *ma-le' vav* הל֯ום.[116]

P, ST and H bring נפלאתי from Ex. 3:20. MV omits the *yod* in error bringing נפלאת.[117]

All our core sources then bring את לבו from Ex. 4:21.

P, MV and H then bring אתה לי from Ex. 4:25. ST extends bringing דמים אתה לי (['bridegroom of] blood you are to me').

7. It is quite difficult to assess the first word on the line that appears at the top of fragment **TS AS 139.158-B** since only the bottom half of the letters remain, and they are faded too. However, based on our reconstruction and the expected position of this instance, it seems to accord with our core sources. **P** and **H** bring אשר על פני המדבר and **MV** and **ST** omit the first word, as this is not in 𝔐, to bring only על פני המדבר from Ex. 16:14. Our scribe may have followed either since the core sources are split equally, but available space suggests that he may have included אשר.

Given all this, our two completely missing lines, 8 and 9, probably read:

Line 8: [ותבל֯ענה • ותחל֯{י}נה • ויסב מעל֯יהם • ל֯עיניהם • ול֯החיות • על֯י רעה •
['and they [the ears] swallowed up' (Gen. 41:7). 'and [the seven years of famine] began' (Gen. 41:54). 'and he turned around from them' (Gen. 42:24). 'before their eyes' (Gen. 42:24). (*Parashat Va-yiggash*) 'and save you alive' (Gen. 45:7). (*Parashat Va-yeḥi*) 'evil against me' (Gen. 50:20).

Line 9: ל֯דעה • וידע אל֯הים • הל֯{ו}ם • נפל֯אתי • את ל֯בו • אתה ל֯י • [7]{אשר} על֯ פני]
(*Parashat Shemot*) 'to know' (Ex. 2:4). 'and God took regard of them' (Ex. 2:25).

---

115 In support of ST, Parma 2427 brings ל֯דעה as does *Ben Mesheq* and *Qiryat Sefer*. Q651–652, Add. MS 11639, MV2 and Parma 1959 omit. **T-S Misc. 24.182** is not extant for this instance.

116 Which Basser does not record, *op. cit.*, p. 100.

117 The *yod* is added back in the transcription in LMV.

'hither' (Ex. 3:5). 'My wonders' (Ex. 3:20). 'his heart' (Ex. 4:21). 'you are to me' (Gen. 4:25). (*Parashat Be-shallaḥ*) 8. '[which] is on the face ...]

We then turn to line 10.

Line 10: המדבר • [נבל֯ • במעל֯[ו]ת • ערותך על֯יו • ל֯פניהם • אל֯הי מסכה • [8]ואל֯הי]
... of the desert' (Ex. 16:14). [(*Parashat Yitro*) '[you will surely] wear yourself out' (Ex. 18:18). 'by steps' (Ex. 20:23). 'your nakedness upon it' (Ex. 20:23). (*Parashat Mishpaṭim*) 'before them' (Ex. 21:1). (*Parashat Ki Tissa'*) 'molten gods' (Ex. 34:17). (*Parashat Qedoshim*) 8. 'and gods [that are] ...]

Reconstructing the rest of line 10, **P**, **MV**, **ST** and **H** all bring נבל from Ex. 18:18.

P, **MV**, **ST** and **H** then all bring במעלות from Ex. 20:23, however, 𝔐 is *ḥaser vav*, so it is unclear what our scribe brought.

P, **ST** and **H** then bring ערותך עליו, also from Ex. 20:23, but **MV** brings only ערותך which is odd, since that word does not have a *lamed* in it.

לפניהם follows in **P** and **H** from Ex. 21:1 and **ST** extends out to אשר תשים ל֯פניהם. However, **MV** disagrees and brings instead לפניכם in the section for *parashat Mishpaṭim*, but this word does not appear in this section or indeed the whole book of Exodus, so this is clearly just a transcription error.[118] We then have a disagreement between our sources.

P, **MV** and **H** then bring אלהי מסכה from Ex. 34:17. **ST** adds an additional descriptor אל֯הי מסכה דתשא ([the] 'molten gods' of [*parashat Ki*] *Tissa'*) to distinguish it from the next instance that it brings ואל֯הי מסכה דקדשים ([the] 'and the molten gods' of [*parashat*] *Qedoshim*) in Lev. 19.4. **MV** also brings ואלהי מסכה, but **P** and **H** omit this second similar instance.[119]

8. Our scribe has clearly not brought the section descriptors from **ST** and we do not know if the מסכה that remains on the next line is from the first or second similar instance. Given the size of the writing and the available space at this point, it is possible that our scribe could well have included this second instance as **ST** and **MV**, but it is a tight squeeze.

---

118 Which **LMV** duly transcribes, incorrectly.

119 Turning to our secondary sources, *Qiryat Sefer* brings אלהי מסכה הלמ״ד מוזרקת ('molten gods' the *lamed* is curved) but as regards the instance in *parashat Qedoshim* speaks only of the *samekh* in מסכה being decorated. Q651–652 also brings ואלהי מס֯כה, but decorates only the *samekh*. **MV2** lists אלהי מסכה in *parashat Ki Tissa'* and ואלהי מסכה in *Qedoshim*, but decorates no letters. Parma 2427, Add. MS 11639, Parma 1959 and *Ben Mesheq* omit either.

T-S AS 139.158-F (left side)—10 lines preserved

Line 11: **מסכה** 9וב[דרך] לא ה[יה • יליד{י}תיהו • ולא יקח שחד • ישראל בת •]
... molten. (Lev. 19:4). (*Parashat Beha'alotkha*) 9. **'and was not on a journey'** (Num. 9:13). ['begotten them' (Num. 11:12). (*Parashat 'Eqev*) 'and He does not take a bribe' (Deut. 10:17). (*Parashat Ve-zo't Ha-berakhah*) the last 'Israel' (Deut. 34:12).

MV then brings an additional instance לצמיתות: בתראה (in perpetuity) in *parashat Be-har* though *ma-le' vav*, as 𝔐 for Lev. 25:30 is לצמיתת. This does not appear in any of the other core sources and our **CG** scribe also omits and, as we showed above, this seems to be a decoration for the *yod*.

9. The next instance is marred by some damage, but likely reads ובדרך לא היה from Lev. 9:13. **P**, **MV**, **ST** and **H** agree.

P and **H** bring ילידתיהו whereas **MV** and **ST** are *ḥaser yod* ילדתיהו from Num. 11:12, as 𝔐.

P, **MV** and **ST** then bring ולא יקח שחד from Deut. 10:17 as 𝔐. **H** brings ולא יקח שוחד, *ma-le' vav* in the last word.

Finally completing the line and the listing for *lamed*, **P** brings ישראל בת̇, the last word of the *Torah*, i.e. Deut. 34:12. **MV** has בתראה, **ST** בתרא and **H** abbreviates to בתר׳. A separate tradition from *Sofrim* 9:7 explains ישראל שבסוף התורה צריך להיות פשוט ולמ״ד שלו צריך להיות זקוף מכל הלמ״ד ('Israel' that is at the end of the *Torah* should be large [lit. obvious] and its *lamed* should be the tallest from all other [letters] *lamed*.)

Our manuscript has preserved only 9 of the possible 44 instances for *lamed* anticipated. The listing for *mem* then begins.

13 Description and Example Forms of the Special Letter *Mem*

The form depicted in the printed Maḥzor Vitry (***LMV***) *is shown right. It shows two* tagin *aloft with dots and one descending* tag *without.*

However, in his rendition of the form in ***T-S NS 287.11-F*** (*right*) *our scribe has brought a* mem *with two lines coming from a quite extended side roof and a further thicker but shorter* tag *from the peak of the letter. This tubbier* tag *shows some similarities to that brought by* **P** *and by* MS *Guenz. 481 below.*

T-S Misc. 24.182 (*right*) *brings three* tagin. *One on the* kaf *part of the body of the letter and one upward and one downwards from the roof of the* vav *part of the letter.*

TABLE 15 Forms for the special letter *mem*. Despite the clear instruction to have three *tagin*, some have four, apparently following **ST** (see below). Even those with three vary quite considerably as there is no agreement on where they should be placed on the letter. Again, because of one *tag* pointing downwards, and an apparent reluctance to do this, other sources elect to only show two *tagin*.

		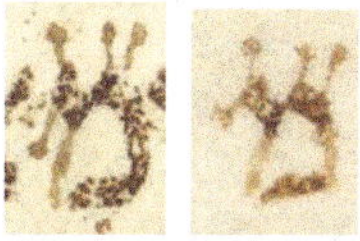		
Maḥzor Vitry Parma 2574 (P)	*Machzor Vitry* Add. MS 27201 (MV)	Shem Tov *Tanakh* *Sefer Tagi* (ST)	*Badey ha-'Aron* Heb. 840 (BH)	*Sefer Tagin* Heb. 837 (H)
Not extant Nr. 5667 (K)	 Parma 2427	 Parma 1959	 Q651–652	 MS Geunz. 481
		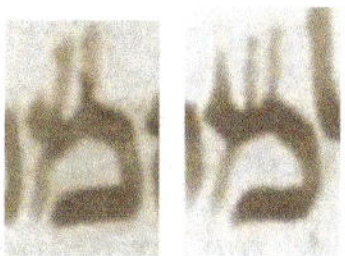		
Maḥzor Vitry Add. MS 27201 (MV2)	Add. MS 11639	Add. MS 26167	Bologna *Torah*	Vat. ebr. 1
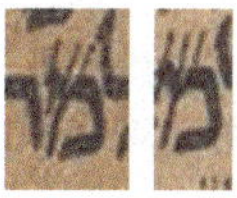 Or. 1463	Not present Alexander *Torah*			

Line 12: שער מׄ טלׄ ב[אור]יתא דגׄ [זיוני למׄראה • למׄאכל • המׄתהפכת •]
Gate of *mem* 39 in the [*To*]***rah*** **that have three** [*tagin* (*Parashat Bere'shit*) 'to behold' (Gen. 2:9) change below. 'to eat' (Gen. 2:9). 'turned over and over' (Gen. 3:24).]

Whilst the word שער may have been added by a later scribe or reader, the מׄ, this time, is part of the original manuscript. Unfortunately, much of the description is damaged, but is in line with the core sources. However, once again our scribe uses the playful reversal of numerals to spell טל (dew) whereas the other sources are more formal. **P**, **MV** and **H** bring מ ל״ט באוריית׳ דג׳ זיוני (*mem* 39 in the *Torah* with three *tagin*). However, **ST** disagrees and brings in the listing for the letter מ דאית לה ארבע זיוני ל״ט באורי׳ (*mem* that has **four** *tagin* 39 in the *Torah*). In the introduction and in **BH** by the same sage we find מ דאית לה ארבעה זיוני תלתין ותשעה באוריתא (*mem* that has **four** *tagin* thirty-nine in the *Torah*), writing the number in full.

14 Listing of Instances for the Special Letter *Mem*

Reconstructing the rest of the line, there is general agreement between all of the core sources. The first instance brought by **P**, **MV**, **ST** and **H** is למראה from Gen. 2:9.

This is followed by למאכל from the same verse as brought by **P**, **MV**, **ST** and **H**.

המתהפכת from Gen. 3:24 likely concludes the line, also brought by **P**, **MV**, **ST** and **H**.

Line 13: **ותאמֿר קניתי**[1] • **והיו ימֿיו**[2] • [{מֿעולם} • וימֿצאו בקעה • מֿגן צריך •]

1. **'and she said "I have gained"'** (Gen. 4:1). 2. **'and his days'** (Gen. 6:3). [{'were of old' (Gen. 6:4) (*Parashat Noaḥ*) 'and they found a plain' (Gen. 11:2). (*Parashat Lekh Lekha*) 'delivered your enemies' (Gen. 14:20).]

1. **P**, **MV** and **ST** agree. **H** agrees, though abbreviating to ותאמ׳ קניתי.
2. **P**, **MV**, **ST** and **H** all agree, bringing והיו ימיו.

The first major deviation regarding the listing for *mem* comes from **ST** which brings an instance that is not in any of the other core sources, מֿעולם ('were of old') from Gen. 6:4. Unfortunately, we do not know whether our scribe included this, though available space on the line would suggest that he did; as otherwise we would have a very short line.[120]

More certain instances on this line are likely to be וימצאו בקעה from Gen. 11:2, as brought by **P**, **MV** and **H**. **ST** brings just וימֿצאו.

P, **MV**, **ST** and **H** then bring מגן צריך from Gen. 14:20.

Line 14: **המֿכסה אני**[3] • **מֿלאכי לפני**[4][ד • מֿנ{י}קתה • למֿה זה אנכי • למֿה לי חיים •]

(*Parashat Va-yera'*) 3. **'shall I hide'** (Gen. 18:17) (*Parashat Ḥayyei Sarah*) 4. **'his**

120 Of our secondary sources, Q651–652 also brings מֿעולם, supporting the possibility. **MV2** also lists אשר מעולם ('that were of old') but does not decorate the letter *mem*. However, Parma 2427, Add. MS 11639, Parma 1959, Add. MS 27167, *Qiryat Sefer* and *Ben Mesheq* all omit.

angel before you' (Gen. 24:7). ['and her nurse' (Gen. 24:59). (*Parashat Toledot*) 'why do I live?'[121] (Gen. 25:22). 'what is life to me?' (Gen. 27:46).]

3. P, MV, ST and H all agree, bringing המסכה אני.
4. P, MV and H agree with our manuscript, however, this is incorrect and only ST brings מ֯לאכו ('his angel') as 𝔐. A simple transcription error where a *vav* has become a *yod* has occurred and the scribes of the other sources, including our *Genizah* fragment, have clearly not verified the text they have copied from.[122]

Once again ST brings another instance that is not in the other core sources תנקה מ֯לאתי ('you will be clear') from Gen. 24:41. Unfortunately, the Shem Tov *Tanakh* is not extant for this listing.[123] Given available space our manuscript probably omitted this, unless the scribe shortened some of the entries, as ST.

Reconstructing the rest of the line, P and H brings מניקתה *ma-le'yod* from Gen. 24:59. MV is doubly *ma-le'*, bringing מיניקתה. ST is the only core source to spell מנקתה *ḥaser yod* as 𝔐.

P, MV and H then bring למה זה אנכי from Gen. 25:22. ST omits אנכי. The line likely concludes with למה לי חיים from Gen. 27:46, as brought by P, MV and H. ST omits חיים.

Line 15: [5]ותעבר המנחה • [6]מהרו ו[עלו • כה תאמ֯רו • ????? [7]ותמ֯לא]
(*Parashat Va-yishlaḥ*) 5. **'so the offering passed'** (Gen 32:22). (*Parashat Va-yiggash*) 6. **'hasten and** [go up' (Gen. 45:9) 'so will you say' (Gen. 50:17). (*Parashat Shemot*) 7. 'and filled ...]

5. P and MV agree and are likewise *ḥaser vav* ותעבר as 𝔐. However, ST and H are *ma-le' vav* ותעבור.
6. P, ST and H agree, bringing מהרו ועלו. MV brings just מהרו. Our scribe has forgotten to indicate the *mem* on both instances 5 and 6.

---

121 Lit. 'why am I this'.

122 Q651–652, Parma 2427 and also bring מ֯לא֯כו again later in *parashat Ḥayyei Sarah* at Gen. 24:40 decorating two letters. Add. MS 11639 brings it as well, but only with regards to the *kaf* ישלח מלאכ֯ו ('will send His angel') which might explain the confusion. However, Add. MS 27167 and Parma 1959 bring only the instance from Gen. 24:40 decorating the *mem* ישלח מ֯לאכו. MV2 lists only ישלח מלאכו, but does not decorate a letter. *Ben Mesheq* and *Qiryat Sefer* omit either.

123 None of the secondary sources appear to lend any support to ST for this additional instance.

Our *Genizah* secondary source **T-S Misc. 24.182** then offers up מ̊ה̊ (what), which, from its positioning, is Gen. 32:27, where Jacob is asked for his name by the angel.[124]

The next instance on this line is likely כה תאמרו from Gen. 50:17, as brought by **P**, **ST** and **H**. **MV**, however, brings כא תאמרון in error.[125]

7. The last word on the line likely joins to the two on the following line. **P**, **MV** and **H** bring only ותמ̊לא but **ST** extends to ותמ̊לא הארץ. Our manuscript has possibly extended even further as otherwise this line is very short. It is highly likely that something else has been added preceding ותמלא, but nothing else is seen in the secondary sources.[126] It is possible that our scribe extended the second or third instance on that line, which also seems unlikely given the secondary sources or perhaps brought the instance from **ST** תנקה מ̊לאתי or the repeat of מ̊לאכו from our secondary sources, but out of sequence. Either would fit. However, this also seems unlikely. It is also possible, given **T-S Misc. 24.182** above, that the missing instance, again out of sequence could be מ̊ה שמך (what is your name) but again unlikely. It may be that the scribe erred and crossed out an entry. This gap is therefore quite problematic and remains unresolved at present.

Line 16: **הארץ אתם • [8]כה תאמר** • [מ̊תו {כל} האנשים • יגרשם מ̊ארצו • [9]{ולא}]
... the land with them' (Ex. 1:7). 8. **'so will you say'** (Ex. 3:14). ['so you will say to the children of Israel' (Ex. 3:14). '{all} the men have died' (Ex. 4:19) 'he will drive them out of his land' (Ex. 6:1). (*Parashat Va-ʾera*ʾ) 9. '{and he will not} ...]

8. **H** brings כה תאמר לבני ישראל ('so you will say to the children of Israel'). **P** and **MV** abbreviate the last word to ישר̇. **ST** just brings כה תאמר and, given available space, our scribe may have done similar (see below). Regardless, he has again omitted to indicate the *mem*.

124 Again, this is likely an error as usually only the *he* is decorated in other core and secondary sources on this word.

125 LMV corrects to כה תאמרו in the transcription.

126 Q651–652 brings only ותמ̊לא. Parma 2427 does extend as our scribe ותמ̊לא הארץ אתם. Add. MS 11639 only decorates the *tav* in the word. **T-S Misc. 24.182**, **MV2** and Parma 1959 omit and *Ben Mesheq* and *Qiryat Sefer* do not employ phrases, so none of our secondary sources support the use of additional words from this phrase. Nor do they bring any additional instances between Gen. 50:17 and Ex. 1:7.

P, MV and H bring מתו אנשים. However, the phrase in Ex. 4:19 is מתו כל האנשים in 𝔐. ST extends further, bringing מ̊תו כל האנשים המבקשים ('all the men have died who sought') but that adds another possible *mem*, though ST does not add a circle on that.

The line likely concludes with יגרשם מארצו from Ex. 6:1 as brought by P, MV, ST and H. However, all of this simply does not fit in the available space, but can be accommodated if we omit לבני ישראל as ST. It is possible that the extension has been omitted and then added in superscript.

Line 17: **ישמ̊ע אליכם קדמׄ** • [10]חמ̊רם קדמׄ • [[11]לא מ̊ת אחד • לא מ̊ת דממקנה • [12]ומ̊ת]
'... listen to you' the first [occurrence]. (Ex. 7:4). 10. **the first 'heaps'** (Ex. 8:10). ['not one died' (Ex. 9:6). the 'did not die' of [the verse containing] 'from the cattle' (Ex. 9:7). (*Parashat Bo'*) 12. 'and died ...]

9. P, MV and H bring just ישמע אליכם and omit קדמׄ. ST also omits that, but extends to ולא ישמ̊ע אליכם ('and you will not listen to them'). Since there is only one occurrence of the phrase in the book of Exodus, קדמׄ is perhaps superfluous and possibly an error given the next instance, where our scribe has omitted the key word and has written it above the line, but is also then followed by קדמׄ.
10. ST and H bring חמרים קדמׄ and P חמרים קדׄ. MV extends bringing חמרים חמרים קדמאה, however, 𝔐 is *ḥaser yod*, חמרם. Because of a split in the parchment, our manuscript is difficult to read; as the last letter could be a *yod* or more likely part of the *mem sofit*.
11. P and H bring לא מת אחד and ST is similar, abbreviating the last word to אחׄ. MV omits this instance.

P brings לא מת דממקנה from the next verse Ex. 9:7. H errs and gives לא מת דמקנה omitting a *mem*. MV omits completely. ST is difficult to read, but likely reads לא מת ומ̊מ̊קנה ב̇ בפׄ. This causes Basser to add ומ̊מקנה ('and from the cattle') from Ex. 9:6, with the decoration on the first *mem* to his listing.[127] Whilst slightly different to the normal usage of בה or בו (in it [the verse]), the phrase ב̇ בפׄ is likely is an abbreviation suggesting twice in the *pasuq* (verse). In fact, looking at the Shem Tov *Tanakh* (above right), we see that he decorates three instances in Ex. 9:6 and 9:7 ומ̊מקנה and לא מ̊ת from the same *pasuq* and then again from the next.[128]

127 Basser, op. cit., p. 101.
128 It is possible ST has erred here, and only the word מ̊ת in both instances should have been

12. CG brings כל בכור בת̊ on the next line and the initial word ומת is not extant this line. P brings ומת כל בכור בת̊. MV brings in full ומת כל בכור • בתראה, but with a superfluous separator. ST brings ומ̊ת כל בכור בתרא̊ and H is similar, but with בתר׳.

Line 18: כל בכור בת̊ • [13]שמ̊ורים [בתרא̊ • מ̊ה זאת עשית לנו • מ̊מ{ו}ת{י}נו]
... every firstborn' the last [occurrence] (Ex. 11:5). 12. [the last] **'watching'** (Ex. 12:42). [(*Parashat Be-shallaḥ*) 'what is this you have done to us' (Ex. 14:11). 'that we should die' (Ex. 14:12).]

13. Many of our core sources seem to put separators between the two word in this instance. ST and MV bring שמורים • בתרא. H gives שמרים//בתרא but is *ḥaser vav* as 𝔐. P is also *ḥaser vav*, but the scribe wrote קד̇ initially and changed it to בת̊ though left the descender of the *qof* in the *bet* so it looks like קת̊.

Reconstructing the rest of the line P, MV and H bring quite a long phrase מה זאת עשית לנו from Ex. 14:11. ST originally omitted this in error, but has written the instance in the margin.

The line likely concludes with an instance from Ex. 14:12. P and H bring ממותינו *male' vav*, and MV brings *ḥaser vav* ממתינו. However, 𝔐 is ממתנו. It is not clear from these source on which *mem* the decoration falls, and our fragment offers no assistance here. ST had also originally omitted, but also brings this in the margin and fortunately adds the circle over the first *mem*, bringing מ̊מתנו קד̇. Since there is only one occurrence of this word in Exodus, the קד̇ must be reinforcing that this is on the first *mem*.[129]

---

brought. However, from our secondary sources, Q651–652 brings לא מ̊ת and והנה לא מ̊ת. Add. MS 11639 brings לא מ̊ת אחד and והנה לא מ̊ת. Parma 1959 brings three instances מ̊ת אחד and מ̊ת מ̊מקנה. MV2 lists only והנה לא מת but does not decorate the letter *mem*. Parma 2427 omits any instances here. *Qiryat Sefer* typically seems to want to decorate more letters bringing מת מת ממקנה כל הממי״ן מתוייגות ('died' 'died' 'of the cattle' all the [letters] *mem* are decorated with *tagin*). *Ben Mesheq* too expands the opportunities to decorate and brings ס״ט ו׳ ב׳ ממי״ן דממקנה מ׳ם דומת ז ג׳ ממי״ן דומת ממקנה (chapter 9, [verse] 6 2 [letters] *mem* of 'from the cattle' [and] *mem* of 'and died' [verse] 7, 3 [letters] *mem* of 'and died' 'of the cattle'). It is difficult to assess the most likely reading with such variation.

129 This is further reinforced by Parma 2427, Q651–652 and Parma 1959 which bring מ̊מתנו. Add. MS 11639 brings מ̊מתינו. *Qiryat Sefer* notes ממתנו חסרים והמ״ם מתוייגת שנים ('that we should die' is *ḥaser* and the *mem* is decorated with two *tagin*). Typically *Ben Mesheq* brings ב׳ ממי״ן דממתינו (two [letters] *mem* of 'that we should die').

Line 19: **[14]אנוסה מ̊פני ישראל • [15]מי** [בעל דברים • וישימ̊הו על הנס]
14. **'let us flee from before Israel'** (Ex. 14:25). (*Parashat Mishpaṭim*) 15. **'who** [ever has a cause' (Ex. 24:14). (*Parashat Ḥuqqat*) 'and he set it upon the pole' (Num. 21:9).]

14. P and H agree, though P abbreviates to ישר̇. **MV** and **ST** omit the word ישראל entirely.
15. P, **MV**, **ST** and H all bring מי בעל דברים and our fragment likely agrees. Our scribe has omitted to indicate the *mem*.

Only one instance is likely completely missing from this line. P, **MV** and H bring וישימהו על הנס from Num. 21:9. ST abbreviates the last word to הנ̇.

Line 20: **[16]במ̊חוקק • [17]מ̊י מנה • [18]מ̊ש**[כנ{ו}תיך • רק השמ̊ר {לך} • מ̊יסרך • במותימ̊ו •]
16. **'hacked out'** (Num. 21:18). 17. (*Parashat Balaq*) **'who has counted'** (Num. 23:10). 18. **'your dwellings'** (Num. 24:5). [(*Parashat Va-ʾetḥanan*) 'only take heed' (Deut. 4:9). (*Parashat ʿEqev*) 'chastens you' (Deut. 8:5). (*Parashat Ve-zoʾt Ha-berakhah*) 'their high places' (Deut. 33:29).]

This line crosses two of our fragments, but is clearer when joined together digitally. We move back to TS-AS 139.144-F on the left side.

T-S AS 139.144-F (left side)—6 lines preserved

16. **ST** agrees and is *ma-leʾ vav* as our scribe. However, P, **MV**, and H are *ḥaser vav* במחקק as 𝔐.
17. P and H agree, however, it is not clear which *mem* to decorate. On the current fragment the top of the letters are cut of, but joining it to T-S AS 139.158-F shows that the first *mem* on מ̊י was decorated. **MV** brings מי מנה בתראה (the last 'who has counted') and since there is only one occurrence of this phrase in Numbers, it must mean the last *mem* in the phrase. This is echoed by **ST**, which brings מי מ̊נה. The secondary sources are of limited use.[130]

130 CG is supported here by Q651–652 which brings מ̊י מנה. Typically *Ben Mesheq* brings ב' ממין ממי מנה (two [letters] *mem* from 'who has counted'). Parma 1959 originally omitted, but added מי מנה in the margin, but decorates neither *mem*. Add. MS 11639 also lists מי מנה with no decoration. Parma 2427 and *Qiryat Sefer* omit.

18. P brings משכנתיך *ḥaser vav* as 𝔐. ST and H bring it *ma-le' vav*, as does MV who also extends to משכנותיך ישר̇.

This is likely followed by רק השמר from Deut. 4:9 as brought by P, MV and H. ST extends to רק השמר לך ('only take heed for yourself') and given available space our scribe may have done so too.

P, MV, ST and H all bring מיסרך from Deut. 8:5.[131]

The last instance on this line is likely במותימו from Deut. 33:29, as brought by P and H. ST conflates the last two instances and reads במותימ̊ו: מו בתרא̇. The suggestion is that the מו means the last two letters in the word, but since the circle is already deployed on the second *mem* in the word, this is obvious.[132] MV is similarly confused, bringing במתימו בת̇ בתראה (the last, the last 'their high places').

Line 21: [19][י']**מי בת̇ שער ם ק̇ל באורית**[א דלא דבקין וג̇ תאגין אית להון • [1]אלהי̊ם]
19. **the last 'days of'** (Deut. 34:8). **Gate of final *mem* 130 in the *Tora***[*h* that do not join and have 3 *tagin*. (*Parashat Bere'shit*) 1. 'God] ...]

19. This last entry for *mem* is the cause of some considerable disagreement. P gives מי בת̇ (the last 'who') which would occur in the same verse as the previous entry—i.e. Deut 33:29. However, this occurs in the verse before the previous word listed and so should be listed prior to that instance. It is H which instead gives ימי בתר' (the last 'days of [mourning]'). This is at Deut 34:8 near the end of the *Torah* during the mourning for Moses, and thus after the previous instance and a significant event for a word to take a decoration. Unfortunately, our fragment is damaged over the key word, however, I would argue that a small blob of ink to the right side of what is most likely a *mem* form is possibly the remains of a *yod*, so our scribe seems to be bringing ימי בת̇ as H. This does seem the most likely instance of the options available.[133]

---

131 The *Ba'al ha-Ṭurim* notes of מיסרך that there are '*tagin* on the *mem* to say that the soul is formed from 40 days and the *Torah* was [similarly] given after 40 days—and if you do not keep the *Torah* which was given after 40 days, [God] will take from you the soul that was formed from 49 days'.

132 Basser, however, takes this as his 39th instance omitting the last instance entirely, op. cit., p. 102.

133 However, Add. MS 11639, Q651–Q652 and Parma 2427, **MV2**, *Qiryat Sefer* and *Ben Mesheq* do not bring this. **T-S Misc. 24.182** is not extant.

15 Description and Example Forms of the Special Letter *Mem Sofit*

We then turn to the listing for *mem sofit.*

The printed Maḥzor Vitry (*LMV*) (*right*) *brings a mem with three tagin, one on the base to the left.*

*However, in his rendition of the form in **T-S NS 287.11-F*** (*right*), *our scribe has brought a* mem *sofit with two lines coming from the roof and and a further* tag *coming from the right of the base of the letter. In other sources where a* tag *comes from the base, it tends to be from the left side. Additionally, it, like most of the sources, brings no break in the letter despite the instruction to not join. It is instead a fully enclosed square shape.*[134] *Indeed if it did not join then it would be* pasul (*invalid*) *by all opinions nowadays.*[135]

T-S Misc. 24.182 (*right*) *often has quite a curved* mem *form that looks more like a* samekh *to modern eyes but tends to have two* tagin *on the roof and one descending from underside of the roof on the left side made in one stroke.*

This is a particularly important entry from our fragment as, whilst there is no disagreement as to the form of their letter, there is some disagreement over how many instances there are for this special *mem sofit*. P explains that קׄגׄ באורייתׄ דלא דבקין וג׳ תאגין אית להון (103 [letters *mem sofit*] in the *Torah*, which do not join and which have 3 *tagin*). MV concurs exactly, as does H which brings קׄגׄ באוריי׳ דלא דבקין וגׄ תאגי׳ אית להון.

It is ST that stands out in contrast, stating that דאית לה תלתא תגין ולא דבקין קׄלׄ באורייתא (that have three *tagin* and do not join—130 in the *Torah*) in the listing. This is echoed by the same sage in BH. In the introduction the entry is very faded, but seems to suggests מאה ותלת[י]ן באורית׳ (one hundred and thirty in the *Torah*). Our scribe here is also clear that the number is 130, agreeing with

134 *Mishnat Sofrim* explains, 'it should initially be rounded at the top on the right side and below it should have a corner on the right and left so that it shouldn't look like a *samekh* (the *Peri Megidim* wrote that it is better that it be square on all sides because it easier to err). And in all cases it should be closed on all sides. And its roof should pass initially outside of the closed part a little like the head of a *vav*. One should not lengthen the roof to the left too much'.

135 Indeed, there is a statement by Rav Hisda in b. *Talmud Shabbat* 104b that explains that the letters carved in the Ten Commandments went through from front to back and the centre of the *mem sofit* and the *samekh* which should have fallen out, but held there miraculously. The *Yerushalmi* instead ascribes this magical occurrence to the *'ayin*, which in Paleo-Hebrew (*Ketav 'Ivri*) letters resembled a stylised 'eye' or 'o' form and would have had a similar issue.

TABLE 16 Forms for the special letter *mem sofit*. Most ignore the break, though some do have this on the left leg where it joins the roof. Sometimes it is a very thin join. Again, there is disagreement on placing the third *tag* with some coming from the underside of the roof's left hand projection and some from the base of the letter. Once again, scribes who do not appear to accept downward *tagin* reduce the number to two, to avoid this.

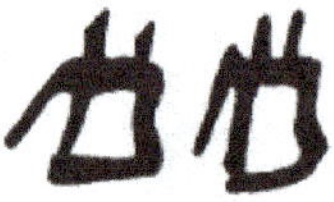	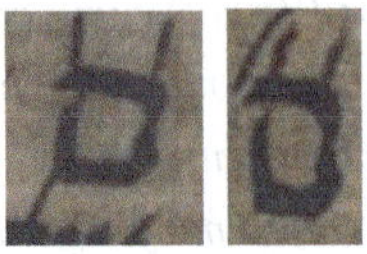			
Maḥzor Vitry Parma 2574 (P)	*Maḥzor Vitry* Add. MS 27201 (MV)	Shem Tov *Tanakh* *Sefer Tagi* (ST)	*Badey ha-'Aron* Heb. 840 (BH)	*Sefer Tagin* Heb. 837 (H)

Not extant Nr. 5667 (K)	Parma 2427	Parma 1959	Q651–652	MS Geunz. 481

Maḥzor Vitry Add. MS 27201 (MV2)	Add. MS 11639	Add. MS 26167	Bologna *Torah*	Vat. ebr. 1
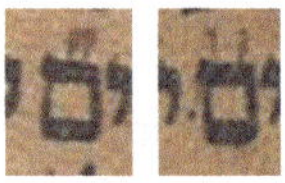				
Or. 1463	Alexander *Torah*			

ST.[136] However, on the first few lines at the end of the reconstructed folio on **T-S AS 139.144-F**, our **CG** scribe does not indicate the *mem sofit* that is to be decorated, so I have not added this into the text and reconstruction that covers this element. On the next folio he does add a vertical line on the top of the letter. Turning to the first instance:

16 Listing of Instances for the Special Letter *Mem Sofit*

1. **P, MV, ST** and **H** all agree with our instance from the first verse of the *Torah*. Unlike other sources, **ST** sets out the word אלהים̊ and relates the next few instances to that word rather than repeating it in each instance.

Line 22: **דבראשית • [2]אלהים דויה**[י אור • אלהים דיהי רקיע • אלהים דיקוו המים •]
... **of** [the verse beginning] **'in the beginning'** (Gen. 1:1). 2. **'God' of the** [verse ending] **'and there was** [light]' (Gen. 1:3). ['God' of the [verse beginning] 'let there be a firmament' (Gen. 1:6). 'God' of [the verse] 'He gathered the waters' (Gen. 1:9).]

2. **MV** agrees with our fragment, bringing אלהים דויהי אור. **P** and **H** give instead אלהים דיהי אור and **ST** דיהי אור. Regardless, it is the same word אלהים̊ that is decorated, but how it anchors to the verse differs—is it 'let there be light' or 'there was light'.[137]

Reconstructing the rest of the line, we see further examples of God in action during creation with P, MV and H bringing אלהים דיהי רקיע from Gen. 1:6. Similarly ST brings דיהי רקיע.

P and H then bring אלהים דיקוו המים from Gen. 1:9 and ST concurs with דיקוו המים. MV shortens to just אלהים דיקוו.

Line 23: **[3]אלהים דתדשא הארץ •** [אלהים ד{יהי} מא{ו}ר{ו}ת • [4]אלהים דישרצו]
3. **'God' that** [precedes in the verse] **'let the earth sprout'** (Gen 1:11). ['God' of [the verse containing] 'let there be lights' (Gen. 1:14).] 4. 'God' of [the verse with] 'let swarm ...

136 However, Basser notes that he has found 132 within Shem Tov's listing/*Tanakh*, op. cit., p. 106.

137 Turning to our secondary sources, Q651–652 brings אלהים̊ יהי אור (and also decorates the *mem* in וירא אלהים̊ את האור ('and God saw the light') from Gen. 1:4. Add. MS 27167, MV2 and Parma 1959 similarly bring ויאמר אלהים̊ יהי אור. Parma 2427 makes no reference to anything other than the אלהים̊ and *Ben Mesheq* similarly just says it is in verse 3, which does not help. Add. MS 11639 and *Qiryat Sefer* omit.

3. **ST** and **H** agree bringing אלהים דתדשא הארץ. **P** and **MV** shorten to אלהים דתדשא.

At this point, we also gain access to the Oxford Bodleian MS. Heb. d. 33/3 fragment, likely 10th/11th century—to which I have assigned the siglum **OB**.[138] Unfortunately, the description and form are not present at the start of this fragment, however, it does preserve the listing from Gen. 1:14 onwards.

In terms of the fully reconstructed instance on this line, **P** and **H** spell דמאורות doubly *ma-le' vav* even though 𝔐 is doubly *ḥaser*. **ST** brings דמאורת. **OB** and **MV** are *ḥaser* but also add a word, bringing דיהי מארת (of 'let there be lights'). We do not know what our scribe brought, but given available space may have extended as in **OB** and **MV**.

4. **P**, **OB**, **MV**, **ST** and **H** all just give אלהים דישרצו. Our manuscript differs from all of the other core sources by adding a further word המים for clarification, which falls onto the next line. However, that does add a potential source of confusion, bringing a further *mem sofit*. Neither are indicated.

Line 24: **המים • [5]אלהים דתוצא • [6]אלהים** [דויכל • אלהים דויברך • בהבראם •]
... the waters' (Gen. 1:20). 5. **'God' that** [precedes the word] **'let bring forth'** (Gen. 1:24). 6. **'God' of** [the verse beginning 'and He completed' (Gen. 2:2). 'God' of [the verse beginning] 'and He blessed' (Gen. 2:3). 'when they were created' (Gen. 2:4).]

5. **P**, **OB**, **MV**, **ST** and **H** all agree, bringing אלהים דתוצא.

Before the next instance, **ST** brings ויברך אתם אלהים ('and God blessed them') from Gen. 1:28. The other core sources bring only the ויברך that relates to Gen. 2:3 (see below).[139] Unfortunately, the Shem Tov *Tanakh* is not extant.

---

138 See part 1 for full description.

139 In support of **ST**, Q651–652 brings both ויברך אלהים and ויברך אתם אלהים, however, it is certainly in the minority, as Parma 2427 brings ויברך אתם but only in relation to the *kaf sofit*, and the next אלהים it decorates is not until after ויקדש אתו ('and he blessed it'), which is Gen. 2:3. Similarly Add. MS 27167 and Parma 1959 bring ויברך אתם אלהים, but also only decorate the *kaf sofit*, and then bring ויברך אלהים decorating the *mem sofit* along with the *he* and *kaf sofit*. **MV2** may be decorating the *mem sofit* in ויברך אתם, but it is not clear as it only has one *tag*. *Ben Mesheq* does not bring an אלהים in relation to Gen. 1:28, but does for Gen. 2:3 referencing כ'ח כ'ף מן ויברך ([verse] 28. the *kaf* from 'and He blessed')

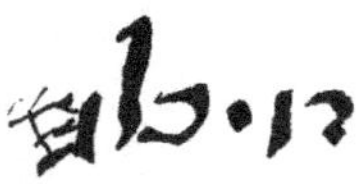

6. We then have a possible disagreement, which, unfortunately, our fragment cannot help solve, since the key word is missing. **P**, **OB**, and **MV** all bring אלהים דויכל which would refer to Gen. 2:2. **ST** similarly brings ויכל אלהים֯ ('and God completed'). However, **H** might disagree bringing, אלהי׳ דויכלו ('God' of 'and He completed') which would be Gen. 2:1 instead. It looks like there is some (not terribly successful) subsequent attempt to cross this out (see drawing right) to agree with the other sources.

Reconstructing the line **P**, **MV** and **H** bring אלהים דויברך apparently from Gen. 2:3. **OB** extends to אלהים֯ דויברך אלהים ('God' of [the verse beginning] 'and God blessed')[140] which seems a little duplicative. **ST** also brings this instance ויב׳ אלהים֯.

ST then brings ברא אלהים֯ ('God created') also from Gen. 2:3. However, no other core sources brings this, and, additionally, there seems to be insufficient room for this on the line of our manuscript.[141]

Instead the likely next instance is בהבראם from Gen. 2:4 as brought by **P**, **OB** and **H**. **ST** extends to בהבראם֯ אלהים (when God created them') adding another possible *mem sofit*, but marks only one. **MV** appears to err, bringing ביום הבראם, which is then also repeated three instances later in its proper place (see below).[142]

Line 25: [7]כי אמר אלהים • [8]אלהים דלאשה • [את שמם • {ביום} הבראם • אלהים אל נח •]

7. **'for God said'** (Gen. 3:1). 8. **'God' of** [the verse containing] **'to the woman'** (Gen. 3:13). ['their name' (Gen. 5:2). '[on the day] when they were created' (Gen. 5:2). (*Parashat Noaḥ*) 'God to Noah' (Gen. 8:15).]

---

which rather suggests that **ST** has added a reference here for a *mem sofit*, when it was only intended for the *kaf sofit*. Add. MS 11639 and *Qiryat Sefer* omit both possibilities.

140 It should be noted that when **OB** writes the word here it uses the *ʾalef-lamed* ligature and omits the *he*.

141 Again, in support of **ST**, Q651–652 brings ברא אלהים֯, as does *Qiryat Sefer*, who explains that אלהים שלשה שבפרשה מתוייגים ג׳ בה׳א וב׳ במ׳ם ('God' [all] three in this section are decorated with three *tagin* on the *he* and two on the *mem sofit*), i.e. Gen. 2:2 and twice in 2:3. **MV2** also supports **ST** and extends to אשר ברא אלהים֯. However, Parma 2427, Add. MS 11639, Add. MS 27167 and Parma 1959 all omit.

142 It is worth noting that MS 27617 and Parma do not bring בהבראם from that verse (Gen. 2:4) but instead ביום עשׂות ייי אלה֯ים֯ ('on the day the Lord God made') from the same verse. **MV2** brings both בהבראם֯ and also עשות ייי אלהים֯. After referring to עשות, *Qiryat Sefer* also brings אלהים ... ושנים במ׳ם הכפולה ('God' ... and two [*tagin*] on the final *mem*). Also Parma 2427 does bring בה֯רבאם֯ but its next instance, based on positioning, is אלה֯ים֯ from Gen. 2:4. *Qiryat Sefer*, however, after referring to המטיר as *ma-leʾ*, explains that ... אלהים ואחד במ׳ם הכפולה ('God' ... and one [*tag*] on the final *mem*), so this suggests Gen. 2:5. **MV2**

7. P, MV, ST and H all agree, bringing כי אמר אלהים. OB omits this instance.
8. This instance is particularly interesting, as only our fragment and OB bring it. Indeed OB extends to אלהים דלאשה מה זאת ('God' of [the verse containing] 'to the woman "what is this?"'). The younger core sources do not include it; and so it may have fallen out of the listing at some point. It has to be after Gen. 3:1 and before Gen. 5:2, and thus the likely candidate is Gen. 3:13, which is the only to have both words in the verse.[143]

It should be noted that ST also brings a couple of instances not in P, MV, H or our fragment at this point. He gives אל האדם ('to the man') in Gen. 3:9 and ביום ברא אלהים ('on the day God created') in Gen. 5:1. The former makes sense as it would be a companion to the previous instance of אלהים דלאשה, though no other core or secondary source brings this.

Looking at the older OB, we also see one additional entry, which does agree with ST as it also brings ביום ברא אלהים.[144]

It seems clear that there are potentially some omissions here in the core texts. These omissions are likely absent from manuscript too; as there just isn't sufficient space, unless they were added in superscript.

Instead, likely inclusions in our reconstruction are based on P, OB, MV and H, which bring את שמם from Gen: 5:2.

P, MV and H then bring ביום הבראם, from the same verse, but it is not clear which *mem sofit* is intended. ST just brings הבראם making it clearer which *mem sofit* takes the decoration. However, whilst OB marks the second *mem sofit* only with a dot, it actually brings ביום הבראם תרו ('[on the day] when they were created' both of them), potentially providing us instead with two instances.[145]

---

does bring a further אלהים which falls between Gen. 2:4 and 2:7, so this is either אלהים על הארץ from Gen. 2:5 or וייצר יי אלהים from Gen 2:7.

143 Supporting our fragment and OB, Q651–652 also brings ויאמר אלהים לאשה. Add. MS 27167 and Parma 1959 instead give אף כי אמר אלהים ('and also God said') also from Gen. 3:1, but would be a different instance of the word אלהים in that verse. Parma 2427 also brings • אלהים • אף • which from positioning would also be different. *Qiryat Sefer* also references this *mem sofit*. Add. MS 11639, MV2 and *Ben Mesheq* omit.

144 From our secondary sources, Q651–652 also brings ביום ברא אלהים. *Ben Mesheq* also agrees, bringing סימן ה' א' ... ה"ם מן אלהים (Chapter 5 [verse] 1 ... the *mem sofit* from 'God'). MV2 brings ביום ברא אלהים, but only decorates the *he*. Similarly from its position in the list MS 27617 and Parma 1959 do bring ברא אלהים, though they too only decorate the *he*. Add. MS 11639, Parma 2427, *Ben Mesheq* and *Qiryat Sefer* omit.

145 From our secondary sources, Q651–652 and Parma 2427 also brings ביום הבראם, marking both. Add. MS 27167 and Parma 1959 bring only הבראם. Conversely, MV2 only decorates the first *mem sofit* bringing ביום הבראם. Add. MS 11639 lists הבראם, but only in relation to it being *petuḥa* (*open*). *Ben Mesheq* omits this reference, bringing only the *mem sofit* of

The line likely concludes with אלהים אל נח from Gen. 8:15, brought by **P, OB, MV, ST** and also **H**, which brings אל׳הי׳ אל נח.

T-S AS 139.152-B (right side)—6 lines preserved

The listing for *mem sofit* then moves to **T-S AS 139.152-B.** The top is very damaged indeed, with very little surviving. Thus our reconstruction is quite speculative, based on character size and line length as well as the other sources. There is a word on line 3 that concurs with the other core sources and by line 4 we are on safer ground. Also, on this folio our scribe has finally started to indicate the letters *mem sofit* to be decorated.

Line 1: [היצאים מן התיבה • כחם היום {תר̇} • לבבכם • עברתם • סאים • עמד]
['that went out from the ark' (Gen. 9:18). (*Parashat Va-yera'*) 'in the heat of the day' [both of them] (Gen. 18:1). 'your heart' (Gen. 18:5). 'you will pass on' (Gen. 18:5). 'measures' (*se'ah* plural) (Gen. 18:6). 'he stood ...]

P, MV, bring היוצאים מן התיבה from Gen. 9:18. **ST** brings just היוצאים. However, **OB** is *ḥaser vav* as 𝔐, bringing היצאים מן התבה.

P then brings two related, but separated instances that follow each other in 𝔐, כחם and היום from Gen. 18:1. **MV** and **H** bring them as one instance כחם היום, so for these two sources, it is not clear which takes the decoration. **OB** clarifies, giving כחום היום תר̇ ('In the heat of the day' [on] both of them), and **ST** brings כחם • היום. Our scribe may have added similar to **OB**, or just brought the two instances.

P, ST and **H** then bring לבבכם from Gen. 18:5. **OB** expands to וסערו לבבכם. **MV** errs and brings לבבכם.

P brings ועברתם from the same verse. **OB, MV** and **H** omit the *vav*, giving עברתם as 𝔐. **ST** does similarly, but links this instance to the previous one, since they are both from the same verse עברתם ב̇ בו ('you will pass on' two in it [the verse]).

Then we likely see סאים from the next verse Gen. 18:6 as brought by **P, OB, MV, ST** and **H**.

From a spacing point of view, the next instance probably splits over two lines with עמד עליהם from Gen. 18:8, as brought by **P, OB, MV, ST** and **H**.

בהרבאם in Gen. 2:4. *Qiryat Sefer* brings five, stating that בראם מתוייג על המ׳ם הכפולה בשנים ('created' the final *mem* is decorated with two [*tagin*]) and also שמם אדם ביום הבראם ארבעתם המ׳ם הכפולה מתוייגת בשנים ('their name Adam on the day they were created' all four final [letters] *mem* are decorated with two [*tagin*]).

RECONSTRUCTION 3 Above, the reconstruction of the folio showing 25 lines with the conclusion of the listing for the first form of *kaf sofit*, that for the second, for *lamed*, *mem* and the start of *mem sofit* that we have considered above. This covers fragments **T-S AS 139.158-F** (left side), **T-S AS 139.158-B** and **T-S AS 139.144-F** (left side), though joined together they all form the right side of this reconstructed page. We have one gap that remains unresolved.

Line 2: [עליהם֯ • על אברהם֯ • בעד כל רחם֯ • ביום֯ הגמל {את יצחק} • {הנער}]
[… by them' (Gen. 18:8). 'upon Abraham' (Gen. 18:19). 'closed up all the wombs' (Gen. 20:18). 'on the day {Isaac} was weaned' (Gen 21:8). '{the lad …]

P, MV, ST and **H** then bring על אברהם from 18:19. **OB** extends to ייי על אברהם, bringing the pyramid of *yodim* that is used instead of the Tetragrammaton.

This is followed by בעד כל רחם from Gen. 20:18 as brought by **P, OB, MV** and **ST. H** brings בעו כל רחם, which is likely just a poor transcription of a short roofed *dalet* from his *Vorlage*.[146]

P, OB, MV and **H** then bring ביום הגמל from Gen. 21:8. However, **ST** extends to ביום הגמל את יצחק ('on the day Isaac was weaned').

P and **H** then bring just הוא שם from Gen. 21:17. **OB** and **MV** adds באשר and **ST** adds הנער באשר. Given available space, our scribe will have extended at least one of these instances, if not both, straddling the lines with the last instance.

Line 3: [{באשר} הוא שם֯ • לבני משם֯ • וי{י}שם֯ לפניו • וינחם֯ • אשור{י}ם֯] [9]ולטו[ש]**ים֯**
[… from where} he is there' (Gen. 21:17). (*Parashat Ḥayyei Sarah*) 'for my son, from there' (Gen. 24:7). 'was set' (Gen. 24:33). 'and [Isaac] was comforted' (Gen. 24:67). ''Ash-shurim' (Gen. 25:3). 9. 'and Leṭu]**shim**' (Gen. 25:3).

P, OB, MV, ST and **H** then bring לבני משם from Gen. 24:7.

P follows with וישם לפניו from Gen. 24:33. **MV** spells ויישם *ma-le' vav* as 𝔐. This is an example of *qeri-ketiv* which 'should' have been spelt ויושם and **OB** and **ST**, in fact, bring the *qeri* ויושם֯ לפניו.

Completing the reconstructive element of the line, **P, MV, ST** and **H** bring וינחם from Gen. 24:67. **OB** extends to וינחם יצחק ('and Isaac was comforted'). **P, OB, ST** and **H** bring אשורים. **MV** spells *ḥaser yod* אשורם as 𝔐, Available space suggest our scribe did not extend as **OB**.

9. **P, ST** and **H** agree. **OB** is *ḥaser vav* ולטשם. Only **MV** brings as 𝔐, which is is ולטושם *ḥaser yod.*

Line 4: [ולא{ו}מ{י}ם֯ • מטעמים֯ קדמׄ • [10]ויפגע במ]**קום֯** • [11]**מה** [נורא המ]**קום֯** •
['and Le'ummim' (Gen. 25:3).[147] (*Parashat Toledot*) the first 'savoury food' (Gen. 27:4) (*Parashat Va-yetse'*) 10. 'and he [Jacob] came upon the] **place**' (Gen. 28:11). 11. '**how** [awesome is this] **place**' (Gen. 28:17).

---

146 Corrected in the transcription of **EPST** to בעד.

147 Three sons of Dedan, a descendant of Abraham by Keturah.

The first instance in the reconstruction of this line is from the same verse Gen. 25:3. **P** and **ST** give ולאומים. **MV** is *ḥaser yod* ולאומם. However, 𝔐 is actually *ḥaser vav* and *male᾿ yod* ולאמים and **OB** and **H** match this. **OB** also adds the abbreviation תל֯ת (all three of them) referring to the ᾿Ash-shurim, Leṭushim and Le᾿ummim that all come from the same verse and **ST** similarly recognises this, though adding the word גם (also) instead. Our **CG** scribe has probably omitted תל֯ת, given available space.

P and **OB** then bring מטעמים קד֯ and **H** and **ST** similarly but קדמ׳ and **MV** gives קדמאה in full, as it tends to. This is from Gen. 27:4, as opposed to its repetitions in verses 7, 9, 14 and 31 in that chapter.

10. **P, OB, MV, ST** and **H** all agree, bringing ויפגע במקום.
11. **P, OB, MV, ST** and **H** all agree, bringing מה נורא המקום.

Line 5: [בית אלהים֯ • וקהל גוים֯ • אלהים֯ {ד}בית אל • התחת אלהי]ם֯ • [12]גר שם֯ • [13]שלום֯

['the house of God' (Gen. 28:17). 'In God's stead' (Gen. 30:2). (*Parashat Vayishlaḥ*) 'a company of nations' (Gen. 35:11). 'God' of [the verse ending] 'Beyt-El' (Gen. 35:15).] **12. 'sojourned there'** (Gen. 35:27). (*Parashat Miqqets*) 13. **'peace'** (Gen. 43:23).

P, MV, ST and **H** bring בית אלהים from Gen. 28:17. **OB** extends to כי אם בית אלהים֯ תרו (‘for this is the house of God' both of them) and whilst it places a circle above only the second *mem sofit*, the qualifier suggests that both are supposed to take the decoration, potentially providing an additional instance.[148] Available space suggests our scribe did not extend similarly.

ST and **MV** then bring התחת אלהים from Gen. 30:2, whereas **P, OB** and **H** bring this later, so there is clearly some confusion that has crept into the manuscripts. This exact phrase also appears in Gen. 50:19, so it may have been that **P, OB** and **H** were referring to this. However, when they eventually do bring this, it is still before instance 12 at Gen. 35:27. Given the surviving letter ם, it is likely that our scribe has also similarly mis-ordered the sequence.

P, OB, MV, ST and **H** bring וקהל גוים from Gen. 35:11.

---

148 In support of **OB**, Parma 1959 brings אם֯ בית אלהים֯ decorating both, and in this does not agree with Add. MS 27167, which brings just בית אלהים֯, even though they usually agree. The available scan of Q651–652 is not clear, but Basser states that it is present (op. cit., p. 189) on אלהים֯ only. *Qiryat Sefer* also only brings the *mem* of אלהים֯. **MV2** lists אם בית אלהים, but decorates neither *mem sofit*. Parma 2427, Add. MS 11639 and *Ben Mesheq* omit either possibility.

P, MV and H then bring אלהים ביתאל from Gen. 35:15, as if בית אל were one word. OB still joins the words, but brings אלהיםֺ דביתאל ('God' of [the verse ending] 'Beyt-El'). 𝔐 has two separate words and only ST makes that clear bringing אלהיםֺ בית אל.[149]

It is only after this that P, OB and H and our scribe bring התחת אלהים.

12. MV and ST agree as 𝔐, bringing גר שם. P and H give as one word גרשם. OB omits here, but has written this beneath the next line down, so does agree that the instance should be included in the listing.

13. P agrees, bringing שלום as a separate entry. MV and H give שלום לכם as one entry without a separator. ST similarly explains שלוםֺ לכםֺ בֺ בה ('peace to you' 2 in it [the verse]). The scribe of OB, however, recognises that there are in fact three instances here and gives שלוםֺ לכםֺ אלהיכםֺ תל ('peace to you' [and] 'your God' three of them) without any separator, which is possibly a remnant of how this was originally brought, as a group of three instances (see below).

Line 6: ‏[לכםֺ אלהיכםֺ {תלתֺ} • עלו לשלוםֺ • ואמרתםֺ אליו • [14]ש]מני אלהים • [15]לאדון
['to you' (Gen. 43:23). 'your God' (Gen. 43:23) {three of them}. 'go up in peace' (Gen. 44:17). (*Parashat Va-yiggash*) 'and say to him' (Gen. 45:9).] **14. 'God put me** [Joseph]' (Gen. 45:9). 15. **'to be lord ...**

P brings לכם from Gen. 43:23 as a separated instance.

P then brings אלהיכם תל from the same verse. ST and H omit the qualifier, bringing just אלהיכם. MV echoing OB, gives in full אלהיכם • תלתיהון, but does separate the two words and the third instance from the first two. Two of our core sources have omitted the reference to תלתיהון presumably because they did not understand why it was there. There are not three occurrences of the word אלהיכם in this section, but instead it means that the last three instances all appear in the same verse, Gen. 43:23. It is highly likely that originally these three were not separated into individual instances. OB is likely the most accurate, but perhaps originally the text may even have run on as a full sentence שלוםֺ לכםֺ אל תיראו אלהיכםֺ תלתיהון ('Peace be to you, fear not, you God' the three of them) in much the same way we have seen K treat instances where they follow in a single verse. Given available space, our scribe likely abbreviated to תלתֺ.

P, OB, MV, ST and H all bring עלו לשלום from Gen. 44:17.

This is likely to be followed by ואמרתם אליו from Gen. 45:9, which is also brought by all the core sources.

149 *Sofrim* 5:10 specifically notes ... אלו שמות הנחלקין בית אל (these names are to be divided: 'Beit El' ...).

14. **P, OB, ST** agree, as 𝔐. **H** puts a separator between the words in error, שמני אלהים //. **MV** gives שימני ~~כהתם~~ אלהים *ma-le'yod.*
15. **P, OB, MV, ST** and **H** just give לכל מצרים. Our scribe has extended the reference adding לאדון, the only core source to do so.

Line 7: [לכל מצרי֯ם • ושמת֯ם שרי מקנה • וינהל֯ם • שדי֯ם [16]ו]רח֯ם • [17][וי{י}]ש֯ם •
[... over all Egypt' (Gen. 45:9). 'put them as rulers over cattle' (Gen. 47:6). 'and he fed them' (Gen. 47:17). (*Parashat Va-yeḥi*) 'breasts' (Gen. 49:25). 'and] **womb'** (Gen. 49:25) [both of them]. 16. **'and they put'** (Gen. 50:26).

P, ST and **H** bring ושמתם שרי מקנה from Gen. 47:6. **MV** omits מקנה. **OB** brings just ושמת֯ם.
P, OB, MV, ST and **H** all bring וינהלם from Gen. 47:17.
P and **MV** then bring שדים from Gen. 49:25, separately.

16. Very faint on our fragment, but likely, under magnification, to be ורחם from the same verse. This is brought by **P** and **MV**. **H**, however, brings the two instances שדים ורחם together without a separator. **OB** links them more formally together giving שדי֯ם ורח֯ם תרו ('breasts and womb' both of them) as does **ST** who **brings** שדי֯ם ורח֯ם ב֯ בה ('breasts and womb' 2 in it [the verse]). Our scribe has not linked them.
17. **P, OB** and **MV** give ויישם as 𝔐. **ST** extends to ויישם בארון ('and they placed him [Joseph] in a coffin') but is *ḥaser yod* as is **H**, bringing וישם.

The reconstruction of the three virtually completely missing lines is, as the first two, somewhat more speculative. Once again, we assume **P** as the base and pay particular attention to the line lengths.

Line 8: [עוד אלהי֯ם {אל משה} • אהיה שלחני אליכ֯ם • ישלכ֯ם • יגרש֯ם] •
[(*Parashat Shemot*) 'God again' (Ex. 3:15). 'I AM has sent me to you' (Ex. 3:15). (*Parashat Va-'era'*) 'he will let them go' (Ex. 6:1). 'he will drive them out' (Ex. 6:1).]

Only a faint part of the top of a *mem sofit* with a decoration remains at the end of our line. To begin the line, **P, OB** and **MV** bring עוד אלהים from Ex. 3:15. However, **ST** extends to עוד אלהים אל משה ('God again to Moses') and it is likely, given available space, that our scribe has extended similarly.

This is then likely followed by אהיה שלחני אליכם from the same verse, as brought by **P, MV** and **H**. **OB** and **ST** both omit אהיה.

Then **P, OB, MV, ST** and **H** all bring ישלכם from Ex. 6:1.

The line likely ends with יגרשם from the same verse, as brought by all the core sources.

Line 9: [{ו}בשפטים • {אשר} אין שם {מת} • {שמרים • מימים} • {פן} ינחם •
בראו{ו}תם •]

['and by judgements' (Ex. 6:6). (*Parashat Bo'*) '{where} there was not {dead}' (Ex. 12:30). {'guarded'} (Ex. 12:42). {'from year'} (Ex. 13:10).} (*Parashat Beshallah*) '{lest} they regret' (Ex. 13:17). 'when they see' (Ex. 13:17).

P, **OB**, **MV** and **H** bring בשפטים from Ex. 6:6, however, **P** brings this twice which suggests a wish to include Ex. 7:4 as well. **ST** brings ובשפטים as 𝔐.[150]

This is likely followed by אין שם from Ex. 12:30, as brought by **P**, **MV** and **H**. **OB** extends to אשר אין שם and **ST** extends to אין שם מת. There is space for our scribe to have added both words.

We then hit a significant split of opinion. **P**, **MV** and **H** bring מימים from Ex. 13:10 which **ST** extends to מימים ימימה ('from year to year'). However, **OB** brings שמרים ('watched [night]') which must be from Ex. 12:42. Either would fit into the sequence with no issue.[151] From an examination of the secondary sources (see notes below), it is possible that both were originally intended.

Back on safer ground, **P**, **MV** bring ינחם from Ex. 13:17, which **OB** and **ST** extend to פן ינחם ('lest they regret').

The last instance on this line is likely בראותם from the same verse, as brought by **P**, **ST** and **OB**. **H** brings בראותם *haser vav* as 𝔐. **MV** appears to bring כראותם, but since it often has a *bet* that looks more like a *kaf*, this may be a similar occurrence, rather than an error.

Line 10: [{כי} אשר ראיתם • לראותם עוד • ילחם • ואתם {תחרשון} • ויהם •]

['{that} you have seen' (Ex. 14:13). 'to see them again' (Ex. 14:13). 'He will fight' (Ex. 14:14). 'and you {will be silent}' (Ex. 14:14). 'and He discomforted' (Ex. 14:24).]

---

150 It is possible that **P** is confusing the repeat of the word with its decorating of the letter *pe* as this is what we find decorated in the secondary sources bar one, Parma 1959, which brings the *mem sofit* as decorated, במשפטים גדלים ('great judgements').

151 From our secondary sources, **OB** finds support in Add. MS 11639, which brings ליל שמורים. מימים ימימה is also listed, but no letters are decorated. *Qiryat Sefer* explains that שמרים חסר וא״ו ושני הממי״ן מתוייגת שנים ('guarded' is *haser vav* and the two letters *mem* are decorated with two [*tagin*]) but also מימים המ״ם הכפולה מתויגת שנים ('from year' the final *mem* is decorated with two [*tagin*]). *Ben Mesheq* also brings both מ׳ם דשמורים (the *mem* [*sofit*] of 'guarded') and also מ׳ם דמימים (the *mem* [*sofit*] of 'from year'). Q651–652 brings שמרים but only to decorate the *mem* and lists מימים ימימה for that concerning the *mem sofit*. **MV2** lists ליל שמורים הוא לייי and also brings מימים ימימה, but decorates no letters in either phrase. Parma 2427 and Parma 1959 omits both possibilities. **T-S Misc. 24.182** is not extant for this section.

P, MV, ST and H bring אשר ראיתם from Ex. 14:13. OB extends to כי אשר ראיתם֯.

P and H follow with לראותם עוד from the same verse. OB, MV and ST omit עוד and these are *ma-le' vav*, when 𝔐 is *ḥaser* לראתם.

The next instance is likely ילחם from Ex. 14:14, as brought by P, OB, MV and ST.

P, OB, MV and H then bring ואתם from the same verse and ST brings ואתם ב̇ בה ('and you', 2 in it [the verse]) linking this to the previous instance.

The line likely concludes with ויהם from Ex. 14:24 as brought by P, OB, MV, ST and H. This is quite a short line, so it is possible our scribe extended some of the entries or there were others.[152]

T-S AS 139.158-F—11 lines preserved

We then move back to our mid section **T-S AS 139.158-F** to pick up the rest of our listing for *mem sofit*.

Line 11: [נ{ו}זלים֯ • כסמו ים֯ • אדירים֯ • לע{ו}לם֯ {ועד} • בת{ו}פים֯ • לא אסים֯ • 17ע[ד
['stood upright' (Ex. 15:8). 'the sea covered them' (Ex. 15:10). 'mighty' (Ex. 15:10). 'forever {and ever}' (Ex. 15:18). 'with timbrels' (Ex. 15:20). 'thrown into the sea' (Ex. 15:21). 'I will not put' (Ex. 15:26).] 17. **'until ...**

P and H bring נוזלים from Ex. 15:8. OB, MV and ST are *ḥaser vav* נזלים as 𝔐.

The next instance is likely כסמו ים from Ex. 15:10, as brought by P, MV, ST and H. OB omits ים, which is odd, given this is the key word that takes the decoration.

P, ST and H then brings אדירים from the same verse as 𝔐. MV, however, is *ḥaser yod* אדירם. OB brings דאדירים (of 'mighty') which would suggest that the scribe had a different word in mind and was using this word as a marker, however, the *mem sofit* is marked in the word.[153]

This is likely followed by לעולם from Ex. 15:18, as brought by P, ST and H. 𝔐, however, is *ḥaser vav*, and this is the case in OB and MV, לעלם, and OB also extends to לעלם ועד ('forever and ever'). Our scribe may have done similarly, given available space.

The same issue appears with the next instance. P and H bring בתופים also *ma-le' vav* from Ex. 15:20 when 𝔐 is *ḥaser vav*, as we see again in OB and MV and this time in ST, בתפים.

---

152 Parma 1959 extends to ואתם תחרשון ('and you will hold your peace'). Parma 2427 also lists לכם֯ ('for you') from Ex. 14:14, but is the only source to do so.

153 *Ben Mesheq* and *Qiryat Sefer* do bring the word במים that precedes as decorated in that verse, so it is possible that may have been the intention of OB, but it is odd that the actual word itself would be omitted.

ST then brings an additional instance רמה בים ('throw into the sea') from Ex. 15:21, which is not in the other core sources.[154] Based on the available space and the general agreement of the other instances in this line, it is unlikely that our scribe supports this.

P, OB, MV and instead bring לא אסים from Ex. 15:26, which ST then brings after its additional instance.

17. P brings עד באם תרׄ. OB is similar but *ma-le' vav* in the second word עד בוא֯ם תרׄ. MV gives the specifics עד באם אל ארץ ('until they come to a land') and עד באם אל קצה ('until the come to the borders'). ST also spells in out in full עד בוא֯ם אל ארץ נושבת ('until they come to a land inhabited'), though also the second word is *ma-le' vav* when 𝔐 is not, and then brings עד באם אל קצה. H has incorrectly transcribed it, bringing עד ביום // תרוויי' confusing the *'alef* for a *yod* and *vav*—which suggests his *Vorlage* had script that might have resembled P where this is an easy error to make. It also separates off the reference to it as being on both letters, as if this were connected to the next instance instead.

Line 12: [ב{ו}א֯ם תרׄ • למסעיה֯ם • זדו עליה֯ם • [18]אשר] ת[שי֯ם • [19]אחרי רב[י֯ם •
… they came'—both [occurrences in the verse (Ex. 16:35). 'by their journeys' (Ex. 17:1). (*Parashat Yitro*) 'proudly against them' (Ex. 18:11).] (*Parashat Mishpatim*) 18. **'which you will set'** (Ex. 21:1). 19. **'after the multitude'** (Ex. 23:2).

P, MV, ST and H then bring למסעיהם from Ex. 17:1. OB extends to למסעיהם על פי ייי ('by their journeys according to the word of God').

P, OB, MV and ST follows with זדו עליהם from Ex. 18:11. H brings זדע עליהם in error.[155]

18. P, OB, MV and ST agree, bringing אשר תשים. H extends to אשר תשים עליהם ('which you will set upon them') which would gives us another *mem sofit* and so confuse the issue. Additionally, 𝔐 gives לפניהם ('before them'), so the scribe of H has erred, possibly because the previous instance has עליהם. There is a line written above the word by the scribe of H, which is likely acting as a cancellation line, so perhaps he has recognised this.[156]
19. P, OB, MV, ST and H all agree, bringing אחרי רבים.[157]

---

154 None of the secondary sources bring this, so ST enjoys no support for this additional instance.

155 Corrected to זדו עליהם in EPST.

156 As has the transcriber of EPST, who removes the word.

157 Basser explains in a footnote that ST extends to אחרי רבים לרעות, but it does not, particularly since 𝔐 is אחרי רבים להטת ('after a multitude to pervert justice'), op. cit., p. 105.

Line 13: [יגש אל{י}הם֯ • ויקם֯ {משה} • {הר} האלהים֯ • הזקנים֯ • ושכנתי בתוכם֯] • [20]**אמתים֯**

['come near to them' (Ex. 24:14). 'and {Moses} arose' (Ex. 24:13). '{mountain} of God' (Ex. 24:13). 'the elders' (Ex. 24:14). (*Parashat Terumah*) 'and I will dwell among them' (Ex. 25:8).] 20. **'cubits' …**

P, OB, MV, ST and H all bring יגש אליהם from Ex. 24:14. However, whilst they are all *ma-le'yod*, 𝔐 is *ḥaser*, יגש אלהם.

This is followed by ויקם in P, MV and H, which is actually from the previous verse Ex. 24:13. OB and ST extend to ויקם֯ משה ('and Moses arose').

Then P, MV and H bring האלהים, which is from the that same verse 13. ST is damaged, but also seems to give האל[ה]ים֯.

OB extends to הר האל[ה]ים֯ ('mountain of God'). Our scribe will have extended one of these last two instances, based on available space. I have selected the first since two core sources bring this.

P, MV, ST and H then bring הזקנים from Ex. 24:14 OB extends to אל הזקנים. This instance should also be before יגש אלהם. The listing is out of sequence generally. We do not know what our scribe did, but presumably erred as in the other core sources.[158]

The last instance in this reconstructed line is likely ושכנתי בתוכם from Ex. 25:8, as brought by P, OB, MV, ST and H.

20. P and OB agree, bringing אמתים קדמׄ. ST and H agree bringing קדמ׳ and MV brings קדמאה in full.

Line 14: [קדמׄ • טבע{ו}תיהם֯ קדמׄ • וקנמן בשם֯ • [21]וק]**נה בשם֯** • [22]**לדו**[רתי]**כם֯** • [23] **יהיה**

—the last [occurrence] (Ex. 25:10). the first 'their rings' (Ex. 26:29). (*Parashat Ki Tissa'*) 'and sweet cinnamon' (Ex. 30:23).] 21. **'sweet kane'** (Ex. 30:23). 22. **'through your generations'** (Ex. 30:31). 23. **'will be …**

In the reconstructed section of the line, P brings טבעותיהם קדׄ from Ex. 26:29, *ma-le'vav*. ST brings טבעותיהם • קדמא, separated as if they were a different instance. H is טבעותיהם קדמׄ. OB omits קדׄ and MV omits completely. 𝔐 is *ḥaser vav*, טבעתיהם.

P, MV, ST and H then bring וקנמן בשם from Ex. 30:23. OB appears to have a different instance not in other sources, bringing בסם֯ מחציתו, but is in fact just a mis-spelling of בשם, as 𝔐 reads וקנמן בשם מחציתו ('and sweet cinnamon, half as much').

158 T-S Misc 24.182 also brings this in reversed order.

21. **P, OB, MV, ST,** and **H** all agree, bringing וקנה בשם.
22. **OB** and **ST** agree, but are לדרתיכם *haser vav* as 𝔐. **P, MV** and **H** omit.
23. **P, MV, ST** and **H** agree, bringing יהיה לכם. **OB** extends to קדש יהיה לכם̊ ('it will be holy to you').

Line 15: [לכם̊ • סמים̊ נטף • תהיה לכם̊ • [24]ברית] **עולם • [25]היא לעלם • [26]{וי}קרא בשם •**
[… [to you]' (Ex. 30:32). 'sweet spices' (Ex. 30:34). 'it will be to you' (Ex. 30:36).]
24. **'everlasting** [covenant]' (Ex. 31:16). 25. **'forever'** (Ex. 31.17). 26. **'and he called by name'** (Ex. 34:5).

Reconstructing the rest of the line, **P, MV** and **ST** bring סמים נטף from Ex. 30:34. **OB** just brings סמים̊. **H** oddly brings סמים // נט' נטף with a space filler, but splitting them as if they were two separate instances and then leaving a sizeable gap after נטף.[159]

This is likely followed by תהיה לכם from Ex. 30:36 as brought by **P, MV, ST** and **H**. **OB** extends to קדשים̊ תהיה לכם̊ and places a dot above each *mem sofit*, thus giving us an additional instance not in the other sources.[160]

T-S Misc. 24.182, brings הם̊ כתבים ('they were written') from Ex. 32:15 from *parashat Ki Tissa'*.[161]

24. **P, OB, MV, ST,** and **H** all agree, bringing ברית עולם.
25. **OB** agrees, bringing היא לעלם as 𝔐. However, it is worth noting that whilst the *qeri* is הִיא the actual *Torah* text *ketiv* is הִוא. **ST** appears to bring הוא לעולם partly agreeing with 𝔐, but with the second word *ma-le' vav*. **P, MV** and **H** bring היא לעולם, *ma-le' vav*.
26. **P, ST, MV** and **H** bring וקראתי בשם ('and I will call in the name [of God]') which would be Ex. 33:19. **OB** brings instead ויקרא בשם ייי ('and called in the name [of God]') which would be Ex. 34:5 instead and enjoys a lots of support from our secondary sources.[162] Our scribe brings instead קרא בשם

---

159 Transcribed correctly as סמים נטף in **EPST**. The gap may have been left to accommodate קדשים as **OB**, but the scribe may not have been able to read it in his *Vorlage* and left a space hoping to work it out later and then forgot about it, leaving the gap. **T-S Misc. 24.182** repeats סמים̊ סמים̊.

160 Amongst our secondary sources, **OB** finds support only from Q651–652 which brings קדשים̊ תהיה לכם̊. **T-S Misc. 24.182** brings both in succession, קדשים̊, decorating only the *qof* and then לכם̊ decorating the *mem sofit*. **MV2** lists קדש קדשי קדשים תהיה לכם, but decorates no letters in the phrase. Add. MS 11639 and *Ben Mesheq* only bring קדשים̊ with a decoration on the *qof*. Parma 2427, Parma 1959 and *Qiryat Sefer* omit.

161 Absent from other sources.

162 Turning to our secondary sources, **OB** finds support from Q651–652, Add. MS 11639 and

which may be a corruption of either of these, but given the space between this and the last instance, I would argue that there are faint residues of the *vav* and *yod*, so likely this manuscript also supports **OB** bringing [וי]קרא בשם. Our scribe has omitted to indicate the decoration on the last three instances.

Line 16: [רחום • לאלפים • שלשים • רב{י}עים • 27והקטיר]ם • 28לדורתיכם • 29משבתיכם •

['merciful' (Ex. 34:6). 'the thousandth' (Ex. 34:7). 'the third' (Ex. 34:7). 'the fourth' (Ex. 34:7).] (*Parashat Va-yiqra'*) 27. **'will make them smoke'** (Lev. 3:16). 28. **'throughout your generations'** (Lev. 3:17). 29. **'all your dwellings'** (Lev. 3:17).

P, **OB**, **MV** bring רחום from Ex. 34:6.

This is likely followed by לאלפים from Ex. 34:7, as brought by **P**, **OB**, **MV**. **H** brings רחום לאלפים as if they were one instance.[163]

Then from the same verse, we likely have שלשים and רביעים, which we find in **MV**, **OB**, and **H**. **P** and **ST** agree with the first, but bring רבעים *ḥaser yod*, as 𝔐.

27. **P**, **OB**, **MV**, **ST**, and **H** all agree, bringing והקטירם, though our scribe again omits the decoration.

OB brings an additional instance חקת עולם ('an everlasting statute') from the same verse Lev. 3:17. This time, our scribe follows **P**, **MV**, **ST** and **H** and omits. However, **OB** enjoys complete support from the secondary sources, and thus this instance was likely originally intended.[164]

28. **OB** agrees, but is *ḥaser vav* לדרתיכם as 𝔐. **P**, **MV**, **ST** and **H** omit at this point.
29. **ST** agrees, bringing משבתיכם. **OB** brings מושבתיכם *ma-le' vav* as 𝔐.[165] **MV** brings מושבתיכם דוכל דם ('their dwelling places' of the verse including 'and all blood') in the listing for *parashat Tsav* which more helpfully locates

---

Parma 1959 who brings ויקרא בשם. Parma 2427 does bring בשם which by its positioning after וירד would also be Ex. 34:5. **T-S Misc. 24.182**, **MV2**, *Qiryat Sefer* and *Ben Mesheq* omit. The secondary sources are fairly aligned to **OB**, and potentially our manuscript.

163 And that is faithfully transcribed as one in **EPST**.

164 Q651–652 brings עולם לדורותיכם marking both, thus supporting **OB**. Add. MS 11639 also brings חקת עולם lending further support. **MV2** lists חקת עולם לדרת׳כם and Parma 2427 lists חקת עולם but neither source marks any *mem sofit* as decorated. *Qiryat Sefer* notes עולם מלא והמ״ם מתוייגת שנים ('world' is *ma-le'* and the *mem* is decorated with two [*tagin*]) and *Ben Mesheq* gives יז ... מ״ם דעולם ([verse] 17 ... the *mem* of 'world').

165 **T-S Misc. 24.182** seems to follow **OB**, also bringing לדרתיכם מושבתיכם.

this as Lev. 3:17. P, and H sort of omit, however, it seems that they have confused the לדורתיכם of Lev. 3:17 with the one of Lev. 10:9 and perhaps that is why they follow with משבתיכם֯ after instance 30.

Line 17: [[לדרתם֯ דביום • משחו אתם֯] • [30]לדורתיכם֯] דיין • [?]**משבותיכם֯** • [31]**לא**
[(*Parashat Tsav*) 'to their generation' of the verse with 'on the day' (Lev. 7:36). 'that they were anointed' (Lev. 7:36).] (*Parashat Shemini*) 30. 'throughout your generations' **of** [the verse beginning] **'wine'** (Lev. 10:9). **'in all your dwellings'** 31. **'you do not ...**

This line is interesting. It is quite clear there is space for certainly two and perhaps three extra instances, but our standard sources P, MV, ST and H all bring nothing in this space[166] between Lev. 3:17 and Lev. 10:9.

Fortunately OB does (see right)[167] and so we can assume what is missing from our fragment is likely לדרתם֯ דביום ('to their generation' of [the verse with] 'on the day') which would make this Lev. 7:36.

The next instance is slightly harder to read because of the stretched *ḥet* and a longer *vav*, but is משחו אתם֯ ('that they were anointed') which is in the same verse, Lev. 7:36, though the word אתם֯ actually occurs before לדרתם֯ so should probably be listed first, even though ביום is earliest in the verse. If this text was extant in our fragment, then we might see that the scribe had reversed these two instances, but it is likely that they were included. Our fragment has been largely in accordance with the other older source **OB** for much of this section on *mem sofit*.

30. P and H agree, bringing לדורתיכם דיין. **MV** agrees too, but oddly brings this instance and the one after at the end of the listing for *yod*, before the decorated *mem sofit* letter that starts the section. **OB** and **ST** are as 𝔐, which is *ḥaser vav* לדרתיכם֯.

The next instance brought in our fragment presents a problem. **OB**, **MV**, H and our scribe all bring משבותיכם *ma-le' vav*. P is *ḥaser vav* משבתיכם. ST, however, is our only core source to omit this completely. If it was to appear, then it must fall between Lev. 10:9 and Lev. 10:17 in our current sequence, but the word does

---

166 Possibly because of the confusion between the apparent double listing of לדורתיכם and משבותיכם.

167 אתם is brought up from the next line in the image for simplicity.

not occur. Indeed, it does not occur until Lev 23:14 where it follows on not quite immediately after the word לדרתיכם but is משבתיכם *ḥaser vav* in 𝔐. It is possible that its proximity to the earlier לדרתיכם has caused the confusion, and arguably the majority of our sources and our scribe are in error. Thus this instance should not be present here and **ST** is correct to omit.[168] Our secondary sources are as varied and confused as the core ones.

31. We return to safer ground as **P, OB, ST,** and **H** all bring לא אכלתם.

Line 18: [אכלתם̊ • {את} חטאתם̊ • {ואת} ע{ו}לתם̊ • [32]{לא} כר]עים̊ • [33]פרומים̊ • [34]שפם̊ • [35]אדמדם̊ •

[... eat' (Lev. 10:17) 'their sin offering' (Lev. 10:19). '{and} their burnt offering' (Lev. 10:19).] 32. **'have jointed'** (Lev. 11:21). (*Parashat Tazria'*) 33. **'rent'** (Lev. 13:45). 34. **'his upper lip'** (Lev. 13:45). 35. **'reddish'** (Lev. 13:49).

P, OB, MV and **H** then bring חטאתם from Lev. 10:19.

The last full missing instance in the line is likely from the same verse. **P, OB, MV** and **H** give עולתם *ma-le' vav*, but 𝔐 is *ḥaser* עלתם. Whilst showing these as separate instances, **ST** does link them together bringing חטאתם̊ ואת עלתם̊ ב̇ בו ('their sin offering' and 'their burnt offering' 2 in it [the verse]). Our scribe may have done the same given available space and may indeed have reflected some of the secondary sources who also expand and similarly link these two instances.[169]

---

168 Turning to our secondary sources we really need to look at this section across *parshiyyot Va-yikra', Tsav* and *Shemini* as a group, rather than individual instances to better understand what was intended. Q651–652 brings עולם̊ • לדורותיכם̊ • מושבותיכם̊ • לדרתיכם̊ • מדוע לא אכלתם̊. It also lists חקת עולם and לדרתיכם דביום משחו, but these do not have a decoration on the *mem sofit*. Parma 2427 brings לדרתיכם̊ • מושבתיכם̊ • והקטירם̊ •. A further instance of both מושבתיכם and לדרתיכם are listed, but these are not decorated. Add. MS 11639 brings חקת עולם̊ • לדורותיכם̊ • עולם̊ • לדרתם̊ • לדרתיכם̊ • לא אכלתם̊. Parma 1959 brings והקטירם̊ • לדרתם̊ זאת • לדרתיכם̊ • את חטאתם̊. *Qiryat Sefer* brings references to עולם, לדרתיכם, מושבתיכם, ולמילוטים, לא אכלתם as having a *mem sofit* with two *tagin*. *Ben Mesheq* brings references to חקת עולם̊, והקטירם̊, לדרתיכם̊, חקת עולם̊ לדרתם, לא אכלתם. Unfortunately, **MV2** is of little help, as no instance of *mem sofit* is decorated in this section, even if a phrase is listed. There is considerable confusion in the secondary sources and none fully match **OB** and what is likely in our manuscript, given the space available.

169 Q651–652, Add. MS 11639 and Parma 1959 all bring את חטאתם̊ ואת עולתם̊. **MV2** also lists את חטאתם ואת עלתם, but does not decorate the letters in that phrase. Parma 2427 omits. *Qiryat Sefer* and *Ben Mesheq* do not bring listings in this format.

32. P, OB, MV, ST, and H all agree, bringing לא כרעים. It is possible our scribe has extended this as some of our secondary sources, given available space.[170]
33. Like our scribe, OB, ST, MV and H are all פרומים, *ma-le' vav*. 𝔐 is *ḥaser vav* פרמים, as brought only by P.
34. P, ST and H agree, bringing שפם. MV may be bringing שפים, but the *yod* is more a blob of ink, so may just be an error that was not erased. OB extends to שפם יעטה ('he will uncover his upper lip').
35. P, OB, MV, ST and H agree, bringing אדמדם. However, H repeats the same word on the next page in error.

Line 19: [באכלם • {את} קדשיהם • וספרתם • [36]הביא]כם • [37]עד תם • [38]ימים תהיה •
[(*Parashat 'Emor*) 'when they eat' (Lev. 22:16). 'their holy things' (Lev. 22:16). ['and you will count' (Lev. 23:15).] 36. **'you brought'** (Lev. 23:15). (*Parashat Behar*) 37. **'until the completion'** (Lev. 25:29). 38. **'days will be'** (Lev. 25:29).

P, MV and H bring באכלם from Lev. 22:16.

P, MV and H then bring קדשיהם from the same verse. OB joins the two instances as באכלם את קדשיהם ('when they eat their holy things') and ST does similar באכלם את קדשיהם ב. Our scribe probably does similar, given available space.

The last fully missing instance is likely וספרתם from Lev. 23:15, as brought by P, OB, MV, ST and H.

36. P, OB, MV, ST, and H all agree, bringing הביאכם. ST links these two instances together, וספרתם בה • הביאכם ב ('and you will count' 'you brought', 2 in it [the verse]).
37. OB, MV and ST agree, bringing עד תם as 𝔐. P and H appear to bring in error, עד תום *ma-le' vav*.
38. P, OB, MV, ST, and H all agree, bringing ימים תהיה.

The next line straddles two fragments, and we start to draw on the right side of **T-S AS 139.144-B**.

170 Q651–652 and Add. MS 11639 bring אשר לא כרעים ('which have jointed') and Parma 1959 brings לא כרעים. MV2 lists אשר לא כרעים, but again with no decoration. Parma 2427 omits. *Qiryat Sefer* and *Ben Mesheq* do not bring listings in this format.

T-S AS 139.144-B (right side)—6 lines preserved

Line 20:]אחזתם֯ • אח{ו}זת עולם֯ • {אחזה} לע{ו}לם֯ • [39]ע]בדיהם֯ • [40]אלהיכם֯ • [41]אלילם֯ •

['of their inheritance' (Lev. 25:32). 'a perpetual inheritance' (Lev. 25:34). 'perpetual {inheritance}' (Lev. 25:46).] 39. **'they are My servants'** (Lev. 25:55). 40. **'your God'** (Lev. 25:55). 40. **'idols'** (Lev. 26:1).

Reconstructing the line **P**, **OB**, **MV**, **ST** and **H** all bring אחזתם from Lev. 25:32.

This is likely followed by a similar themed instance אחזת עולם from Lev. 25:34 as 𝔐, as brought by **MV** and **ST**. **P** and **H** bring אחזת עולם *ma-le' vav*. **OB** extends to כי אחזת עולם ('for a perpetual inheritance').

For the last full missing instance **P** and **MV** brings לעלם from Lev. 25:46 as 𝔐. **OB**, **ST** and **H** are *ma-le' vav*, לעולם. This is also related thematically, since it is preceded by the word אחזה in 𝔐, even though the core sources do not call it out specifically. This is quite a short line otherwise, and it is possible that our scribe did include this related word.[171]

39. Our scribe has erred in his spacing, bringing the two words that look like one. 𝔐 is עבדי הם and this is what is brought by **P**, **MV**, **ST** and **H**. **OB** also brings עבדי but the next part is missing because of a hole in the fragment.
40. **P**, **MV**, **ST** and **H** agree, bringing אלהיכם. **OB** has only יכם֯ survive, but likely agrees.
41. **P**, **ST** and **H** bring אלילים. However, 𝔐 is *ḥaser yod*, as our scribe brings. **MV** omits.

Line 21:]{לא} תתנו בארצכם֯ • אם֯ בחקתי • מאסתים֯ • [42]געל]תם֯ • [43]לכלותם֯ •

['{do not} place in your land' (Lev. 26:1). (*Parashat Be-ḥuqotai*) 'if in My statutes' (Lev. 26:3). 'reject them' (Lev. 26:44).] 42. **'abhor them'** (Lev. 26:44). 43. **'to destroy them'** (Lev. 26:44).

P, **OB**, **MV** and **H** bring תתנו בארצכם from Lev. 26:1. **ST** extends to לא תתנו בארצכם ('do not place in your land'). Our scribe may have done similarly, given available space.

P, **OB**, **ST** and **H** then bring אם בחקתי from Lev. 26:3. **MV** omits.

P, **OB**, **MV**, **ST** and **H** all bring מאסתים from Lev. 26:44.

42. **P**, **OB**, **MV**, **ST** and **H** all bring געלתים *ma-le' yod* as 𝔐. Our scribe appears to have omitted the *yod*.

171 In the listing for Parma 2427 the word does precede, but it is separated off.

43. **OB**, **ST** and **MV** agree with our fragment, bringing לכלותם *ma-le' vav*. However, 𝔐 is *ḥaser vav* לכלתם and **P** and **H** accord with this.

The listing for *mem sofit* concludes on the next line where the letter *nun* is introduced. **P**, **OB**, **MV**, **ST** and **H** all bring וזכרתי להם from Lev. 26:45.

Overall our fragments have preserved some 43 of the 130 instances of the special *mem sofit* that **ST** and our scribe suggest should be present.

17 Description and Example Forms of the Special Letter *Nun*

Turning to the letter *nun*, unfortunately, our manuscript fragment has only part of the description, bringing בזנביה נ באורית (in its tail—50 in the *Torah*). In this it accords with a number of the core sources, but not all as there is a specific difference of opinion over a core word. Our base text **P** appears to read נ דאקים בחכיה נ באוריית׳. This is echoed by **H** which definitely brings נ דאקים בחכיה נ באורי׳. חך is related to a fish-hook[172] and so this could translate as 'stands up/raised in its hook'. **MV** differs, apparently agreeing with our fragment, giving instead דעקים בזנביה נ׳ באורייתא (that is bent in its tail—50 in the *Torah*). This is duly transcribed in **LMV**. However, it is interesting to note that in **MV** the second ב looks more like כ in the word comparing it against the first ב in that same word.

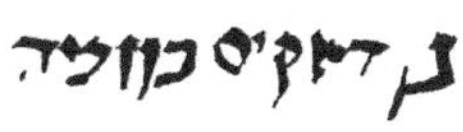

This confusion, I would contend, is because the ח of בחכיה has perhaps been mistaken by the **MV** scribe as two separate letters a ז and נ. This is not unreasonable, as the scribe of **P**, for example, has formed a particularly poor ח looking a bit like a ו and ז not joined and with a smudge over the letter too (see above right). It is possible that an early transcription error on some manuscripts perpetuated confusion amongst scribes with copies of *Sefer Tagin* over what this word actually was. בכחיה has possibly morphed into בזנביה or vice versa. In the listing and introduction **ST** gives a very different reading to those considered thus far, דאקים כרעיהון לבתריהון חמשין באורי׳ (that their leg/knees are standing up/raised to their backs, fifty in the *Torah*). As would be expected, **BH** concurs, bringing באוריתא in full.

We also continue to enjoy access to the Oxford Bodleian MS. Heb. d. 33/3 fragment—**OB**—which preserves the *nun* listing. Unfortunately, it gives us no actual description, reading just נ ֹנ באוֹ (*nun*—50 in the *Torah*), so we know

172 Jastrow, op. cit., p. 461.

it agrees with the number of instances, but the description is omitted in favour of a drawing of a *nun* with three *tagin* and a curl below (above right) similar to most of the other forms in the table below.

The example brought in the printed Maḥzor Vitry (*LMV*)*, shown right, is perhaps a little poorly rendered, as the curve touches the base of the letter which does not happen in the manuscripts.*

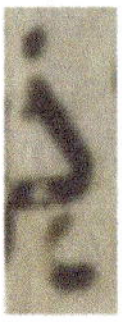

Through his listing our scribe places his indicator tag *on the bottom of the letter rather than on other letters on the roof, acknowledging that the decoration is below. This is confirmed in his rendition of the form in* **T-S NS 287.11-F** (*right*)*. However, oddly, he does not join the curl to the letter itself and places it under the middle of the base. He also adds a dot above it, which we have suggested elsewhere means that he might have felt some difficulty with how to draw the form.*

However, as we see below, the other sources are generally quite happy to attach the curl to the base of the letter on the left side. The curl on the nun *in* **T-S Misc. 24.182** (*right*) *is generally quite flat.*

All the core sources agree there are fifty instances, which makes perfect sense, given numerically *nun* = 50.[173]

Line 22: [וזכרתי להם   שער נ   דאקים] **בזנביה נ באורית**[1]נעש]ה
['and I will remember for their sake' (Lev. 26:45). //// Gate of the *nun* //// [*Nun*] that is standing up/raised] **in its tail, 50 in the *Torah*.** (*Parashat Bere'shit*) 1. **'let us make …**

18 Listing of Instances for the Special Letter *Nun*

1. **P**, **OB**, **MV**, **ST**, and **H** all agree, bringing נעשה אדם, and our scribe appears to, with the instance going into the next line.

Line 23: אדם • בצלמ{י}נו • כדמות{י}נו • [2]בינ֯י וב{י}נ֯יכ[ם תרו֯ • [3]**וענו אתם** • [4]**בריתי**
[… man' (Gen. 1:26). 'in our image' (Gen. 1:26). 'after our likeness' (Gen. 1:26). (*Parashat Noaḥ*) 2. 'between you and them'] **on both of them** (Gen. 9:12). (*Parashat Lekh Lekha*) 3. **'and they will afflict them'** (Gen. 15:13). 4. **'My covenant …**

Reconstructing the missing elements, we see that **P**, **OB**, **MV** and **ST** bring בצלמנו as 𝔐, but **H** brings בצלמינו *ma-le' vav*.

173 Baer brings instead 55, op. cit., p. 24.

TABLE 17 Forms for the special letter *nun*. By and large these all have a curl under the base, some plain and some more ornate. **P** brings two forms, with one more of a line going up and down from the base, than a curl. **H** curls upwards from the base, but also adds a line downwards and MS Geunz 481 places the curl on the roof instead. Interestingly, many omit the normal three *tagin* that are usually on the *nun* form. The instruction makes no reference to these.

 *Maḥzor Vitry* Parma 2574 (**P**)	 *Maḥzor Vitry* Add. MS 27201 (**MV**)	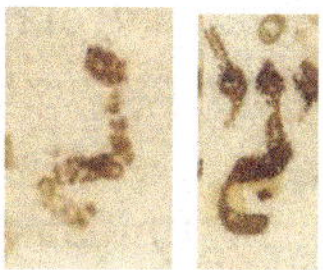 Shem Tov *Tanakh* *Sefer Tagi* (**ST**)	 *Badey ha-ʾAron* Heb. 840 (**BH**)	 *Sefer Tagin* Heb. 837 (**H**)
Not extant Nr. 5667 (**K**)	 Parma 2427	 Parma 1959	 Q651–652	 MS Geunz. 481
 *Maḥzor Vitry* Add. MS 27201 (**MV2**)	 Add. MS 11639	 Add. MS 27167	 Bologna *Torah*	 Vat. ebr. 1
 Or. 1463	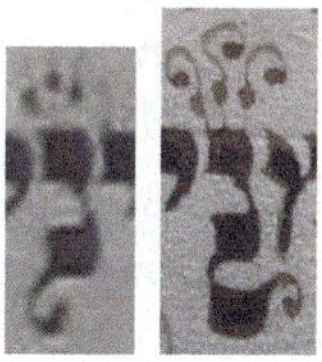 Alexander *Torah*			

P, MV and H then bring כדמותינו also *ma-le' vav*, whilst OB and ST are *ḥaser* כדמותנו as 𝔐. Our manuscript could have been either *ma-le'* or *ḥaser*. Both are from the same verse as the first instance and follow on. This line is quite widely spaced but there are no additional words to fill that space.

2. Given the element extant, our scribe probably brings ביני וביניכם as P, MV and ST and H, *ma-le' yod* as 𝔐 or ביני ובניכם as OB. MV brings תרויהון in full, but puts a separator before it as if stands alone as an instance. H brings תרווי׳.
3. P and OB agree, bringing וענו אתם, as 𝔐. MV and H are *ma-le' vav* וענו אותם, as is ST, who extends to וענו אותם ארבע ('they shall afflict them four [hundred years]').
4. P brings ברית ביני ובינך תרׄ. H is similar but תרווי׳, both having a missing *yod* in the first word of the instance. MV brings בריתי ביני ובינך תרויהון correctly, with the *yod* in בריתי. ST disagrees and brings instead בריתי בינ֯י ובינ֯יכם בׄ בו ('covenant between me and between you' 2 in it [the verse]), but this seems an error and is easily explained by the similar instance in the previous line.[174] All of them are *ma-le' vav* in ובינך whereas 𝔐 is *ḥaser*, ובינך. Our manuscript likely brings some variant on this. However, **OB** differs more significantly, in that it connects the first word to a different word and gives instead ואתנ֯ה בריתי ('and I will make/give') providing an additional instance before that is not seen in the rest of the core sources.[175]

Line 24: **[ביני ובינ{י}ך תרו • על פנ֯יו ויצחק • [5]הלבן מא]ה יולד שנ֯ה • [6]מאת שנ֯ה •**
[... between you and I' on both of them] (Gen. 17:2). 'upon his face and laughed' (Gen. 17:17)] 5. **'shall a child be born to one a hundred years** [old]' (Gen. 17:17). (*Parashat Va-yera'*) 6. **'year'** (Gen. 21:5) 7. **'one hundred years** [old]' (Gen. 21:5).

Reconstructing the line, P, OB, MV, ST and H all bring על פניו ויצחק from Gen. 17:17.

5 and 6. There follows some considerable confusion in the core sources around instances involving the word שנה. Our fragment does not make any distinction between the instances so it does make things a little

---

174 Basser makes no reference to this error and instead brings ובינך even though ST does not, *op. cit.*, p. 107.

175 From our secondary sources, Q651–652 lends some support to OB bringing אתנ֯ה ברית בינ֯י ובינ֯יך with all three letters *nun* being decorated. In Add. MS 11639 the whole phrase is listed but none of the letters *nun* are decorated. Add. MS 27167, Parma 1959, MV2, *Qiryat Sefer* and *Ben Mesheq* omit this additional instance.

harder here and it may have the word order wrong. Reviewing our sources in turn, P brings three instances הלבן מאה שנה • שנה • מאת שנה. As P, **MV** brings the first two as part of its entry in *parashat Lekh Lekha* and then adds the third under *parashat Va-yera'*. הלבן מאה שנה is clearly from Gen. 17:17. מאת שנה appearing in *Va-yera'* (and related to Isaac's birth) would thus be Gen. 21:5. However, there are three occurrences of the word שנה between these two instances. It is **ST** that provides a clearer solution, though slightly out of sequence, as it brings שנ̊ה יולד (Gen. 17:17) מאת שנ̊ה (Gen. 21:5) and then brings תשעים שנ̊ה תלד ('ninety years [old] and she bore') back in Gen. 17:17.[176] **OB** extends the first instance, likely agreeing with our manuscript, as it brings הלבן מאה שנ̊ה יולד ('shall a child be born to him who is one hundred') and then after a separator dot brings only the third instance, though associating Sarah in error to this and also spelling the second word with a *he* שרה מאה שנ̊ה. H, however, is by far the most defective of our sources and brings only one instance here הלבן מאה שנה. None of our core sources are wholly accurate,[177] but between the various sources, we can posit that the original intention was likely:

הלבן מאה שנ̊ה יולד • שרה הבת תשעים שנ̊ה תלד • מאת שנ̊ה

Based on available space on lines 22 and 23, our scribe has possibly got the sequence and word order wrong and possibly orders as **ST**, bringing what should be the second instance in the third position at the start of the next line, but may only have the word שנ̊ה as P.

Line 25: **[שנ̊ה • לבנ̊י דואשביעך • לבנ̊י מש]ם • [7]אדני מאד • [8]נ̊קרא • [9]מנ̊קתה •**

[(*Parashat Ḥayyei Sarah*) 'to my son' of [the verse beginning] 'and I will make you swear' (Gen. 24:3). 'for my son from there' (Gen. 24:7). 7. '{blessed}] **my master greatly'** (Gen. 24:35). 8. **'we will call'** (Gen. 24:57). 9. **'and her wet nurse'** (Gen. 24:59).

---

176 Again Basser makes no reference to this error of sequencing, op. cit., p. 107.

177 Turning to our secondary sources, we similarly have to look at these as a block of instances. Q651–652 brings מאה שנ̊ה • הבת תשעים שנ̊ה • מאת שנ̊ה. Parma 2427 brings מאה שנ̊ה • תשעים שנ̊ה • מאה שנ̊ה. Add. MS 27167 brings שנ̊ה תלד only, however, Parma 1959 brings שנ̊ה יולד שנ̊ה תלד. MV2 brings ואברהם בן מאת שנ̊ה with the *nun* decorated, but lists הלבן מאה שנה with no decoration, and lists ה̊ב̊ת תשעים שנה, decorating two different letters instead (that are not generally decorated). *Qiryat Sefer* brings שנה שנה הנוני"ן מוזרקות למע[ל]ה ... מאה שנה הנו"ן מוזרקת מלמעלה ומלמטה ('year', 'year' the letters *nun* are curled above ... 'one hundred years' the *nun* is curled above and below). *Ben Mesheq* brings פי"ז שנה שנה (verse 17 'year' [and] 'year'). Add. MS 11639 omits all these instances.

Reconstructing this line, we see yet more disagreement between the core sources. **P** and **H** bring לבנ֯י דואשה ('to my son' of the verse including 'and the woman'), but there is no such reference in the Genesis. **OB** and **ST** are perhaps clearer, bringing לבנ֯י דואשביעך from Gen. 24:3. **MV** brings the same, but there is a poor spacing between the *shin* and *bet* that make it look like a word break. Given available spacing, I suspect our scribe brought the correct instance, unless he lengthened the previous instance instead.

P, **MV**, **ST** and **H** then bring לבני משם from Gen. 24:7. **OB** omits.

7. **P**, **MV**, **ST** and **H** agree, bringing אדני מאד. **OB** agrees with the instance, but frames differently as ברך את אדנ֯י ('blessed my master').
8. **P**, **MV** and **H** agree, bringing נקרא. However, **OB** extends to נ֯קרא לנ֯ערה ('we will call the girl') thus providing us with yet another instance, the inclusion of which enjoys some limited support in the secondary sources.[178] 𝔐 is לנער, as this is a *qeri-ketiv*. **ST** partly agrees as it abbreviates to נקרא לנ:, but does not indicate a second instance.
9. Our scribe brings as 𝔐 *ḥaser yod*, but none of the other sources do. **P**, **OB** and **ST** bring מניקתה.[179] **MV** brings מינקתה and **H** is doubly *ma-le'* with מיניקתה writing the *tav* again over above the word since it was originally written as a *ḥet* in error, and was poorly corrected.

Line 26: **[הוא אד{ו}ני • וינחם {יצחק} • נ֯ת]ן • [10]בעודנ֯י חי • [11]לעבדך לאבינו •**
['he is my master' (Gen. 24:65). 'and {Isaac} was comforted' (Gen. 24:67). 'gave' (Gen. 25:6).] 10. **'while he still lived'** (Gen. 25:6). 11. **'your servant, our father'** (Gen. 43:28).

Reconstructing the line **P** and **H** bring הוא אדוני *ma-le' vav* from Gen. 24:65. **OB**, **MV** and **ST** bring instead הוא אדני, *ḥaser vav* as 𝔐.

P, **MV**, **ST** and **H** then bring וינחם from Gen. 24:67. **OB** extends to וינחם יצחק ('and Isaac was comforted').

P, **OB**, **MV** and **H** bring נתן אברהם from Gen. 25:6, and this time, it is **ST** that extends to נ֯תן אברהם מתנות ויש: ('Abraham gave gifts and he sent them away'), which potentially

178 Basser again makes no reference to this addition bringing just נקרא, op. cit., p. 107. Turning to our secondary sources, Q651–652 lends support to **OB**, bringing ונ֯קרא לנ֯ערה decorating both. *Qiryat Sefer* also brings נקרא לנער הנונין מוזרקות למעלה ולמטה ('we will call to the girl', the [letters] *nun* are curled above and below). *Ben Mesheq* too lists this פנ"ז ונקרא לנערה ... כעין הנו"ן של בצלמנו דבראשית (verse 57, 'and we will call to the girl' ... like the *nun* of 'in our image' from *Bere'shit*.) Parma 2427 brings ונ֯קרא לנערה, but decorates only the first. Add. MS 11639, Add. MS 27617 and Parma 1959 omit both.

179 Whereas Basser normally corrects **ST** to the reading in 𝔐 when it differs, he does not do in this case, op. cit., p. 107.

introduces a further *nun*, but it is clear that only the first is intended. Also 𝔐 is *ḥaser vav* מתנת. However, since there is a *nun sofit* present on the fragment, it would appear that our scribe has omitted the word אברהם. Since this would still create a short line, it is possible that he has followed **OB** in the previous instance and added the word יצחק. None of the secondary sources bring לאברהם which is the word that precedes נתן in 𝔐, so this is unlikely to have been added. To fill the line, it is also possible that our scribe has transposed אברהם and נתן in error.

10. There is general agreement about the instance, but some disagreement over the spelling. **P** and **ST** are as 𝔐, bringing בעודנו חי. Our manuscript ends the second word with a *yod* and not a *vav*. **MV** crosses out his first attempt ~~בעדיני~~ and then errs, as our manuscript, bringing בעודני חי. Possibly the *vav* was too short in their *Vorlage* and the scribes did not check it.[180] **H** brings בעודנו חיי doubling the *yod* in the last word.[181]

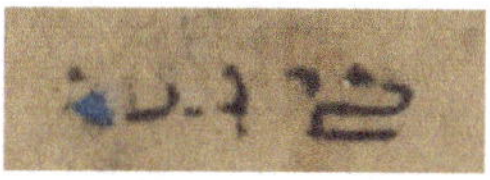

T-S Misc. 24.182 may or may not bring an additional instance concerning *nun* at this point (see right). From its positioning it would need to fall between Gen. 40:12 and Gen. 40:16, but it is not clear that the first letter is a *nun*, even though the decoration is that for the *nun. The* only word that beings with a *nun* in that section is נא ('I beseech you') followed by עמדי ('with me') from Gen. 40:14, which does not fit the ink remains. What does fit is כי גנב ('for I was stolen away') from Gen. 40:15, and this is more likely, but it is not clear why the *kaf* has been decorated in the same way as normally reserved by this scribe for a *nun*.

11. Our last extant example from *nun* on our **CG** fragments is largely common across all core sources. **P**, **OB**, **ST** and **H** agree, whilst **MV** omits.

As mentioned above there is some discussion over whether there are 50 or 55 instances. Unfortunately, our fragment's listing of instances of *nun* finishes here, and cannot add to this debate.

19 Description and Example Forms of the Special Letter *Tav*

Our last **CG** section comes from the top of a full folio **T-S NS 287.11-F** which fortunately does not need reconstruction. However, we are missing the descrip-

---

180 The printed **LMV** corrects it in the transcription.

181 Corrected in the transcription in **EPST**.

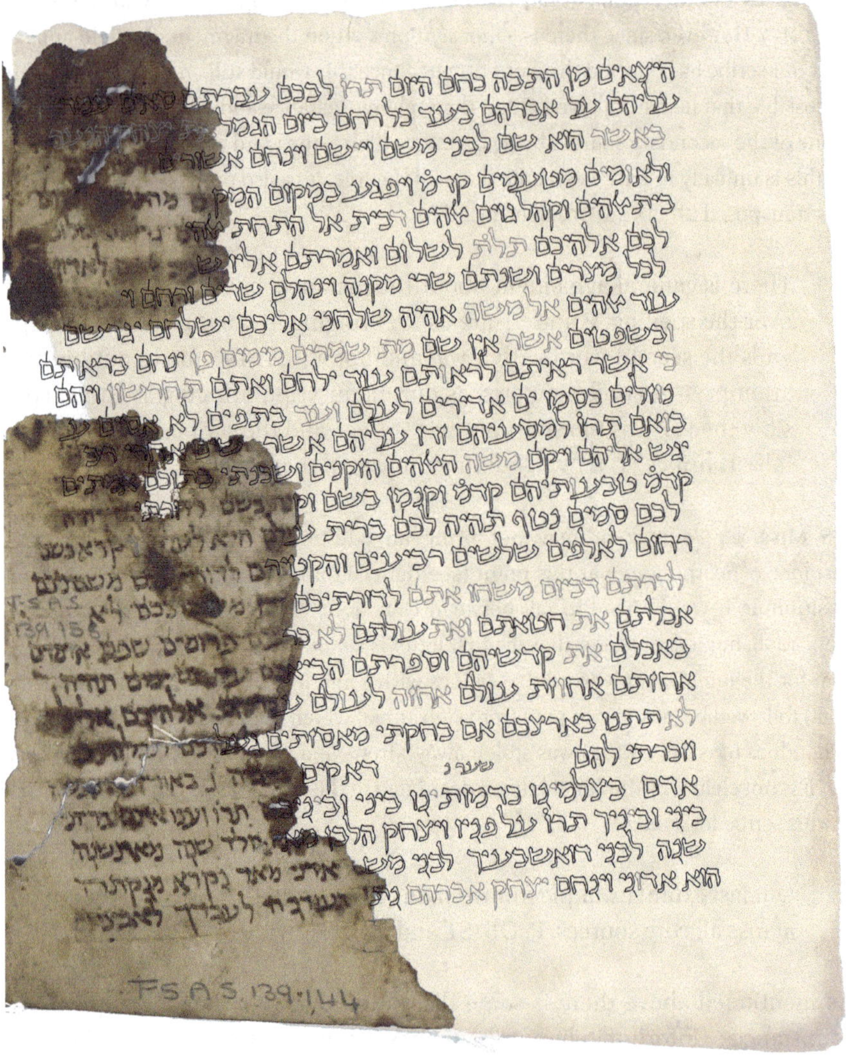

RECONSTRUCTION 4 Above, the reconstruction of the folio with 26 lines, showing the conclusion of the listing for the *mem sofit* and the start of *nun* that we have considered above. This covers fragments T-S AS 139.152-B (right side), T-S AS 139.158-F and T-S AS 139.144-F (right side), though joined together they all form the left side of this reconstructed page.

tion, number and first four instances of the letter *tav* that would have been on the previous page. Nonetheless, we do have all the examples of the letters forms at the end of the listing for *tav*, which we have seen through this monograph.

P explains that ת כׄבׄ באוריית׳ דמדלי רישיהון מכולהו׳ (*Tav*—22 in the *Torah* where their heads are extended/suspended/raised more than others). **MV** gives the last word in full, ת כׄבׄ באוריית׳ דמדלי רישיהון מכולהון and **H** abbreviates elsewhere giving, ת כ׳ב׳ באורי׳ דמדלי רישיהון מכולהון. It is only in the introduction and listing for **ST** that we see a slight variant ת דמדלי רישיהון מן כולהון עשרין ותרין באורייתא, ordering the phrase slightly differently, with the full version of the Aramaic numbers and using מן rather than the contraction מ. **BH**, as one would expect given the same author, is as **ST**.

The printed Maḥzor Vitry (*LMV*)*, shown right, brings a fairly standard example of the special* tav *with a* tag *coming from the right side of the roof.*

From our **CG** *fragments, though we do not have the description, we do have the form drawn below within* **T-S NS 287.11-F** (*right*) *and it is very similar to those in the other sources and so we can fairly safely assume that the description was the same.*

T-S Misc. 24.182 (*right*) *has a long line coming out of the roof in line with the leg.*

Our scribe has seemingly abandoned indicating which letter in the word carries the decoration, but in all cases this is obvious.

20 Listing of Instances for the Special Letter *Tav*

As noted, we are missing the first four instances in the list that must have been listed on the previous folio from *parashat Bere'shit*. P, MV, ST and H bring מרחפת ('hovered') from Gen. 1:2.

P, MV, ST and H then brings עשות ('made') from Gen. 2:4.

From *parashat Ki Tissa'* P brings two instances חרות • על הלוחות from Ex. 32:16 where both instances of the letter *tav* are to be decorated. **ST** shows this decoration specifically in its listing חרות̊ • על הלוחות̊, making it very clear what the intention is. **H** brings as one entry חרות על הלוחות. **MV** also brings them together חרות על הלחת ('graven upon the tablets') and is the only one of the core sources to match 𝔐 with the last word doubly *ḥaser vav*.[182]

182 Our *Genizah* secondary source **T-S Misc. 24.182** is also doubly *ḥaser*, bringing חרות̊ and then הלחת̊.

TABLE 18 Forms for the special letter *tav*. Generally these add a line on the left end of the roof of the letter, sometimes with a round *tag*, sometimes with a flag shape. Add. MS 11639 brings a very dramatic diagonal line going above and below the roof. MS Geuntz. 481 and the Bologna *Torah* bring two *tagin*. Parma 1959 adds 3 *tagin* and Parma 2427 oddly extends the length of the left leg instead.

 *Maḥzor Vitry* Parma 2574 (P)	 *Maḥzor Vitry* Add. MS 27201 (MV)	 Shem Tov *Tanakh* *Sefer Tagi* (ST)	 *Badey Ha-'Aron* Heb. 840 (BH)	 *Sefer Tagin* Heb. 837 (H)
Not extant Nr. 5667 (K)	 Parma 2427	 Parma 1959	 Q651–652	 MS Geunz. 481
 *Maḥzor Vitry* Add. MS 27201 (MV2)	 Add. MS 11639	Not deployed Add. MS 27167	 Bologna *Torah*	Not present Vat. ebr. 1
 Or. 1463	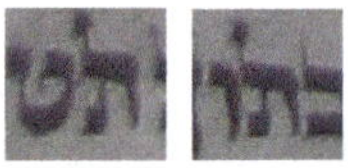 Alexander *Torah*			

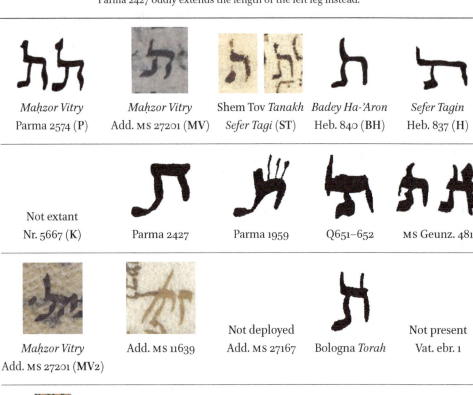

It is worth noting, in passing that our *Genizah* secondary source **T-S Misc. 24.182** also brings ושמתם from Gen. 47:6, but this is likely an error since this is usually only associated with a decoration on the *mem sofit* in the core and secondary sources. It uniquely also brings a further instance ונתת ('and you will put'). However, from its positioning seems could be either its use in Ex. 30:16, or one of its two uses in Ex. 30:18. Either way, it enjoys no other support from core or secondary sources.

T-S NS 287.11-F—5 lines of interest

We start at the top of T-S NS 287.11-F with three linked instances from within one verse.

Line 1: [1]וסלחת • [2]לחטאתינו • [3]ונחלתנו • [4]וחטאתיכם • [5]תטהרו • [6][שבת • [7]שב]תון •
(*Parashat Ki Tissa'*) 1. **'and pardon'** (Ex. 34:9). **2. 'and our sins'** (Ex. 34:9). 3. '[take] **us for Your inheritance'** (Ex. 34:9). (*Parashat 'Aḥarey Mot*) 4. **'and your sins'** (Lev. 16:30). 5. **'you shall be cleansed'** (Lev. 16:30). [(*Parashat 'Emor?*) 6. 'sabbath' (Lev. 23:32).] 7. **'of sabbaths'** (Lev. 23:32).

1. **P**, **MV**, **ST** and **H** all agree, bringing וסלחת.
2. **P**, **MV**, **ST** and **H** give ולחטאתינו. Our scribe has omitted a *vav* at the start of the word, in error. However, none of the sources are correct, since they are all *ma-le' yod*, whilst 𝔐 is *ḥaser*, ולחטאתנו.
3. **P**, **MV**, **ST** and **H** all agree, bringing ונחלתנו. **ST** then adds ג׳ בו: (three in it [the verse]), linking these three instances. It is possible, given previous examples where the word has been replaced by **ST**, that Shem Tov saw תלתיהון in his *Vorlage*.
4. **P** and **H** give וחטאתם ('and their sins'), but this word does not occur till Num. 15:25, so that would mean it was in the wrong order in the list. Our scribe here almost agrees instead with **MV** and **ST** who bring חטאתיכם ('your sins') from Lev. 16:30. Having omitted one *vav* a mere two instance previously, this time our scribe brings a superfluous *vav* at the start of the word.
5. **P**, **MV**, **ST** and **H** all agree.

6 and 7. These are also linked. **P** brings them separately, שבת • שבתון, **ST** decorates each letter *tav*, שבת̊ • שבת̊ון הוא, however, **MV** and **H** put both together as one entry שבת שבתון. Whilst there is no disagreement in the core sources as to which words should be decorated, there is a disagreement as to the position of these two instances and indeed the next two as well. This is because the same words appear in the same sequence, both in *parashat 'Aḥarey Mot* in Lev. 16:31 and also in *parashat 'Emor* in Lev. 23:32. **MV** places these all in *'Emor*. This is substantiated by **ST** which adds the word הוא which would also place them in *'Emor* and this is further supported by the entry in the Shem Tov *Tanakh*. Lev. 16:31 gives היא. However, the secondary sources tend to place them in *'Aḥarey Mot*.[183]

183 Turning to our secondary sources, Q651–Q652 brings שבת̊ שבת̊ון in *parashat 'Aḥarey*

Line 2: [8]ועניתֹ[ם] • [9]נפשתיכם • [10]חקת • [11]את שמי • [12]ואספת • כברכת • ת[הי]ה • תזל???

8. 'and you will afflict' (Lev. 23:32) 9. **'your souls'**[184] (Lev. 23:32). 10. **'statute'** (Lev. 24:3) 11. **'My Name'** (Num. 6:27). 12. **'and you will gather'** (Deut. 11:14). **'according to the blessing'**, **'will be' 'shall drop'**, (likely errors)

8. P and H agree, bringing ועניתם, as 𝔐. ST extends to ועניתֹם את, but is clear which letter takes the decoration. **MV** appears to be *ma-le' yod*, bringing ועניתים.
9. **MV, ST and H** agree, bringing נפשתיכם, as 𝔐. **P** brings instead נפשותיכם *ma-le' vav*. **ST** then brings an additional qualifier ד בפסו (4 in [one] verse), linking instances 6–9, as they do indeed appear in one verse, in both possible locations.
10. **P and H** brings חקה אחת ('one statute') which would be referring to one law for the born Jew and the same for the convert/stranger from Num. 9:14, and which would suggest that the decoration is on the second word. This would be quite out of sequence. **ST**, however, brings חקתֹ עולם ('an everlasting statute') which is either from Lev. 16:31 from *parashat 'Aḥarey Mot* or from Lev. 24:3 from *parashat Tsav*, but the Shem Tov *Tanakh* only decorates the instance in *parashat 'Emor*. Our scribe seems to agree with **ST** and **MV** bringing חקת, but provides no additional clarification as to its location. **MV** claims that חקת occurs twice and both in the *sedra* of *'Emor*, but since it appears at the end of folio 213r and then again at the top of folio 213v, it is likely that this is a repetition error rather than intentional.[185]

Mot. Parma 1959 lists this in the section he begins ואחר which is *parashat 'Aḥarey Mot* and shows שבתֹ שבתֹון יהיה לכם ('a sabbath of sabbaths it will be to you'). *Qiryat Sefer* brings both in *'Aḥarey Mot* שבת בשלשתם התי״ו מתייגת שנים, שבתון מלא והתי״ו מתייגת שנים ('sabbath' in the three of them the *tav* is decorated with two [*tagin*], 'of sabbaths' is *ma-le'* and the *tav* is decorated with two [*tagin*]) and only the one on שבתון in *'Emor*, שבתון מלא והתי״ו מעגלת ('of sabbaths' is *ma-le'* and the *tav* is curled). Similarly *Ben Mesheq* lists seven letters *tav* in the *'Aḥarey Mot* section, which includes these two. However, *Ben Mesheq* also lists the letters *tav* of שבתֹ שבתֹון in *parashat Be-har* and refers back to their occurrence in *parashat 'Aḥarey Mot*. MV2 only lists שבת שבתון in *'Aḥarey Mot*, but does not decorate either word. Parma 2427 and Add. MS 11639 do not list these two instances in either location.

184 i.e. fast.

185 Q651–652 does bring the phrase חקתֹ עולם in the listing for *parashat Tsav*, but only decorates the *qof*. Instead it decorates the *tav* in חקתֹ עולם that occurs in *'Aḥarey Mot*. Parma 9159 too lists חקתֹ עולם in *'Aḥarey Mot* as does Add. MS 11639, which brings a very dramatic *tag*. *Qiryat Sefer* also brings this in *'Aḥarey Mot*, חקת התי״ו מתייגת שנים ('statute' the *tav*

11. **P**, **ST** and **H** agree, bringing את שמי, but **MV**, confused by this listing, brings two instances joined together and gives it instead as occurring in *parashat ʾEmor* as את שמי שלמית בת ('My name *'Shelomit* the daughter [of *Divri*]') from *Lev.* 24:11, but that is not in *ʾEmor*, or what is meant.
12. **ST** agrees, bringing ואספתֿ. **P** brings ואספת • דוהיה אם שמוע as if they are two separate instances, but **H** is clearer, bringing ואספת דוהיה אם שמוע ('and you may gather' of 'and if you listen') in Deut. 11:14. **MV** is similar, bringing ואספת • ד'היה אם שמע, though the first *vav* in **MV** was omitted and suspended and also adds a separator that is unnecessary. However, **MV** is the only source to accord with 𝔐 where שמע is *ḥaser vav*. Additionally, והיה אם שמע is, in fact, Deut. 11:13, so it must imply that it is in the section rather than the verse,[186] hooking it to the nearest significant descriptor.

Our scribe has apparently omitted an instance and this has been written in subsequently. We can just about make out the first word כברכת but there are additional words after, but these are not at all clear, with really only a ת at the end obvious. However, he brings this instance again on the next line. It is possible that whoever added the smaller writing intended to repeat and meant the first occurrence in Deut. 12:15, but this is unlikely, given our other sources. Our scribe also appears to have written תהיה and תזל on this line, which he then repeats on the next line. It is possible that the fading here was not a matter of the passing of time, but instead a deliberate, though only partial, erasure.

Line 3: [?]תהיה • [13]כברכת בתׁ • [14]שלומית • [15]תזל • [16]אמרתי • [17]רבבות
'will be' (likely an error). (*Parashat Reʾeh*) 13. **the last 'according to the blessing'** (Deut. 16:17). 14. **'Shelomit'**—likely an error, possibly (*Parashat Ki Tavoʾ*) **'unhewn'** (Deut. 27:6). (*Parashat Haʾazinu*). 15. **'shall drop'** (Deut. 32:2). 16. **'my speech'** (Deut. 32:2). (*Parashat Ve-zoʾt Ha-berakhah*). 17. **'myriads'** (Deut. 33:17).

is decorated with two [*tagin*]) and not in *ʾEmor*. It is also in the listing of seven instances brought by *Ben Mesheq* for *ʾAḥarey Mot*. **MV2** only lists חקת עולם in *ʾAḥarey Mot*, but does not decorate the *tav*.

186 Verse numbering are a late Christian innovation. The system that was generally accepted was by Robert Estienne (Robert Stephanus), his verse numbers entering printed editions in 1551 (New Testament) and 1571 (*Tanakh*). However, the 'division of the Hebrew Bible into verses is [also] an ancient Jewish tradition reflected in the accentuation system, which marks the end of every verse by placing the accent *silluq* under the last word of each verse', Penkower, Jordan S. *Verse Divisions in the Hebrew Bible* from *Vetus Testamentum, vol. 50, no. 3*, 2000, p. 379. JSTOR, www.jstor.org/stable/1585296. Accessed 22/1/20. I have employed the Jewish system throughout.

Our scribe then brings תהיה again, this time implying an actual instance. However, this is not brought in any of the other core sources. Given its position in the list, if it is an actual listing, then it would need to occur between Deut. 11:13 and Deut. 16:17, which would make it Deut. 13:10, כי הרג תהרגנו ידך תהיה בו ('and you will stone him with stones, your hand be upon him') rather than the numerous occurrences in the rest of Deuteronomy. However, given no other sources bring this, and the fact that it follows on from ואספת in both lines, I would be inclined argue that this is in fact a corruption of דוהיה where the דו has been mis-transcribed into a ת, perhaps copied from a poorly written *Vorlage*.

13. P brings כברכת בת̇ and H similar כברכת בתר' implying this is only on the second occasion it occurs. However, ST brings just כברכת̊. **MV** brings כברכת בתראה in *parashat Re'eh* where both occur. This would imply Deut. 16:17, as opposed to the earlier occurrence in Deut. 12:15.[187]
14. P and H agree with our fragment, bringing שלומית but this word does not occur in Deuteronomy. ST brings instead שלומים ואכלת̊ ('peace offerings and you will eat') from Deut. 27:7. Basser notes[188] that in the margin of the Shem Tov *Tanakh* the letters כ̇ב̇ (22) are written opposite שלמים ואכלת̊ and he decorates the *tav* there. ST has clearly tried to find an alternative option. However, given the other sources do not reference ואכלת, I would argue that an alternative possible instance would be שלמות ('unhewn'), merely one verse earlier in Deut. 27:6, since it would be much easier to confuse a *vav* and *yod* than a *tav* and *mem sofit*.[189] This is one occasion where I feel that **all the sources are corrupt** and do not show the likely original intention.
15. P agrees, bringing תזל. MV, ST and H extend to ת̊זל כטל ('shall drop as dew').
16. P, **MV**, ST and H all agree, bringing אמרתי.
17. All our sources, as one might hope, agree with the very last instance of *Sefer Tagin*, P, **MV**, ST and H agree with our scribe, bringing רבבות̊.

Adding the 17 instances listed here to the 4 we anticipate were on the previous folio gives us 21, one short of our expected 22. Indeed P and H also list only 21.

187 Parma 1959 brings כברכת̊ ײ אלהיך in the end of the list for *Re'eh*, which also suggests the last one based on positioning. Q651–652, Parma 2427, Add. MS 11639, MV2, *Qiryat Sefer* and *Ben Mesheq* all omit either possibility.

188 Basser, op. cit., p. 144.

189 Unfortunately, none of the secondary sources bring any reference here to either possibility.

MV is not useful here as it omits instances, because of its format of listing by *parasha*. If we accept תהיה as an instance, then our scribe would bring 22 but this is not likely as we have seen. Instead it is down to **ST** to provide us with the most likely missing instance מרבבוֹת (‘from the myriads’) from Deut. 33:2, though 𝔐 is *ḥaser vav* מרבבת.[190] It is possible it was excluded by the others because of its similarity to the final instance. Including this would give us our penultimate instance, and bring our total to 22.

21 Conclusion of *Sefer Tagin*

Our **CG** scribe then adds the phrase סליק ספר תאגי (conclusion of *Sefer Tagi*). As mentioned previously, he does not bring the section on *BeYah Shemo* which is added to the end of **P** and **H**, though not in **ST**.[191] **MV** instead runs into a listing of the large letters. It seems clear that for *BeYah Shemo* and the *ʾOtiyot Gedolot/Rabati*, these are just an accident of proximity and it is much more likely that *Sefer Tagin* itself originally only consisted of the listing of the descriptions and instances of the letters. Our *Genizah* manuscript **CG** certainly supports this contention.

Our scribe then ends with his interpretation of the letters forms which we have examined as we have encountered them. As we have discussed, it is telling that some forms are ignored and dots are simply placed above the letters, suggesting that our **CG** scribe was uncomfortable with some of the forms, or just did not know how to properly display them.

---

190 From our secondary sources, Parma 2427 lists מרבבת but does not decorate a letter. **MV2**, Q651–652, Add. MS 11639, Parma 1959, *Qiryat Sefer* and *Ben Mesheq* all omit.

191 After the listing, **ST** concludes with the following: דע אתה המעיין כי כל תג ותג הרמוז על כל אות ואות שנרמז בספר הזה הנכבד רשמתי אותו במקומו אחר דקדק גדול ועמל יתר וחפוש מופלג בספרים רבים מדבקים ובחבורים קדמונים: (Know that the source of each *tag* that over each letter that is alluded to in this respected book, I copied it in its [right] place after great precision and labour and incomparable searching in many books accurate and ancient texts). This suggests Shem Tov may have undertaken some cross referencing between texts as opposed to just copying one primary *Vorlage*, and thus amended some entries, if he was unhappy with them. However, it is worth noting that in *Badey ha-ʾAron*, Shem Tov claims that finding even one copy of *Sefer Tagin* proved troublesome and took him some considerable time and effort.

22 Summary—CG Joined Fragments

These collective fragments from the Cairo *Genizah* collection held in CUL represent an important witness to *Sefer Tagin*. The scribe of **CG** most often echoes **P** or **OB**, and on a number of occasions has helped clarify disagreements between the core sources, though sadly remaining silent on others where parts of the manuscript are damaged or missing. The activity of reconstructing the folios of **CG** has helped address some of these, bringing an additional witness to this relatively small corpus of authoritative core texts concerning *Sefer Tagin*.

PART 3

Oxford Bodleian MS. Heb. 33/3 (fol. 9)

1 Critical Analysis of MS. Heb. d. 33/3

Continuing our listing, we now turn to the Oxford fragment given the siglum **OB**. As a reminder, the physical description notes that it is 'Syr. squ. Rabb. char.; oblong, vellum. It was bought from the Rev. G.J. Chester, 1891 (from the Cairo *Genizah*)'. The listing is under MS. Heb. d. 33/3 (fol. 9) where it is described as follows by the Bodleian, '(fol. 9) the Masorah finalis beginning with words ending in ם (אלהים דיהי מארת) to ע (ואל רשעו), not as in the printed text.' However, no mention is made of it being part of *Sefer Tagin*.

Each folio itself has writing that has faded to brown. Folio 9a consist of 22 lines. The second side 9b has only 21 lines but has a catchword to the next page.

MS Heb. d.33/9b—21 lines preserved

Lines 1, 2 and most of line 3 of this page of **OB** are treated above in part 2 under the listing for *nun*. Thus we begin our at the end of line 3 continuing entries for *nun*. Images for the special *nun* from various core sources are also given in part 2 above in table 17, but right is that of **OB**. In common with many examples from other sources, there is a curl emanating from the base of the *nun*.

2 Continuing the Listing for the Special Letter *Nun*

Line 3: **אדנ̊י • וינ̊חם יצחק • נ̊תן אברהם • בעדנ̊ו חי • לעבדך לאבינ̊ו • [1]עודנ̊ו חי • [2]אתי**
The first five instances are treated above in part 2. (*Parashat Miqqets*) 1. **'he is yet alive'** (Gen 43:28). 2. **'me …**

1. Related to a previous occurrence of the same phrase, **P**, **ST** and **H** agree, bringing עודנו חי. **MV** disagrees and brings instead פנעה • פותי פרע בתרא. ([Tsafnat] Paneaḥ [in the verse with the] last Poti Phera') in the listing for *parashat Miqqets*. The metathesis serves to confuse as 𝔐 gives פענח and this only occurs once in Gen. 41:45, thus the reference to the last 'Poti

 | DOI:10.1163/9789004426368_007

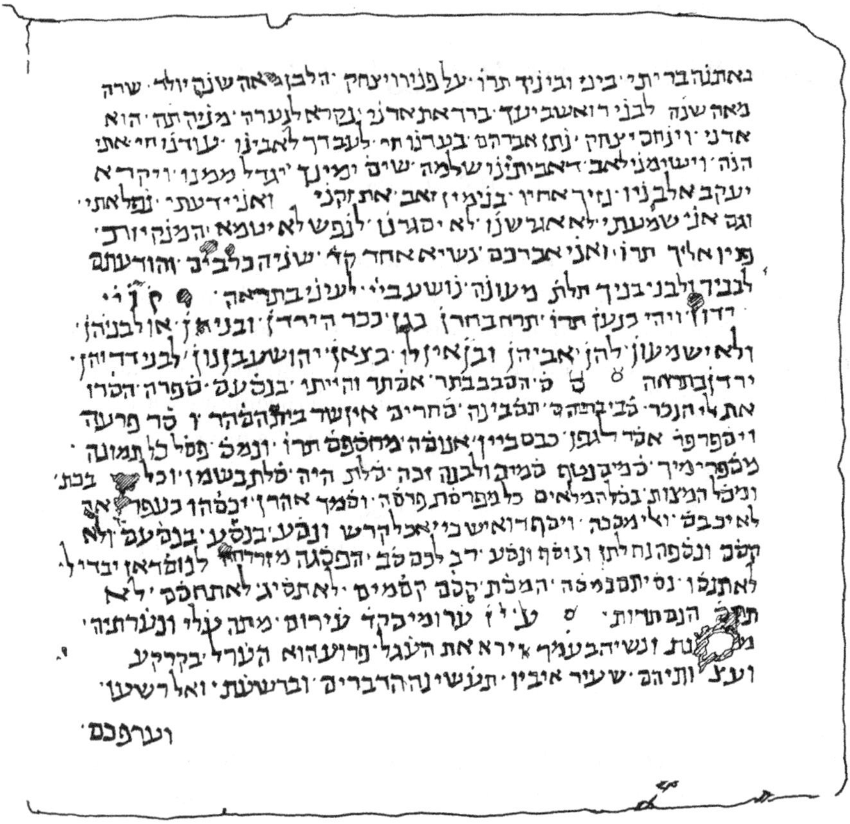

FIGURE 21 My drawing of MS Heb. 33/9b that covers part way through *nun* through to the first *'ayin* form. It is this side of the fragment that concerns us within this section, commencing a few lines in.
DRAWING © MARC MICHAELS. THIS IMAGE IS AVAILABLE TO VIEW IN COLOUR AT HTTPS://GENIZAH.BODLEIAN.OX.AC.UK/FRAGMENTS/FULL/MS_HEB_D_33_9B.JPG

Phera‘’ is somewhat redundant. No other core sources bring this, nor do the secondary ones.[1]

2. **P, MV** and **H** agree, bringing אתי הנה, as 𝔐. ST is *ma-le' vav* אותי הנֹה.

---

1 It is possible that **MV** here is confusing which letter is to be decorated since the *pe* in this word is one of those that is *melufefet* (curled). Turning to our secondary sources, the scan of Q651–652 is obscured. Parma 2427, Add. MS 27167, Add. MS 11639, Parma 1959, **MV2**, *Qiryat Sefer* and *Ben Mesheq* omit any reference to a special *nun* here. **MV** enjoys no other support.

Our *Genizah* secondary source **T-S Misc. 24.182** brings a further עוד֯נו, presumably the one that follows in Gen. 44:14.

Line 4: **הנ֯ה • [3]וישימנ֯י לאב • [4]דאבותינ֯ו שלמה • [5]שים ימינ֯ך • [6]יגדל ממנ֯ו • [7]ויקרא**
… here' (Gen. 45:8). 3. **'and he placed me as a father'** (Gen. 45:8). (*Parashat Va-yiggash*) 4. **of 'our fathers' complete** (Gen. 46:34 or 47:3). (*Parashat Va-yeḥi*) 5. **'put your right [hand]'** (Gen. 48:18). 6. **'greater than he'** (Gen. 49:19). 7. **'and Jacob called …**

3. Following on in the same verse, **OB** has also extended the instance adding לאב. **P**, **MV**, **ST** and **H** just bring וישימני.
4. It appears that the scribe of **OB** has erred, as the use of of ד would suggest that something preceded that word, and indeed that is what we find in the other core sources. **P**, **MV** and **H** bring גם אנחנו דאבותינו (also [the] 'we' from [the verse with] 'our father') though it is not clear which word the *nun* applies to. Or is it both? **ST** helps clarifies this by bringing גם אנחנ֯ו • דאבותינו, marking the second *nun* only. However, it is not clear which verse in *parashat Va-yiggash* this is, since the phrase appears twice: in Gen. 46:34 𝔐 reads גם אנחנו גם אבתינו בעבור תשבו (also us, [and] also our fathers, that you may dwell) and in Gen. 47:3 𝔐 reads רעה צאן גם אנחנו גם אבותינו (shepherds, also us, [and] also our fathers, that you may dwell). It is worth noting that all the core sources bring אבותינו *ma-le' vav* in 𝔐, which might suggest Gen. 47:3. Unfortunately, the Shem Tov *Tanakh* is not extent for either. It also is not clear why the word שלמה (complete) is present in **OB**, as this word does not appear in either verse, but it is possible that in this case it is referring to this *vav* being present. However, the secondary sources do not necessarily agree with that positioning, or even with which word should be decorated.[2]
5. **P**, **MV**, **ST** and **H** all agree, bringing שים ימינך.

---

2 Turning to our secondary sources, **T-S Misc. 24.182** brings אבותינ֯ו which from its position is Gen. 47:3 and Parma 2427 brings only גם אבתינ֯ו, *ḥaser vav*, which does not assist. However, Add. MS 27167 brings אבתינ֯ו בעבור and Parma 1959 which, as we have established, is copied from the same tradition seems to err and brings אבתיכ֯ו בעבור, but this is perhaps just a poorly formed *nun*. This would place this instance earlier in Gen. 46:34 instead. This is further supported by *Qiryat Sefer* which brings אבתינו חסר וא״ו והנו״ן מוזרקת למעלה ולמטה, בעבור מלא ('our father' is *ḥaser vav* and the *nun* is curled above and below, 'that you may' is *ma-le'*). These secondary sources decorate the *nun* in אבתינו rather than אנחנו. Q651–652, Add. MS 11639, **MV2** and *Ben Mesheq*, omit either possibility, likely because of the confusion.

6. P, MV, ST and H **all** agree, bringing יגדל ממנו.
7. **OB** extends the instance. **P, MV, ST** and **H** just bring אל בניו.

Line 5: **יעקב אל בנ̊יו • [8]נ̊זיר אחיו • [9]בנ̊ימין זאב • [10]את זקנ̊י יש̊ • [11]ואנ̊י ידעתי • [12]נ̊פלאתי •**

... to his sons' (Gen. 49:1). 8. **'a prince** [amongst] **his brothers'** (Gen. 49:26). 9. **'Benjamin is a wolf'** (Gen. 49:27). (*Parashat Shemot*) 10. **'the elders of Israel'** (Ex. 3:16). 11. **'and I know'** (Ex. 3:19). 12. **'My wonders'** (Ex. 3:20).

8. **P, MV, ST** and **H** all agree, bringing נזיר אחיו.
9. **P, MV, ST** and **H** are all *ḥaser yod*, bringing בנימן זאב. 𝔐 is *ma-le'* as our scribe in **OB**.
10. **ST** brings just זקנ̊י whilst **P, MV** and **H** omit. Basser notes that Shem Tov may have included it 'from his imagination, because it is similar to זאב'.[3] However, this is clearly an intentional inclusion supported by **OB** and is present in many secondary sources.[4]
11. **P, MV, ST** and **H** all agree, bringing ואני ידעתי.[5]
12. **P, MV, ST** and **H** all agree, bringing נפלאתי.

Line 6: **[13]וגם אנ̊י שמעתי • [14]לא אגרשנ̊ו • [15]לא יסגרנ̊ו • [16]לנ̊פש לא יטמא • [17]המנ̊קיות •**
(*Parashat Va-'era'*) 13. **'and also I heard'** (Ex. 6:5). (*Parashat Mishpaṭim*) 14. **'I will not drive them out'** (Ex. 23:29). (*Parashat Tazria'*) 15. **'he shall not shut him out'** (Lev. 13:11). (*Parashat 'Emor*) 16. **'for the dead he will not defile himself'** (Lev. 21:1). (*Parashat Be-midbar*) 17. **'and the jars'** (Num. 4:7).

13. **OB** extends the instance with וגם. **P, MV, ST** and **H** bring just אני שמעתי.
14. **P** and **H** just bring אגרשנו, which immediately sets up a problem as the word occurs in both Ex. 23:29 and 23:30. However, the extension by **OB**

3 Basser, op. cit., p. 108, note 315.

4 Turning to our secondary sources, Parma 2427 brings quite a long instance לך ואספת את זקנ̊י ואמרת אלהם ('go and gather the elders and say to them') missing the word ישראל but supporting **OB** and **ST**. Q651–652 also supports, bringing לך̊ ואספת את זקנ̊י. MV2 brings the phrase לך ואספת את זקני ישראל but does not decorate any letters. *Qiryat Sefer* brings זקני הנו"ן מוזרקת למעלה ולמטה ('elders' the *nun* is curled above and below). Basser claims *Ben Mesheq* does not bring this (op. cit., p. 197, note 297), but in fact brings the word in a list of others in *parashat Shemot* ס"ג י"[ו] זקני ... כנו"ן בצלמנו דבראשית (Chapter 3, verse 10 [probably 17 with a letter missing since the word is not in verse 10] 'elders' ... like the *nun* in 'in our image' from *Bere'shit*). T-S Misc. 24.182, Add. MS 11639 and Parma 1959 omit.

5 The *Ba'al ha-Ṭurim* comments here, ''and I'—the *nun* is bent, alluding to the 50 plagues [at sea]', that we read about in the *Pesaḥ Haggada* and other midrashic sources.

shows this is actually referring to the previous verse, Ex. 23:29, where we find לא אגרשנו and is paralleled by the next instance which also has לא. **ST** brings אגרשנ̊ו מן הא̇ ('drive them out' from the land [?—the abbreviation is unclear]), however, the Shem Tov *Tanakh* brings the decoration on the *nun* on אגרשנו from Ex. 23:30.[6]

15. **P** and **H** bring just יסגירנו *ma-le' yod.* **ST** is also *ma-le' yod* but does bring לא יסגירנ̊ו. 𝔐 is *ḥaser yod* as our scribe in **OB. MV** omits.
16. **P, ST** and **H** agree, bringing לנפש לא יטמא. **MV** omits.
17. **P, ST** and **H** agree, bringing המנקיות. **MV** omits.

Line 7: **18/19פנ̊יו אליך תרו̇ • 20ואנ̊י אברכם • 21נ̊שיא אחד קד̇ • 22שנ̊י הכרבים • 23/24/25והודעתם**

(*Parashat Naso'*) 18/19. **'face upon you' both of them** (Num. 6:25 and Num. 6:26). 20. **'and I will bless them'** (Num. 6:27). 21. **'each prince' the first** [occurrence] (Num. 7:11). 22. **'two *cherubim*'** (Num. 7:89). (*Parashat Va-'etḥanan*) 23/24/25. **'and make them known ...**

18 and 19. This is apparently referring to two occurrences of this phrase in close proximity in Num. 6:25 and Num. 6:26 in the *Birkat ha-Kohanim* (Priestly Blessing). **P** brings פניו אליך תר̇, **H** similarly פנ̊יו אליך תרוו׳. **ST** lists פניו אליך • פניו אליך separately, and then, after a further separator dot, adds תרויהון to make sure. **MV** omits both.

20. This is followed by the statement after the blessing, that this is how God will bless the people. **P, ST** and **H** agree, bringing ואני אברכם. **MV** omits.
21. The phrase appears twice in Num. 7:11, so this is suggesting the first only. **P** agrees and **H** is similarly נשיא אחד קדמ̇. **ST** extends and clarifies bringing נ̊שיא אחד ליום • קדמ̇, but with a superfluous separator dot. **MV** omits.
22. **P** and **OB** agree bringing שני הכרבים, *ḥaser vav* as 𝔐. **ST** is *ma-le' vav* שנ̊י הכרובים as is **H** who abbreviates שני הכרובי׳. **MV** omits again, having omitted all instances in *parashat Naso'*, likely an error rather than deliberate.

6 Which is presumably why Basser notes this as occurring at Ex. 20:30, and that there is some confusion over which occurrence (op. cit., p. 108). Turning to our secondary sources, Q651–652 brings both options לא אגרשנ̊ו מפניך ('I will not drive them out from before you') from Ex. 23:29, decorating an additional *nun* and then מעט אגרשנ̊ו ('little [by little] I will drive them out') from the next verse. Similarly, *Qiryat Sefer* explains that אגרשנו שניהם הנו״ן מוזרקת למעלה ולמטה ('I shall drive them out' both of them, the *nun* is curled above and below). Conversely, Parma 1959 brings only אגרשנ̊ו מפניך which could be either. Add. MS 11639 places it in verse 30 bringing מעט מעט אגרשנ̊ו. **MV2** bring the same phrase מעט מעט אגרשנו, but does not decorate any letter. *Ben Mesheq* brings סכ״ג כ׳ט אגרשנו ... כנו׳ן בצלמנו דבראשית placing this firmly in verse 29 only, supporting **OB**. Parma 2427 omits either possibility.

A danger of the transition letter to *parasha* order, as we have seen, but very pronounced in this section.

23, 24 and 25. This is a grouping from Deut. 4:9. **OB** extends by adding והודעתם ('make them known') and also adds תלת to specifically frame the group of three. **P** is the same without והודעתם. **H** is similar לבניך ולבני בניך תלתא. **ST** separates out each instance, bringing לבניך • ולבני • בניך and then adds ג בו (3 in it [the verse]). **MV** lists the word ואתחנן ('and I petitioned') from Deut. 3:23 before לבניך ולבני בניך, However, it is not clear whether this is intended as an actual instance or just a reference to the *parasha* in which the listing takes place.[7]

Line 8: **לבנ̊יך ולבנ̊י בנ̊יך תלת̇ • 26מעונ̊ה • 27נ̊ושע ביי • 28לעינ̊י בתראה • //// ן ו̇ י̇ •**
... to your children and to your children's children'—three of them (Deut. 4:9). (*Parashat Ve-zo't Ha-berakhah*) 26. **'dwelling place'** (Deut. 33:27). 27. **'saved by God'** (Deut. 33:29). 28. **'before the eyes' the last** [occurrence] (Deut. 34:12).

26. **P**, **MV**, **ST** and **H** all agree with **OB** and all are *ma-le' vav*, whereas 𝔐 is *ḥaser* מענה.
27. **P**, **MV**, **ST** and **H** all just bring נושע. **OB** extends.
28. The final verse of the *Torah* marks our last listing for *nun*. **P** brings לעיני בת̇, **H** is similar לעיני בתרא, **MV** לעיני בתראה in full and **ST** extends the reference לעינ̊י כל יש̇ בת̇ (the last 'before the eyes of all Israel').

3 Description and Example Forms of the Special Letter *Nun Sofit*

The end of the line is a little confused, in that the description for the special *nun sofit* is not present. Instead, we see a ו̇ and then a י̇. Likely this refers to there being sixteen instances in the *Torah* as brought by the other sources, even though the Hebrew numerals are reversed.

P brings ן דאקים רישיהון ולא מזייני י̇ו̇ באוריית̇ (*nun sofit* where their heads are standing up/raised and they are not decorated [with *tagin*]—16 in the *Torah*). **H** is similar, bringing ן דאקים רישיהון ולא מזייני י״ו באור׳. **ST** is difficult to read in

7 It is transcribed and included as an instance in **LMV**, but this is likely an error. The *Ba'al ha-Ṭurim* comments on these instances, והודעתם לבניך ולבני בניך ג נונ״ן הפוכין לומר שכל מי שהוא ובנו ובן בנו תלמידי חכמים שוב אין התורה פוסקת מזרעו ('and make them known to your children and to your children's children' 3 [letters] *nun* are reversed to say that all who is [themselves] and whose children and grandchildren are scholars, then the *Torah* will never depart from their descendants).

TABLE 19 Forms for the special letter *nun sofit*, as brought by the halakhic texts, along with some other examples. Many have curls, some pronounced, some more subtle on the top of the letter bending backwards, either from the top of side of the roof of the letter. Others have become a *qof* shape. The scribe of the Alexander *Torah* is perhaps the most understated merely bringing a small curl at the base of the letter.

 *Maḥzor Vitry* Parma 2574 (P)	 *Maḥzor Vitry* Add. MS 27201 (MV)	 Shem Tov *Tanakh* *Sefer Tagi* (ST)	Omitted in error *Badey ha-'Aron* Heb. 840 (BH)	 *Sefer Tagin* Heb. 837 (H)
Not extant Nr. 5667 (K)	 Parma 2427	 Parma 1959	 Q651–652	 MS Geunz. 481
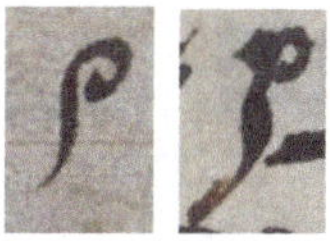 *Maḥzor Vitry* Add. MS 27201 (MV2)	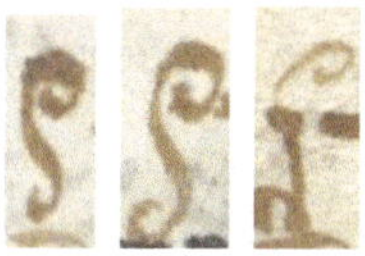 Add. MS 11639	 Add. MS 27167	 Bologna *Torah*	 Vat. ebr. 1
 Or. 1463	 Alexander *Torah*			

the introduction section, but brings, ן דקאים רישיהון לבתריהון ולא מזיינן שיתא עשר באו׳ (*nun*—where there heads are standing/rising[8] to their backs and they are not decorated [with *tagin*], sixteen in the *Torah*), but does add the qualifier לבתריהון (to their backs) and the number sixteen in full. Before the listing, the word order is slightly different, ן דקאים רישיהון לבתריהון י״ו באור׳ ומז׳׳, and it may disagree, in that it suggests the letter does have *tagin*, but the image is not clear. However, it may be that **ST** is merely transposing a couple of letters in the first word and intends דאקים. Nonetheless, the meaning is more or less identical. Oddly, this letter form is completely omitted from **BH**. **MV** disagrees slightly, bringing ן דעקים רישיהון ולא מזייני with an *ʿayin*, suggesting instead that the heads are bent.

A major problem with the forms brought for the special nun sofit *is that sometimes they just are so far removed from the appearance of a* nun sofit *that they resemble a* qof. *The printed* Maḥzor Vitry (*LMV*), *shown right, is a case in point but there are others that are much more problematic from a modern day scribal halachic viewpoint.*

*Our scribe in **OB**, shown far right, brings a* nun sofit *that certainly resembles a* qof *and is similar to Q651–652 shown below. Turning to our other* Genizah *fragments, the nun sofit of **T-S NS 287.11-F** (centre right) has no decoration, merely a dot, which may suggest that scribe of **CG** was unsure as to how to decorate it. The* nun sofit *from **T-S Misc 24.182**, shown near right brings a very pronounced* tag *from the roof of the letter that loops round on itself at the top. Only one is present in the extant fragments, that of* לבניהן*.*

4 Listing of Instances for the Special Letter *Nun Sofit*

Line 9: ידון[1] • ויהי כנען תרו[2/3] • תרח בחרן[4] • כגן[5] • ככר הירדן[6] • ובני דדן[7] • או לבניהן[8] •
(*Parashat Bereʾshit*) 1. **'abide'** (Gen. 6:3). (*Parashat Noaḥ*) 2/3 **'and let Canaan'—both of them** (Gen. 9:26 and Gen. 9:27). 4. **'Teraḥ in Ḥaran'** (Gen. 11:32). (*Parashat Lekh Lekha*) 5. **'like the garden'** (Gen. 13:10). 6. **'plain of the Jordan'** (Gen. 13:11). (*Parashat Ḥayyey Sarah*) 7. **'the sons of Dedan'** (Gen. 25:3). (*Parashat Vayetseʾ*) 8. **'or for their children'** (Gen. 31:43).

1. P and H agree, bringing ידון. **MV** and **ST** extend to ידון רוחי ('My spirit will [not] abide').

8 Jastrow, op. cit., p. 1306.

2 and 3. There are two occurrences of this phrase in Gen. 9:26 and Gen. 9:27. P errs, however, since it brings ויהי הענן תר׳ (and it was the cloud—both of them). H errs similarly, ויהי הענן תרוי״. MV brings ויהי כנען תרויהון, agreeing with **OB**. ST, however, brings ארור כנען from Gen. 9:25, followed by what is the first ויהי כנען.[9] The Shem Tov *Tanakh* is not extant for these verses.[10]

ST then adds an additional instance בצאת מחרן ('when he went out from Ḥaran') which would be Gen. 12:4, and then follows with the second ויהי כנען. This would be quite seriously out of sequence. ST then notes סֹז דנח (chapter 7 [though it is 9] of *Noaḥ*), perhaps recognising and 'correcting' the sequencing issue, before turning to the rest of the listing. Unfortunately, the Shem Tov *Tanakh* is not extant for Gen. 12:4.[11]

4. ST agrees, bringing תרח בחרן. P and H bring just בחרן. MV brings בחרן in *parashat Noaḥ* and then lists it again in *Lekh Lekha*.
5. P, MV, ST and H all agree, bringing כנן.
6. P, MV, ST and H all agree, bringing ככר הירדן.
7. It would seem our scribe in **OB** has omitted a *dalet* in error. P, MV, ST and H all bring ובני דדן.
8. P, MV, ST and H just bring לבניהן.

5 The 'Upside Down' *Nun Sofit* of Ḥaran

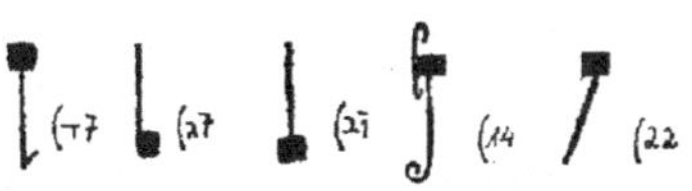

It is worth noting that instance 4 has taken on an independent life, with a tradition that the final *nun* in Ḥaran is to be written upside down/reversed. *Torah Shelemah* Vol. 29 shows numerous forms, a selection of which are shown above right.[12]

9 Basser notes that 'perhaps the printed version and handwritten *Maḥzor Vitry* omitted it because of the similarity to 'and there was in Canaan'', op. cit., p. 109, note 323.

10 Turning to our secondary sources, there is little support here for ST. Q651–652 brings ארור כנען but only to decorate the letters *resh*. Parma 2427, Add. MS 11639, MV2, Add. MS 27617, Parma 1959 and *Ben Mesheq* all omit. *Qiryat Sefer* explains that כל כנען שבתורה הנו״ן הכפולה מוזרקת למטה (all [mentions of] Canaan that are in the *Torah*, the final *nun* is curled below). This technically supports ST but is unlikely to reflect the original intention of *Sefer Tagin*. It is worth noting that Add. MS 27167 (and Parma 1959) frame the instances differently to all other sources, bringing instead כנען עבד • כנען עבד (Canaan [will be] a slave).

11 Basser makes no mention of the order issue, op. cit., p. 109. Turning to our secondary sources, there is no support here for ST, with none of the secondary sources bringing this as an instance.

12 *Torah Shelemah*, op. cit., p. 165.

TABLE 20 A selection of the *nun sofit hafukha* from a number of *Sifrey Torah* that have passed my drawing board. Three of these follow the *Mishnat 'Avraham* (see below).

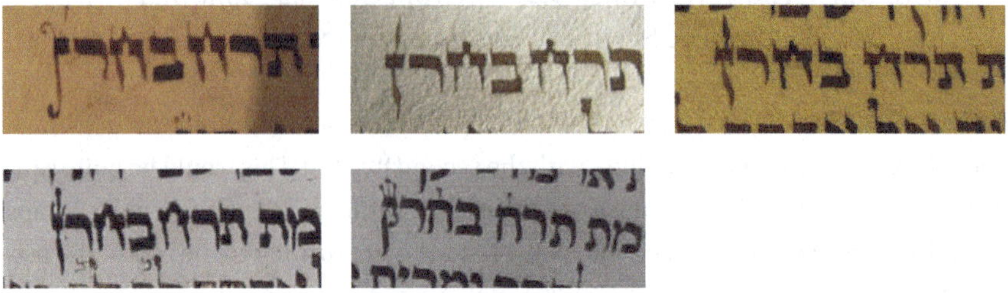

I have also encountered quite a few examples of this in *Sifrey Torah* that I have repaired over time. A selection of these are shown above from those where the *regel* (leg) is repeated coming up from the roof, those involving curls and slants and one with a curl that makes it look like a *qof*.

There is also a great deal of commentary on this particular instance. I have translated a couple of quite extensive sections below, but this is by no means comprehensive.

The *Minḥat Shai*[13] explains that:

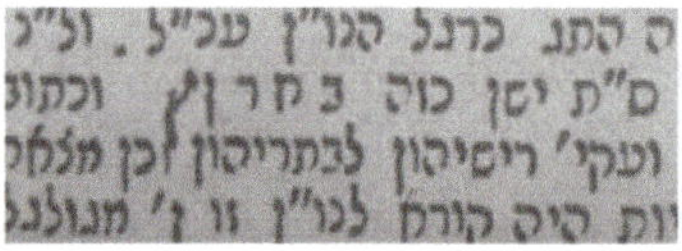
ה התג כרגל הנו"ן עכ"ל. ונ"ל
ס"ת ישן כזה בחרן וכתוב
ועקי' רישיהון לבתריהון וכן מלכא
ות היה קורם לנו"ן זו ז' מגולגל

> 'Rashi writes that the *nun* is upside down etc. and so it is written in the printed *Masorah*. But the *'Or Torah*[14] wrote that he does not know what was implied by upside down—as in all the books [he has seen] it was upright without any difference. In an old book, I have found that it has a *tag* on its head and it is brought about this [subject] that [there are letters] *nun sofit* where their heads are bent—seventeen in the *Torah* and perhaps this is the upside down [that is meant] for the root [meaning] of the inversion is that it appears at the *leg* of the the *nun* [*sofit*].[15] And thus the real 'upside down' is as as I have found in *Sefer Tagin* and also in

13 A masoretic commentary by Rabbi Yedidyah Shelomo ben 'Avraham Norzi (1560–1626) including grammatical treatises on the *Tanakh* and noting variant readings and special letters worth of comment. First published in Mantua, 1742–1744, but extensively revised.

14 *'Or Torah* is a compilation of the teachings of Rabbi Dov Baer ben 'Avraham of Mezeritch, known as the Maggid of Mezritch, as recorded by his students. The book was first published in Koretz in 1804.

15 Indeed some of the forms do look like the leg has been repeated on top of the roof.

> the *tikkun* of an old *Sefer Torah* where it looked like this [see below right]. And it is written in at the start of *Sefer Tagin* that are in the *Torah*—17 letters *nun* [*sofit*] with this appearance that do not have *zayin* type decorations and their heads are bent behind them and so I have found [???][16] to discover this number. And Rabbi Aqiva, who explained the letters,[17] called this *nun*, a curled *nun* and explained about it that all who are humble and plain of spirit [then] the Holy One, blessed be He, makes his life successful and restful his life, for there is no better *midda* (character trait) in the world than humility and fear of sin. And in a small printed [book] from Sabbioneta[18] it was really upside down and distorted. And this is similar to what the Rashba[19] *z"l* in wrote in his responsa brought from the Rabbi [Yosef] Karo[20] in the *Ṭur* 14, end of paragraph 275 and [also] our rabbi Baḥya [ben 'Asher].'[21]

It is also noteworthy that the *Minḥat Shai* brings the opinion that there are 17 instances and not 16. It thus seems highly likely that this tradition has stemmed from its inclusion in *Sefer Tagin* originally, and perhaps it survived when the other instances fell into disuse, since the form for the *nun sofit* brought by most sources is highly questionable, usually resembling some kind of *qof*. Though why only this one should have been given special treatment, over the others in the list, is a subject for further study.

The *Mishnat 'Avraham*[22] similarly treats the *kashrut* of such a form at great length. He writes:

---

16 Unclear abbreviations א' לא'.

17 In the *Midrash deRabbi 'Aqiva al ha-Tagin vehaZiyyunin*, also treating on the ornamentations of the letters of the alphabet. A good clear version can be found in Harley MS 5510, part of a collection of kabbalistic treaties. The section concerning the *tagin* on the letters letters occurs from f. 198r to f. 198v. held in the British Library. It is also published in Jellinek's *B.H.* v. 31–33. This is a separate work from the two versions of *'Otiyot deRabbi Aqiva*, a *midrash* on the letters of the alphabet, attributed to the same sage.

18 Sabbioneta is a 'town in Lombardy, Italy, in the former duchy of Mantua. Jewish settlement in Sabbioneta dates from the 15th century' and it is 'best known ... for its Hebrew press, which was founded in 1551', *Encyclopedia Judaica, Second Edition, Volume 17*, p. 630.

19 Shelomo ben 'Avraham 'ibn 'Aderet (1235–1310) designated as El Rab d' España (The Rabbi of Spain). He served as rabbi of the Main Synagogue of Barcelona.

20 Yosef ben 'Ephraim Karo, (1488–5335). Author of the *Shulḥan Arukh* which is the mainstay of normative Orthodox Jewish practice. He is often referred to as *ha-Meḥabber* (The Author) or in Aramaic as *Maran* (Our Master).

21 Baḥya ben 'Asher 'ibn Halawa, also known as Rabbeynu Beḥaye, (1255–1340), one of the most distinguished of the Biblical exegetes of Spain and a pupil of the Rashba, who had just been mentioned.

22 שער הנון *Sha'ar ha-Nun* (Gate of the *Nun*) chapter 24, written by 'Avraham ben Tsvi Yafeh. Quoted from the 1868 edition, p. 119.

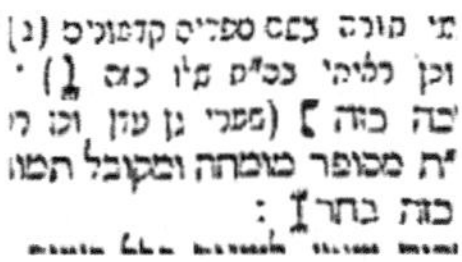

16: There are those who say one must be careful to make the body of the *nun* upside down in 'and Teraḥ died in Ḥaran'. But if he did not do this it is valid (Rashi and our rabbi Shimshon[23] and our rabbi Bacḥya [ben Asher] and the *Paneaḥ Razeh*[24] and the Rashba and the Maharal[25] and the *'Or Torah* in the name of the *Masorah* and *Laḥmey Toda*[26] that he saw in the *Sefer Torah* of an old, great *mequbal* [receiver of tradition]. And the *Ṭa'amey Torah* in the name of [many] ancient books). And R. Shabbetai of Roshkover[27] in a written responsum. And so I have seen in his *Sefer Torah* like this [see above right]. And there are those who write it upside down like this [similar to those used around the *Va-yehi Binsoa'* section][28] (*Sha'arey Gan 'Eden*[29] and so I saw in old books). And I have seen in the *Sefer Torah* of an expert *mequbal* scribe a spiky image like this [see above right].

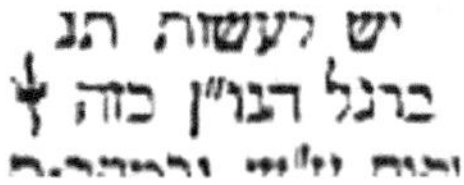

17: And there are those who disagree about this and say one does not change the rule for this because of the difference, it should only be as all the other letters *nun* [*sofit*] that are in the *Sefer Torah* and that if it were changed it is fitting to erase it (*'Or Torah* and *Leqet ha-Qemaḥ*[30] and *Leḥem ha-Panim*[31] and *Tiqqun Sofrim* and *Minchat Kelil*). And there are those who say that if one find this *nun* upside down one does not invalidate it and one does not correct it. And thus is found in several *Sifrey Torah* and one does not forbid it here (*Torah 'Or* and *Sha'arey 'Ephraim*[32] and the *Beyt 'Aharon*[33]) and at

---

23 Written by Yitsḥak ben Yehudah ha-Levi, also known as the Riba, he was the earliest known *tosafist*, a pupil of Rashi. He operated in Speyer during the 11th century.

24 Shimshon ben 'Avraham (c. 1150–c. 1230) a French *tosafist* in France, also known as the HaRaSH of Sens.

25 Judah Loew ben Bezalel, (c. 1512/1526–1609), known as the Maharal of Prague.

26 Possibly the one written by Tsvi Hersh ben Pinḥas Horowitz, though there is also a *Laḥmey Toda* written by Isaiah ben Israel Hezekiah Basran.

27 Rabbi Shabbetai Marshakov was a kabbalist and a scribe, a member of the first generation of the Ḥassidic movement, he lived in Rzeszow in Bessarabia.

28 For much more detail on this letter form, see my book, Michaels, M., *Sefer Binsoa* (*The Book of Binsoa*), Kulmus Publishing, London, 2010.

29 *Sefer Sha'arey Gan 'Eden*, contains kabbalistic essays regarding Paradise, Purgatory and repentance, by R. Moshe Romi, published in Venice, 1589.

30 *Sefer Leqet ha-Qemaḥ* is an abridged version of responsa and halachic rulings on the *Shulḥan 'Arukh, 'Orekh Ḥayyim*, by Rabbi Moshe Chagiz. Amsterdam (1707).

31 Possibly the title suggested by the abbreviation here ולחה"פ.

32 Written by 'Ephraim Zalman Margolios (1762–1828) in 1820. A Galician rabbi born in Brody.

33 *Sefer Beyt 'Aharon*, on the *Torah* and service of God, by 'Aharon Perlow of Karlin (1736–1772), Brody, 1875.

> every time one does not have to bring out another [*Torah*] but one should correct it [afterwards]. And in every place [if you want to do it] one should make a long *tag* in the centre as if it is upside down, and the *tag* appears like the leg of the *nun* like this (*'Or Torah*). And in the *Sha'arey 'Ephraim* is copied a bent *tag* because of this, and in my opinion this is is not a good method.

He then starts to reference the instructions in *Sefer Tagin* and the *Minḥat Shai*, which we have already discussed.

6 Continuing the Listing for the Special Letter *Nun Sofit*

Returning to our core text of **OB**:

Line 10: **[9]ולא ישמעון̊ • [10]להן̊ • [11]אביהן̊ • [12]ובן̊ אין לו • [13]כצאן̊ • [14]יהושע בן נון̊ • [15]לבני דדיהן̊ •**

(*Parashat Shemot*) 9. **'and do not listen'** (Ex. 4:9). (*Parashat Pinḥas*) 10. **'to them'** (Num. 27:7). 11. **'their father'** (Num. 27:7). 12. **'and he had no son'** (Num. 27:8). 13. **'as sheep'** (Num. 27:17). 14. **'Joshua son of Nun'** (Num. 27:18). (*Parashat Mase'ei*) 15. **'to the sons of their uncle'** (Num. 36.11).

9. **P** and **ST** bring the same instance, but frame it as ישמעון לקולך ('listen to your voice'). **MV** and **H** are similar, but bring ישמעון לקלך *ḥaser vav* as 𝔐.
10. **P**, **MV**, **ST** and **H** all agree, bringing להן̊. **ST** then adds פׄאׄ דפׄ נח which does not quite make sense in this context.[34]
11. Our **OB** scribe brings an additional instance, אביהן̊, that is slightly out of sequence, since it should appear before instance 10 as one word follows the other in that verse, concerning the inheritance of the daughters of Zelofḥad. **H** agrees, also bringing this out of sequence, but the secondary sources are very supportive of the instance being included. **P**, **MV** and **ST** omit.[35]

---

34 Basser makes no mention of this. It may stand for *pasuq* (verse) 1 from *parashat Noaḥ*. But that is not likely, since we are within the listing for *parashat Pinḥas*.

35 More evidence that H is not directly copied from P. Turning to our secondary sources, Q651–652, Parma 2427, Add. MS 11639 bring אביהן̊ להן̊ ('their father to them'). *Qiryat Sefer* brings אביהם ... בנו״ן כפולה והיא מעגלת וכן הנו״ן הכפולה שבתיבת להן ('their father' ... [written] with a final *nun* [i.e. אביהן] is curled and so it the final *nun* that is in the word 'to them') and *Ben Mesheq* lists these two words too סכ״ז ז״ [א]ביהן להן ... נוני״ן כנו״ן של ערותן דפ׳ [א]חרי מות (27:7 'their father to them' ... the [letters] *nun* are like the *nun* of 'their

12. P, MV and H agree, bringing ובן אין לו, as does ST who brings the decoration solely on ובן̊ agreeing with OB, but there is another *nun sofit* in the phrase which could be decorated.[36]

13. P, MV and H agree, bringing כצאן. ST brings כצאן • צ̊ע. It is unclear what this addition is as the next word in the verse is אשר (which).[37]

14 and 15. Our scribe in OB brings a further instance not listed in the other core sources, יהושע בן נון̊. This has two possible letters *nun sofit* that could be decorated, but only decorates one of these. It has to be between Num. 27:17 and Num. 36.11. In which case this would be Num. 27:18 in the next verse. It would seem that P and H have conflated two instances bringing נון דדודיהן (the *nun* of 'their uncle'). ST brings דודיהן̊ and MV just brings דדהן, whereas 𝔐 is, as we see in OB, דדיהן. OB enjoys a great deal of support in the secondary sources.[38]

Line 11: ירדן̊ בתראה[16] • //// ס̊[1] הס̊בב בתר׳ • אס̊תר[2] • והייתי בנס̊עם[3] • ס̊פרה[4] • הס̊רו[5]
(*Parashat Ha-'azinu*) 16. **the last 'Jordan'** (Deut. 32:47) //// 60 [in the *Torah*] (*Parashat Bere'shit*) 1. **the last 'surrounds'** (Gen. 2:13) 2. **'I will be hidden'** (Gen. 4:14). (*Parashat Noaḥ*) 3. **'and it was when they travelled'** (Gen. 11:2). 4. **'towards Sephar'** (Gen. 10.30) out of sequence. (*Parashat Va-yishlaḥ*) 5. **'put away ...**

16. P brings ירדן בתרא̊ and H ירדן בתרא̊, both missing the *he*, as our scribe in OB. ST, more accurately, gives הירדן̊ • בתרא̊ as 𝔐, but with a superfluous separator dot. MV omits.

---

nakedness' of *parashat 'Aḥarey Mot*). Parma 1959 shows both words but only decorates one אביהן להן̊. MV2 lists both, but decorates neither. There is much support for OB and H to include this instance.

36 Turning to our secondary sources, Add. MS 11639 brings כי ימות ובן̊ אין̊ לו ('for he died and he had no son'). MV2 lists this same extended phrase but does not decorate the letters. Parma 1959 brings ובן̊ אין̊ לו and Parma 2427 decorates both ובן̊ אין̊ similarly. Q651–652 instead elects to decorate the second *nun sofit*, ובן אין̊ לו which is supported by *Ben Mesheq* which lists אין relating to the special *nun sofit*. *Qiryat Sefer* omits.

37 Again Basser makes no mention of this.

38 Turning to our secondary sources, Q651–652 and Add. MS 11639 bring קח לך את יהושע בן̊ נון̊ ('take to yourself Joshua son of') decorating both. *Qiryat Sefer* brings בן נון הנו״ן הכפולה בשניהם כרוכה מעט בראשה לצד פנים ומוזרקת ('son of Nun' the final *nun* in both of them bends a little to the face side and is curled). *Ben Mesheq* lists וסי״ח בן. נו׳ן. (and verse 18 'son of Nun') relating to the special *nun sofit* for both. Parma 1959 decorates only one יהושע בן נון̊. MV2 lists בן נון but does not decorate. Parma 2427 omits. In terms of the next instance, Q651–652 and Add. MS 11639 are as OB bringing לבני דדיהן̊. Parma 1959 brings לבני דדהן̊ *ḥaser yod*. Qiryat Sefer notes דדיהן חסר וא״ו והנו״ן מוזרקת ('their uncle' is *ḥaser vav* and the *nun* is curled). *Ben Mesheq* lists פ״א דדיהן (verse 11 'their uncle'). MV2 lists לבני דדיהן לנשים ('to their uncles as wives') but does not decorate any letter. Parma 2427 omits. OB seems to be the only core source that is accurate here.

Nun sofit has relatively few instances recorded as being specially decorated, and yet our **OB** scribe has brought two very different examples out of the sixteen. It is also quite possible, given the comment of *Minḥat Shai* and the similarity of a *vav* (ו) and a *zayin* (ז) in a handwritten text, that the original intention may have been seventeen, though ST does specifically state שיתא עשר (sixteen) in full text.

7 Description and Example Forms of the Special Letter *Samekh*

We turn now to the letter *samekh* and once again we see that our scribe in **OB** has omitted the full description, only pointing out that there are 60, echoing the numerical value of the letter *samekh*. However, whilst most agree, one core source disagrees with this.

P brings ס ס̇ באוריית ד̇ד זיוני ולא דבקין (*Samekh*—60 in the *Torah* that have 4 *zayin* type decorations and are not joined). H similarly brings ס̇ באורי׳ ד̇ד זייני ולא דבקין. ST brings a slightly reordered description ס דאית להו̇ ארבע זיוני ולא דבקין שתין באורי׳ (*samekh* that they have four *zayin* type decorations and are not joined— sixty in the *Torah*) in the listing for the letter and in the faded introduction ס דאית לה ארבע זיוני ולא דבקין שתין באור̇ and BH ס דאית לה ד̇ זיוני ולא דבוקין שתין באוריתא. MV, however, brings ס״ז באוריית דד זיוני ולא דבוקין (67 in the *Torah* with 4 *zayin* type decorations and are not joined).

The major halachic issue for modern scribes is that the samekh *described is supposedly open on the side, which similar to the instructions for* mem sofit[39] *would make the form* pasul (*invalid*). *Thus we can see in the printed* Maḥzor Vitry (*LMV*), *shown right, that the form is drawn closed, regardless of the instruction.*

*This is often the case with other examples of the form brought in other manuscripts. There is a general reluctance to draw the form as described. Our scribe from **OB**, right, has deliberately left a break in his version of the form.*

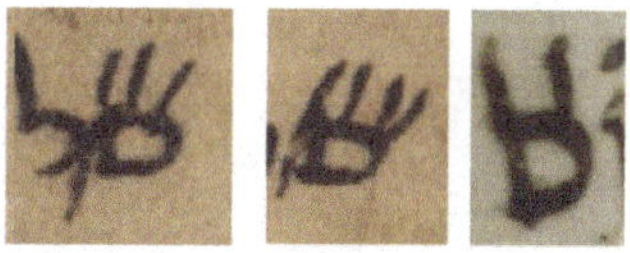

Turning to our other Genizah *manuscripts, we see the scribe of **CG** in **T-S NS 287.11-F** (far right) brings only two* tagin *on the roof of the letter and closes the form. **T-S Misc. 24.182** (near and centre right) also ignores the instruction to break the* samekh *and usually brings four* tagin, *three on the roof and one pointing downwards form the left side of the roof. However, the same scribe also has one with four* tagin *above and one, less confident one, descending.*

39 See part 2 for further discussion of this.

TABLE 21 Forms for the special letter *samekh*, as brought by the halakhic texts to which we have compared our manuscript, along with some other examples. The number and placing of the *tagin* differ significantly with 2, 3 or 4. If one is brought, the placing of the downward *tag* also varies.

 *Maḥzor Vitry* Parma 2574 (P)	 *Machzor Vitry* Add. MS 27201 (MV)	 Shem Tov *Tanakh* *Sefer Tagi* (ST)	 *Badey ha-ʾAron* Heb. 840 (BH)	 *Sefer Tagin* Heb. 837 (H)
not available Nr. 5667 (K)	 Parma 2427	 Parma 1959	 Q651–652	 MS Geunz. 481
 *Maḥzor Vitry* Add. MS 27201 (MV2)	 Add. MS 11639	 Add. MS 27167	 Bologna *Torah*	 Vat. ebr. 1
 Or. 1463	 Alexander *Torah*			

8 Listing of Instances for the Special Letter *Samekh*

1. P agrees bringing הסבב בת, **MV** lists הסבב בתראה in full. H is הסבב בתרא. All of these sources, including **OB** are *ḥaser vav*. It is only **ST** that accords with 𝔐, which is *ma-le' vav*, bringing הסובב.
2. P, **MV** and **ST** agree, bringing אסתר. H omits.
3. P agrees, but both this and **OB** are in error, as the phrase in 𝔐 is ויהי בנסעם. **MV**, **ST** and H just bring בנסעם.
4. P, **MV**, **ST** and H all agree, bringing ספרה.

ST then adds a further instance not in the other core sources, וסעדו לבבכם from Gen 18:5. Unfortunately, the Shem Tov *Tanakh* is not extant for this verse.[40]

5. **OB** has omitted the letter *he* in error in the penultimate word. P brings הסירו את אלהי הנכר *ma-le' yod* in the first word though 𝔐 is *ḥaser yod* הסרו as **OB**. H abbreviates last word to הנכ'. **MV** just brings הסירו את אלהי and runs into the next instance without a separator.[41] **ST** brings הסירו את אלהי.

Line 12: **את אלי הנכר • [6]סביבתיהם • [7]תסבינה • [8]סחרים • [9]אין שר בית הסחר • [10]ויסר פרעה •**

... the foreign gods' (Gen. 35:2). 6. **'round about them'** (Gen. 35:5). (*Parashat Va-yeshev*) 7. **'came round about'** (Gen. 37:7). 8. **'merchants'** (Gen. 37:28). 9. **'the keeper of the prison did not [look]'** (Gen. 39:23). (*Parashat Miqqets*) 10. **'and Pharaoh took off'** (out of sequence Gen. 41:42).

6. P agrees, bringing סביבתיהם. **MV**, **ST** and H bring סביבותיהם *ma-le' vav* as 𝔐. However, H has brought סביבות as a line filler on the previous line, as it were an additional instance.[42]

---

40 Turning to our secondary sources, none of them decorate the *samekh* in וסעדו, though the *mem sofit* in לבבכם is generally decorated. ST enjoys no support for this inclusion and it likely an error and confusion with the *mem sofit*. Nonetheless, Basser chooses to include this, following Shem Tov, even when the evidence suggests otherwise. Basser, op. cit., p. 110.

41 Though transcribed with the separator in LMV.

42 And indeed this line filler is transcribed incorrectly into EPST as a separate instance.

ST brings a further instance not in the other core sources, פסים קד (the first 'long-sleeved[43] [coat]') from Gen. 37:3 in *parashat Va-yeshev*, but has no support from the secondary sources.[44]

7. **P**, **MV** and **H** agree, bringing תסבינה. **ST** brings תס֯ובינ *ma-le' vav*.
8. **P**, **MV** and **H** agree, bringing סחרים. **ST** runs out of space and brings ס֯חרי.
9. **P**, **ST**, **MV** and **H** agree, bringing אין שר בית הסחר, though the last word in **MV** is very damaged.
10. There is an issue with ordering with the related instances 10 and 11 in our core sources. It should be ויספר פרעה followed by ויסר פרעה. **OB** reverses them as does **P** and **H**. **ST** orders correctly, the only core source to do so. **MV** omits both.

Line 13: **[11]ויס֯פר פר֗ • [12]אס֯רי לגפן • [13]כבס֯ ביין • [14]אנוס֯ה • [15/16]מחס֯פס֯ תרו֗ • [17]ונמס֯ • [18]פס֯ל כל תמונה •**

11. **'and Pharaoh told** [them]' (out of sequence Gen. 41:8). (*Parashat Va-yeḥi*) 12. **'binding** [his foal] **to the vine'** (Gen. 49:11). 13. **'he washed** [his garments] **in wine'** (Gen. 49:11). (*Parashat Be-shallaḥ*) 14. **'let us flee'** (Ex. 14:25). 15/16. **'scale-like' both of them** (Ex. 6:14). 17. **'and it melted'** (Ex. 16:21). 18. (*Parashat Yitro*) **'graven images and all likenesses'** (Ex. 20:4).

11. See note above on instance 10.
12. **P**, **ST** and **H** and agree, bringing אסרי לגפן. **MV** omits.
13. **P**, **ST** and **H** agree, bringing כבס ביין. **MV** omits.

Basser then includes another instance אסרה, as 𝔐, from Ex. 3:3, which is not in the other core sources. A bit damaged, but **ST** does indeed bring אס֯ורה but *ma-le' vav*. However, this may well be a misspelling/mis-transcription of the next instance of אנוסה. That

43 Whilst it is generally and popularly referred to as a 'coat of many colours' this is not a good translation of כתנת פסים and various commentators have suggested alternatives such as 'a full-sleeved robe', 'a coat reaching to his feet', 'an ornamented tunic' etc.

44 Turning to our secondary sources, Q651–652 lists this, but only to decorate the *pe* in פ֯סים. Similarly, Add. MS 11639 also lists כתנת פ֯סים. Parma 2427 brings כתנת פסים, but decorates not letters. **MV2** extends the phrase ועשה לו כתנת פסים ('and he made him a long-sleeved coat'), but decorates no letters. Add. MS 27167 and Parma 1959 bring the longer phrase כתנתו את כתנת הפ֯סים ('his coat, the long-sleeved coat'), which places it in Gen. 37.3 instead. **T-S Misc. 24.182** also brings הפ֯סים, similarly placing it in Gen. 37.3, but only decorating the *pe*. *Qiryat Sefer* and *Ben Mesheq* make no reference to a *samekh* but both mention a special *pe*. **ST** enjoys no support for this additional instance of a special *samekh*.

said, ST does bring אנוסה later in its listing, so this may be deliberate, and enjoys some support from secondary sources.[45]

14. P, MV and H agree, bringing אנוסה. ST omits at this point.

15 and 16. P brings מחספס תר׳. ST just lists מחספס but decorates both. MV is not clear but appears to bring מחספס תרויהון. H brings מחספס // תרויי׳ //, as if they were two separate instances.[46]

17. P, MV, ST and H all agree, bringing ונמס.

ST now brings אנוסה in the correct sequence. the other sources have erred in their ordering of the instances.

18. P and MV agree, bringing פסל כל תמונה.[47] ST and H bring פסל וכל תמונה as 𝔐 with a *vav* in the second word. H abbreviates to תמונ׳. OB has omitted a letter.

Line 14: [19]מספר ימיך • [20]סמים נטף • [21]סמים ולבנה זכה • [22]סלת יהיה • [23]סלת בשמן • [24]וסלת [מ]רבכת •

(*Parashat Mishpaṭim*) 19. **'number of your days'** (Ex. 23:26). (*Parashat Ki Tissa'*) 20. **'sweet spice'** (Ex. 30:34). 21. **'spices with pure frankincense'** (Ex. 30:34). (*Parashat Va-yiqra'*) 22. **'shall be of fine flour'** (Lev. 2:1). 23. **'fine flour in oil'** (Lev. 2:5). 24. **'fine flour soaked'** (Lev. 7:12)

19. P and H agree, bringing מספר ימיך. ST extends to מספר ימיך אמלא (number of your days, I will fulfil). MV omits.

20. P and MV agree, bringing סמים ולבנה זכה. ST brings סמים דנטף ('spices' of [the verse with] 'sweet').

21. P brings סמים ולבונה the last word *ma-le' vav* and omitting זכה. MV brings סמים ולבנה *ḥaser vav*. ST brings סמים דלבונה ('spices' of [the verse with] 'frankincense'). 𝔐 is *ḥaser vav*, ולבנה. H breaks the two related instances 20 and 21 in the wrong place סמים // נטף סמים // ולבונה, as if there are three.[48]

---

45 Turning to our secondary sources, ST finds support with Q651–652 which brings אסרה נא ('I will turn aside now') and *Ben Mesheq* which lists ג. סמך דאסרה (3. *samekh* of 'I will turn aside'). MV2 lists אסרה נא but does not decorate a letter. Add. MS 11639 brings אסרה נא but only decorates the *he*. *Qiryat Sefer* only references the *he* too, so this may be the source of confusion over this instance. Parma 2327 and Parma 1959 omit.

46 Transcribed incorrectly as two separate entries in EPST.

47 Though the LMV transcription amends this to פסל וכל תמונה.

48 Corrected in the EPST transcription as סמים נטף • סמים ולבונה.

22. P, MV and H agree, bringing סלת יהיה. ST extends to ס̊לת יהיה קרבנו ('his offering shall be of fine flour').
23. P and H bring instead סלת בלולה בשמן. However, MV and ST both disagree, bringing two separate instances here. Both give סלת בלולה and then follow with סלת בשמן. Our scribe in **OB** has likely omitted one instance, and **P** and **H** have likely conflated two instances into one.
24. **OB** is damaged, so it is difficult to see the full words here. **P**, **MV** and **ST** bring סלת מרבכת. **H** similarly brings וסלת מרב מרבכת, though the second word is a line filler.[49]

Line 15: **[25]ומס̊ל המצות • [26]בס̊ל המילאים • [27/28]כל מפרס̊ת פרס̊ה • [29]וס̊מך אהרן • [30]וכס̊הו בעפר • [31]אם**

25. **'and from the basket of unleavened bread'** (Lev. 8:26). 26. **'in the basket of consecration'** (Lev. 8:31). (*Parashat Shemini*) 27/28. **'all that have cloven hooves'** (Lev. 11:3). 29. **'and Aaron will place'** (Lev. 16:21). 30. **'and cover it with dust'** (Lev. 17:13). 31. **'if ...**

25. **P**, **MV** and **ST** agree, bringing ומסל המצות as 𝔐. **H** brings ומסלת המצות with a superfluous *tav* in error.
26 **P**, and **H** bring בסל המילואים *ma-le' yod* and *vav*. **MV** brings בסל ~~המליאי~~ crosses through and then המלואים. **ST** is also בסל המילואים, *ma-le' vav*. None of the sources are as 𝔐, which reads בסל המלאים.
27 and 28. **P** agrees, bringing כל מפרסת פרסה. **ST** brings כל מפרסת פרסה ב̇ בו ('all that have cloven hooves' two in it [the verse]). **H** deliberately breaks into two instances // כל מפ מפרסת // פרסה. **MV** just brings כל מפרסת, thus missing one instance.
29. **P**, **MV**, **ST** and **H** all agree, bringing וסמך אהרן.
30. **P** and **MV** agree, bringing וכסהו בעפר as 𝔐. **H** is *ma-le' yod* וכסיהו בעפר. **ST** is the shortest version, bringing only וכס̊הו.

ST then brings another instance from Lev. 17:15 וכבס̊ בגדיו ('and washes his clothes') which is clearly very similar thematically to the next instance from the same verse and could easily have been omitted from a list because of that similarity. However, no other core sources bring this, and there is minimal support from the secondary sources.[50]

---

49 Transcribed without the filler word in EPST.

50 Turning to our secondary sources, they all omit this additional instance with the exception of *Ben Mesheq* who brings וסי״ז ט״ו סמ״ך דוכבס ב״ת לעיל ות״א לרע (and chapter 17 [verse] 15 the *samekh* of 'and washes' 2 *tagin* above and 1 *tag* below).

31. **P**, **MV** and **H** bring ואם לא יכבס as 𝔐. **OB** has omitted a *vav* in error. **ST** shortens to just לא יכבס֯.

Line 16: **לא יכבס֯ • [32]ואלי מס֯כה • [33]ויס֯ף דואיש כי יאכל קדש • [34]ונס֯ע • [35]בנס֯ע •**
[36]בנס֯עם •

… **he did not wash** [them]' (Lev. 17:16). (*Parashat Qedoshim*) 32. **'molten Gods'** (Lev. 19:4). (*Parashat 'Emor*) 33. **'and he shall put' of** [the verse beginning] **'if a man ate holy'** (Lev. 22:14). 34. **'shall set forward'** (Num. 2:17). 35. **'when it set forward'** (out of sequence Num. 10:35). 36. **'when they set forward'** (out of sequence Num. 10:34).

32. **P**, **MV**, **ST** and **H** bring ואלהי מסכה, without the *'alef-lamed* ligature making things clearer than **OB**, which has also omitted the *he*.
33. **ST** agrees, bringing ויס֯ף דואיש כי יאכל קדש. The other sources shorten the instance. **P** and **MV** bring ויסף דואיש כי יאכל, and **H** extends to ויסף חמש' דאיש כי יאכל ('and he shall put the fifth part' of [the verse beginning] 'if a man ate holy').[51]
34. **P**, **MV** and **H** agree, bringing ונסע. **ST** extends and clarifies to ונס֯ע אהל מו' ('and the tent of meeting will set forward').
35. **P** agrees, bringing בנסע. **H** brings בנסוע, *ma-le' vav*.
36. **P** and **H** agree, bringing בנסעם. **MV** has both these instances, but reversed the order בנסעם • בנסע, which is correct. **ST** also brings them in the correct sequence and extended, though adds an extraneous separator dot בנסעם • קדמ֯ • בנסע הארן ('when they set forward'. the first. 'when the ark set forward'). **OB** has erred in sequence, as **P** and **H**.

Line 17: **[37]ולא קס֯ם • [38]ונס֯פה נחלתן • [39/40]ונוס֯ף ונס֯ע • [41]רב לכם ס֯ב •**
[42]הפס֯גה מזרחה • [43]לנוס דאז יבדיל •

(*Parashat Balaq*) 37. **'and no divination'** (Num. 23:23). (*Parashat Mase'ei*) 38. **'and their inheritance will be added'** (out of sequence Num. 36:4). 39. **'and will be added'** (out of sequence Num. 36:3). (*Parashat Devarim*) 40. **'and journeyed'** (Deut. 2:1). 41. **'you have surrounded enough'** (Deut. 2:3). 42. **'of *Pisgah* eastward'** (Deut. 3:17). (*Parashat Va-'etḥanan*) 43. **'to travel' of** [the verse beginning] **'and then** [Moses] **separated'** (Deut. 4:42).

51 Transcribed in EPST as ויסף חמשתו דואיש כי יאכל even though 𝔐 is חמשיתו, *ma-le' yod*.

37. P, **MV** and H agree, bringing ולא קסם. ST brings just קסׄם.
38. P just gives ונספה, **MV** and H are *ma-le' vav* ונוספה only, but this is as 𝔐. ST brings ונסׄפה על *ḥaser vav*, but which also suggests an omitted word[52] as the phrase is ונוספה נחלתן על ('then their inheritance will be added to').
39 and 40. P agrees, bringing both instances, ונוסף • ונסע, but unlike **OB** correctly places a separator between them. **MV** also brings them separately, as they belong to different *parashiyyot*. ונוסף is listed in the section on *Mase'ei* and ונסע is listed in the section on *Devarim*. ST brings ונוסׄף as a separated instance, though it is hard to make out. What is unclear from P, **MV** and **OB** is whether this ונסע is referring to Deut. 1:19 or Deut. 2:1. ST brings initially ונסׄע מחרב ('and we journeyed from Ḥorev') from Deut 1:19. This is also present in the Shem Tov *Tanakh* and does find some considerable support amongst secondary sources.[53] ST, then gives ונפן ונסׄע ('we turned and we journeyed') which would place this as Deut. 2:1.[54] H brings ונוסף and then adds some confusion, as it brings ונסע רב לכם as if it is one instance, but actually the last two words belong to the next instance, though it is missing the key word סב.[55] Viewing the secondary sources suggests that if there is only one instance, it is more likely Deut. 1:19.
41. P and ST agree, bringing רב לכם סב. **MV** does also, but only after a corrected error bringing רב לכם ~~צפנה~~ סב writing another word from that verse and then crossing it through. H, as we have seen, has conflated two instances and omitted the key word from the second in error.[56]

---

52 Basser lists just ונוספה making no reference to the extra word or the *ḥaser vav*, op. cit., p. 111.

53 Turning to our secondary sources, Q651–652, Add. MS 11639 and Parma 1959 bring ונסׄע מחרב. *Qiryat Sefer* also brings ונסע הסמ"ך מתוייגת, מחרב חסר ('and journeyed', the *samekh* is decorated [with *tagin*], 'from Ḥorev' is *ḥaser*). Parma 2427 brings ונסׄע in the right position and thus all these support ST. **MV2** and *Ben Mesheq* omit (though the latter does elsewhere note a extended/suspended/raised *'ayin* in ונסע).

54 Turning again to our secondary sources, Q651–652 and Parma 2427 do bring ונפׄן but not ונסע. Add. MS 11639 and **MV2** list ונסע ונפן but decorate no letters. Parma 1959, *Qiryat Sefer* and *Ben Mesheq* omit reference to a *samekh*. ST enjoys no support amongst the secondary sources.

55 Additionally, the transcription of H in EPST is very different, giving פנו וסעו לכם ('turn and take your journey'), which would instead be Deut. 1:7.

56 The *Ba-al ha-Ṭurim* lists this instance, ''you have surrounded enough', *tagin* on the *samekh*—because he [Esau] honoured his father who was sixty years old when they were born and therefore in the future [Esau] was destined to destroy the Temple for it was sixty cubits').

42. P, and H agree, bringing הפסגה מזרחה. MV and ST bring just הפסגה.
43. P, ST and H agree, bringing לנוס דאז יבדיל, though the *bet* in H is very stretched. MV looks like it is bringing two instances, but they are the same one לנוס שמה • דאז יבדיל ('to travel there'—of [the verse beginning] 'and then [Moses] separated'). 𝔐 is *ḥaser vav* לנס, thus none of the core sources match this. Also the verse containing אז יבדיל is the previous verse 41, so verses 41 and 42 may have been considered one unit at the time this was written.

Line 18: [44]לא תנס֯ו • [45/46]נס֯יתם במס֯ה • [47]המס֯ת • [48/49]קס֯ם קס֯מים • [50]לא תסיג • [51]לא תחסם • [52]לא

44. **'you will not try'** (Deut. 6:16). 45/46. **'as you tried Him in Massah'** (Deut. 6:16). (*Parashat 'Eqev*) 47. **'the trials'** (Deut. 7:19). (*Parashat Shofeṭim*) 48/49. **'one who uses divination'** (Deut. 18:10). 50. **'you will not remove'** (Deut. 19:14). (*Parashat Ki Tetse'*) 51. **'you will not muzzle'** (Deut. 25:4). 52. **'no ...**

44. P and MV bring ולא תנסו. H also, but has crossed out some errors after ולא תנסו. ST omits the *vav* to bring לא תנסו as OB, and, as is found in 𝔐.
45. and 46. OB here brings two instances from the same verse joined together. ST agrees with נסיתם • במס֯ה ב֯ בפסו ('as you tried Him'—'in Massah' 2 in the verse.) but separates them. P also brings both separating them, but brings נסתם *ḥaser yod*. MV brings both separated, but gives נסיתים doubly *ma-le'* and H brings both separated, but spells ניתיסם also doubly *ma-le'* but wrong. 𝔐 is as OB and ST, נסיתם במסה.
47. P, ST and H bring המסות *ma-le' vav*. MV lists this under *mem* in error.
48. and 49. P and MV bring קסם קסמים together. H brings them a separate instances // קסמים // קסם, which is confirmed by ST who brings קסם קסמים • ב֯ בו ('one who uses divination'. 2 in it [the verse]).

ST brings a further instance here ויס֯פת לך ('and you will add to yourself') from Deut. 19:9 and this is in the Shem Tov *Tanakh*. The other core sources disagree, but there is some support from the secondary sources.[57]

57 Turning to our secondary sources, in support of ST, Parma 2427 does bring ויס֯פת decorating the *samekh*. However, Q651–652 and Add. MS 11639 also bring ויספ֯ת לך but decorate only the *pe*, and this may be the source of confusion. MV2 lists ויספת, but decorates no letter. *Qiryat Sefer* brings ויספת הסמ"ך מתוייגת שנים והפ"א לפופה ('and gather'—the *samekh* is decorated [with] two *tagin*] and the *pe* is curled). Similarly *Ben Mesheq* brings ס'פ בויספת suggesting both the *samekh* and *pe* are decorated. Parma 1959 omits.

50. H, ST and MV agree, bringing לא תשיג as 𝔐. P brings ולא תשיג with a superflous *vav*. MV brings this before קסם קסמים. ST adds וגֹ (etc.).
51. P agrees, bringing לא תחסם as 𝔐. ST and H are *ma-le' vav* לא תחסום. MV spells this incorrectly, bringing לא תחמס.
52. OB is not clear because of a nearby hole in the parchment, but seems to give לא תחס *ḥaser vav* as **MV**. P and H bring לא תחוס ז *ma-le' vav*, but with an additional *zayin* after the entry for no apparent reason. ST is just לא תחוס as 𝔐.

Line 19: **תחס̊ • [53]הנס̊תרות • ע יז [1]ע̊רומים קד • [2]ע̊ירום • [3]מתה ע̊לי • [4]ונע̊רתיה •**
... pity will your [eye] have' (Deut. 25:12). (*Parashat Nitsavim*) 53. **'the secret things'** (Deut. 29:28). ***'ayin*** 17 [in the *Torah*] (*Parashat Bere'shit*) 1. **the first 'naked'** (Gen. 2:25). 2. **'naked'** (likely Gen. 3:11) (*Parashat Va-yeḥi*) 3. **'[Rachel] died unto me'** (Gen. 48:7). 4. **'and her maidens'** (Ex. 2:5).

53. P, MV, ST and H all agree, bringing הנסתרות.

9 Description and Example Forms of the First Special Letter *'Ayin*

Our fragment **OB** does not bring the descriptor for this letter *'ayin*, the first of three *'ayin* forms shown in *Sefer Tagin*, only the number of occurrences. P brings ע דתל כתר רישיהון יז באוריית (*'ayin* that the crown of its head is suspended/raised[58]—17 in the *Torah*), **MV** similarly brings ע דתל כתר רישיהון י״ז באוריית. H brings ע דתל כתר רישיהון יֹזֹ באוריתֹ. ST, in the introduction, gives ע דתאלי רישיהון בתראֹ שבעה [עשר] באוריֹ and before the listing ע דתאלי רישיהון בתראֹ יֹזֹ [עשר] באוריתֹ. BH echoes, writing in full ע דתאלי רישיהון בתראה שבעה עשר באוריתא showing the number of instances in Hebrew rather than Aramaic.

The printed Maḥzor Vitry (*LMV*)*, shown right, brings a* vav *shape on top of the left roof of the letter.*

Rather than just extending the left arm, which many sources do, the scribe of **OB***, shown right adds an additional thick swirl, similar to a few of the other sources shown below.*

58 Jastrow, op. cit., p. 1670. It is not entirely clear what the word means but it certainly implies something higher.

TABLE 22 Forms for the first special letter *ʿayin*, as brought by the halakhic texts to which we have compared our manuscript, and some other examples. Once again, a wide variety of interpretations, only some of which extend the left arm. Some preserve the three *tagin* on the ascender, usually when this is merely a stretching of the left arm as opposed to having a *vav* shaped addition on the left arm

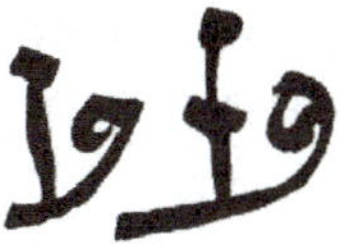

Maḥzor Vitry
Parma 2574 (P)

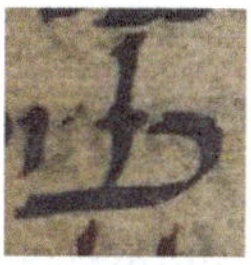

Maḥzor Vitry
Add. MS 27201 (MV)

Shem Tov *Tanakh*
Sefer Tagi (ST)

Badey ha-ʾAron
Heb. 840 (BH)

Sefer Tagin
Heb. 837 (H)

Not extant
Nr. 5667 (K)

Parma 2427

Parma 1959

Q651–652

MS Geunz. 481

Maḥzor Vitry
Add. MS 27201 (MV2)

Add. MS 11639

Add. MS 27167

Bologna *Torah*

Not found
Vat. ebr. 1

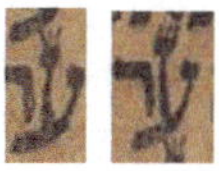

Or. 1463

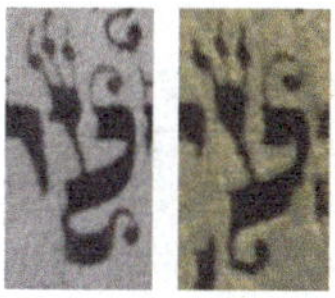

Alexander *Torah*

Turning to our other Genizah *fragments, the scribe of* **CG** *clearly knows there is some kind of ascender, but in* ***T-S NS 287.11-F***, *shown right, places it above the centre of the letter rather than attached to the left arm.*

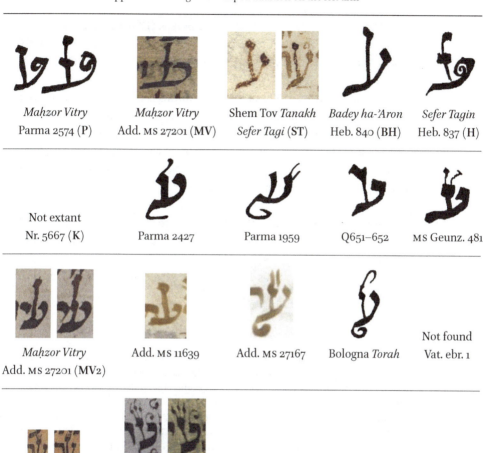

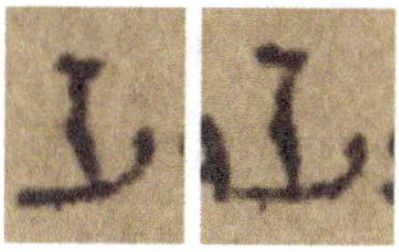

T-S Misc. 24.182 *(shown right) sometimes adds a* vav *shape and sometimes a* zayin *shape onto the top of the letter on the left side. Our older* Genizah *sources do not show the 'normal' three tagin on the ascender. Some others continue to add those* tagin *to the letter, most remove them.*

10 Listing of Instances for the First Special Letter *'Ayin*

1. P agrees, bringing ערומים קד̊. H abbreviates to ערומים קדמ׳. MV separates the words, as if there are two instances ערומים • קדמאה and ST does similarly ע̊רומים • קדמא.
2. P, MV and H are *ḥaser vav* עירם, as 𝔐, whereas OB has added a superfluous *vav*. This is either Gen. 3:10 or 3.11, as the word appears in both. ST brings כי ער̊ום אתה ('that you were naked') which places this as Gen. 3:11.[59]

However, the spelling of ערום in ST has added some further confusion. Basser notes that the Shem Tov *Tanakh* adds a further instance ע̊רום ('subtle') from Gen. 3:1, which conceivably dropped out of the core sources including ST from the same author, because it is similar to the next instance. There is certainly some support for its inclusion from our secondary sources. However, including this takes the total to eighteen, when we are told explicitly by the sources that there are seventeen.[60]

3. MV agrees, bringing מתה על̊י. P and H extend to מתה עלי רחל ('Rachel died unto me'). ST frames this differently as עלי • דרחל ('unto me'—of 'Rachel') with another unnecessary separator dot.
4. H agrees, bringing ונערתיה as 𝔐. P, MV and ST are *ma-le' vav* ונערותיה.

59 Basser states that 'even though in the *Tanakh* of Rabbi Shem Tov he suspends it over [the reference [in verse 10, in his copy [of the listing] he suspends it over verse 11', op. cit., p. 140, note 26. As we will see in the next note, Q651–652 brings this as Gen. 3:11, whilst Parma 2427 brings both.

60 Turning to our secondary sources, Q651–652 brings ע̊רום but also adds a second כי ע̊רומים ('that [they were] naked') from Gen. 3:7 (though 𝔐 is כי עירמם) as well כי ע̊רם אתה *ḥaser yod* from Gen. 3:11. Parma 2427 and MV2 bring והנחש היה ע̊רום and decorates the *'ayin*. However, Parma 2427 uses a swirl on the right roof rather than the elongated left roof, which is the wrong form, so it is possible that it should have been included in a different listing. *Ben Mesheq* also includes this with a very long description ס׳ג פ׳א ערום ראש השני של העין גבוה וסוף הרגל של עין מקום שמתחיל להיות משופע ב׳ תגין עקומים זה מול זה בעין ב׳ חצי עגולים (Chapter 3 verse 1 'subtle' the second head of the *'ayin* is tall and the end of the the leg of the *'ayin* is a place where there starts to be 2 *tagin* sloping, bent *tagin* one against the other in the *'ayin*, two semi circles) similar to that brought earlier for ערומים, which is an interesting descriptor for the form. Parma 2427 also brings a number of other instances but does not decorate them, ידע עירמם which is probably from Gen. 3:11, even though 𝔐 is וידעו כי עירמם ('for they knew they they were naked') then כי ערם ('that [I was] naked') from Gen. 3:11, even though 𝔐 is עירם and finally עירם אתה ('you were naked') from Gen. 3:11. MV2 brings only ע̊רומים as another instance. For this grouping, MS. Add. 27167 and Parma 1959 bring only שניהם ע̊רומים ('both of them were naked') from

Line 20: [5]מ[צר]ענת • [6]ונשיא בעמך • [7]וירא את העגל • [8]פרוע הוא • [9]הערל • [10]בקרקע •
5. **'leprous'** (Ex. 4:6). (*Parashat Mishpaṭim*) 6. **'a ruler of your people'** (Ex. 22:27). (*Parashat Ki Tissa'*) 7. **'he saw the calf'** (Ex. 32:19). 8. **'were broken loose'** (Ex. 32:25). (*Parashat Be-ḥuqotai*) 9. **'uncircumcised'** (Lev. 26:41). (*Parashat Naso'*) 10. **'on the floor of'** (Num. 5:17).

5. OB is damaged with a hole. P, ST and H brings מצרעת as 𝔐. MV is *ma-le' vav* מצורעת. OB appears to bring a superfluous *nun* shaped form before the *tav*. It is possible that it is the additional *vav* out of place.
6. P, ST and H all agree, bringing ונשיא בעמך. MV does also but is quite water damaged.
7. P, MV and H agree, bringing וירא את העגל. ST frames differently as העגל ומחל ('the calf and the dancing'), but it is the same reference.
8. P, MV and H agree, bringing פרוע הוא. ST brings פרע, *ḥaser vav* as 𝔐.[61]
9. P, MV, ST and H all agree bringing הערל.
10. P, MV and H agree, bringing בקרקע. ST extends to אשר יהיה בקרקע ('that is on the floor').[62]

Line 21: [11]ועצמותיהם • [12]שעיר איביו • [13]תעשינה הדברים • [14]וברשעת • [15]ואל רשעו •
11. **'and their bones'** (Num. 24:8). 12. **'Seir, his enemies'** (Num. 24:18). 13. **'as bees do'** (Deut. 1:44). 14. **'for the wickedness of'** (Deut. 9:4). 15. **'nor to their wickedness'** (Deut. 9:27).

11. MV and ST agree, bringing the word *ma-le' vav* as OB. P and H bring ועצמתיהם *ḥaser vav* as 𝔐.[63]

Gen. 2:25. MS. Add. 11639 omits. There is considerable difficulty over the spelling of the key words on both core and secondary sources, which has added a degree of confusion.

61 T-S Misc. 24.182 also brings פרע *ḥaser vav*.

62 The *Ba-'al ha-Ṭurim* comments on this instance, 'on the floor of the Tabernacle' the *'ayin* is extended/suspended/raised, because [of the allusion to the *soṭah* (suspected adulteress) in the verse] 'the adulterer's eye awaits the night, saying, 'no eye will see me (Job 24:15)''.

63 Though oddly EPST transcribes adding a *vav* that is not present in H as ועצמותיהם. The *Ba'al ha-Ṭurim* comments on this instance, 'and their bones' the *'ayin* is suspended, to say top you that the seven [Caananite] nations will be uprooted and in the time to come the other 63 nations [will be uprooted] as this [verse says], 'all of it is dross, together they have become depraved' (Ps. 53:4), playing on the סג = 63.

12. P brings שער איביו. MV, ST and H are *ma-le' vav* שער אויביו.[64] However, all these sources omit the *yod* from שעיר, unlike **OB** who maintains it, bringing שעיר איביו as 𝔐.
13. P, MV, ST and H all agree, bringing תְּשִׁינה הדברים.
14. P and H agree, bringing וברשעת. MV does too, but lists this instance under the wrong *'ayin* form. ST extends to וברשעת הגוים ('for the wickedness of the nations').[65] The inclusion of the *vav* at the start of the phrase is key as the next verse Deut. 9:5 includes ברשעת הגוים. It is odd that one is decorated and not the other.
15. P, ST and H agree, bringing ואל רשעו. MV omits.

Finally a catchword at the bottom of the page on the left provides us with the sixteenth instance, וערפכם ('and your necks [be no longer stiff]') from (Deut. 10:16). P, MV and ST all agree. H has added ועד on the previous line as a line filler.

Though not shown on the folio of **OB**, to be as comprehensive as possible, it is worth noting that all the core sources agree on the seventeenth entry concerning the first *'ayin* form. P, MV, ST and H all bring ויבעט ('and kicked/trampled') from Deut. 32:15.

11 Summary—Oxford Heb. 33/9

OB has provided a further useful *Genizah* source extending our understanding of these four letters, *nun* through to the first *'ayin* form, helping to clarify the intention of a number of instances where there is query and disagreement. Even though it is of comparable age to the Cambridge *Genizah* fragments, **CG**, (treated in the first two sections), **OB**, like all the core sources is not free from error. Thus, it is only by careful individual examination and comparison of all these core sources and the secondary sources against 𝔐, that one can establish where the errors may have crept in over time, and assess the likely original intention of the author of *Sefer Tagin*.

It is entirely possible that within the large and not fully charted *Genizah* contents, spread far and wide amongst various institutions, there are yet other fragments and pages from these, and other manuscripts of *Sefer Tagin*, that would equally add to our understanding of this key scribal text.

64 Transcribed and corrected in LMV to שעיר איביו, but still shown incorrectly in EPST as שער אויביו.

65 Nonetheless, Basser gives only וברשעת, op. cit., p. 112.

Transcription and Annotation of T-S Misc. 24.182

Whilst most of the fragments of T-S Misc. 24.182 are perfectly visible and legible, not everything has been fully preserved. Since this is a new and important partial witness to a composite version of *Sefer Tagin*, I have transcribed, annotated and, where necessary, reconstructed the text below.

The reconstructed areas are drawn from the core and secondary sources. The conventions employed for the earlier reconstruction are continued. The special letters are decorated with a circle as before and a separator added for clarity, even though this is not present in the manuscript.

T-S Misc. 24.182 P2-B—22 lines preserved

Line 1: ה[פ]ריד • [עד]רים • העטפים • מק[נה] [א]ביכם • נקדים

'separated' (Gen. 30:40). **'droves'** (Gen. 30:40). **'the feebler'** (Gen. 30:42). **'the cattle of your father'** (Gen. 31:9). **'speckled ...**

Line 2: וברדים • ותגנב • ויגנב • ותנהג • ואלהי אביכם •

... and spotted' (Gen. 31:10). **'and she stole'** (Gen. 31:19). **'and he stole'** (Gen. 31:20). **'carried away'** (Gen. 31:26). **'and the God of your father'** (Gen. 31:29).

Line 3: הל[ך] • הכר לך • וקח • לוא שכלו • בנתי • בני • צאני •

'gone' (Gen. 31:30). **'you discern'** (Gen 31:32). **'and take'** (Gen. 31:32). **'not miscarried'** (Gen. 31:38). **'my daughters'** (Gen. 31:43). **'my sons'** (Gen. 31:43). **'my flock'** (Gen. 31:43).

Line 4: לבניהן • והמצפה • אלהי • בהר • ~~אלהם~~ אלהים • מחנים •

'for their children' (Gen. 31:43). **'and Mitspah'** (Gen. 31:49). **'God of'** (Gen. 31:53). **'in the mountain'** (Gen. 31:54). **'God'** (Gen. 32:2). **'camps'** (Gen. 32:3).

Line 5: וישלח פ • קטנתי עַבְדֶּךָ • הצילני • והכני • עמך •

'and he sent' ***petuḥa*** (open section). **'I am small'** (Gen. 32:11). 'your servant' (Gen. 32:11).[1] **'deliver me'** (Gen. 32:12). **'and smite me'** (Gen. 32:12). **'with you'** (Gen. 32:13).

1 On the face of it, the inclusion of this word seems odd. Firstly, it includes pointing when this is not present elsewhere. Secondly it carries no decoration. The vowel points are not entirely clear but looks like עַבֲדֶךָ; 𝔐 is עַבְדֶּךָ with a silent *sheva* under the *bet*. It is possible our scribe

 | DOI:10.1163/9789004426368_008

Line 6: אכפרה • לפני • פני • השחר • השחר • אשלחך • מה •

'I will appease' (Gen. 32:21). **'before me'** (Gen. 32:21). **'my face'** (Gen. 32:21). **'the dawn'** (Gen. 32:25). **'I will [not] let you go'** (Gen. 32:25).[2] **'what'** (Gen. 32:28).

Line 7: [ישראל] • ויחבקהו • וישקהו • ויבכו • קח • ויפצר •

['Israel'] (Gen. 32:29) **'and he hugged him'** (Gen. 33:4). **'and he kissed him'** (Gen. 33:4).[3] **'and they wept'** (Gen. 33:4). **'take'** (Gen. 33:11). **'and he urged'** (Gen. 33:11).

Line 8: [וד]פקום • ולרגל • ותצא ס • להם • וייטבו • כאבים •

'and if they overdrive them' (Gen. 33:13). **'and according to the pace'** (Gen. 33:14). **'and she went out'** ***setuma*** (closed section) (Gen. 44:1). **'to them'** (Gen. 44:7). **'and they pleased'** (Gen. 44:18). **'in pain'** (Gen. 44:25).

Line 9: בישב • מתי • אלהים דקום פ • סביב'תיהם • וירא פ •

'unto the inhabitants' (Gen. 34:30). **'few'** (Gen. 34:30). **'God'** of [the verse with] **'arise'** (Gen. 35:1) ***petuḥa***. **'round about them'** (Gen. 35:5). **'and He appeared'** (Gen. 35:9) ***petuḥa***.

Line 10: לו אלהים • ישראל • פרה • ורבה • גוים • מחלציך •

'God [said] to him' (Gen. 35:11). **'Israel'** (Gen. 35:10).[4] **'be fruitful'** (Gen. 35:11). **'and multiply'** (Gen. 35:11). **'nations'** (Gen. 35:11). **'from your loins'** (Gen. 35:11).

Line 11: יצאו • לאברהם • אלהים • ותמת • הימם • [??] • וישב פ •

'will emerge' (Gen. 35:11). **'to Abraham'** (Gen. 35:12). **'God'** (Gen. 35:15). **'and she died'** (Gen. 35:19). **'hot springs'** (Gen. 36:24). [??].[5] **'and he dwelt'** (Gen. 37:1) ***petuḥa***.

Line 12: מגורי • תלדות יעקב • חלום • ~~ויוספו~~ ויוספו • [ח]למתיו •

'sojournings' (Gen. 37:1). **'generations of Jacob'** (Gen. 37:2). **'dream'** (Gen. 37:5).[6] **'and they added'** (Gen. 37:5).[7] **'for his dreams'** (Gen. 37:8).[8]

---

here is making a point that he disagrees with the vowels and is preserving an alterative reading. *Minḥat Shai* does not bring any alternative.

2 Though no special letter is indicated.

3 An example of the *ʾotiyot menuqqadot* (dotted letters).

4 Out of sequence.

5 A very badly damaged section. It is possible the word מי (*Mey-*[*Zahav*]) is there from Gen. 36:39, since that would be an expected inclusion at this point.

6 Out of sequence.

7 Out of sequence.

8 Out of sequence.

Line 13: רעה֯ • אל אביה֯ם • נצ֯בה • תס֯בינה • את • ח֯[יה]
'evil' (Gen. 37:2). **'to their father'** (Gen. 37:2). **'stood upright'** (Gen. 37:7). **'came round about'** (Gen. 37:7). '[indicating definite article]' (Gen. 37:12).[9] **'beast'** (Gen. 37:20).[10]

Line 14: ה֯לזה֯ • הפ֯סים • ס֯חרים • ל֯ישמעאל֯ים • ו֯יכרה •
'this' (Gen. 37:19). **'the long-sleeved'** (Gen. 37:23). **'merchants'** (Gen. 37:28). **'to the Ishmaelites'** (Gen. 37:28). **'and he knew it'** (Gen. 37:33).

Line 15: ו֯יקרע • ו֯יקמו • ו֯ימאן • לפו֯טיפ֯ר • ה֯טבחים • ויהי ס •
'and he rent' (Gen. 37:34). **'and they arose'** (Gen. 37:35). **'and he refused'** (Gen. 37:35). **'to Poitphar'** (Gen. 37:36). **'of the guard'** (Gen. 37:36). **'and it came to pass'** (Gen. 38:1) ***setuma*.**

Line 16: עדל֯מי • ותשרף֯ • פ֯[רצ]ת • ויוסף ס • אל֯יה • להי֯ות • ו֯יהי •
'Adullamite' (Gen. 38:1). **'be burnt'** (Gen. 38:1) **'breach for yourself'** (Gen. 38:29). **'and Joseph'** (Gen. 39:1) ***setuma*.** **'towards her'** (Gen. 39:10). **'to be with'** (Gen. 39:10). **'and it was …**

Line 17: כשמע • [אין ש]ר בית הס֯חר • עשה֯ יי • ויהי פ •
… when he heard' (Gen. 39:19). **'the keep of the prison did not** [look]**'** (Gen. 39:23). **'God made'** (Gen. 39:23). **'and it was'** (Gen. 40:1). ***petuḥa*.**

Line 18: ויפ֯קד • [ש]רי֯גם • השרגי֯ם • כ֯י גנב • ח֯רי • ה֯לדת •
'and he charged' (Gen. 40:4). **'branches'** (Gen. 40:10). **'the branches'** (Gen. 40:12). **'for I was stolen away'** (Gen. 40:15).[11] **'white bread'** (Gen. 40:16). **'birth**[day]**'** (Gen. 40:20).

Line 19: ו֯ישכחהו • ויהי מקץ פ • ו֯יה֯י בבקר • ויס֯פ֯ר • חלמו֯ •
'but forgot him' (Gen. 40:23). **'and it was at the end'** (Gen. 41:1) ***petuḥa*.** **'and he told them'** (Gen. 41:8). **'his dream'** (Gen. 41:8).

Line 20: ה֯טבחים • ה֯נה֯ • [וי]ל֯בש • ל֯פניו • צפ֯נת פ֯ענה • פ
'of the guard' (Gen. 41:12). **'behold'** (Gen. 41:29). **'and they dressed'** (Gen. 41:42). **'before him'** (Gen. 41:43). **'Tsafnat Paneaḥ'** (Gen. 41:45).

9 Another example of the *ʾotiyot menuqqadot* (dotted letters).
10 Out of sequence.
11 As already mentioned, it is not clear why the decoration for the *nun* has been applied to a *kaf*.

Line 21: פוטיפרע • חדל • ותבלענה • ותחלנה • את האלה[י]ם
'Potiphera' (Gen. 41:45). **'they left off'** (Gen. 41:49). **'and they** [the ears] **swallowed up'** (Gen. 41:7). **'and** [the seven years of famine] **began'** (Gen. 41:54). **'God'** (Gen. 42:18).

Line 22: מעליהם • ויקח • לעיניהם • והכֵן • שלום • לכם
'around from them' (Gen. 42:24). **'and he took'** (Gen. 42:24). **'before their eyes'** (Gen. 42:24) **'and prepare'** (Gen. 43:16).[12] **'peace'** (Gen. 43:23). **'to you'** (Gen. 43:23).

In addition, a further word has been written vertically down the left side of the folio, מחלציך ('from your loins') from Gen. 35:11, which was already listed, but this time the *lamed* is also decorated.

Our listing continues on the next folio.

T-S Misc. 24.182 P2-F—21 lines

Line 1: אלהיכם • ואלהי • לאבינו • עודנו • אחיכם הקטן • ויורדו •
'your God' (Gen. 43:23). **'and the God'** (Gen. 43:23). **'to our father'** (Gen. 43:28). **'still'** (Gen. 43:28). **'your little brother'** (Gen. 43:29). **'and they took down'** (Gen. 44:11).[13]

Line 2: בנימן • עודנו • לשלום • ויגש ס • היש • קשורה • ולא •
'Benjamin' (Gen. 44:12). **'still'** (Gen. 44:14). **'and he came near'** (Gen. 44:18) *setuma*. (Gen. 44:19). **'have** [you]' (Gen. 44:19). **'bound'** (Gen. 44:30). **'was not** [able]' (Gen. 45:1).

Line 3: ולהחיות ל • הנה • וישימנו • מהרו • ואמרתם • אלה[י]ם •
'and to save alive' (Gen. 45:7).[14] **'here'** (Gen. 45:8). 3. **'and he placed me'** (Gen. 45:8). **'hasten'** (Gen. 45:9). **'and say'** (Gen. 45:1). **'God'** (Gen. 45:9).

Line 4: מצרים • עיניכם • כי פי • לכם הוא • ותחי • רוח • מרדה •
'Egypt' (Gen. 45:9). **'and regard** [not]' (Gen. 45:20).[15] **'for the mouth'** (Gen. 45:12). **'are yours'** (Gen. 45:20). **'and revived'** (Gen. 45:27). **'spirit'** (Gen. 45:27). **'to go down'** (Gen. 46:3).

12 The scribe has added the *tserei* vowel.
13 Listed, but no letter is decorated.
14 This is followed by an erroneous *lamed*, which has been partially erased.
15 Out of sequence.

Line 5: מצ֯ר֯ימה • אר֯ד • מצר֯ימה • ואלה סׄ • אמותה֯ • ה֯פעם •

'to Egypt' (Gen. 46:3). **'I will go down'** (Gen. 46:4). **'to Egypt'** (Gen. 46:4). **'and these'** (Gen. 46:8) ***setuma***. **'let me die'** (Gen. 46:30). **'once'** (Gen. 46:30).

Line 6: אחר֯י • ר֯אותי • אבותינ֯ו • לפניך ה֯וא • במיט֯ב • ושמת֯ם֯ •

'after' (Gen. 46:30). **'I have seen'** (Gen. 46:30). **'our fathers'** (Gen. 46:34 or 47:3). **'it is before you'** (Gen. 47:6). **'the best of'** (Gen. 47:6). **'and put them'** (Gen. 47:6).

Line 7: מק֯נה • אשר ל֯י • כמה֯ • במיט֯ב • וינהל֯ם • ויהי סׄ •

'cattle' (Gen. 47:6). **'which I have'** (Gen. 47:6). **'how many'** (Gen. 47:8). **'in the best of'** (Gen. 47:11). **'and he sustained them'** (Gen. 47:17). **'and it was'** (Gen. 47:28) ***setuma***.

Line 8: ויה֯י • וישתחו ישר֯אל • ה֯מטה • ויהי פׄ • ע֯לי • וי֯גש •

'and it was' (Gen. 47:28). **'and Israel bowed'** (Gen. 47:31). 'the bed' **'and it was'** (Gen. 47:31). **'and it was'** (Gen. 48:1) ***petuḥa***. **'unto me'** (Gen. 48:7). **'and he brought** [them] **near'** (Gen. 48:10).

Line 9: שניה֯ם • ועיני יש֯ראל • המלא֯ך • יבר֯ך • כי זה֯ •

'both of them' (Gen. 48:13). **'and the eyes of Israel'** (Gen. 48:10).[16] **'the angel'** (Gen. 48:16). **'shall bless'** (Gen. 48:20). **'for this'** (Gen. 48:18).

Line 10: ימינ֯ך • ממנ֯ו • ה֯גוים • ישמ֯ך • אלה֯ים • ויקרא פׄ •

'your right hand' (Gen. 48:18). **'than he'** (Gen. 48:19). **'the nations'** (Gen. 48:19). **'may He make you'** (Gen. 47:20). **'God'** (Gen. 48:20). **'and he called'** (Gen. 48:18), ***petuḥa***.

Line 11: בנ֯יו • בקה֯לם • קשתה֯ • אריה֯ • ומחק֯ק֯ • יקה֯ת •

'his sons' (Gen. 49:1). **'in their assembly'** (Gen. 49:6). **'cruel'** (Gen. 49:7). **'lion'** (Gen. 49:9). **'and [his] staff'** (Gen. 49:10). **'obedience of'** (Gen. 49:10).

Line 12: אס֯רי • עירה֯ • כבס֯ • סותה֯ • יה֯י גד • וה֯וא • שמנה֯ •

'binding' (Gen. 49:11). **'his foal'** (Gen. 49:11). **'washes'** (Gen. 49:11). **'clothes'** (Gen. 49:11). **'Gad shall be'** (should be 'Dan shall be' from Gen. 49:17).[17] **'and he'** (Gen. 49:19). **'fat'** (Gen. 49:20).

16 Out of sequence.

17 Likely an error here from our scribe, given the typical instance brought by all the other sources.

Line 13: הנתן • חצים • ותשב • קשתו • ישראל • ויערך •
'he gives' (Gen. 49:21). **'arrows'** (Gen. 49:23).[18] **'and abode'** (Gen. 49:24). **'his bow'** (Gen. 49:24). **'Israel'** (Gen. 49:24). **'shall help you'** (Gen. 49:25).[19]

Line 14: ויברכך • ברכת • ברכת • שדים • ורחם • ברכת •
'He shall bless you' (Gen. 49:25). **'blessings of'** (Gen. 49:25). **'blessings of'** (Gen. 49:25). **'of breasts'** (Gen. 49:25). **'and the womb'** (Gen. 49:25).

Line 15: על ברכת • יטרף • בבקר • כל אלה • תאמרו •
'beyond the blessings' (Gen. 49:26). **'that rends'** (Gen. 49:27). **'in the morning'** (Gen. 49:27). **'all these'** (Gen. 49:28). '[so] **will you say'** (Gen. 50:17).

Line 16: פשע • לפשע • ואלהים • וימת • ויישם •
'transgression' (Gen. 50:17). **'to the transgression'** (Gen. 50:17). **'and God'** (Gen. 50:17). **'and he died'** (Gen. 50:26). **'and they placed him'** (Gen. 50:26).

Line 17: //// ואלה שמות ////
//// **'and these are the names'** //// (Ex. 1:1).[20]

Line 18: ויקם פ • הנה עם • נתחכמה • פן • ירבה • וישימו •
'and there arose' (Ex. 1:8) *petuḥa*. **'behold the people'** (Ex. 1:9). **'let us deal wisely'** (Ex. 1:10). **'lest'** (Ex. 1:10). **'and they set'** (Ex. 1:11)

Line 19: יענו • ירבה • יפרץ • קשה • הע[ב]ריות • פתס • ויצו •
'they afflicted' (Ex. 1:12). **'they increased'** (Ex. 1:12). **'they spread'** (Ex. 1:12). **'hard'** (Ex. 1:14). **'the Hebrew women'** (Ex. 1:16). **'Pithom'** (Ex. 1:11).[21] **'and he commanded'** (Ex. 1:22)

Line 20: וילך ס • טוב • ותצפנהו • ותחמרה • ותתצב • ונערתיה •
'and he went' (Ex. 2:1) *setuma*. **'goodly'** (Ex. 2:1). **'and she hid him'** (Ex. 2:2). **'and she daubed'** (Ex. 2:3). **'and she stood'** (Ex. 2:4). **'and her handmaids'** (Ex. 2:5).

Line 21: תפתח • העברים זה • היליכי • משיתהו • ויהי פ • עזבתן •
'and she opened' (Ex. 2:6). **'this is** [one of] **the Hebrews'** [children]' (Ex. 2:6). **'take away'** (Ex. 2:9). **'drew him out'** (Ex. 2:10). **'left'** (Ex. 2:20).[22]

18 בעלי חצים (lit. masters of arrows)—i.e. archers.
19 Our scribe has omitted the *zayin* from ויעזרך.
20 Introducing the new book.
21 Out of sequence.
22 Another scribe has added an additional instance in a poorly formed book-hand.

T-S Misc. 24.182 P1-F—23 lines

Line 1: ואכ֯בתי֯ את • וצ֯רתי֯ • צ֯ררי֯ך • בארצ֯ך֯ • מס֯פ֯ר • [ימי]ך֯

'I will be an enemy' (Ex. 23:22).[23] **'and an adversary'** (Ex. 23:22). **'your adversaries'** (Ex. 23:22). **'in your land'** (Ex. 23:26). **'number'** (Ex. 23:26). **'your days'** (Ex. 23:26).

Line 2: וברך֯ • את לחמך֯ • מימיך֯ • והסרתי֯ • מקרבך֯ • משכלה ס֯ •

'He will bless' (Ex. 23:25). **'your bread'** (Ex. 23:25). **'your water'** (Ex. 23:25). **'I will take away'** (Ex. 23:25). **'from amongst you'** (Ex. 23:25). **'miscarry'** (Ex. 23:26) ***setuma***.

Line 3: לפנ[י]ך֯ • וה֯מתי • ערף֯ • ה֯צרעה • אגרשנ֯ו • תפ֯רה • על משה פ֯ •

'before you' (Ex. 23:27). **'and will discomfit'** (Ex. 23:27). **'nape'** (Ex. 23:27). **'I will drive them out'** (Ex. 23:30). **'you are increased'** (Ex. 23:30). **'and to Moses'** (Ex. 24:1).[24]

Line 4: [~~דברי~~ יה֯וה֯ • יה֯וה֯] • דבר יה֯וה֯ • ויק֯ם֯ משה • ה֯אלה֯ים •

[~~'words'~~ **'God' 'God'**] **'God has spoken'** (Ex. 24:7).[25] **'and Moses arose'** (Ex. 24:13). **'God'** (Ex. 24:13).

Line 5: ה֯זקנים • ש֯בו • בזה֯ • מ֯י בעל • אלה֯ם֯ • ומראה֯ • כבוד יה֯וה֯ •

'the elders' (Ex. 24:14). **'remain'** (Ex. 24:14). **'here'** (Ex. 24:14).[26] **'whoever has cause'** (Ex. 24:14). **'to them'** (Ex. 24:14). **'and the appearance'** (Ex. 24:17). **'glory of God'** (Ex. 24:17).

Line 6: משה בה֯ר • וידבר פ֯ • וש֯כנתי • ועשו ס֯ • כפ֯רת •

'Moses in the mountain' (Ex. 24:18). **'and He said'** (Ex. 25:1), *petuḥa*. **'and I will dwell'** (Ex. 25:8). **'and make'** (Ex. 25:10) ***setuma***. **'cover'** (Ex. 25:17).

---

23 Our scribe has written a *kaf* instead of a *yod* for ואיבתי, but has added a vertical line to indicate the error.

24 This is an error, as 𝔐 gives ואל משה.

25 Our scribe intended to write דבר יהוה but wrote דברי and then the Tetragrammaton twice. It is likely that the doubling was caused by a misunderstanding of the instruction seen in the core sources, תרויהון (both of them) referring to both letters *he*. It is possible our scribe misread and wrote the whole word twice. He then crossed through the first word, but unable to do so with God's Holy Name, he put a box around them to indicate that they should not be there. As mentioned, the prohibition of erasing the written Name of God is derived from a reading of Deut. 12:1–7, the key phrases being ונתצתם את מזבחתם ושברתם את מצבתם ואשריהם תשרפון באש ופסילי אלהיהם תגדעון ואבדתם את שמם מן המקום ההוא: לא תעשון כן ליהוה אלהיכם ('and you shall shatter their altars, and break their pillars, and burn their *ʾasherim* with fire, and cut down the statues of their gods, and destroy their names from that place. You shall not do thus to the Lord your God').

26 Lit. 'in this'.

Line 7: ואת המשכן • והיה • המשכן • כרכב המזבח •

'and the Tabernacle' (Ex. 26:1). 'and it will be' (Ex. 26:6). 'the Tabernacle' (Ex. 26:6). 'the ledge of the altar' (Ex. 27:5).

Line 8: הראה • חצר ס • יתדת החצר • ואתה תצוה ס •

'been shown' (Ex. 27:8). 'court' (Ex. 27:9), *setuma*. 'pins of the court' (Ex. 27:19). 'and you will command' (Ex. 27:20), *setuma*.

Line 9: להעלות • נר • לכהנו לי • תשבץ • לכהנו לי • טור אדם •

'to burn' (Ex. 27:20). 'flame' (Ex. 27:20). 'to minister to me' (Ex. 28:1). 'chequered' (Ex. 28:4). 'to minister to me' (Ex. 28:4). 'a row of carnelian' (Ex. 28:17).

Line 10: לזכרון • אל חשן ס • עון הקדשים • ושבצת • ירכים

'as a remembrance' (Ex. 28: 29).[27] 'to the breastplate' (Ex. 28:30) *setuma*. 'iniquity of holy things' (Ex. 28:38). 'and you will weave' (Ex. 28:39). 'loins ...

Line 11: יהיו • המצנפת • כהנה • וקדש הוא • לריח ניחוח •

... they will be' (Ex. 28:42).[28] 'the mitre' (Ex. 29:6). 'priesthood' (Ex. 29:9). 'and he will be made holy' (Ex. 29:21). 'as a sweet savour' (Ex. 29:25).[29]

Line 12: כי תרומה הוא • אל אהל • כי קדש הם • כל הנגע •

'for it is a heave-offering' (Ex. 29:28).[30] 'to the tent' (Ex. 29:30). 'for they are holy' (Ex. 29:33). 'whoever touches' (Ex. 29:37).

Line 13: מזבח פ • והקטיר • וכפר • בשנה • ליהוה • ונתת •

'altar' (Ex. 30:1) *petuḥa*. 'and he will burn' (Ex. 30:7). 'make atonement' (Ex. 30:10). 'in the year' (Ex. 30:1). 'to God' (Ex. 30:10). 'and you will give' (Ex. 30:16 or 18).[31]

Line 14: לפני • לכפר • העשיר • ממחצית • לכפר • כפר •

'before' (Ex. 30:16). 'to atone' (Ex. 30:17). 'the rich' (Ex. 30:16). 'than half' (Ex. 30:16). 'to atone' (Ex. 30:17). 'atonement' (Ex. 30:12).[32]

---

27 However, 𝔐 is *ḥaser vav* לזכרן.

28 𝔐 is *ḥaser vav* ירכים.

29 It is not clear which is the special letter but the *ḥet* indicated is written slightly differently to the others. This instance is not in the standard listings for *Sefer Tagin*, so it is difficult to assess which is intended.

30 No letter appears to be indicated as special.

31 There are three possibilities here, with two in verse 18.

32 All the instances listed in line 14 are standard for *Sefer Tagin*, but are very out of sequence.

Line 15: כיור • לרחצה • ורחצו • להקטיר • ורחצו • וקנמן •
'laver' (Ex. 30:18). 'for washing' (Ex. 30:18). 'and they will wash' (Ex. 30:19). 'to kindle' (Ex. 30:20). 'and they will wash' (Ex. 30:21). 'and cinnamon' (Ex. 30:23).

Line 16: בשם • וקנה • בשם • וקדה • רקח • מרקחת • רקח •
'sweet' (Ex. 30:23). 'reed' (Ex. 30:23). 'sweet' (Ex. 30:23). 'cassia' (Ex. 30:24). 'aromatic' (Ex. 30:25). 'perfume' (Ex. 30:25). 'perfumer' (Ex. 30:25).

Line 17: לדרתיכם • לכם • ~~והקטרת~~ • סמים • סמים • זכה •
'throughout your generations' (Ex. 30:31). 'to you' (Ex. 30:32). ~~'and the incense'.~~[33] 'spices' (Ex. 30:34). 'spices' (Ex. 30:34). 'pure' (Ex. 30:34).

Line 18: קט[ר]ת • רקח • הדק • קודש • קדשים • לכם • והקטרת •
'incense' (Ex. 30:35). 'perfume' (Ex. 30:35). 'crush' (Ex. 30:36). 'holy' (Ex. 30:36). 'most holy' (Ex. 30:36). 'to you' (Ex. 30:36). 'and the incense' (Ex. 30:37).

Line 19: ~~וה~~ ראה ס • עולם • לעלם • לחת כתבים • אלהים •
[34]'see' (Ex. 31:2) *setuma*. 'perpetual' (Ex. 31:16). 'forever' (Ex. 31:17). 'tablets written' (Ex. 31:18). 'God' (Ex. 31:18).

Line 20: ויקהל • והביאו • ויתפרקו • ויביאו • וידבר פ •
'and they gathered' (Ex. 32:1). 'and bring them' (Ex. 32:2). 'they broke off' (Ex. 32:3). 'and they brought them' (Ex. 32:3) 'and He said' (Ex. 32:3) *petuḥa*.

Line 21: ערף • ויפן פ • הם כתבים • והמכתב • חרות •
'[stiff]necked' (Ex. 32:9). 'and he turned' (Ex. 32:15) *petuḥa*. 'were they written' (Ex. 32:15) 'and the writing' (Ex. 32:16). 'graven' (Ex. 32:16).

Line 22: הלחת • יהושוע שמע • העגל • ומחלת • וישבר •
'the tablets' (Ex. 32:16). Joshua hear (prob. Ex. 32:17).[35] 'the calf' (Ex. 32:19). 'and the dancing' (Ex. 32:19). 'and he broke' (Ee. 32:19).

Line 23: ההר • פרע • פרעה • ליהוה • העם • היום • ברכה •
'the mountain' (Ex. 32:19). 'broken loose' (Ex. 32:25). 'let them loose' (32:25). 'for God' (32:26). 'that day' (32:28). 'blessing' (32:29).

---

33 Our scribe has erred, bringing the instance from Ex. 30:37 too early and crosses it out.
34 Our scribe may have started to write והקטרת again and corrected himself after two letters.
35 Likely an error by our scribe, and the intention was וישמע יהושע ('and Joshua heard') with the name *ḥaser vav*, as 𝔐.

T-S Misc. 24.182 P1-B—22 lines

Line 1: ח֯ט[א]ה • ו֯יגף֯ • עש֯ה • ערף֯ • ערף֯ • ונט֯ה לו • ר֯אה

'sin' (Ex. 32:31). **'and he smote'** (Ex. 32:35). **'made'** (Ex. 32:35). **'[stiff]necked'** (Ex. 33:3). **'[stiff]necked'** (Ex. 33:3). **'and to pitch it'** (Ex. 33:7). **'see ...**

Line 2: אתה • וה֯נחתי • ה֯לא • ט֯ובי • פ֯ניך • את פ֯ני • ה֯נה •

... you' (Ex. 33:12). **'and I will give rest'** (33:14). **'is it not'** (Ex. 33:16).[36] **'my goodness'** (Ex. 33:19). **'your face'** (Ex. 33:19). **'My face'** (Ex. 33:20) **'behold'** (Ex. 33:21).

Line 3: וי֯רד • בש֯ם • יה֯וה • ויק֯רא • רחו֯ם • לאלפי֯ם • וחט֯אה •

'and He descended' (Ex. 34:5). **'in the name'** (Ex. 34:5) 'of God' (Ex. 34:5). **'and proclaimed'** (Ex. 34:6). **'merciful'** (Ex. 34:6). **'to the thousandth'** (Ex. 34:7) **'and transgression'** (Ex. 34:7).

Line 4: של֯שים • רבעי֯ם • ויק֯ד • ארצ֯ה • ער֯ף • וסלח֯ת •

'third' (Ex. 34:7). **'fourth'** (Ex. 34:7). **'and he bowed to the ground'** (Ex. 34:8). **'[stiff] necked'** (Ex. 34:9) **'and pardons'** (Ex. 34:9).

Line 5: ולחטאת֯נו ֯ • ה֯נה • מעש֯ה • עש֯ה • לאל אח֯ר •

'and our sin' (Ex. 34:9).[37] **'behold'** (Ex. 34:10). **'the work'** (Ex. 34:10). **'to do'** (Ex. 34:10). **'to another god'** (Ex. 34:14).[38]

Line 6: אל֯הי • ה֯אדן • יה֯וה֯ • אל֯הי • מפ֯נ[י]ך • לר֯אות אל֯היך •

'God of' (34:17). **'the Lord'** (Ex. 34:23). **'God'** (Ex. 34:23). **'God of'** (Ex. 34:23). **'from before you'** (Ex. 34:24). **'to see'**[39] (Ex. 34:24). **'your God'** (Ex. 34:24).

Line 7: דברי ה֯ברית • קר֯ן • עו֯ר • עו֯ר פניו • בה֯ר • יצו֯ה • ור֯או •

'the words of the covenant' (Ex. 34:28). **'beams'** (Ex. 34:29). **'skin'** (Ex. 34:29). ^**'skin'**^ (Ex. 34:30).[40] **'in the mountain'** (Ex. 34:32). **'he was commanded'** (Ex. 34:34) **'and they saw'** (Ex. 34:35).

---

36 Our scribe is *ḥaser vav*, whereas 𝔐 is *ma-le'* הלוא.

37 By the side of the *vav* our scribe has added a ֯ to indicate a missing instance.

38 Our scribe also indicates the accepted tradition for the large *resh* in this word that ensures that this is read as אחר *'aḥer* (another) and not אחד *'eḥad* (one). The counter to this is the large *dalet* in *'eḥad* in the first line of the *Shema'*.

39 In the sense of appearing before God.

40 Added in above the next word by another scribe who clearly felt that עור should be listed from both verses, where it appears in succession. Interestingly, this is normally listed twice, but involving the *pe* from פניו in both verses.

Line 8: פני משה֯ • המסוה֯ • על פ֯ניו • ויקהל ס֗ • תבער֯ו •

‘the face of Moses’ (Ex. 34:35). **‘the veil’** (Ex. 34:35). **‘and he assembled’** (Ex. 35:1) ***setuma.*** **‘kindle’** (Ex. 35:3).

Line 9: יביאה֯ • תנופ֯ת זהב • מסוה֯ • נדבה ליי׳ • קרא יה֯וה֯ •

‘let him bring’ (Ex. 35:5). **‘an offering of gold’** (Ex. 35:22). **‘did spin’** (35:25).[41] **‘free-will offering to God’** (Ex. 35:29) **‘God called’** (Ex. 35:30).

Line 10: לקרבה • ויעשו. ס • ה֯משכן • מזבח ה֯קטרת • ובצלאל •

‘to come near’ (Ex. 36:2). **‘and they made’** (Ex. 36:8) ***setuma.*** **‘the Tabernacle’** (Ex. 36:8). **‘the altar of incense’** (Ex. 37:25). **‘and Betsalel’** (Ex. 22:23).

Line 11: צוה • כל הזהב ס • לכה֯נת • ובק֯רבתם • הענן פ֗ •

‘commanded’ (Ex. 38:22). **‘all the gold’** (Ex. 38:24) ***setuma.*** **‘[everlasting] priesthood’** (Ex. 40:15). **‘and when they came near’** (Ex. 40:32). **‘the cloud’** (Ex. 40:34) ***petuḥa.***

Line 12: את ה֯משכן • יש֯ראל • בכל מסעיה֯ם •

‘the Tabernacle’ (Ex. 40:35). **‘Israel’** (Ex. 40:38) **‘through all their journeys’** (Ex. 40:38).

Line 13: //// ספר ויקרא ////

The book of *Va-yiqra’*

Line 14: ונרצה֯ • לכפ֯ר • אשר פ֯תח • אה֯ל • והפ֯שיט • על

‘and it will be accepted’ (Lev. 1:4). **‘to make atonement’** (Lev. 1:4). **‘that is at the opening’** (Lev. 1:5). **‘of the tent’** (Lev. 1:5). **‘and he will flay’** (Lev. 1:6). **‘on …**

Line 15: ה֯מזבח • וה֯קטיר • אשה֯ • ריח ניחוח • צפ֯נה •

… the altar’ (Lev. 1:7 or Lev. 1:8).[42] **‘and he make smoke’** (Lev. 1:9). **‘sweet savour’** (Lev. 1:9).[43] **‘northward’** (Lev. 1:11).

41 This is likely an error by our scribe, since the expected instance here is מטוה with a *ṭet*, rather than the *samekh* as written. The word מסוה֯ (veil) is not present between verses 22 and 29, but was in the line above and so he may have erred, writing this instead.

42 Other sources suggest this is Lev. 1:8.

43 However, no letter appears to be decorated. It is likely that the scribe omitted a reference to ס֗ *setuma* here.

Line 16: והסיר֯ • ~~איש~~ אשה ניחח • ונפש סׄ • מאשי

'and he will remove' (Lev. 1:16). ~~man~~[44] 'made by fire a sweet [savour]' (Lev. 1:17).[45] 'and anyone' (Lev. 2:1) ***setuma***. 'fire offerings …

Line 17: יה֯וה֯ • מנחה סׄ • ה֯וא • ס֯לת • אלה֯ מזבח • אלה֯יך •

… of God' (Lev. 2:3) 'meal offering' (Lev. 2:6) ***setumah***. 'it is' (Lev. 2:6). 'flour' (Lev. 2:7). Likely 'and to the altar'[46] (Lev. 2.12). 'your God' (Lev. 2:13).

Line 18: בכורים סׄ • מנחה֯ • אשה֯ לייי • שלמים סׄ • אשה֯ •

'first-fruits' (Lev. 2:14) ***setumah***. 'meal offering' (Lev. 2:14) 'made by fire to God' (Lev. 2:16). 'peace offering' (Lev. 3:1) ***setuma***.[47] 'made by fire' (Lev. 3:5).

Line 19: הצאן פׄ • לחם אשה֯ • עז פׄ • והקטירם֯ • לחם

'the sheep' (Lev. 3:6) ***petuḥa***. 'bread' 'made by fire' (Lev. 3:11). 'goat' (Lev. 3:12) ***petuḥa***. 'and he will make them smoke' (Lev. 3:16). 'bread …

Line 20: אשה֯ • לדרתיכם֯ • מושבתיכם֯ • וידבר פׄ • ה֯משיח •

… made by fire' (Lev. 3:16). 'throughout your generations' (Lev. 3:17). 'in all your dwellings' (Lev. 3:17). 'and He spoke' (Lev. 4:1) ***petuḥa***. 'the anointed' (Lev. 4:3).

Line 21: את ה֯פר • פ֯ני • פ֯רכת • ה֯קדש • ישפ֯ך • ואם כל

'the bullock' (Lev. 4:4). 'in front' (Lev. 4:6). 'the curtain' (Lev. 4:6). 'the holy' (Lev. 4:6). 'he will pour out' (Lev. 4:7). 'and if the whole …

Line 22: עדת פׄ • אצ֯בעו • הפ֯רכת • ואם נפש פׄ •

… the congregation' (Lev. 4:13) ***petuḥa***. 'his finger' (Lev. 4:17). 'the curtain' (Lev. 4:17). 'and if any one' (Lev. 4:27) ***petuḥa***.

As noted in the footnotes, the scribe has also added vertically **ונחל֯תנו** ('for Your inheritance') from Ex. 34:9 in the right margin. He has indicated its position in the main text with a circle ֯. The word is also written **~~ונלה~~** but crossed through, as there was a clear metathesis.

In transcribing and annotating this particular manuscript it is obvious the scribe has omitted some considerable number of instances that are found in the core sources

44 Our scribe has erred and crossed out the error.

45 Likely the word ריח ('savour') has been omitted in this instance.

46 It is highly likely our scribe has erred here, and what was intended was ואל ה֯מזבח and he has omitted the *vav* and added the *he* to the first word.

47 This is, in fact, a *petuḥa*.

of *Sefer Tagin*, as is the case with quite a few of the secondary sources. His *Vorlage* may have been defective or he was constructing this from multiple sources and erred. Conversely **T-S Misc. 24.182** has also brought quite a few instances which are not present in any of the other sources examined for this monograph, so he may have been constructing this from a particular *Sefer Torah*, which had additional decorations. These have been outlined above as they relate to the specific letters covered by the main manuscript **CG**, that we have been reconstructing, and are worth further study, as other letters in *Sefer Tagin* are explored in future work.

APPENDIX 2

Enhanced Imagery of *Sefer Tagin* from Sassoon 82 (JUD. 022)

Reproduced with kind permission of Jacqui E. Safra. Manuscript held in his private collection.

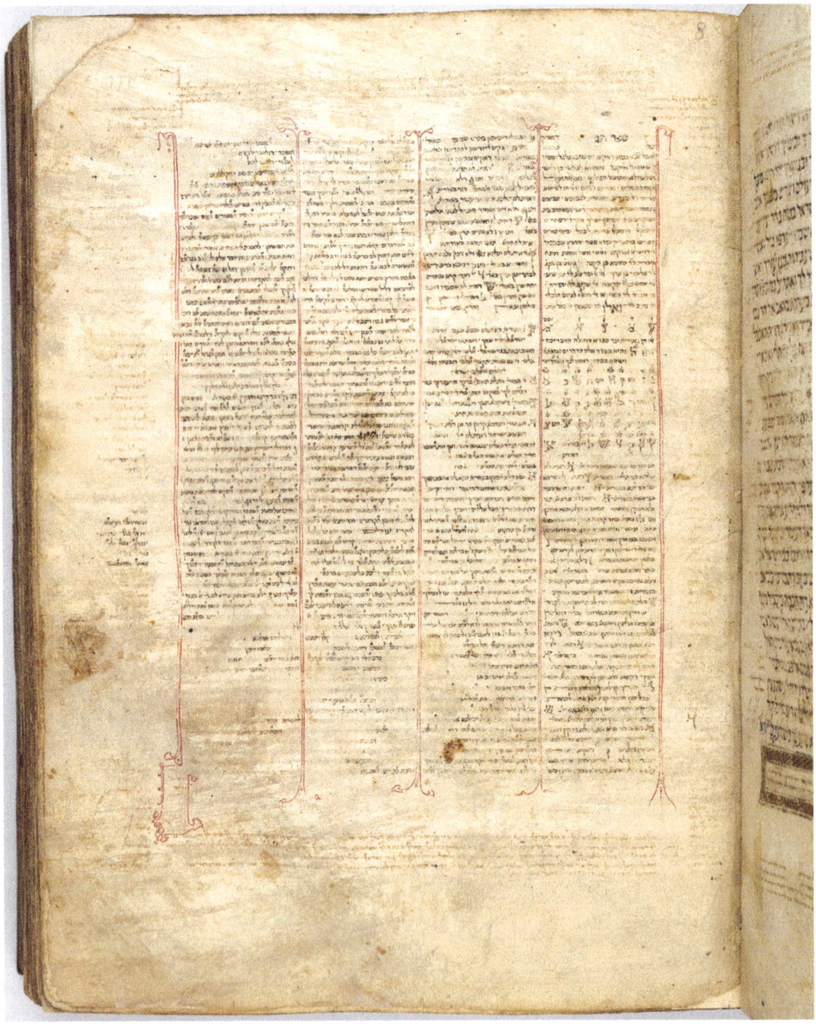

FIGURE 22 Sassoon 82 (JUD. 022) page 177

DOI:10.1163/9789004426368_009

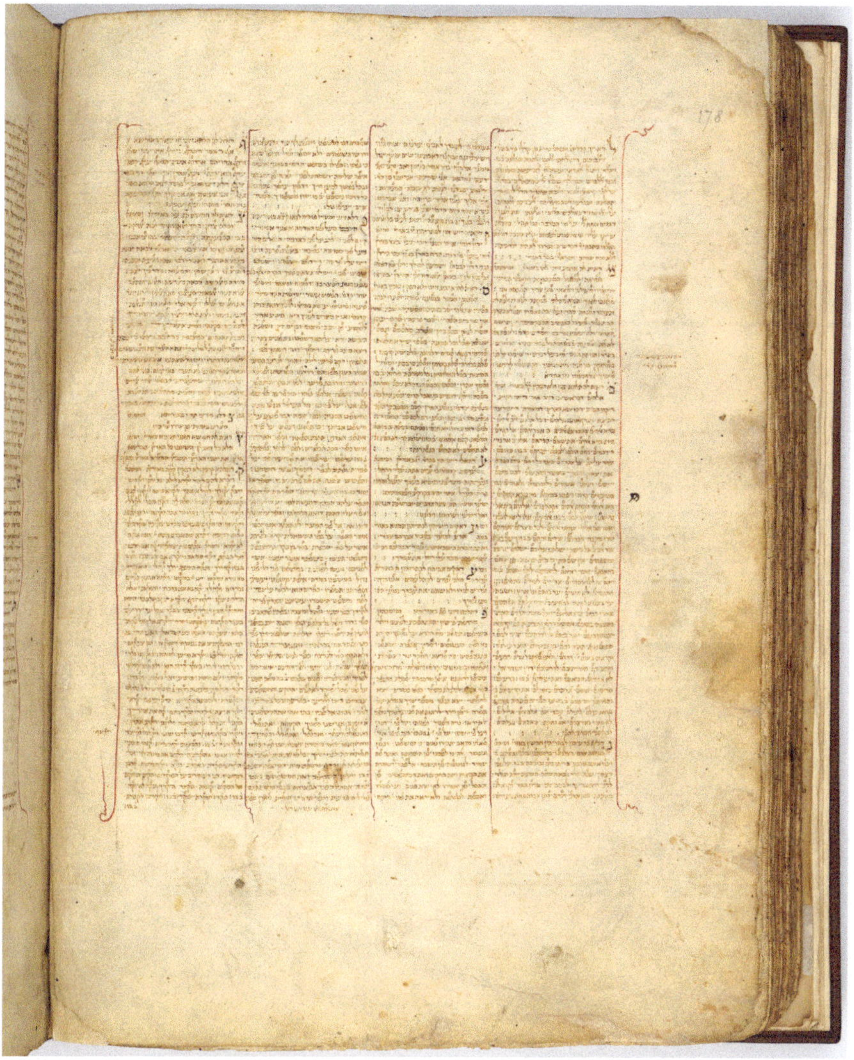

FIGURE 23 Sassoon 82 (JUD. 022) page 178

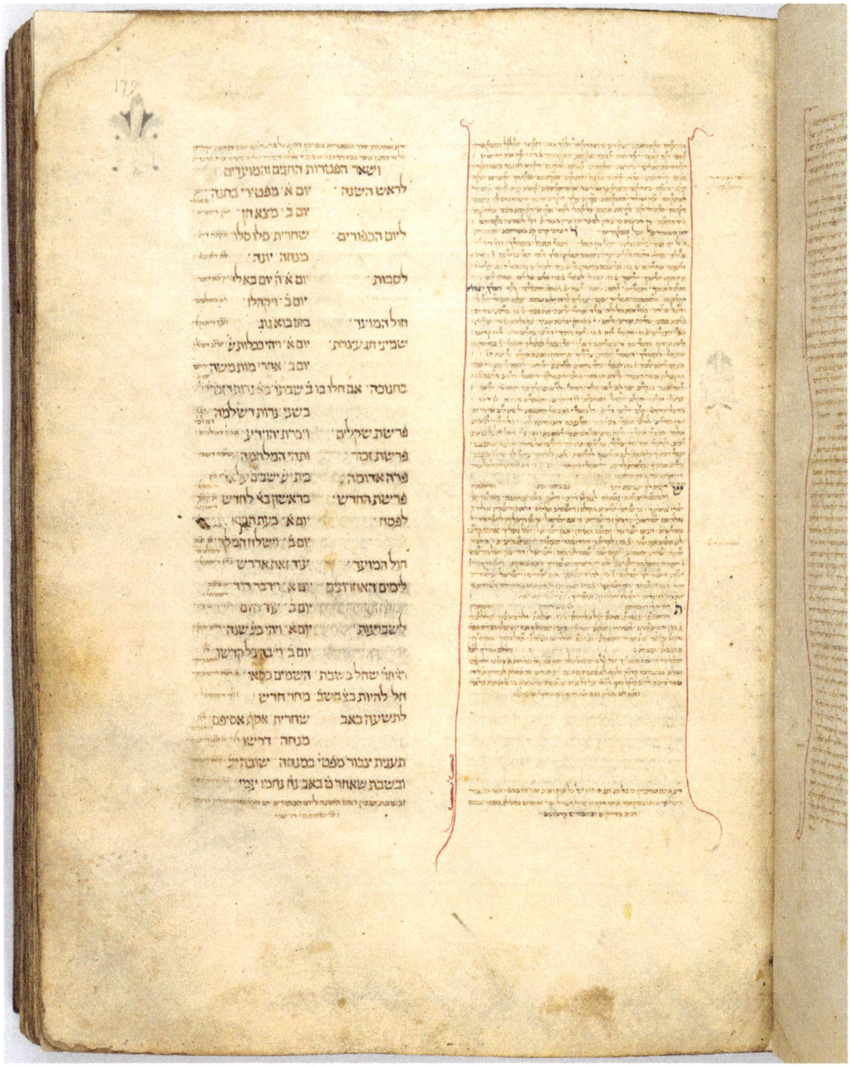

FIGURE 24 Sassoon 82 (JUD. 022) page 179

Bibliography

Primary Sources (Core and Secondary Manuscripts)

References as quoted above in the text and footnotes.

Books

Antonio, B., De Tata, R. and Perani, M., *Il Rotolo 2 dela Biblioteca Universitaria de Bologna, il Pentateuco piÙ antica del mondo*, BUB, 2015.

Baer, S., תקון הסופר והקורא (*Copyist Guide for the Scribe and for the Reader*), Frankfurt a. M (früher Rödelheim), Druck and Verlag von M. Lehrberger & Co., 1900.

Barges, J.J.L. (ed.), *Editio princeps* of *Sepher Taghin* (ספר תגין), *Liber Coronularum*, Paris, 1866, pp. 1–28 (with a Hebrew preface by Senior (Shneur) Sachs).

Basser, Y., *Sefer Tagi*, Israel, 2010.

Beit Arié, M., *Transmission of Texts by Scribes and Copyists: Unconscious and Critical Interferences*, John Ryland University Bulletin, Vol. 75, Issue 3, 1993.

Beit Arié, M. (ed. Leiter, T.), *Hebrew Codicology, Primary Sources*, The Hebrew and Jewish Studies University of Oxford, 2008.

Beit Arié, M., *Hebrew Codicology* (Preprint internet version 0.9 Hebrew and 0.2 English (April 2018)).

Beit Arié, M., (in collaboration with Engel E. and Yardeni, A.), אסופות כתבים עבריים מימי—הבינים כרך א: כתב מזרחי וכתב תימני, (*Specimens of Medieval Hebrew Scripts, Part 1; Oriental and Yemenite Scripts*), The Israel Academy of Sciences and Humanities, Jerusalem, 1987.

Ben Mesheq: Tiqqun Sofrim ve'Iṭur Sofrim, 'Eliezer ben 'Eved-'el Yitsḥaq, Prague, 1658/9

Berlin, Adele & Brettler, Marc Zvi, *The Jewish Study Bible, 2nd Edition*, Oxford University Press, 2014.

Biblia Hebraica Stuttgartensia, (Ed. Rudolph, W. & Elliger, K.), Deutsche Bibelgeselleschaft, Stuugart, 1997.

Bloom, A., ספר אור המלך (*The Book of the Light of the King*), Jerusalem, 2000

Brown, F., Driver, S.R. & Briggs, C.A., *A Hebrew and English Lexicon of the Old Testament with an Appendix containing the Biblical Aramaic*, The Riverside Press, Cambridge, 1906

Caspi, E., מקורות דרשניים לאותיות המתויגות והמשונות בתורה (*Interpretive Sources for the Tittled and Strange Letters in the Torah*), from קובץ חצי גבורים—פליטת סופרים, מאסף תורני, ח, עלול תשע"ה

Caspi, E. and Weintroyb, M., על זמנו של ספר תגין (On the Time of *Sefer Tagin*) from ירושתינו, Vol. 5, *Makhon Moreshet 'Askenaz*, Bene Beraq, 5771.

Encyclopaedia Judaica, Keter Publishing House, Jerusalem, 1971, Crawford, H. and Eisenstein J., *Tagin* from *The Jewish Encyclopedia, Volume 11*. Funk & Wagnalls. New York, 1901–1906.

Ginsburg, Christian D., *The Massorah, Vol. 11*, London 1880.

Ginzburgh, Y., *The Art of Education: Internalizing Ever-new Horizons*, Gal Einai Publication Society, 2005.

Holtz, B., *Back to the Sources*, Summit Books, 1984.

Hurwitz, S., *Maḥzor Vitry leRabbeynu Simḥa*, Nuremberg, 1923, 2 vols.

Jastrow, M., *Dictionary of the Targumim, Talmud Babli, Yerushalmi and Midrashic Literature*, Judaica Press, New York, 1989.

Kasher, M. and Razhabi, Y., *Torah Shelemah Leviticus Vol. 29*. American Biblical Encyclopedia Society Inc. Jerusalem, 1978.

Khan, Geoffrey, *The Tiberian Pronunciation Tradition of Biblical Hebrew, Volume 1*, Cambridge (FAMES), UK: Open Book Publishers, 2020, https://doi.org/10.11647/OBP.0163, pp. 608–610

Liss, Hanna, *A Pentateuch to Read in: The Secrets of the Regensburg Pentateuch*, De Gruyter, 2017.

Meiri—R. Menachem ben Shelomo, *Qiryat Sefer*, Izmir, 1881.

Melamed, E.Z., *Aramaic Hebrew English Dictionary of the Babylonian Talmud*, Feldheim Publishers, Jerusalem, 2005.

Michaels, M., *Sefer Binsoa* (*The Book of Binsoa*), Kulmus Publishing, London, 2010.

Michaels, M., *The Torah in the Wardrobe*, Kulmus Publishing, London, 2017.

Michaels, M., *Adventures in Practical Halachah no. 3: Neither Clever nor a Simpleton*, Kulmus Publishing, 2019.

Michaels, *Adventures in Practical Halachah no. 4: To a Place Destruction*, Kulmus Publishing, 2019.

Munk, M., *The Wisdom in the Hebrew Alphabet*, Artscroll, 1983.

Narkiss, B., *Hebrew Illuminated Manuscripts*, Macmillan/Keter Publishing House, Jerusalem, 1969.

Neubauer, Adolf, Cowley, Arthur Ernest, *Catalogue of the Hebrew Manuscripts in the Bodleian Library*, Oxford Clarendon Press, 1906,

Orenstein, A. (ed.), Ḥafets Ḥayim, *Mishnah Berurah Volume 1(B)—The laws of Tefillin*, Feldheim Publishers, 1982. (Includes *Mishnat Sofrim*).

Paz, Yakir, קושר כתרים לאותיות: מנהג סופרי אלוהי בהקשרו ההיסטורי (*Binding Crowns to the Letters—A Divine Scribal Practice in Its Historical Context*) from רביץ—רבעון למדעי היהודית, שנה פו, חוברת ב—ג (תשע"ט)

Penkower, Jordan S. *Verse Divisions in the Hebrew Bible* from *Vetus Testamentum, vol. 50, no. 3*, 2000, pp. 379–393.

Perani, M., *The Rediscovery of the Most Ancient Entire Sefer Torah at the Bologna University Library (12th Century) A Rare Witness of the Masoretic Babylonian Graphic and Textual Tradition*, University of Bologna, 2016.

Perani, M., *Part 2: The Oldest Complete Extant Sefer Torah Rediscovered at the Bologna University Library: Codicological, Textual, and Paleographic Features of an Ancient Eastern Tradition* in *The Jews of Italy: Their Contribution to the Development and Diffusion of Jewish Heritage*, Academic Studies Press, Boston, 2019.

Perani, M. (ed.), *The Ancient Torah of Bologna: features and history*, Brill, Leiden, 2019.

Richler, Benjamin (ed.), *Hebrew Manuscripts in the Biblioteca Palatina in Parma*, Jewish National and University Library, Jerusalem, 2001.

Rosenwasser, Moshe, האותיות המשונות שבתורה (*The Odd Letters that are in the Torah*), from המעין (The Spring), *Nisan* 5766. pp. 22–40.

Sassoon, D.S., *Ohel David. Descriptive Catalogue of the Hebrew and Samaritan Manuscripts in the Sassoon Library, vol. 1, London, 1932.*

Schechter, A. and Aurbach, U., פתחי שערים החדש—אוצר הלכות מזוזה, (*The New Opening of the Gates—collection of laws of Mezuzah*), Jerusalem, 1990.

Sirat, C., *Hebrew Manuscripts of the Middle Ages*, Cambridge University Press, 2002.

Sofer, Ḥatam, *Keneset Sofrim*, reprinted in Jerusalem by Makhon Bene Moshe, 2005.

Sutcliffe, E.F., *One Jot or Tittle*, MT. 5, 18. *Biblica*, vol. 9, no. 4, 1928, pp. 458–460. *JSTOR*, www.jstor.org/stable/42613750.

Timm, E., Birnbaum E., and Birnbaum D. (ed.), *Solomon A. Birnbaum: Ein Leben fur die Wissenschaft A Lifetime of Achievement*, Vol. II Palaeography, De Gruyter, Germany, 2011,

Touger, E. and Gold, A., *Ba'al haTurim Chumash, The Davis Edition*, Mesorah Publications (1999–2004).

Touger, E. (trans. and notes) Maimonides, Mishneh Torah: Hilkhot Tefillin uMezuzah veSefer Torah, Hilkhot Tzitzit, Moznaim Publishing Corporation, Jerusalem, 1990.

Tov, Emanuel, *Textual Criticism of the Hebrew Bible, 3rd Ed.*, Fortress Press, 2012.

Van der Toorn, Karel, *Scribal Culture and the Making of the Hebrew Bible*, Harvard University Press, Massachusetts, 2007.

Yardeni, Ada, *The Book of Hebrew Script: History, Palaeography, Script Styles, Calligraphy & Design*. Carta, Jerusalem, 2010.

Zucker, Shlomo, *A Torah-Scroll from Northern Spain Following the Tradition of Curved Letters, from a Circle of 13th Century Kabbalists*, Jewish National and University Library, 2013.

ליקוט ספרי סת׳ם *Liquṭ Sifrey S"TaM I, (incorporating Keset ha-Sofer, Lishkat ha-Sofer, 'Alpha Beta, Shoneh Halakhot, Kol Sofrim, Mishnat Sofrim, Tiqqun Tefillin-Baruch She'amar, Da'at Qedoshim* (*Levush, Mikdash Me'at*), Collected by R.T. Kohuna.

Various volumes from the Soncino Press Hebrew-English edition of the *Talmud*, notably *Shabbat, Gittin, Ketubot, Menaḥot and Masekhtot Qetanot* (minor tractates)—*Sofrim, Sefer Torah and 'Avot deRabbi Natan.*

Printed in the United States
By Bookmasters